REPRINTED BY

CH'ENG WEN PUBLISHING CO.,

TAIPEI 1970

ANNALS & MEMOIRS OF THE COURT OF PEKING

E. BACKHOUSE AND J.O.P. BLAND

REPRINTED BY

CH'ENG WEN PUBLISHING CO.,

TAIPEI 1970

ALPHABETICAL LIST OF THE PRINCIPAL PERSONS HEREINAFTER NAMED

ABTAI, elder brother of Emperor T'ai Tsung.
AO PAI, regent during K'ang Hsi's minority.
AO PAO, Grand Secretary under Ch'ien Lung.
AN TE-HAI, Tzŭ Hsi's pet eunuch during the first Regency.

BORJIKIN, Mongol consort of Shunchih and Empress Dowager of K'ang Hsi.

CHANG CHIH-TUNG, scholar and statesman of Kuang Hsü's reign.
CHANG CHIH-WAN, Grand Councillor in Kuang Hsü's reign.
CH'ANG FU, son of Emperor Wan Li; Prince of Kueiyang.
CHANG HSIEN-CHUNG, Li Tzu-ch'eng's chief rebel colleague.
CH'ANG HSUN, Prince Fu, son of Wan Li, slain by Li Tzu-ch'eng.
CHANG KUO-CHI, adopted father of Hsi Tsung's Empress.
CH'ANG LO, or KUANG TSUNG, son of Wan Li, reigned one month.
CHANG PEI-LUN, one of the "Puritans," under Tzŭ Hsi; son-in-law to Li Hung-chang.
CHANG T'ING-YÜ, 1670–1756, great scholar under Ch'ien Lung.
CHANG YIN-HUAN, friend of Kuang Hsü, banished by Tzŭ Hsi in 1898, and executed by Prince Tuan's order in 1900.
CHANG YUAN-FU, eunuch favourite of Lung Yü, commonly called Hsiao Chang. He is believed to have stolen her pearl shoes before the breath was out of her body.
CHAO CH'I-LIN, a famous censor under Tzŭ Hsi.
CHAO SHU-CH'IAO, allowed to commit suicide in 1900 for supposed anti-foreign proclivities.
CHAO ERH-HSÜN, ex-Viceroy of Manchuria and opponent of the Republic.
CHAO HUI, a Manchu General of Ch'ien Lung.
CH'EN, LADY, the mistress of Wu San-kuei.
CHENG, LADY, favourite concubine of Wan Li and mother of Prince Fu.

PRINCIPAL PERSONS NAMED

CHENG, PRINCE, one of the conspiring Regents, 1861.
CHENG TÊ, reign title of Wu Tsung, Emperor from 1506 to 1522.
CH'ENG TÊ, a Manchu who attempted to slay the Emperor Chia Ch'ing.
CHEN HSIN-CHIA, Ch'ung Chen's Minister of War.
CH'EN PI, corrupt Minister under Hsüan T'ung, now adviser to the President, Yuan Shih-k'ai.
CHEN PAO-CHEN, one of the "Puritan" party, later tutor to Emperor Hsüan T'ung.
CHIA CH'ING, reign title of Jen Tsung, who succeeded Ch'ien Lung.
CH'I CHÜN-TSAO, Grand Councillor under Tao Kuang.
CH'I HSIU, Boxer leader, decapitated in 1901.
CHING LIN, decapitated by Old Buddha for cowardice.
CH'IN, MADAME, Li Tzu-ch'eng's personal attendant.
CHIN, PRINCE, a descendant of Yung Lo.
CH'ING YI-K'UANG, PRINCE, Prime Minister under Tzŭ Hsi for si years, and later under the Regent.
CHIN KUEI, a traitor famous in history.
CH'I SHAN, or KISHAN, Viceroy of Canton in 1841.
CHOU, EMPRESS, wife of Ch'ung Chen.
CHOU KUEI, a statesman in the last days of the Mings.
CHU CHIH-FENG, Governor of Hsüan Hua under Ch'ung Chen.
CH'UNG HUA, Manchu official in Formosa in 1812.
CHÜ HUNG-CHI, rival to Prince Ch'ing from 1903 to 1907, enemy of Yuan Shih-k'ai and ally of Ts'en Ch'un-hsüan.
CHU HSIEN, leader of White Lily sect.
CHU KUEI, tutor and valued servant of Chia Ch'ing.
CH'UN, PRINCESS, mother of Kuang Hsü and sister of Tzŭ Hsi.
CH'UNG CH'I, father of A Lu-te, consort of Emperor T'ung Chih, friend of Yung Lu, slew himself in Paotingfu.
CH'UNG HOU, signed the Treaty of Livadia in 1878.
CH'UNG LI, Commander of Peking gendarmerie in 1900 and pro-Boxer.
CHU SHIH, Grand Secretary of Ch'ien Lung.
CHU YÜAN-CHANG, canonised as T'ai Tsu or the Exalted Ancestor, founder of the Ming dynasty.

DEPORTMENT CONCUBINE, one of Hsi Tsung's consorts, a tool of Madame K'o.
DORGUN, PRINCE JUI, brother of Manchu dynasty's founder and Regent to Shun Chih.

FAN CHING-WEN, Ch'ung Chen's Grand Secretary.
FAN WEN-CHENG, high official under T'ai Tsung.
FANG TSUNG-CHE, Grand Secretary of Wan Li.

PRINCIPAL PERSONS NAMED

FENG HSIU, friend of Jung Lu and father of the Yü Fei, or "Gem" Concubine, at first known as Hui Fei.
FU CH'ANG-AN, *protégé* of Ho Shen.
FU K'ANG-AN, a prominent General under Ch'ien Lung and rival of Ho Shen.

HO LIN, brother of Grand Secretary Ho Shen, under Ch'ien Lung.
HO SHEN, or HO K'UN, the all-powerful Minister of Ch'ien Lung, put to death by his successor Chia Ch'ing.
HO SHIH-TAI, official deputed to receive the Amherst Mission.
HSIAO CHEN, TZŬ AN, Tzŭ Hsi's colleague, Empress of the Eastern Palace.
HSIAO TE, EMPRESS, wife of Hsien Feng, who died before he became Emperor; canonised as his chief Consort.
HSÜ CH'ENG-YÜ, son of Hsü T'ung, decapitated by the Allies in 1901.
HSÜ SHIH-CH'ANG, Viceroy and Grand Councillor, formerly Yuan Shih-k'ai's *protégé*. When his patron was dismissed, Hsü characteristically did nothing to help him.
HSÜ SHU-MING, a partisan of the Old Buddha in 1898.
HSÜ T'UNG, Boxer leader, enemy of Kuang Hsü, slew himself in 1900 on fall of Peking.
HUAI T'A-PU, kinsman of Old Buddha and of Jung Lu.
HU NG KUANG, nominated successor to the last Ming Emperor Ch'ung Chen at Nanking in 1644.
HUANG SOU-LAN, Vice-President of Board of War in 1900.
HUANG T'IEN-PA, a well-known theatrical hero.
HUNG HSIU-CH'ÜAN, the "heavenly king," a Tai Ping leader.
HU YÜ-FEN, high official in Peking under Kuang Hsü, and friendly to foreigners.

I-CHIANG-A, Governor of Shantung and *protégé* of Ho Shen.

JIRHALANG, or CHIERHALANG, first cousin of T'ai Tsung, Prince Cheng.
JUI CH'ENG, Viceroy of Wuchang in 1911, grandson of Ch'i Shan.
JUNG LU, kinsman of Tzŭ Hsi, devoted adherent and patriotic Manchu.

K'ANG, PRINCE, cousin to K'ang Hsi.
K'ANG YU-WEI, reformer loathed by Tzŭ Hsi.
KAO T'IEN-TE, and KOU WEN-MING, leaders of the White Lily rebels in Ch'ien Lung's and Chia Ch'ing's reigns.
K'O, MADAME, Hsi Tsung's wet nurse, the "Lady of Divine Worship," who resided in what is now the Naitzŭ-fu, or "Foster-mother's Palace."

PRINCIPAL PERSONS NAMED

K'o, Prince, descended from Nurhachi's second son.
K'ou Lien-ts'ai, a eunuch decapitated by the Old Buddha.
Kuang Hui, official deputed to receive the Amherst Mission.
K'uei Chün, a chamberlain to the Court under Tzŭ Hsi and Lung Yü.
Kuei Hsiang, father of Lung Yü and younger brother of Tzŭ Hsi.
Kung, Prince, senior, died 1898.
Kung, Prince, junior; P'u Wei, haughty and hostile to House of Ch'un. Opposed the abdication; thought he should have succeeded Kuang Hsü. Now lives in Tsingtau, leading the Tsungshetang or Restoration Society.

Lai Pao, commander of Peking gendarmerie under Ch'ien Lung.
Li, Concubine, favourite Consort of Kuang Tsung.
Liang Ch'i-ch'ao, one of the leading reformers in 1898; subsequently a refugee in Japan.
Liang K'uei, adopted son and heir of Jung Lu.
Liao Shou-heng, Minister on Grand Council under Tzŭ Hsi, and anti-Boxer.
Li Chia-chü, Manchu bannerman of Canton, sometime Speaker of the Senate.
Li Chih, personal name of Kao Tsung, Emperor of T'ang dynasty in A.D. 655.
Li Chien-t'ai, Grand Secretary under Ch'ung Chen; the richest man in Peking of that time.
Li Ching-shu, eldest son of Li Hung-chang.
Lien Wen-chung, clerk in Grand Council who drafted decree of 20th June 1900 declaring war against the Powers.
Lien Yüan, Manchu and anti-Boxer, decapitated in 1900.
Li Hsi-chang, Prefect of Peking under Li Tzu-ch'eng.
Li Hsiu-ch'eng, the leader of the Taiping rebellion.
Li Hung-chang, the famous Viceroy of Chihli.
Li K'o-yung, a General at close of T'ang dynasty, who afterwards usurped the Throne.
Li Kuo-p'u, a Grand Secretary of Hsi Tsung.
Li Lien-ying, âme damnée and Chief Eunuch of Tzŭ Hsi.
Lin Hsü, reformer under Kuang Hsü, put to death by Tzŭ Hsi.
Lin Tse-hsü, Viceroy of Canton, who burned the opium and defied Great Britain, thus precipitating the first China War.
Li Shih-min, the ideal ruler, second Emperor of the T'ang dynasty, seventh century A.D.
Li Ping-heng, anti-foreign and Boxer leader.
Li Ting-kuo, brigand chief, supporter of Yung Li, fugitive Ming Sovereign.

PRINCIPAL PERSONS NAMED

Li Tzu-ch'eng, rebel leader and usurping Emperor.
Liu Ch'üan-chih, Chia Ch'ing's Grand Secretary.
Liu Chu-hsuan, Prefect of Peking under Hsi Tsung.
Liu Kuang-fu, Censor under Wan Li.
Liu K'un-yi, Viceroy of Nanking under Tzŭ Hsi.
Liu Lin, *alias* Liu Ch'ing, leader of Palace conspiracy in 1813.
Liu Te-ts'ai, eunuch implicated in Chia Ch'ing's Palace conspiracy.
Liu Tsung-min, a rebel General under Li Tzŭ-ch'eng.
Li Yen, one of Li Tzŭ-ch'eng's Generals.
Li Yu-heng, Commander-in-chief of Szechuan under Tzŭ Hsi.
Lo Pao, Manchu General under Chia Ch'ing.
Lu, Prince, cousin of Yung Li, the last of the Mings.
Lu Ch'uan-lin, a patriotic statesman at the close of the Manchu *régime*.
Lung K'o-to, maternal uncle of Emperor Yung Cheng.
Lung Wu, successor to Hung Kuang, slain at Foochow.
Lu Yuan-ting, taotai of Shanghai under Kuang Hsü.

Ma Shao-yü, Ming Peace Commissioner to Manchus.
Meng Ch'uan-chin, a censor who impeached Po Sui.
Mien En, Prince Ting, nephew of Chia Ch'ing.
Mien K'ai, third son of Chia Ch'ing.
Mu Ch'ang-a, Chief Minister under Tao Kuang.

Nieh Ch'i-kuei, Provincial Judge under Tzŭ Hsi.
Nien Keng-yao, a famous General, ordered to commit suicide by Yung Cheng.
Ning, Prince, rebelled against the Ming Emperor Cheng Tê.
Nurhachi, founder of the Manchu dynasty.

Pan Shih-tsu, Grand Councillor under Tao Kuang.
Pao Ning, Governor-General of Ili.
Pao Tai, Resident at Lhasa under Ch'ien Lung.
Pao Yün, Grand Secretary under Tzŭ Hsi.
Po Sui, Grand Secretary, executed by Hsien Feng.
P'u An, father of Na T'ung, decapitated for improper conduct whilst serving on an examination commission.
P'u Shan, an Imperial Duke, flogged by Lung Yü's eunuchs.

San Kuniang, Ch'ien Lung's literary courtesan.
Shen Kuei-fen, Grand Councillor during Kuang Hsü's minority.
Shen Liu-t'ing, one of Lung Yü's eunuchs.

PRINCIPAL PERSONS NAMED

SHIH HSÜ, Grand Councillor under Tzŭ Hsi, afterwards chief guardian to Emperor on Manchu downfall.

SHIH K'O-FA, patriotic Grand Secretary of the Ming Emperor Hung Kuang.

SHOU FU, an Imperial Clansman of Kuang Hsü's party, son-in-law of Lien Yüan.

SHUN CHIH, first Manchu Emperor, said to have taken vows as a bonze and to have lived to extreme old age.

SU, PRINCE, an anti-republican Manchu.

SULINGA, father-in-law of Ho Lin, Grand Secretary under Ch'ien Lung.

SUN CHIA-NAI, Kuang Hsü's tutor.

SUNG YÜN, resident at Lhasa under Ch'ien Lung.

SUN SHIH-YI, Envoy to Burmah under Ch'ien Lung.

SU SHUN, President of Board of Revenue and Grand Councillor, Imperial Clansman and boon companion of Hsien Feng, put to death by the two Empress-Regents for treason, in 1861.

SUN TI-A, poet of the T'ang dynasty.

SUN TZU-SHOU, one of Kuang Hsü's tutors.

SUN YÜ-WEN, Grand Councillor under Tzŭ Hsi.

TAI HUNG-T'ZU, first Cantonese to enter Grand Council, died 1910.

T'AN CHIAO-T'IEN-ERH, the most famous actor in China under Tzŭ Hsi.

TAO KUANG, reign title of Mien Ning, canonised as Hsüan Tsung, or Distinguished Ancestor.

TENG CH'ENG-HSIU, a Puritan party man of the Reformers of 1898.

T'IEH PAO, famous scholar under Ch'ien Lung.

TIEN WEN-CHING, favourite Minister of Yun Cheng.

TSAI CHEN, son of Prince Ch'ing, and Envoy to the Coronation of George V; he complained at not being given a higher precedence, and had photographs published of himself as Crown Prince, which he was not, and could not be.

TSAI FENG, Prince Ch'un, the ex-Regent.

TSAI HSÜN, Prince Chuang, Boxer leader.

TSAI LAN, Boxer leader and brother of Prince Tuan.

TSAI LIEN, son of Prince Tun, implicated in the Boxer rising.

TS'AI MOU-TE, defender of the city of Tai Yuan against Li Tzu-ch'eng.

TSAI YING, son of Prince Kung, implicated in Boxer movement.

TSAI YUAN, one of the conspiring Regents, 1861.

TS'AO PIN-CHOU, tutor to Hsien Feng.

TSO TSUNG-T'ANG, General and statesman under Tzŭ Hsi.

TSENG KUO-FAN, statesman and soldier who overcame the Taipings.

TUAN CH'I-JUI, a favourite and *protégé* of Yuan Shih-k'ai.

PRINCIPAL PERSONS NAMED

TUAN FANG, Viceroy and amateur in curios. decapitated in Szechuan by his troops.

TU HSÜN, eunuch who betrayed Peking to Li Tzu-ch'eng.

TUN, PRINCE, fifth son of Tao Kuang (*vide* Manchu genealogical tree).

TUNG CHIA, EMPRESS, mother of K'ang Hsi.

TUNG FU-HSIANG, Boxer leader, who falsely claimed until his death that he was obeying Jung Lu's orders in attacking the legations.

TUNG T'U-LAI, prominent Chinese supporter of Manchu Emperor T'ai Tsung.

TU SHOU-T'IEN, tutor of Tao Kuang.

TZŬ HSI, the Empress Dowager, Old Buddha, or Western Empress.

WANG CH'ENG-EN, eunuch Commander-in-chief of Peking, who died with his master, the Emperor Ch'ung Chen.

WANG P'ENG-YÜN, a censor under Kuang Hsü.

WANG WEN-SHAO, favourite of Tzŭ Hsi and sometime Viceroy of Chihli. Grand Councillor under Tzŭ Hsi.

WAN LI, reign title of Shen Tsung, died 1620.

WEI CHUNG-HSIEN, originally called Wei Chin-chung, an infamous eunuch under the late Mings.

WENG T'UNG-HO, famous scholar and tutor to Kuang Hsü, who was dismissed by Tzŭ Hsi in 1898 for alleged hostility to herself.

WU CHAO-PING, a Canton merchant who traded with the barbarians under Ch'ien Lung.

WU HSIANG, father of Wu San-kuei.

WU HSIUNG-KUANG, promoted to be Grand Councillor by Ch'ien Lung.

WU SAN-KUEI, made a Prince by the Manchus, afterwards adopted reign title of his own and rebelled against them.

YANG HSIAO-LOU, palace actor under Lung Yü.

YANG HSIU-CH'ING, famous General of the Taiping rebellion.

YANG JUI-LIEN, a famous scholar under Yung Cheng and Ch'ien Lung.

YANG LIEN, loyal official who impeached the eunuch Wei Chung-hsien.

YEN HSIU, Manchu President of Board of Ceremonies in 1886.

YI YUAN-LU, high officer who slew himself at the fall of Peking in 1644.

YÜ, PRINCE (son of T'ai Tsung), Manchu Commander-in-chief at siege of Yang Chou-fu in 1643.

YUAN CHIA-SAN, grandfather of Yuan Shih-k'ai.

YUAN CH'UNG-HUAN, patriotic Ming General, and ancestor of Yuan Shih-k'ai.

YUAN SHIH-K'AI, born in 1859 of old official family. Viceroy of Chihli, now President of the Republic.

YÜ HSIEN, Manchu Governor of Shansi who massacred the missionaries.

PRINCIPAL PERSONS NAMED

Yü Lu, Viceroy of Tientsin in 1900.
Yün Chih, eldest son of K'ang Hsi by a lower concubine.
Yung Cheng, son of K'ang Hsi and successor to that Monarch.
Yung Kuei, Grand Secretary under Ch'ien Lung.
Yung Li, reign title of last Ming Prince, grandson of Wan Li, who reigned in the south from 1645 to 1659.
Yung Lo, fourth son of first Ming Emperor, who usurped the throne from his nephew.
Yu Te, Grand Secretary under the Old Buddha.

INTRODUCTION

The enduring interest displayed by many readers in the character of China's great Empress Dowager Tzŭ Hsi, and the generous appreciation accorded to our work on her life and reign,[1] have prompted the belief that the present work, covering a wider stretch of space and time, should prove interesting, and of some value, to those who desire to study the causes, immediate and remote, of recent and current events in the Far East. Until we understand something of the mainsprings of thought and action which determine the governance and daily life of a people—something of their atavistic memories and instincts, of their social, religious and economic systems, it is not possible to sympathise with them in their perils and crises of change, or to render them the assistance which appreciation of their motives and intelligent anticipation of their needs might supply. And to see the Chinese world steadily and see it whole, to trace cause and effect back to the deeply buried foundations of their philosophy and civilisation, it is necessary to look at things from their point of view, to hear them speaking, amongst themselves, of many things which the West has forgotten, but which are still part of the very soul of the East. It is for this reason that, in the present work, as in the life of Tzŭ Hsi, we have thought it best to reproduce the actual form and substance of the words in which China's Sovereigns, annalists, commentators and despatch-writers have recorded the events

[1] *China under the Empress Dowager*, 1910. (Heinemann).

INTRODUCTION

of contemporary history, hoping thus to create in the mind of the European reader something of the atmosphere in which they lived and moved.

The purpose of the present work is to present a faithful picture of life at the Court of Peking, beginning with the period at which the decline of the Ming dynasty had definitely set in and the rise of the Manchu power had begun—that is to say, from the middle of the sixteenth century down to the passing of the Manchus, to the chaos of degeneration and disruption, which obtains in China to-day under the name of a Republic. We have not attempted to construct a consecutive chronological record of the Empire's internal history or foreign relations, but only to present a series of impressions, taken from life, serving to illustrate the personal and domestic relations of China's rulers with their Court, and of the Court itself with the government of the country; to trace in these relations (vitally important under China's patriarchal system) alternating causes of national growth and decay; to watch, during the space of a few generations, the sowing of the seeds, and the reaping of the harvests, of good and evil.

Our object being to reproduce as fully and as truthfully as possible the atmosphere of the Court of Peking, throughout the period which has culminated in the present paroxysm of demoralisation, we have allowed the narratives of Chinese writers to stand, as a rule, without attempting to amend or curtail them to meet the conventions of reticence imposed, in certain directions, upon European writers. Here and there (notably in the narrative of the sack of Yang Chou-fu) we have thought it advisable to omit some of the worst details of horrors inseparable from the orgies of bloodshed and lust which mark the rise and fall of power in China. As a whole, however, we have assumed that the student of history prefers to see things as they are, rather than as

INTRODUCTION

the moralist would prefer them to be; that he can, and will, approach this study of Eastern life, described by Orientals, in the same spirit of detachment, with the same recognition of fundamental humanities and moralities, as that with which we approach the brutal frankness of the Chronicles of the Kings of Israel—things written for our learning.

There exists a small and happily diminishing class of moralists who would rather not look upon the mirror of history, or face the unpleasant realities of life, lest perchance they be disturbed from their comfortable fireside conceptions of the universe. One such there was —the manager of an American agency for supplying improving literature for the home circle—who recently asked us for a series of articles on China and the Chinese; but he stipulated, amongst other conditions calculated to preserve the moral dignity of his subscribers, that "they should contain no reference to concubines, secondary wives or other forms of immorality." The present Annals and Memoirs of the Chinese Court are no more suitable to the libraries of these dwellers in the walled garden of cherished illusions than Job, fresh from his place amongst the ashes and scraping himself with a potsherd, would be fit company for their drawing-rooms. Nevertheless, Job, his afflictions and philosophy, remain to this day commonplaces of existence in the Far East, and he who would truthfully depict the life of this people must take them into account. As it was in the beginning, so it is now; while men speak glibly of parliaments and representative institutions, the "stupid people" are "born unto trouble as the sparks fly upward," because of an ancient social system not to be uprooted by any philanthropic devices of the West. Within the last few months, many a walled city of China has known once more the abomination of desolation, has heard again the familiar voice of Rachel mourning for her children.

INTRODUCTION

Railways, telephones, forts and ships—all the paraphernalia of Europe's material civilisation, have availed nothing to save the citizens of Nanking from the hand of the destroyers, men of their own race. As it was in the time of the Sabeans and the Chaldeans, so it remains to-day in the East; the sons of Han " are far from safety; they are crushed in the gate, neither is there any to deliver them : whose harvest the hungry eateth up, and taketh it even out of the thorns, and the robber swalloweth up their substance." To these hereditary victims of an outworn patriarchal system, the words of Job are everyday truths. " Terrors make them afraid on every side. Their strength is hunger-bitten, and destruction stands ever ready at their side. The king of terrors dwells in their tabernacles and brimstone is scattered upon their habitations."

The annals and memoirs used in compiling the present work have been selected as typically representative of the Oriental outlook on life and death, and the business of government. We have not sought by any means to emphasise the brutalities, debaucheries and cruelties of the Forbidden City; we have not looked for horrors, nor reproduced anything which the Chinese themselves would consider to be outside the range of common experience. We have aimed simply at reproducing from Chinese sources a series of impressions true to life—not life as the sentimental humanitarian prefers to imagine it, but life as it was yesterday, and will be to-morrow, in the light that beat upon the Dragon Throne, and in the dark shadows behind it. To do this, we have endeavoured to steer a middle course between the Scylla of the Chinese chroniclers' brutal realism and the Charybdis of our conventional and often prurient reticences.

The reader will best appreciate the historical value and the significance of these Chinese records, who, in studying them, is able to detach himself for a while from

INTRODUCTION

Western modes of thought and standards of actions; who, clearing his mind of conventions and cant, endeavours to understand the fundamental differences between the moralities of East and West, and to weigh their results without prejudice or passion. It is impossible, for instance, for any one who regards polygamy as a form of "immorality" to study Chinese history with intelligent sympathy; or even to appreciate the motives which chiefly influence individuals and determine policies amongst the ruling class at this moment. To get the correct point of view, we must, in fact, assume for the study of China's institutions and history the frame of mind in which we approach the lives of the Hebraic patriarchs and rulers; cheerfully accepting for them customs which we, the heirs of all the ages, have decided to modify or to reject. Better still if, in adopting this attitude of detachment, we can bring ourselves to recognitoin of the truth that the Western World's convictions and conventions concerning the moralities are neither final nor necessarily superior, as a whole, to those of the East. Beneath the cruelties and rapacities of life, the brooding soul of the East preserves, with its infinite capacity for suffering, the dignity of a philosophy and the beauty of ideals which the West has never equalled, and from which it has derived many of its noblest inspirations and religions. Inferior to the European in many things that make for intellectual and material progress, the Oriental in general, and the Chinese in particular, can claim superiority in this, that in remaining nearer to nature, he has escaped the shameful hypocrisies and conventional falsehoods, which play so large a part in the social systems of the Western World. Admitted, that the East's immemorial acceptance of polygamy, with all its multitudinous paternity and chaotic domesticity, represents a lower ideal than that which finds expression in the monogamous West; admitted, that, as practised by the

INTRODUCTION

rulers of China, it has been the cause of many and great evils; yet, so soon as we regard the question dispassionately and without reference to our own standard of conduct, we are compelled to admit that polygamy, with all its evils, has preserved the Chinese from many things which they justly condemn and despise in our social system—from the terrible human traffic of our streets, from the unsexed or superfluous woman and the militant Suffragette, from the network of sordid sex problems and intrigues which honeycomb European society and reflect themselves in its literature and drama. The East is by tradition and temperament tolerant, reluctant to discuss the immortal Gods, and, for the rest, judging the tree by its fruits; willing to see good in every creed which preaches benevolence and gentleness; yet even the Chinese cannot avoid comparing some of the results of Christianity's civilisation with their own, and realising with satisfaction that the daily records of our divorce and police courts have no parallels in the East. And again, although we may disagree with the principles and practice of ancestor worship, we cannot deny that it has inculcated reverence for parents with definite ideals of duty and produced a race of women which instinctively prefers death to dishonour. The Chinese, with no desire to argue about worlds unseen or the road thereto, would be more than human if they took no comfort from comparing these results of the Confucian philosophy with those of our European systems; if they failed to perceive the undeniable fact that (as de Tocqueville observed in America) democracy affords neither time nor place for that profitable meditation which makes for the peace of a man's, or a nation's, soul. In studying Chinese history it is well to remember these things.

One of the most conspicuous results of the Chinese educational and philosophical systems confronts us in the family likeness impressed by classical traditions upon

INTRODUCTION

the seven ages of their literature. All the annalists of the Mings, like their forbears under the Sung dynasty, and their descendants under the Manchus, use the same stock phrases, metaphors and arguments, derived one and all from the classical authors of antiquity. Age can never wither, nor custom stale, the perennial vitality of their venerable quotations. The more remote their ancientry, the better do they become in the eyes of a race of scholars who

"Though they wrote in all by rote,
Could never write it right."

All Chinese literature is sicklied o'er by the pale cast of the Confucian tradition; therefore it is, that in the Ming chroniclers of the sixteenth century, as in those of the T'ang dynasty, we find the same set phrases, the same artificial gestures and ready-made emotions, as we find in the presidential mandates of Yuan Shih-k'ai to-day. Throughout the whole course of Chinese history, events, as recorded by the Hanlin annalist, become stereotyped in fixed groves and rigid patterns. The Confucian scholar sees and interprets the whole human comedy in rigid terms of classical allusions. For him there is, indeed, no new thing under the sun; nothing in heaven or earth, concerning which the Four Books and the Five Classics have not said the first and last word. In the fifteenth century, a somewhat similar attitude obtained amongst the rank and file of European scholars; indeed there is reason to believe that it survives, to this day, in certain slumbering backwaters of our universities. The mind which lives for and by Latin odes or Greek elegiacs at Oxford is surely the same, in its causes and effects, as that which rejoices in the production of antithetical couplets at Peking; fortunately for itself, however, it has to deal with a different public. The absence of a healthy spirit of criticism, due to the Middle Kingdom's splendid

INTRODUCTION

isolation and self-sufficiency, gradually evolved a type of scholarship amongst the Chinese which displays all the erudition of a Montaigne, a Bacon or a Burton, but lacks their saving graces of humour and humanity. Thus it is that the mandarin scholar, century after century, has seen and described men and events in a dull monotone of conventional platitudes. Borne down by the weight of the classical tradition, all things in heaven and earth are associated in his mind with the odes of Confucius, the stilted periods of some Sung philosopher, or the poems of Li Tai-po. It is not surprising, therefore, that we find official annalists of the present day using precisely the same expressions as those which were in vogue amongst the writers of the Ming period; or that, throughout the dynastic annals, we find evidence of a tendency, on the part of the chroniclers, to make history conform, as far as possible, to the precedents established by the old times before them.

Judged in the light of its achievements, and even of its avowed aims, Young China stands at present condemned of futility. With a fair field and much favour, it has failed to seize its splendid opportunities; it has been weighed in the balance and found wanting. But even whilst we recognise that its shrill-voiced iconoclasm and loud beating of imported drums present but little justification for optimism, yet this, at least, must be placed to its credit, that its fervour of zeal for Western learning has been, and is, an intelligent protest—a conscious reaction—against the petrefaction of the Confucian system, against "the letter which killeth"; a wholesome breeze of dawn, stirring the dead bones in the dark valleys of Chinese tradition. The lamp which they have lighted can never again be extinguished; the old order must pass, giving place to the new. It will be well for China and for the world if, in destroying the fetters of the past, the leaders of the people find grace and wisdom to seek once

INTRODUCTION

more the pure well of moral philosophy from which the early sages drew their sweetness and their light.

Amongst such morals and conclusions as the reader may draw from study of these three centuries of Chinese history, one of the most obvious is to be found in the persistent coincidence of periods of demoralisation in the State with the ascendancy of eunuchs at Court. The Chinese have always realised the truth of this matter; scholars, historians and moralists never fail to declare that the Empire's crisis of private corruption and public disorder, the decline and fall of dynasties, have been caused or greatly hastened by the interference and intrigues of these Court menials in affairs of State. The first Manchu rulers perceived clearly the evils of a eunuch-ridden Court, and took wise precautions against them. In the fate of the Mings, the lesson was writ plain for them to learn, adding one more to the many warnings of history against the insidious dangers of the Court's excessive polygamy and the atmosphere of debauchery and enervation thereby created. They could see for themselves to what a pitiful state the Throne and Court had been brought by the tyrannous cruelty, treachery and greed of the eunuchs who infested the Forbidden City and projected the " poisonous miasma " of their influence to the farthest frontiers of the Empire. It is noteworthy that, amongst that many emasculated Palace officials who rose to place and power under the Mings and again under the latter Manchus, few displayed the fidelity and the civic virtues which seem to have distinguished those of the Court of Babylon, or those which Herodotus attributes to the eunuch magnates of Persia. Fidelity to the person of the Emperor we find, indeed (though none too frequently), combined with literary and histrionic talents of a high order and great intellectual vigour; but the history of China, during the period with which we are dealing, produces no eunuch general or statesman com-

INTRODUCTION

parable to that Hermias, Governor of Atarnea, to whose manes Aristotle offered sacrifice and sincere reverence.

If we compare the condition of China's civil service and military organisation of to-day with that which obtained in the reign of Ch'ien Lung, we are compelled to seek for specific causes to account for so complete a demoralisation of the ruling caste and so swift decay of the nation's civic and patriotic instincts. A century and a half ago, Chinese armies, organised under the rigorous military system of the Manchus, were steadily fighting one successful war after another, thereby extending the frontiers of the Empire and the benefits of its well-ordered administration to independent Tartary, Thibet, Nepal, Burmah and Sungaria. Studying the history of this great Monarch's long reign, and that of his immediate successors, we perceive that the chief cause of the swift decline and fall of the Manchu power, and of the consequent demoralisation of the whole system of government, lay (as Tzŭ Hsi admitted on her deathbed) in the corruption of public and private morals which set in, so soon as the " rats and foxes " of the Court were permitted to interfere in affairs of State. So long at the Palace eunuchs were kept in the place wisely assigned to them by Shun Chih, and debarred from all high offices, the Court retained its virile dignity and the public service its efficiency. The luxury, nepotism and venality introduced during the *régime* of Ch'ien Lung's favourite, the Grand Secretary, Ho Shen, restored to the Palace eunuchs opportunities which they had not enjoyed since the overthrow of the Ming dynasty. Fifty years later, their ascendancy at Court was completely established. Henceforward, they were able to exercise once more their traditional functions as the tempters of youth, the debauchers of age, in the profound seclusion of the Forbidden City, until gradually the Son of Heaven on his Throne became a defenceless puppet in their supple bloodstained hands. Steep is the ascent

INTRODUCTION

of Olympus, rapid the descent to Avernus; the structural character of a people moves onward and upward only by slow processes of evolution, but its destruction is often brought about by swift and direct factors of demoralisation. Seldom is this truth thrown into relief so clear as that in which we see it against the background of China's history, during the periods immediately preceding the downfall of the Ming and Manchu dynasties.

PART I
THE MING DYNASTY

CHAPTER I

A CHINESE HAROUN AL RASCHID

WHEN, in 1368, Chu Yüan-chang, Buddhist priest, administrator and fighter, established the Ming dynasty by his successful rebellion against the degenerate descendants of Kublai Khan, and thus shattered the last remnants of the great Mongol Empire, he laid down certain principles for the government of China which proved him to be a statesman of the first order. He realised clearly that the rulers of the Celestial Empire must govern rather by moral than material force, and that the consent of the governed will always be withdrawn from those who lack the moral qualities which the people reverence and expect in their rulers. During his reign and that of his illustrious nephew, Yung Lo, literature, education, arts, industries and commerce were systematically encouraged, with results that conferred great glory on the dynasty and prosperity on the people. The founder of the great Ming dynasty, whose throne was established by the sword, knew that the pen is a mightier weapon against the vicissitudes of Time—by its aid he hoped to revive a patriotic spirit and the instincts of nationalism, long dormant in the Chinese people. He therefore reorganised the whole system of the public service and competitive examinations, revised the penal code, regulated taxation, and introduced a national currency. More important than all, as has since been repeatedly proved, he forbade the official employment of eunuchs at the capital.

In subsequent chapters, dealing with the decline and fall of the Ming dynasty, the rebellion of Li Tzŭ-ch'eng, and the establishment of the Manchu power, the reader will perceive that the Ming rulers' failure to observe this fundamental principle of government (upon which the great Tzu Hsi insisted as she lay dying in 1908), was the chief cause of their final overthrow and of countless calamities to the nation at large. It was in the year 1430, that the Emperor Hsüan Tsung, grandson of Yung Lo, adopted the well-meant but disastrous course of raising the status of the Palace menials, and giving them the advantages of a first-class literary education. During the reign of his successor, the power of the eunuchs and their interference in affairs of State steadily increased, and from this time the decline of the great Ming dynasty may be said to have commenced.

Before proceeding to describe, from contemporary annals and State papers, the dark days of anarchy and bloodshed which preceded the subjugation of China by the Manchus, let us narrate the following episodes from the life of the Ming Emperor Chang Tê, who reigned from 1506 to 1522. The story is taken from a contemporary memoir, now very scarce; it throws instructive light on the life and manners of the Court of those days, before the energies of the Mings had been sapped to the extent of making the Emperor little better than a puppet in his gilded prison of the Forbidden City.

The Emperor Chang Tê (a reign title, meaning "Orthodox Virtue") is described by Chinese historians as a sensual and thriftless monarch. He may have been; but he would seem at least to have been superior to many of his successors in possessing a will of his own, a sense of humour, a taste for adventure, and other redeeming qualities, as shown by the following incidents of his reign.

In the year 1508, the graduate-doctors of the lowest degree, or Hanlin bachelors, were undergoing a test examination before a Commission in the Palace to qualify for metropolitan or provincial posts. The Emperor himself was present and took an active part in the examination.

One of the candidates, a bachelor of the Hanlin Academy, named Lin Chi-shih, a native of Fuhkien Province, was addicted to the use of arbitrary or archaic forms in the writing of characters. When the essays were handed in, His Majesty objected to Lin's style of writing and asked what was his authority for such affectations. Lin replied that they were archaisms. At this, the Emperor wrote out a spurious character of his own invention and asked him to give it a name. Lin said he did not know it, whereupon His Majesty observed: "If one character may be written topsy-turvy, why not another? You are evidently not a scholar of the standard required in the Hanlin Academy. I order that you return to your native place to study for three years, at the end of which time you may come to Peking and compete again at the examinations."

Lin thanked the Emperor and withdrew. His friends and relations all looked upon him as a victim of Imperial displeasure, and refused to have any further dealings with him. Being very poor, he could not afford to pay the cost of the journey back to Fuhkien, and no official in Peking would give him employment as tutor, owing to his having incurred Imperial censure. He therefore proceeded to earn his livelihood by writing scrolls at a stand in the street just outside the Ch'ien Men, the main gate of the Tartar city, leading to the Palace.

As his writing was admirable, he attracted much attention from literary men. One day, about a year later, the Emperor, walking about as he loved to do, incognito, was passing the scribe's stand, when his curiosity was aroused by the large crowd of scholars, who were pressing round and uttering admiring comments.

Anxious to learn the cause of the commotion, the

Emperor made his way through the crowd and observed a young man wielding his pen with extraordinary rapidity and skill. His caligraphy and the style of his composition showed plainly that he was a master of the literary language, and the Emperor (no bad judge) was delighted with his work. He had forgotten the man's face, being at that time completely absorbed in the charms of the latest favourite in his harem.

So, coming nearer, he said to the writer: "I perceive that your caligraphy and composition are alike excellent; why do you not compete at the examinations, instead of wasting your talents in this humble occupation?" Lin looked up and failed to recognise His Majesty, but perceived at once that it was no common person who thus addressed him; so, rising from his place, he bowed low and invited him to be seated. "My name," said he, "is Lin: I, all unworthy, passed for the Hanlin Bachelorship." The Emperor replied: "It is not fitting that a member of so honourable a body as the Hanlin Academy should engage in what is really a form of street hawking." "At the Court examination held last year for conferring official appointments upon Hanlin bachelors," said Lin, "I failed to recognise a character written by His Majesty, and was by him commanded to return home to Fuhkien and study." "Why, then, have you disobeyed the order and remained in the capital?" "Because," said Lin, "I come of a very poor family and could not afford to pay for my journey home. My present employment was the only livelihood left to me." The Emperor asked why he did not seek a position as tutor. Lin answered: "All the world knows that I am in disgrace, and so no one dares engage my services." The Emperor then said: "I will recommend you for a post as secretary in a neighbouring province, which will at least be an improvement on your present vocation."

Lin gratefully bowed his thanks and asked the Emperor's

title and address, in order that he might call and return thanks for his kindness. "Never mind that," said His Majesty, "wait here to-morrow for a messenger from me." With that he turned away. None of the spectators had recognised him, though all were surprised at his kindness to Lin. Next day, a eunuch from the Palace arrived bearing a sealed yellow envelope and a hundred taels. These he handed to Lin, saying: "Yesterday an official personage told me to hand these to you, sir, and to direct you to follow the instructions written on this envelope. On no account are you to open it, lest evil befall you. This money is for your travelling expenses." The eunuch then took his departure, leaving no name. Lin examined the envelope and read the inscription writ large: "To be delivered in person to the Governor of Shantung and to be opened by him."

Lin joyfully closed his stand, hired a cart and proceeded with his former servant to Chi-nan fu. At that time the substantive post of Governor was vacant, and was temporarily filled by the Treasurer. Arrived at the provincial capital, Lin took up his quarters at an inn, changed his clothes and proceeded with his servant to the Governor's yamên. The Acting Governor had a high reputation as an honest official and a strict disciplinarian; his underlings dared not accept bribes, so it was no easy matter to gain access to his presence. For three days in succession Lin tried unsuccessfully to send in his card, and at last said reproachfully to one of the gate-keepers: "I have a secret message from Peking which I must deliver in person. Why do you obstruct me like this?" The underling then informed the official in charge of the gate, who ordered Lin to approach, but, on observing his somewhat common raiment, came to the conclusion that he was merely a suppliant for favour. Therefore he shook his head contemptuously, saying: "My master is Acting Governor of this province and far too busy to see any former friend of his less prosperous days. Any letter you may have for him I will deliver; meanwhile, get you to your lodging and wait until you hear from me." Lin was obliged to hand him the yellow envelope and went sorrowfully back to the inn.

Scarcely had he reached his room, when the landlord came rushing in and made obeisance before him. "I did not recognise Your Excellency," he said, "and have failed in respect to your attendants, I deserve to die a thousand deaths." Indignantly Lin answered: "Why do you mock my poverty?" The landlord was about to explain, when a great commotion was heard outside the inn; gongs were beaten and crackers fired. An aide-de-camp from the Governor had arrived, attended by a large retinue, and was kneeling reverently at the inn door. When the ceremony was completed, he rose and addressed Lin: "The provincial Treasurer bids us invite Your Excellency the Imperial Commissioner to proceed to his office."

Lin, completely dumbfounded, felt as if he were walking on air. However, he was assisted, almost by force, into a sedan-chair borne by eight men. Preceded by a long line of insignia bearers and followed by troops of horsemen, he was carried into the yamên, just outside the main hall of audience. Here, the provincial Treasurer (that was Acting Governor) was awaiting him in full dress. Alighting from the sedan he observed an altar upon which incense was burning; on it lay the yellow envelope which had been entrusted to him for delivery. The Treasurer knelt before the altar and saluted His Sacred Majesty's communication; then, bowing to Lin, he said: "Will Your Excellency the Imperial Commissioner be pleased to read aloud the sacred decree?" Lin opened the envelope and read: "The Governorship of Shantung is at present vacant. WE command Lin Chi-shih to act as Governor." Realising that it was the Emperor himself who had befriended him, he kotowed nine times in the direction of the Forbidden City. The Treasurer then came forward with his congratulations, apologising for not having met him at some distance from the city. So Lin became Governor of Shantung and, as in duty bound, drafted a memorial of thanks to His Majesty and requested an audience. Not long after he received the Imperial rescript: "WE saw that you possessed capacity and WE therefore conferred this appointment upon you. Do your duty diligently in all things, so as to do credit to Our choice. In three years time return to Peking and give an account of your Governorship."

At the expiry of the appointed time Lin returned to the capital and had audience with the Emperor, who said: "You have now acquired a literary efficiency: WE appoint you Hanlin compiler. Study three years more at the Academy, and WE shall then see what higher appointment you may deserve."

On another occasion, the Emperor entered the quarters in the Palace where the Grand Secretaries were wont to transact business after audience, and found all the officials there assembled at breakfast. They rose at his entrance, and the Emperor said: "Come all of you to my private apartments, after you have finished, that we may talk." In due course they joined His Majesty, who bade them be seated. "You have all been eating rice," said he; "do you know anything about the method of its cultivation and the difficulty of producing a crop? Before I succeeded to the Throne, I used to fancy that cereals were produced like weeds, that they grew of themselves without any trouble being bestowed on them. However, now that I often roam about the country and have seen with my own eyes the hardships which the peasants endure, I realise the truth of the old saying: 'Every grain of the rice on your plate is won by the sweat of the brow.' You, my ministers, come from various parts of the Empire, and the customs of North and South differ greatly. I desire now to extend my knowledge, and I therefore request that each of you will state fully for my information the methods of sowing, weeding and harvesting rice in your respective parts of the Empire." It so happened that most of the Ministers of the day had begun life as farmers' sons and peasants, so they were able to supply the Emperor with the information he desired. But there was one president of a Board, by name Chang Chin, of an ancient and aristocratic family, who was quite ignorant of the subject. To him His Majesty scornfully said: "How can you perform the functions of your office if you are so grossly ignorant about the production of the very food you eat? Can you possibly attend to the daily business of your Board without committing some serious blunder or dereliction of duty?"

The President was so much alarmed that he could only kotow, and then in his confusion he mumbled: "I am Chief of the Ministry of Civil Appointments; this morning I attended office, and the last business we dealt with was the filling of a vacancy in Kiangsu Province for the post of Deputy Assistant District Magistrate (the lowest post in the Empire carrying official rank). My ministry has the right to nominate for this post on this occasion, as on the last occasion the Governor of the Province conferred the appo ntment." [1]

His Majesty roared with laughter: "Is this wretched piece of routine business all you can cite in answer to my question?" With that he shook his sleeve, dismissing the ministers. The President's colleagues asked him why he had made such a stupid reply. "I was so greatly bewildered," said he, "that my mind refused to think of anything else."

[1] Posts below a certain rank in the provinces are filled alternately on the invitation of the Peking Ministry and of the provincial authorities.

THE COURT OF PEKING

A few days later a decree was issued: " The post of Deputy Assistant District Magistrate at T'ai-hu in Kiangsu is hereby given to President Chang Chin!" On reading the decree he was greatly distressed. Turning to his colleagues, he said: " What can it mean and what shall I do? The lowest post in the official list is given me; naturally I must proceed to take up my new duties, but would it be right for me to ask for a farewell audience before leaving Peking?" His colleagues, greatly tickled at the Imperial jest, replied: " What right has an official of the lowest rank to demand an audience? All you can do is to prostrate yourself at the Gate of Mid-day,[1] and thank His Majesty. There they will give you the warrant authorising you to take over the post. But as the decree says nothing about your being cashiered or reduced in rank, you will have to go on wearing your first-class button and official robes."

On arrival at the provincial capital, he found the Governor and all the local officials awaiting to greet him in the suburbs as a mark of respect. But he begged them to desist and go home, while he proceeded on foot to pay his respects to the various officials, presenting to each his visiting card, drawn up in the humblest form like that of a petitioner. This made all the officials rather uncomfortable, as he was superior in rank to them all, so they begged him to remain in residence at the provincial capital and not to trouble about taking up his post. He replied; " How dare I disobey the Imperial mandate. I shall proceed thither on the first auspicious day." Thereupon the Prefect and Magistrate of T'ai-hu decided in all haste to decorate and alter his official residence, so as to make it resemble as closely as possible, and so far as size would allow, the yamên of a governor. Outside they mustered a great number of lictors and runners, with a forest of

---

[1] The southern gate of the Forbidden City.

insignia and bands of musicians, and they placed *chevaux de frise* in front of the main entrance.

On his arrival, the President-Magistrate observed that his new residence was surrounded on three sides by rice-fields, and thus it came to him that His Majesty desired him to learn by practical experience the hardships of a farmer's life. So he dismissed all his underlings and retinue, and thereafter made it his daily business to go, simply dressed, amongst the people, visiting the adjoining villages and chatting with the elders concerning the condition of the peasantry. He made careful study of their grievances, and took note of wrongs that might be put right. Five years he lived amongst them, acting as mediator and arbitrator in their disputes, so that he earned the respect of all men and their goodwill.

When, in 1519, Prince Ning, a kinsman of the Emperor, rebelled, His Majesty came South in person to chastise him, and arrived in due course at Soochow, the provincial capital of Kiangsu Province. The ex-President, hearing of his impending arrival, hurried to Soochow and said to the Governor: " I who have held one of the highest posts in the Empire am in duty bound to wait upon His Majesty when he arrives here, but official etiquette forbids that one who holds so humble a post as that of Deputy Assistant District Magistrate should proceed to the provincial capital and absent himself from his duties. What do you advise me to do ? "

The Governor and his colleagues replied : " As regards official duties you are, it is true, our subordinate, but in rank you are our superior. You should, therefore, go to meet His Majesty, wearing your robes and insignia of the highest rank, but you should take up a position in our rear." To this the President agreed. As the Imperial cortège drew near, His Majesty, who was on horseback, recognised him from a distance, and bade him approach, " Do you now understand," said he, " the hardships of a

THE COURT OF PEKING

farmer's life?" The President kotowed and thanked the Emperor for the lesson he had given him. His Majesty bade him join the Imperial party at the travelling lodge, and there questioned him concerning the fulfilment of his charge. The President gave him full details of the various reforms he had initiated, which so pleased His Majesty that he promoted him to a rank even higher than that which he had previously enjoyed, namely, to be Assistant Grand Secretary.

During this same expedition against Prince Ning, while the Imperial barge was moored one day at Ch'ing ho on the Grand Canal in Kiangsu, His Majesty went incognito and afoot to an adjacent teashop, desiring to hear something of the local gossip. As he sat there, he heard many grievous complaints concerning the squeezing and barefaced robbery which travellers were suffering at the hands of certain military officers and their underlings. Every boat passing up and down the canal at this point, whether laden with merchandise or personal baggage, was liable to detention until it paid their extortionate charges, and if the " squeeze " was not promptly forthcoming, all the contents of the boat were often confiscated and the boat itself smashed to pieces. Travellers and traders were loud in their helpless wrath at this state of affairs, and many expressed their hope that the rebel prince would defeat the Imperialist forces, for any change must be for the better.

The Emperor made up his mind to look into these matters for himself, so he bought a small boat, dressed himself as a trader, and with only one body-servant and a young eunuch, proceeded down the canal. On reaching the Customs station which lies outside the important city of Yang chou-fu, close to the Yangtsze, the Emperor saw hundreds of boats drawn up in rows, which were being searched by the river police and petty Customs officers.

A large Customs barge was moored to the bank where the tolls were fixed and protests heard. From each boat heavy payment was being exacted in the name of the Emperor, and ostensibly for the purpose of providing funds to suppress the rebellion. All the merchants meekly paid "squeeze" to the underlings, who were rapidly making their fortunes. When the time came for the Emperor's boat to be searched, His Majesty lay prone in the stern and when summoned to rise paid no attention. The runners, therefore, seized him roughly and brought him to the Customs barge, where he saw an official in full robes surrounded by lictors and seated at a table, as if he were presiding at a court. As the Emperor approached, this official began angrily to upbraid him: " What manner of man are you who dare interfere with His Majesty's servants in the execution of their duty? Has the law no terrors for you; do you not fear the heavier bamboo?" At this the Emperor smiled contemptuously, so the official bade his lictors strip him and apply the heavy bamboo to his person. Happily His Majesty's body-servant was a particularly lusty fellow, and he succeeded in putting fear into the myrmidons for the time being, so that the Emperor suffered no insult. But the official grew angrier than ever. He shouted: " This is evidently some notorious river pirate or cut-throat. Go and arrest his boatman." They did so, and flogged him cruelly to make him confess that he knew the Emperor to be a robber.

Meanwhile, His Majesty had drawn from his breast a tablet of jade and told the eunuch to take it to the Lieutenant Governor of the province (who at that time resided at Yang chou) and bid him come quickly. Very soon, in obedience to the Imperial command, the Governor came hurrying up in a panic of nervous fear. On seeing him approach the Customs official knelt at the gangway to receive him, and was just beginning to tell him how he had captured a notorious pirate, when the Governor perceived

THE COURT OF PEKING

the Emperor standing near the main mast. Reverently he fell upon his knees, and prostrated himself in the dust, imploring forgiveness.

The Emperor remained silent, but made signs to his body-servant to remove the offending official's hat and button. These he presented to the boatman, who thus attained to official rank. Said he: "This hat is to compensate you for the pain you have suffered." Next he ordered that the official be arrested and made to disgorge his ill-gotten gains, after which he was duly decapitated. All the higher officials of the town were punished for having failed to put a stop to these exactions, and from this time forward the boats of travellers were allowed to pass in peace.

On the last night of the year after the Emperor's return to Peking from the expedition against Prince Ning, he left the Forbidden City to make a round of the various government offices, for he knew that they would then be practically deserted, as the officials would be seeing the old year out at their own homes. But when he reached the Board of Appointments (Li pu) he heard sounds of cheerful song proceeding from the main hall, as if a large party of revellers were gathered together. The song was of the South.

The Emperor entered and, to his astonishment, found only one petty official, who was singing to himself, with a plate of meat before him and a wine kettle. This man rose as the visitor entered, and politely offering him a seat, proffered a cup of wine. The Emperor asked him: "What is your official rank and why are you here all alone?" He replied: "I am a native of Chekiang and am on duty at this Board as a clerk. The seals being locked up for the New Year holiday, all the officials are away at their homes, drinking and feasting with their families. I thought it wrong and dangerous that such a mass of official documents and archives should remain unguarded, so I have remained here on watch and will not desert my post." The Monarch said: "Very good. I shall see you to-morrow." With that he departed, the clerk attended him to the door, and then resumed his solitary vigil.

Next morning, when the whole Court and the chief metropolitan officials proceeded to the main Palace hall to offer their New Year congratulations, the Emperor turned to the President of the Board of Appointments (the same man who had just returned from learning the hardships of a farmer's life in the T'ai hu magistracy), and asked: "What is the name of the clerk who was on watch at your Board last night? Let him attend our audience at once."

The President promptly dispatched a Board secretary to command the clerk's presence. So he came to the Throne Hall, and after making the nine obeisances, looked up and perceived in the Emperor his guest of the previous evening. He trembled all over, but His Majesty reassured him. "Be not alarmed. Your diligent performance of duty and faithfulness to the trust imposed upon you, are worthy of the highest praise. What is the highest promotion to which you would be entitled at the end of your present term of office?" The clerk answered: "If my conduct has been blameless for five years and no black marks are recorded against me, the most I could expect would be to be eligible for selection as an official of the secondary ninth rank."[1] His Majesty said: "What post do you covet?" "What your unworthy servant covets is the post of Deputy Assistant District Magistrate at T'ai hu in Kiangsu, because it has been temporarily held of late by the President of my Board. It would be an extraordinary honour to obtain it, because recent events have caused it to loom large in the public eye. But as my

[1] This is the lowest rank entitling the holder to be classed as an "official."

time of duty at my present post is still unexpired, it would be contrary to precedent."

His Majesty smiled: "If WE command you to proceed, what has precedent to do with the case?" The clerk, overcome with joy, exclaimed: "Wan Sui!" (Ten thousand years) "May Your Majesty live for ever!" So the Emperor bade the President prepare the necessary papers and arrange for the clerk's immediate departure to take up his new post.

In 1517, the Emperor, whose eccentricities and excursions were the despair of the Court, took it upon himself to proceed incognito to Hsüan-hua fu (about 120 miles north of Peking). The fairest damsel in that city was "Sister Phœnix," then in her seventeenth year; she was the daughter of a wine distiller named Li, and she kept his shop. One day, when her father was out, the Emperor, passing by on one of his walks, observed her dazzling and queenly beauty. At the charm of a glance, sufficient of itself to overthrow a kingdom, His Majesty felt as if he were losing control of his senses. He entered and called for wine. The maiden brought it, and the Emperor, supposing her to be an ordinary courtesan, seized her in his arms and bore her to the inner chamber. She was shouting for help, when His Majesty placed his hand over her mouth and said: "WE are the Son of Heaven. Trust yourself to Us, and wealth and power are yours from this day forward."

Now it so happened that Sister Phœnix had recently dreamed more than once that she was changed into a white pearl and carried off by a divine dragon. But there the dream had always stopped. She now understood its meaning, and believing the Emperor's word, submitted to his august wishes. His Majesty was enraptured to know that she was no courtesan, but a pure maiden.

When, in response to her first cry for help, her father had come upon the scene, he found the door fast bolted, and as her cries had ceased he believed that his beloved daughter had been the victim of a cruel outrage. He ran, therefore, to summon the guard; but as they came rushing up the Emperor opened the door and came out. He revealed his identity to the excited Li, whereupon all present made humble obeisance. His Majesty then bade them conduct Sister Phœnix to the quarters occupied by his concubines. To her father he gave a thousand ounces of gold and raised him to the rank of a high official. It was his wish to bestow upon Sister Phœnix the rank of an Imperial Concubine of the second grade, were she so inclined. Humbly she declined the honour. "Your maidservant," said she, "has but a little measure of good fortune to expect: she is not long for this world. Were I to accept the rank which Your Majesty's divine goodness would bestow upon me, it would hasten my death. Have I not had the immeasurable honour of finding favour in the sight of the 'World Honoured One'? Is not that a sufficient reward for my humble merits? In all humility I would beseech Your Majesty to consider your duty to your people and to return speedily to the capital. By so doing you will give me far greater happiness than by conferring honours upon me."

The Emperor realised that her simple peasant's attire served only to enhance her radiant beauty, and so he did not urge her to exchange it for the robes of a concubine. She was ever at his side in those days, serving him at table and sharing his couch. But she never ceased to beg him to return to Peking and at last, won by her gentle entreaties, he consented to fix the day for his departure.

Sister Phœnix travelled by his side until the cortège reached the Great Wall (forty miles from Peking). Here a terrible storm broke upon them, and the party took shelter at a house just inside the gate of Chü-Yung kuan. Suddenly Sister Phœnix saw that the images of the Four Heavenly Kings, or Defenders of Buddhism, which stand guarding the entrance, seemed to be endowed with life, and that they turned angry glances in her direction. At the sight she fainted and fell to the ground. Gently the Emperor raised her and had her borne to a temple outside the barrier. He watched by her bedside until she recovered consciousness, when she said: "Your handmaid knew full well that she was not destined long to enjoy the sweets of life, or to wait upon Your Majesty in the Forbidden City. Let me now leave you and return to my home." The Emperor answered: "I cannot grant that prayer, for I would rather abandon my Empire than be deprived of your sweet and gracious person." Sadly she gazed at him, and then, with a deep sigh, expired.

His Majesty mourned long and deeply over the death of his favourite, and commanded that she be buried with Imperial honours at the summit of the pass. So they built a huge mound of yellow earth over her tomb, but, to the amazement of all, in one night the yellow earth became white; so powerful her virtuous will, even after death. The Emperor pondered long over her advice concerning his duty to attend to State affairs. Said he: "If even a maiden could realise the responsibility of the head of the State towards his people, surely I should profit by her advice." With that he returned straightway to Peking. The historians record that the Emperor had paid no heed to the repeated entreaties of his officials, that he should be pleased to leave Hsüan-hua and resume his place at the capital: how strange, they say, that a humble peasant girl should have been able to persuade him to return to the path of duty! Is it not an example of what the Canon of History calls "The softness of the feminine nature overcoming a strong man's will"?

In the year 1508 the triennial autumn examination took place in Peking for the Masters' degree. As usual, thousands of scholars from all parts of the provinces had assembled in the metropolis. The soothsayers and fortune-tellers were all busily plying their trade in booths just outside the Ch'ien Men; one of them attracted particular attention by proclaiming, in a well-written notice exhibited outside his booth, that he challenged comparison with the most famous magicians known to history. He boasted that he could tell at once the rank and antecedents of any official who might come to him incognito, and that he had never made a mistake. As the days went by this fame increased, and there was always a crowd around his booth. Soon His Majesty came to hear of him, and passing by his booth one day, joined the crowd and watched him at his trade. The time was 11 a.m. on the 8th day of the 8th moon. Suddenly there was noise and commotion. The crowd swayed and parted, and through it there came rushing a scholar who seized hold of the fortune-teller and shouted: "You have ruined my career for good and all. Either you or I shall die for it." The spectators tried to separate the combatants, but without success. The Emperor motioned to his attendant, a man of powerful physique, to separate them, and proceeded to inquire what all the excitement was about.

The soothsayer replied: "A few days ago this man came here to consult me with regard to his prospects in the impending examination, and I promised that he would win the first place. Now, having failed to take his place in the examination hall, he comes here forsooth and blames me for his own unpunctuality. Much learning has made him mad."

At this, the scholar broke in and said: "Because you foretold that I should come out at the head of the list, my friends gave me a banquet, at which I became very drunk. When at last my servant managed to arouse me, I got up and hurried to the examination hall, but the gates were already barred.[1] Did you ever hear of a non-competitor coming out at the head of the list? Are you not, then, the sole cause of my undoing?"

The two men continued loudly disputing, until the Emperor said to the soothsayer: "Cease your brawling! Supposing I get this scholar admitted to the examination hall and he fails to come out at the head of the list, to what punishment will you submit?"

The soothsayer replied: "You may gouge out one eye." "All right," said the Emperor, "that's a bargain." He then took up pen and paper from the table, wrote a few words, and sealed the document with a small seal which he wore at his girdle. He then bade his attendant go with the scholar and deliver the paper. To the soothsayer he said, "Farewell: I shall return in a fortnight to prove your words." The soothsayer guessed that it was the Emperor, and promptly folded his tent and departed.

Meantime, the attendant and the scholar proceeded to the examination hall, some two miles away. The Imperial messenger then commanded the drums to be beaten, as a signal that he was the bearer of a decree from His Sacred Majesty. The seals upon the gates were speedily removed and the locks opened, whereupon the officials on duty outside the hall sounded a gong. This brought an usher from within, who escorted the attendant and the scholar up to the main hall, where the Imperial examiners were seated. As the Imperial messenger approached they all knelt: he strode to the daïs and there, facing South, read the decree. Having done so he left to report the fulfilment of his mission.

A censor and an inspector then conducted the scholar

[1] A competitor was excluded from participation once the gates had been closed, as they could not be re-opened until after the examination.

to one of the vacant cells. Examiners and candidates alike marvelled that the Emperor should thus send a *protégé* of his to take part in the examination. Naturally, the chief examiners paid particular attention to his papers, and finding that his composition was quite good and his principles sound, they said one to another : " This candidate having been specially recommended by the present occupant of the Throne, it would be disrespectful to His Majesty if we were to place any other name ahead of his on the class lists." So they passed him at the top of his year, and in reporting the fact to the Emperor, warmly praised the excellence of his style and his exceptional gifts. They seized the occasion to congratulate the Emperor on being so good a judge of talent.

The Emperor laughed loudly : " This is surely Fate," said he. As a matter of fact he had originally intended that the scholar should be ploughed, in order that he might triumph over the soothsayer, but, as luck would have it, he had been so much engrossed in dalliance with the latest favourite of his harem, that the whole thing had escaped his memory, and he had forgotten to send word to the chief examiner. Now that the scholar had come out at the head of the list, he was deeply impressed with the soothsayer's prophetic skill and desired to engage his services for the Court. So, after sending messengers in vain, he set out in state, at the head of a large retinue, to look for him; but the soothsayer had vanished and was never seen again.

Early one spring morning, the Emperor had just left the harem, and was taking a drive in the city before holding his daily audience in the Palace, when he met a bridal procession on its way to the bridegroom's house. The insignia were borne by an army of attendants, and the magnificence of the equipages and of the escort showed that the bridegroom was of a distinguished family. Much impressed, the Emperor stopped his cart and, standing by the roadside, watched the long cavalcade go by. Just as the bride's chair drew near, he saw a black giant, twenty feet high, standing in front of it as if to bar her way. His features were cruel and repulsive in the extreme; he was clad in armour and wielded a huge club. Insolently he stood there, until suddenly he perceived the Emperor, when he seemed to hesitate, and finally hurried away to the head of the cortège. The Emperor's cart-driver had seen nothing of this monstrous apparition. Greatly wondering, His Majesty bade the man drive on, following in rear of the procession, until they came to the bridegroom's house, which he perceived to be the stately mansion of some ancient and respected family. The Emperor alighted and went in towards the main hall. The black giant had preceded the bride's chair and was standing in the courtyard, but when he saw the Son of Heaven approach, he covered his face and vanished. His Majesty then remembered that this particular day was unlucky, owing to the power therein of the Spirit of Disaster; no doubt it was this spirit which had so strangely crossed his path. He thought that whoever had chosen such an unlucky day for a marriage was greatly to blame, and determined to find out who was responsible for so disastrous a selection.

So he waited, while the bride descended from her chair and the newly wedded pair made obeisance to heaven and earth in the inner chamber. After the bride had been duly conducted to the nuptial apartment the banquet was served, and the host came forward to invite the wedding guests to take their seats. In all sixteen tables were prepared, and the guests sat down in their order of seniority and precedence. The host could see that the Emperor was no ordinary visitor, so invited him to the seat of honour at the central table, and himself came and sat beside him. As he did so, his limbs trembled as if he were in the presence of some divine being; he dared not even ask his guest's honourable name.

The Emperor asked him who the person was who had selected this day for the wedding. The host pointed to a venerable man at the second table, and said: " He was formerly a director at the Court of Astronomy, now retired. He is a past master of his art; any family wishing to fix a date for an auspicious event invariably secures his services. He has never yet been known to fail."

" Ask him to come here," said the Emperor, who thus addressed the astrologer: " I am told that you are an expert in selecting auspicious days. What made you invoke disaster to-day by your cabalistic arts? " The old man replied: " Not so: it is quite true that between the hours of three and five this morning the black Spirit of Disaster, the so-called ' Ruler of the Evil Stars,' was due to descend into the world, but at the same hour the Fortunate Star of Good Omen was also destined to appear among mortals. His benign influence routed the forces of evil, and has made the occasion auspicious in the extreme. So far from portending ruin, the event is the harbinger of much future prosperity."

The Emperor could think of no way of refuting his words, so he said: " I have just composed the first verse of an antithetical couplet; if you can supply me with the second half, matching mine exactly, I will forgive you the punishment which you deserve, if only for bandying words so plausibly. Here is my verse:

"The ruler of the evil stars hath encountered the ruler of all mortal men."

The old man asked to be excused on the plea of his old age and failing faculties. " Will you permit the bridegroom to try his skill in my stead? " The Emperor agreed, so the bridegroom was summoned. On hearing the first verse, he replied without a moment's hesitation:

THE COURT OF PEKING

"The bright Star of Good Omen[1] has shone upon the fortunate bridegroom!"

The Emperor was delighted at the prompt and fitting antithesis and said to the assembled company: "Some day he will become a doctor of the Hanlin Academy." The old man then bade the bridegroom prostrate himself on the ground and thank His Majesty, who, seeing that his disguise had been discovered, mounted his carriage and departed.

The bridegroom had already attained his Master's degree; after passing the next year for the doctorate, he attended at Court, together with the other successful competitors, to be presented. The Emperor recognised him, and appointed him to be a Hanlin compiler, saying: "WE were an intruder at your wedding banquet: this, though belated, is Our wedding present."

[1] The star thus named is often used as a figurative appellation of the Son of Heaven.

CHAPTER II

AN INFAMOUS EUNUCH

READERS of *China under the Empress Dowager* may remember how, when the great Tzŭ Hsi lay dying, the watchers by her bedside asked her, in accordance with ancient custom, to pronounce her last words. " Never again," she said, " allow any woman to hold the supreme power in the State. It is against the house-law of our dynasty and should be strictly forbidden. Be careful not to allow eunuchs to meddle in Government matters. The Ming dynasty was brought to ruin by eunuchs and its fate should be a warning to my people."

Tzŭ Hsi knew well the law, though she observed it not herself. She was deeply read in the history of China, but in the matter of the eunuchs' power at Court, she failed to benefit by its teaching. Although her edicts frequently denounced the corrupt and demoralising influence of the " rats and foxes " who infested her Palace, describing them as " fawning sycophants " and " artful minions," against whom the Throne must ever be sternly vigilant, she nevertheless allowed her favourites, An Te-hai and Li Lien-ying, to wield an authority only little inferior to her own. She knew that, not only under the Mings but under the Han and Tang dynasties, the authority of the Sovereign had been usurped and degraded by these myrmidons, to the ruin of the State. Yet she took no steps to rid her own Court of evils which all her best advisers denounced and which, under her successor, Lung

Yü, became no small factor in the final decline and fall of the Manchu power.

When Tzŭ Hsi spoke of the ruin of the Ming dynasty by the eunuchs, she had in mind the history of the Emperor Wan Li and his three successors, the last of the Mings, and that of the infamous Chief Eunuch Wei Chung-hsien, whose memory is universally execrated to this day by the Chinese people. The tale of this foul creature's evil deeds and of the calamities which he brought upon the Throne and people of China, sheds no little light on the dark places of life in the Forbidden City, where, beneath the dignities and splendours prescribed by venerable tradition, lie grim shadows of death-dealing intrigue, of cold-blooded cruelty and lust and greed; where, close to the polished surface of Sacred Edicts and Confucian philosophy, lurk the elemental passions and insatiable ambitions of Oriental despotism. The life story of Wei Chung-hsien reveals the seamy side of China's imperial tapestry of state-craft. It serves to remind us, firstly, that it is the human equation, the impulses and instincts of dominant individuals which, far more than any theories of government, shape the destinies of peoples; secondly, that the human equation, predetermined in its essentials by climatic and economic environment, remains unchanged, and to a great extent unchangeable, beneath the surface of national life.

The Emperor Wan Li ascended the Throne in 1573 as a child, and being educated under the influence of the women and eunuchs of the Palace, remained under that influence all his days. During the last twenty years of his reign he refused to transact affairs of State through the proper officials, conducting all the business of Government through his principal eunuchs, and through the Imperial Concubine Cheng, who was the mother of his favourite son, Prince Fu.

Wan Li's eldest son, Ch'ang Lo, was a Prince of high

promise, of strong and virtuous disposition, but the evil influence of Lady Cheng and the eunuchs poisoned the Emperor's mind against him, so that the two rarely saw each other. Eventually, in 1615, when Ch'ang Lo was thirty-four years of age, the Lady Cheng, desiring to secure the succession for her dissolute son, Prince Fu, conspired with her brother Cheng Kuo-tai and two eunuchs, named Pang Pao and Liu Ch'eng, to have the Heir Apparent murdered. Their plans were laid with great care and subtlety, but they failed, owing to the stupidity of their hired assassins and to the courage of Ch'ang Lo's personal attendants. This attempt on the life of the Heir Apparent created a profound impression on the public mind, not only at Peking but in the provinces; it revealed to the nation the true state of affairs in the Palace, and laid the foundations of that distrust and disrespect for the dynasty which were subsequently manifested in Li Tzŭ-ch'eng's rebellion. Shortly before sunset of an evening in June 1615, a man, armed with a stout cudgel of jujube wood, forced his way into the residence of the Heir Apparent, the Palace of Benevolent Blessings, and having felled the eunuch on guard at the outer door, made his way to Ch'ang Lo's private apartments; but there, hesitating, he was overpowered and disarmed. Cast into prison, at first he feigned madness, but subsequently attempted to explain his action. His name, he said, was Chang Ch'ai, and he lived in a small village not far from the Imperial Eastern Mausolea. The Lady Cheng had sent some of her eunuchs to build a shrine near to the tombs, and these men had made a brick kiln there, close by a pile of brushwood which he had collected for fuel. Some one had set fire to the brushwood. Enraged at the loss, he had come to Peking to lodge a complaint at the Palace, and on entering the Forbidden City had met a man who told him that he must carry a cudgel as a sign that he was bearing a petition. On reaching the Heir Apparent's residence he had been angered by the eunuch, but meant no harm to the Prince.

Complying with the Heir Apparent's request, the Emperor ordered a formal inquiry into the case. The officials entrusted with the examination of the prisoner, shrewdly suspecting that the Lady Cheng and her brother were at the bottom of the affair, endeavoured to hush it up and to treat it as the work of a lunatic. One member of the Court of Inquiry refused, however, to agree with the rest, who wished to have Chang Ch'ai beheaded without further ado. He insisted on a thorough investigation, and examined the prisoner in private. Eventually a confession was extracted; the attempt at murder had been instigated by one of the eunuchs, with promise of rich reward.

This evidence being reported to the Court, a new Commission was appointed, which, after applying torture, elicited a further confession. The instigators of the crime were declared to be the eunuch Pang Pao and another named Liu Ch'eng, both henchmen of the Lady Cheng. Chang admitted that he had been in their pay for three years, and that they had told him if he succeeded in killing the Prince he should never want for meat and drink.

At this stage of the case public indignation began to be displayed in the capital, and a Censor was emboldened to accuse the Lady Cheng's brother of connivance in the crime. In a plain-spoken memorial he urged that the Emperor should order the immediate arrest of the two men named by the prisoner and, if implicated, the Imperial Concubine's brother; and it would be her duty to request the Emperor to have him decapitated. If the prisoner Chang were now put out of the way, and the case hushed up, the world would know that the Lady Cheng and her brother were guilty.

The Emperor was greatly disturbed by this memorial. Being himself of a lazily gentle disposition, he had no conception of the depths of cruelty and villainy about him, and would have wished to avoid the further inquiries that threatened to involve the good name of his favourite consort. But the officials and Censorate continued to urge that the case must be thoroughly investigated; the city was in a ferment of excitement, and the Palace gates were closed. A Censor now asked that the market days of the Forbidden City should be temporarily suspended, and that a strict watch of police be maintained at the Palace gates, to guard against further attacks. The Court declined to close the market, but ordered that for the time being no metal utensils or weapons be sold therein.[1]

At this juncture, the Grand Secretary Fang Tsung-che intervened, and bluntly warned the Emperor that any further hesitation in regard to the open trial of Chang Ch'ai could not fail to produce a bad impression and probably dangerous consequences. He reminded the Sovereign that one of the conspirators, Liu Ch'eng, had already been accused of witchcraft against His Majesty. Wan Li was so greatly impressed by this, that he turned against his favourite concubine and angrily bade her "look out for herself." Terrified at the turn affairs were taking, the Lady Cheng sought out the Heir Apparent and begged his forgiveness and help. The Prince magnanimously forgave her.

On the following morning, His Majesty went to the Heir Apparent's Palace and held an audience of the entire Court. In the presence of all, he took his son by the hand and said: "You all see this dutiful son of mine. Know that I love him dearly. Had I intended to kill him, I should have done so long ago. Why do you all try to create discord between father and son?" Then

[1] Under the Ming dynasty, the gates of the Palace were always opened on these so-called market-days, to allow of the removal of refuse accumulated in the Forbidden City.

he called the Chamberlain to summon the Heir Apparent's three sons, who were conducted to the daïs by the Emperor's side. He bade the Court look well at them. "These three grandsons of mine are now grown lads," he exclaimed; "what nonsense is this that you talk?" He asked Ch'ang Lo whether there was anything he wished to say : " Tell me the whole truth and conceal nought." The Heir replied : "This wretched lunatic Chang Ch'ai ought to be put to death at once, and so let the matter end." Then, turning to the Court, the Prince went on : " All of you can see the affection which exists between my father and me. These nonsensical rumours which you have been spreading make you to appear as disloyal Ministers and me as an unfeeling son." Wan Li called out : " Do you hear what the Prince has said?" He repeated these words thrice, and the whole Court made obeisance.

Next day the wretched Chang Ch'ai was decapitated and, at the intercession of Ch'ang Lo, the instigators of his crime were pardoned. Dearly was the magnanimous Prince to pay for this act of short-sighted clemency. For the time being, the eunuchs conspired no more against his life, content with the power they enjoyed under his father; but their enmity against him brooded, biding its time, in the dark places of the Forbidden City.

In 1620, Wan Li lay upon his death-bed, but by order of the Lady Cheng his Ministers of State and the Heir Apparent were not permitted to enter the Presence. Once more rumour flew, trumpet-tongued, through Peking, and a brave Censor, named Yang Lien, urged the Grand Secretaries to do their duty and to insist upon admission. The Grand Secretary Fang, after much persuasion, proceeded, at the head of his colleagues, to the Emperor's bedchamber. His Majesty was evidently moribund. Yang Lien and another honest Censor, Tso Kuang-tou, seeing this, insisted that the Heir Apparent, who was anxiously waiting without, should be summoned to receive his father's last commands, to tend him at the last; and to " taste his medicine." He was brought in just as Wan Li expired.

Ch'ang Jo, known in history by the dynastic title of Kuang Tsung (Glorious Ancestor), might have saved the dynasty had he been able to protect himself against the murderous hatred of the Lady Cheng and her eunuch confederates, but his life lasted less than two months from the date of his accession. He died of slow poisoning by arsenic, undoubtedly administered by his eunuch attendants.

The Lady Cheng, as usual, played craftily for safety, whilst steadily pursuing her ambitious designs. Shortly after the new Emperor's accession, she sent him gifts of great price, jade and pearls and eight beautiful maidens; at the same time she made friends with his favourite concubine, the Lady Li, and urged her to persuade the Emperor to confer upon herself the title of Empress Dowager, a suggestion which evoked immediate and unanimous opposition from the Board of Ceremonies.

The Emperor's illness rapidly increased; it was aggravated shortly before his death by one of the eunuchs (Tsui Wen-sheng) administering an extremely violent purgative. The Court became seriously alarmed, whilst in the city the report was spread that the Son of Heaven was being done to death by the Imperial Concubines. Once more the brave Censors Yang Lien and Tso Kuang-tou came forward, demanding that, in conformity with inviolable tradition, the Lady Cheng be compelled to depart from the Palace of Celestial Purity (in which Wan Li had died) where no female is allowed to sleep. The Lady Cheng at first refused to move, but eventually, fearful of popular clamour, she complied.

Yang Lien next proceeded to impeach the eunuch who had administered the purgative to His Majesty. " This villain is no physician," he said, " and ought not to be allowed to conduct his wanton experiments upon the divine person. If he knew anything about medicine, he must be aware that tonics, and not purgatives, are needed in a weakening complaint. What the Emperor requires is strengthening physic, at a time when he is naturally suffering from the shock of his sire's death and is also overworked with State affairs. It is at such a time that the eunuch gives an aperient. Rumours declare that the Emperor is not in good hands, and that there are designs against his life. Ts ui Wen-sheng excuses himself on the ground that the Emperor's weakness is due to debauchery, but the truth is that he calumniates His Majesty's morals as well as increasing his sickness. Such a man deserves to be eaten. Why does Your Majesty allow such traitors at your elbows?" Another Censor urged the Grand Secretary to take more care of the Emperor's sacred person, and added that a wrong prescription had evidently been given.

The Court officials were all summoned to the Imperial bedchamber, a side apartment in the Palace of Celestial Purity. A special decree had previously ordered Yang Lien to repair thither for audience. The courtiers grouped themselves about the Emperor's bedside. The dying Monarch looked closely at Yang Lien as if he meant to consign his sons to his protection. He then addressed the Court: "I am glad to see you all," he said. The Grand Secretary replied: "Pray, Sire, be more careful about the medicine you are receiving." The Monarch rejoined: "I have taken none for ten days." He then appointed the concubine Li to be secondary Consort. The lady thereupon sent for the Heir Apparent, and in the presence of the Court asked him to demand for her the title of Empress. He did so, but his father refused to grant the request and closed the audience. The Court was greatly astonished at her audacity.

The Emperor lingered on, growing daily worse. Five

days later the last agony had begun, and once more he summoned his Ministers to a farewell audience. As they pressed him to nominate his successor, he pointed to his eldest son, and said: "Help him to be a good man." Then he spoke of the Imperial tomb. The courtiers pretended to misunderstand, and asked if he referred to his father's tomb north of Peking. "No, I mean my own." They answered: "May Your Majesty live for ever; why speak of this now?" The Emperor then asked: "Where is the official from the Court of Banquets who was to give me some medicine?" The Grand Secretary replied: "The Secretary Li K'o-shao claims that he possesses a marvellous remedy, but we dare not recommend it." The Emperor bade him be sent for, to feel his pulse. He was ushered in, gave a very fluent diagnosis of the disease, and suggested his remedy. The Emperor was pleased, and agreed to take the drug. Li was told to discuss the matter with the doctors and the Ministers, but they came to no decision. The Grand Secretary Liu Yi-ching remarked that this particular remedy had been taken by two men in his native place: one had recovered and the other had died, so it could not be called an infallible prescription. The Board of Rites thought it would be dangerous to administer it, but while they were still discussing they were again summoned to the Emperor's presence. Li K'o-shao then hastily compounded the medicine, the famous red pill, and gave it to the Emperor, who swallowed it. He gasped slightly and exclaimed: "My loyal servants!"

After taking the medicine, the Emperor dismissed his Ministers, who waited in an ante-chamber. In a short time a decree was brought out to them, which said: "Our person is much better." At sunset Li K'o-shao was permitted to administer another red pill, and at dawn next day the Monarch "ascended on the dragon," aged thirty-nine.

Upon the Emperor's death, his would-be Empress, the

concubine Li, threw off all disguise and came boldly to the front with her chief henchman, the eunuch Wei Chin-shang (who subsequently received from the new Emperor the name of Wei Chung-hsien, meaning, Wei, the loyal and good). These two and their troop of eunuchs now held the Palace against all comers, kept close watch on the Heir to the Throne, and issued orders forbidding the usual mourning of Ministers at the deceased Sovereign's bier. Once more the Censor Yang Lien braved the powers of darkness in high places. Forcing his way through the eunuchs, he demanded to see the Heir Apparent. The concubine Li sent word that the young Emperor had left the Palace, but that he would soon return. She then actually endeavoured to smuggle him out of the Forbidden City, but his movements were discovered, and he was conducted back to his Palace. Under the direction of Yang Lien he ascended the palanquin and received the obeisances of the Court. It was proposed that he should formally ascend the Throne without delay, but Yang Lien deprecated unceremonious haste, since the succession was not contested. At the same time he took vigorous steps to preserve law and order in Peking.

The young Emperor T'ien Ch'i (known in history as Hsi Tsung) was but fifteen years of age when called to ascend the Dragon Throne; a weakly lad, of small stature, and utterly lacking in strength of character. From the date of his accession, the power of the eunuchs, hitherto kept in check by the firmness and moral dignity which his grandfather, Wan Li, had always displayed at critical moments, increased beyond all bounds, until their leader, Wei Chung-hsien, became the autocratic ruler of the Empire. With the death of Kuang Tsung, the Lady Cheng could no longer hope to secure the Throne for her son, the dissolute Prince Fu, so that gradually her influence and her interest in Palace politics became less personal and less aggressive.

Immediately upon the death of Kuang Tsung, a struggle for supreme power began between the concubine Li and the new Emperor's foster-mother, the fascinating and notoriously wicked woman known to history as Madame K'o. The Emperor's mother having died years before, it was the ambition of Lady Li, through her influence over him and by the power of the eunuchs, to arrogate to herself the position of an Empress Dowager, and to rule the Empire. To this end she began by ignoring the dynastic law which required her to remove from the Palace of her late lord, announcing her intention of residing there with the young Emperor, and she was able to enlist on her side the sympathies of the Grand Secretary Fang Tsung-che. But the Censor Yang Lien and his colleague Tso Kuang-tou, backed by an honest eunuch named Wang An, were not disposed to acquiesce in such irregularities. They protested most energetically, and put in a joint memorial demanding that the concubine Li should forthwith take her departure from the Central Palace to that of the Whirring Phœnixes. Tso pointed out that an Emperor of fifteen required no mother to attend him, and that if such a breach of custom were permitted, China might be afflicted by another usurpation of power like that of the Empress Wu in the T'ang dynasty.

At this the Lady Li was very wroth, and sent a eunuch to summon Tso to her presence; but he declined, saying: " I am the servant of the Son of Heaven; his orders only will I obey." Yang Lien, discussing the matter angrily with the Grand Secretary, observed: " Even if the Emperor's own mother were alive, he must take precedence over her. What manner of woman is the concubine Li that she dares thus insult the dignity of the Throne?"

As some of eunuchs showed signs of a desire to support Lady Li's action, Yang announced his intention of re-

THE COURT OF PEKING

maining in the Palace until she had moved out. To those who sided with the Grand Secretary he said: "Let the woman Li go to the Temple of Ancestors and state her demands before the sacred shrines. Are you all in her pay? Let her kill me if she can. I will not move until he does."

Faced with this crisis, on a clear issue where public opinion and the law were all against her, the Lady Li made a virtue of necessity and evacuated the Palace, but not before her retainers had looted much of its store of gold ingots. The chroniclers report that Yang's hair and moustache turned completely white during these days of danger. But he had won the day and from this point the influence and activities of Lady Li waned rapidly at Court. Certain of the eunuchs of her immediate following endeavoured to enlist for her the sympathies of the high officials of the Court, by spreading rumours that it was her intention to commit suicide in order to escape further persecution. Hereupon a Censor demanded that the Emperor should definitely communicate to the Grand Secretariat his decision in regard to her, in order to allay these unseemly rumours of the eunuchs. There is every reason to believe that this action of the Censor's was inspired not, like Yang Lien's, by pure motives of loyalty to the Throne, but by the party of the eunuch Wei Chung-hsien, who now abandoned the cause of Lady Li and became the close confederate of Madame K'o, the foster-mother. Beyond all doubt feminine jealousy and the hand of Madame K'o were behind the decree which the boy Emperor proceeded to issue in reply to the Censor's memorial. It said:

"When I was a boy the Lady Li used so to bully my sacred mother that she fell sick and died. To the end of my days I shall bear her ill-will for this. Also, when my father lay dying, she laid violent hands on my person and demanded to be made Empress Consort. At that time I was living in the Palace of Benevolent Blessings; every day she would send her two Chief Eunuchs to compel me to submit all State papers for her perusal. I have now transferred her to the Palace of Whirring Phœnixes, in filial remembrance of the love my father bore to her. I do not propose to involve her in the punishment which will be meted out to her satellites for stealing valuables from the Palace."

A little later and the Lady Li's downfall was complete. Another decree of the Emperor deprived her of her rank as concubine, "in order to comfort his mother in heaven," while continuing her maintenance grant, "in order to show honour to his father," a typical Chinese "face-saving" solution. From this moment Wei Chung-hsien and his confederate Madame K'o stand forth in absolute and almost undisputed authority. Under Wan Li, the Chief Eunuch had ruled the capital and chastised the Court with whips; he now proceeded to chastise it with scorpions.

The first noteworthy indication of their vengeful and bloodthirsty power was given when they did to death the loyal eunuch Wang An, who had dared to support the Censor Yang Lien in his fight for clean government. Wei Chung-hsien forged and uttered an Imperial decree condemning Wang to death, and in order to prevent any chance of his being reprieved, had him murdered in prison. Yang Lien, who might have saved this honest man, had already left Peking, and gone into retirement at his home. In applying for permission to resign, he had boldly told the young Emperor that, having done his duty in cleansing the Palace of the usurping concubine, he desired only to leave the capital, for his straightforward nature could not brook the sycophants and traitors who surrounded the Throne. He was to pay dearly for his courage.

The young Emperor was only too willing to allow all

THE COURT OF PEKING

the business of the State to pass into the hands of the masterful eunuch and of the woman K'o, who exercised so baneful an influence over him. He devoted himself continually to his hobby of carpentry, which Wei Chung-hsien encouraged. The eunuch would wait until he was busy with plane and saw and then go to him asking for instructions concerning some routine question of government or one of the day's memorials. Hsi Tsung, hating to be disturbed, would tell him to settle the business as he thought fit; and thus, little by little, the eunuch usurped all the functions of the Sovereign. The Emperor Ch'ien Lung, commenting on the causes of the Ming dynasty's ruin, ascribed it partly to " Hsi Tsung's infatuate interest in mean and cunning handicrafts, which brought him into competition with workmen. Eunuchs," he wrote, " have always tried to engage their Sovereign's attention in ignoble pursuits, so that they might freely pursue their ambitious designs. In all ages, bad men are the same in their ways; the pity is that Sovereigns should be so blind as to fall into the snares prepared for them."

During the seven years of his calamitous reign, one good influence, and one only, saved the young Emperor from utter degradation, and led good men occasionally to hope that he might in time cast off his bondage and assert the Imperial dignity of his Throne. This was the influence of his consort, the " Precious Pearl," in whom dignity, virtue and high courage were combined to a degree which make her one of the most admirable women in China's history, and indeed in the history of the world. Her gentle and steadfast character shines brightly to this day against the dark background of those evil times, her lofty ideals, patience and loyalty smell sweet and blossom, even now, amidst the dust and ruins of that degenerate age. Seldom indeed has history recorded a nobler life, a more pathetic death. We make no apology for digressing at this point, to tell the romantic story of her youth and of her selection to be the Empress Consort of China's weak and dissolute Monarch.

In the winter of the year 1612, a student of K'ai Feng-fu, named Chang Kuo-chi, found lying by the roadside a little girl, aged six, and taking her to his home, adopted her as his daughter, by the name of Chang Yen. Her " style " was " Precious Pearl." He attended carefully to her education and she proved remarkably intelligent and diligent in study. Chang Kuo-chi had intended her to marry his son, but was dissuaded from this course by a Buddhist priest who, after casting her horoscope, foretold for her a far more exalted position. In 1620, the year of the death of Wan Li, the dissolute Prince Fu (son of Lady Cheng) came to take up his fief of Honan, and forthwith sent eunuchs to search through the city of Kaifeng for damsels worthy to enter his harem. One of the eunuchs came to Chang's house and seeing " Precious Pearl," then aged fourteen, bade her accompany him to the Prince's Palace, but the girl indignantly repelled him, threatening that if he laid a hand upon her she would commit suicide.

In the year (1621) following the death of the Emperor Wan Li and his unfortunate son, the Emperor Kuang Tsung, the young Emperor Hsi Tsung, then aged sixteen, proclaimed his intention of solemnising his marriage. The whole Empire was notified that comely maidens between the ages of thirteen and sixteen were eligible; after which the eunuchs made an eliminating inspection. Those whose height or figure failed to reach the required standard were weeded out, until the number was reduced to 4000. On the following day a much more careful scrutiny was conducted by the two head eunuchs, who made copious notes of each damsel's features, size of nose, colour of hair, shape of waist and length of foot. Each maiden was required to state clearly her name, lineage and age; if the *timbre* of the voice did not satisfy the eunuchs, she was at once rejected. Stammering or thickness of speech was regarded as an insuperable defect. As a result of this scrutiny, only 2000 remained eligible, and on the following day further physical measurements were made, in addition to which each candidate was required to walk a hundred paces, in order that her deportment might be observed. Any slovenliness of gait or lack of dignity disqualified the candidate; after this test only 1000 remained. These were then taken into the Inner Palace where they were subjected to a searching scrutiny by discreet and elderly women of the Palace, who compelled them to strip so that their persons might be scanned from head to foot. Three hundred were ultimately chosen to undergo a month's probation as Palace handmaidens. Those amongst them who showed signs of stubbornness or of frivolous disposition were weeded out, until at the end of the month only fifty remained, all of whom were appointed to be Imperial concubines.

The Chief Eunuch in charge of the Ceremonial Department was greatly impressed by " Precious Pearl's " beauty, and placed her at the head of the list to be presented to the Senior Concubine, Lady Chao, who had been one of the Emperor Wan Li's chief wives, and was at present acting as Empress Dowager. This lady, an accomplished scholar, tested each candidate in caligraphy and other accomplishments. Finally three were chosen as candidates for the position of Empress, of whom " Precious Pearl " was one; the other two young ladies were named Wang and Tuan.

In accordance with ancient custom, the Lady Chao enveloped the heads of the three chosen ones in turbans of black crape, and fastened the arms of each with a bracelet of jade and gold. They were then taken into an inner chamber for a final examination by the women of the Palace, to make sure that they were without spot or blemish.

In due course their report was submitted. The official chronicler gives from it a detailed list of the future

Empress's charms, some of which is unprintable. Her complexion was as the dawn, her eyes like autumn waves, her lips like cherries; her teeth, numbering thirty-eight in all, were perfect, her chin ample, and she was free of birthmarks.

Lady Chao hastened to report to His Majesty, and conducted the three maidens to his apartments, where his foster-mother, the evil Madame K'o, was waiting to help the Emperor to make a final choice. At this time, K'o was about thirty-three, a woman of great physical beauty and charm. The Emperor had already bestowed upon her the title of the "Holy Lady of Ch'in." [1]

Madame K'o took an immediate and instinctive dislike to "Precious Pearl" and began to criticise her. "For a girl of fifteen," she said, "her figure is too stout; she won't improve as she gets older. She is good-looking after a fashion, but quite unworthy to be your Consort." Pointing to Miss Wang, she exclaimed, "That's the wife for you." The Emperor, however, was evidently attracted by "Precious Pearl," but following the prescribed custom, he asked the Lady Chao's advice. She replied: "All three are exceptionally comely, but Miss Chang ('Precious Pearl') surpasses the others in dignity of demeanour."

Thereupon, nothing loth, His Majesty chose "Precious Pearl" for his Consort. Miss Wang was given the title of "Virtuous Concubine" and Miss Tuan that of "Pure Concubine." The eighth day of the fourth Moon following was fixed by the astronomers as auspicious for the Emperor to ascend his nuptial couch; and three weeks later the new Empress received her patents. The Emperor asked her many questions about her family and past life. Her replies greatly pleased him, and she speedily acquired

[1] Ch'in, the classical name of the province of Shensi, of which she was a native. The ruins of Madame K'o's private residence are still visible just outside the Tung An Gate of Peking, and the site is popularly known as the "Foster-Mother's Palace."

over him that influence for good which became the one redeeming feature of his weak nature. Her father (by adoption), Chang Kuo-chi, was ennobled as an "Earl of exalted strength," and other members of her family received suitable honours.

A few days after the marriage, Hsi Tsung and his Consort proceeded to the Ancestral Temple, where Her Majesty performed obeisance before the Imperial shrine. Hsi Tsung was at this time only sixteen and of very diminutive stature; his Consort towered above him. As the Empress's influence increased, Madame K'o showed unmistakable signs of jealousy and wrath; nevertheless, she continued to visit His Majesty daily in the Palace of Heavenly Purity.

In spite of the Emperor's devotion to his beautiful bride, it was evident to all the Court that he was becoming more and more subject to the influence of the Chief Eunuch, Wei Chung-hsien, who had attended him since early infancy. This man and Madame K'o gradually established their authority as the real rulers of China, and maintained it throughout his reign. Completely dominated in regard to affairs of State by the eunuch, Hsi Tsung showered honours upon him; meritorious officials were tortured and executed to gratify his lightest whim. Wholesale proscriptions were made by Wei against those who had criticised him, so that it came to pass that even the great Viceroys vied with each other in currying favour with the all-powerful eunuch. In nearly every province shrines were erected to him during his lifetime and he was worshipped as a deity. In Kiangsi a temple which had been built centuries before in honour of one of the most eminent disciples of Confucius was dismantled, and Wei Chung-hsien's tablet was set up in its central hall. He was likened to the Sage for virtue and learning: nay, his merits were even exalted beyond those of the Sage, and he was accorded the highest place in the national

Pantheon. The Governor of Shantung gravely informed the Throne that a *chi lin* [1] had been captured in Confucius' native province, near to the Sage's grave, an auspicious event which he attributed to the fact that near to the Throne there stood a person of Wei Chung-hsien's consummate virtue. (The *chilin's* rare appearances, like angels' visits, only occur when the Empire is governed by a perfect ruler.) The eunuch was called Lord of 9000 years, and the Emperor's decrees, which Wei invariably drafted, began with the words: " WE and OUR eunuch Minister, decree as follows . . ."

In all things the infatuated Monarch submitted to the will of Wei Chung-hsien, except only when the eunuch and Madame K'o endeavoured to poison his mind against his beloved Consort, to whom he remained devotedly faithful all his life. Whenever the Emperor, under her good influence, showed signs of wishing to devote himself to study or serious pursuits, K'o and Wei would lure him back into paths of sensual dissipation. The Empress feared and disliked them both, but she could not persuade Hsi Tsung to free himself from their control.

Shortly after His Majesty's marriage, certain Censors began to send in outspoken memorials against Madame K'o, urging that she should not be permitted to spend so much of her time in the Forbidden City in close attendance upon the Sovereign; it being contrary to etiquette that a woman should be allowed to enter the Palace of Heavenly Purity. The Emperor, in reply to these memorials, declared that his wife's extreme youth required the guiding hand of a foster-mother. The Censors returned to the charge, pointing out that a woman of K'o's low antecedents was unfit to minister to a person so virtuous as the Empress. "How," said one of them, " can this woman be permitted to usurp the authority which belongs

---

[1] A fabulous animal, of origin probably similar to our unicorn.

of right to Your Majesty's Consort?" K'o was eventually compelled to leave the Palace, and for a time she remained at her own residence, but the weakling Emperor felt her absence so deeply that he lost his appetite and became greatly dejected. In spite of the remonstrances of the Censors, he soon recalled her, and thereafter her influence grew greater than before. Waxing proud, she began openly to ill-treat those of the concubines who were not on her side, and supported by Wei Chung-hsien, dared to show open contempt for the Empress. Shortly after her return, the Emperor celebrated her birthday with royal splendour. Proceeding in person to her residence, he burned incense before her tablet and offered up prayers for her long life. All the eunuchs and concubines of the Court were ordered to prostrate themselves in obeisance before her. Sumptuous theatricals were held in her honour for three days, and the best musicians in the capital were specially engaged. In the following month the Empress's birthday occurred, but no entertainments were given in the Palace, nor were any promotions conferred. Even in the tea-houses, men knew where lay the power behind the Throne.

Thus things went on, from bad to worse. K'o and Wei were served with the richest viands from the Imperial kitchens, while the Empress was frequently kept waiting for her simple meals. She fully realised the dangers that threatened the decadent dynasty at the hands of these evil-doers, and frequently remonstrated with the Emperor against his flagrant violation of the dynastic laws. K'o and Wei now tried to lay snares for the Empress, and set one of their eunuch minions, Ch'en Ti-jun, to spy upon her in her Palace of Feminine Tranquillity, endeavouring all the time to turn the Emperor against her. But the, blameless and pure of heart, paid no heed. She spent most of her time in reading and in penmanship, wherein she was highly expert; to the more intelligent of the

Palace concubines she gave lessons in history and philosophy. A devout Buddhist, she spent many hours in prayer before the altar of the Goddess of Mercy. Frequently she attired herself as a nun and gave herself over to pious meditation. She knew full well that her enemies were plotting against her, but she relied upon her gentle influence over the Emperor, which never failed to hold him, although she used no feminine arts to win his favour.

Her Lord the Emperor being without an heir, she would recommend various concubines to his notice, but usually excused herself from receiving his conjugal attentions on the plea of ill-health. The Emperor was wont to say to her: "Your influence over me is wonderful: you are so brave, so good. If I but look at you I feel a different man. Your face seems to say that you should easily be won. How comes it, then, that I find it so difficult to woo you?"

At times he would invite her to a boating excursion upon the lake adjoining the Forbidden City; His Majesty himself rowing and endeavouring to please her by good-humoured badinage. But she would use these occasions to remonstrate with him for his wild life, urging him to study State papers and to give daily audiences to his Ministers. "You ought to make friends with scholars and attend lectures on the classics," she would way, "instead of dallying with these sycophants." For a time the Emperor would obey her advice, but he speedily relapsed into evil ways. Madame K'o supplied him with drugs to stimulate his passions; whilst "Precious Pearl" warned him against all forms of indulgence, and would throw the drugs down the well. Wei Chung-hsien arranged lewd theatrical performances for His Majesty's amusement, but whenever the play was indelicate, the Empress would rise from her place and leave the theatre in disgust.

In the hope of securing her deposition, Wei and K'o bribed a man named Sun-erh, a Honanese, who was lying under sentence of death in the Board of Punishments, to say that the Empress was his child and that he had given her to her father by adoption, Chang Kuo-chi. To the Emperor they said that a criminal's daughter ought not to be his Consort and that she should be deposed, Chang-Kuo-chi receiving the punishment he merited. The Emperor was impressed by the story, and went straight to his Consort's apartment to ask her about it. But at sight of her tranquil beauty he was abashed, and could only say in an embarrassed way: "Are you really the daughter of that wretched villain Sun-erh?" The Empress blushed slightly and paused before replying. Then she said: "If Your Majesty believes such foolish rumours, why should I continue to defile the Palace with my presence? Pray let me be deposed and make room for another more worthy." The Emperor thereupon hurriedly apologised and made amends, all doubt having been dispelled from his mind. That night he supped with the Empress and next day warned Wei Chung-hsien against uttering idle reports.

Many were the wiles and stratagems by which these two evil conspirators endeavoured to injure the Empress in the eyes of her lord, and at times—so weak a nature was Hsi Tsung's—they seemed to be on the verge of success. On one occasion, the Chief Eunuch devised a crafty plot, supported by lying witnesses, against Her Majesty's adopted father, and induced the Emperor to issue a decree reprimanding him and ordering the Empress to meditate for three days on his conduct. Later, Madame K'o introduced into the harem a creature of her own, named Jen, of bad character but pleasing appearance, and persuaded the Emperor to grant her high rank amongst the Imperial concubines. Here again they were nearly successful, for Hsi Tsung became infatuated with the woman; yet she did not succeed in completely supplanting "Precious Pearl" in his affections.

In 1624, the Chief Eunuch was at the height of his insolence; none were safe from his rapacious and vindictive power. It was at this time that he took a fearful revenge upon the Censor Yang Lien and the others who had denounced him and his former confederate, the concubine Li.

Yang Lien, it will be remembered, had retired from the Court to his native place in 1622, shortly after the death of Wan Li. In 1624 he returned to Peking and, moved to righteous indignation by the evil deeds of Wei and his accomplices, he handed in the denunciatory memorial which eventually cost him his life. This famous impeachment of the notorious eunuch is too long to quote in full, but it reveals so clearly the condition of the Court, and the power wielded by these " rats and foxes," and their effect on the government of the country, that we must reproduce its most important clauses.

The memorial begins thus: "The founder of our dynasty desired that eunuchs should not interfere in governmental affairs, and that evil-doing should not be condoned. But the eunuch Comptroller General of the Eastern Court [1] behaves with overweening arrogance, and treats the dynastic ordinances with contempt. I venture to set forth his chief crimes as follows:

"1. He is a lewd fellow of common extraction who, after being emasculated in middle life, won a position in the Palace by sheer intrigue. He wheedled his way into Imperial favour by displaying zeal in trivial matters, and thereafter developed into a most consummate traitor and villain, until he has become practically a dictator, even issuing his own decrees, whereby the Government has often been thrown into utter confusion. Ancestral tradition requires that the Grand Secretaries shall issue all

---

[1] A bureau under eunuchs which had become virtually the Supreme Court of the Empire, which drew up decrees, and completely superceded the Grand Secretariat.

decrees; but since Wei Chung-hsien's assumption of dictatorship, he has either issued Imperial edicts verbally or has himself appended the vermilion rescript. Thus are the traditions of two centuries defied.

"2. When His late Majesty lay dying, Liu Yi-ching and Chou Chia-mo were the recipients of his last testament, but Wei was able to secure their abrupt dismissal, because he feared that they might clip his power. In this way Your Majesty was made to act undutifully in the removal of your august predecessor's faithful servants.

"3. Wei dismissed Sun Shen-hsing and Tsou Yuan-piao, honest patriots both, who had drawn public attention to the poisoning of the late Emperor by eunuchs. He bestowed a dragon robe on the henchman of the concubine Li, the man who administered the dose of red pills which killed His Majesty. He is a friend to traitors, and the foe of good and loyal men.

"4. He has removed all honest officials from your Court, until not a soul is left who dares to warn Your Majesty. He has prevented you from employing worthy men lest they frustrate his schemes.

"5. It is a common saying in Peking that Your Majesty, the Son of Heaven, can be easily appeased, but that the wrath of Wei Chung-hsien cannot be placated. At a word from him you dismiss every one who incurs his displeasure.

"6. Thus far I have referred only to officials. Last year it was stated that one of the lower concubines ('honourable persons') had won your favour by her purity and virtue. Wei became jealous and fearful that she should undermine his influence and expose his infamies; she died, therefore, of a sudden and mysterious sickness. Your Majesty is unable to protect even your cherished favourites.

"7. Thus far I have spoken only of concubines of lowly rank. Lately the senior concubine 'Abundant' was expecting her confinement, and every one hoped that Your Majesty was about to be blessed with an heir. Wei hated her because she was not of his party. He issued a forged decree which brought about her suicide. Your Majesty is powerless to protect even ladies of exalted position in your Palace.

"8. Thus far I have referred to consorts, but there are worse crimes. Your Empress had given birth to a son, but it died straightway, as the result of Wei's plottings. It is common knowledge that Wei and Madame K'o brought about this death. You cannot even protect your own son.

"9. During the forty years in which your father was Heir Apparent his position was one of grave peril, but he had one faithful henchman, the eunuch Wang An. When your father died mysteriously of the fatal red pills it was Wang An who saw to your protection and helped to secure your safe succession to the Throne. This man deserved well of Your Majesty, but Wei issued a forged decree and had him beheaded in the Hunting Park. And not only did Wang An suffer, but hundreds of your father's attendants have been slain or banished.

"10. Each day sees him rejoicing in fresh honours: shrines are built in his honour at which he, a living man, is to be worshipped. There is no limit to his evil influence with Your Majesty. In conferring distinctions on such a man the words of the Emperor are defiled. At his native place of Ho Chien-fu he has erected triumphal arches in his own honour, on which are carved Imperial dragons and heaven-soaring phœnixes. His sepulchre in the Western hills is built on the scale of an Imperial mausoleum and covered with a yellow roof.

"11. He fills official posts with youths still smelling of their mothers' milk, or with illiterate members of his own family, like Wei Liang-pi, Wei Liang-tsai and Wei Liang-ch'ing.

"12. He has inflicted humiliating punishment on the fathers of Imperial concubines and beheaded their servants by scores. He has done his best to ruin the Empress's father and to shake even Her Majesty's position. Had it not been for the courageous opposition of one of the Grand Secretaries, Her Majesty's father would have perished on the scaffold.

"13. The 'Eastern Court' was established for the purpose of protecting the Throne from treason, but in Wei Chung-hsien's hands it has become a deadly machine for the removal of rivals by general proscription. He keeps a box there into which anonymous complaints may be dropped, and traps are set night and day to betray those who oppose him. Let but a word be whispered against his doings and forthwith a warrant is issued and the offender is dragged to trial at the T'ung Wen-kuan.

"14. Dynastic ordinance forbids that eunuchs should form bands of soldiers as bodyguards to the Sovereign. For this enactment there are urgent reasons, but Wei has got together a troop of his own creatures, who are drilled in the Palace. To this band drift naturally all dangerous and desperate characters; what is to prevent an assassin being found amongst them who would attempt Your Majesty's life?

"15. When Wei was sent to perform sacrifice at Chochin, the road was cleared for him as for an Imperial progress. Heralds announced his advance, and yellow earth was spread upon the highway, so that the people believed that he was the Emperor himself. On his Eastern journey he was borne in a chariot drawn by four horses, Imperial banners and insignia were carried in the procession. His bodyguard surrounded him on both sides to screen his sacred person from the vulgar gaze. In every respect his passing resembled a progress of Your Majesty! Numbers of persons offered their petitions to him or made offerings of tribute, prostrating themselves in the dust. What manner of man does this Wei fancy himself to be?

"16. It is well known that, if too much royal favour be shown, conceit is thereby engendered, and that excess of Imperial grace usually breeds resentment in its recipient against the giver. Thus it came to pass that this spring Wei dared to ride on horseback in front of Your Majesty. Amazed at his effrontery, Your Majesty shot the horse dead; Wei's offence was speedily pardoned. He showed no contrition, but carried himself the more haughtily in your presence and, outside the Palace, spoke despisingly of you. He has now surrounded himself with armed men, prepared to resist in case of his arrest. Traitors and rebels desire only to attain the goal of their nefarious ambitions, and nothing stops them until they have gained it. Why should you nourish a tiger to work his evil will at your very elbows? Even if Wei's carcase were hacked into mincemeat, his sins would remain unexpiated.

"The tale of his crimes and treasonable designs is blazoned abroad in all men's eyes; yet none of your courtiers dare speak against him, lest they incur doom. Their tongues are tied; not one dare memorialise you. Should, perchance, any have the courage to reveal Wei's treasons, the 'Lady of Divine Worship,' Madame K'o, stands at Your Majesty's side to gloss over his guilt. These two are sworn allies; each aids and abets the other, if one calls, the other comes to the rescue.

"Humbly I implore Your Majesty now to display the might of your high displeasure and to appoint a commission of the ablest nobles and highest officials, with power to subject Wei to relentless examination, in order that the law of the land may be vindicated. Also, I beg you to have the 'Lady of Divine Worship' removed from out the precincts of the Forbidden City, in order to guard you from further danger. Then, though your servant die, yet shall he live."

THE COURT OF PEKING

Wei was greatly alarmed at the revelations of this bold memorial and begged the Grand Secretary Han K'uang to defend him. Han refused, so Wei hurried to the Emperor's presence and abjectly asked to be allowed to resign the Comptrollership of the Eastern Court. Madame K'o then used all her wiles, imploring the Emperor not to give his ear to calumny, while one of the Grand Secretaries was found to intercede for the eunuch. For a moment Wei's fate hung in the balance, but in the end the unfortunate Emperor, in his purblind folly, listened to Madame K'o, and issued a complimentary decree retaining Wei at his post. On the following morning he issued another edict sternly rebuking Yang Lien for his temerity. It had been the latter's intention to see the Emperor at the morning audience and to recount the eunuch's crimes in the Monarch's presence, but Wei induced his master to suspend the Court for that day. Baulked of this opportunity, and realising the danger of further delay, Yang handed in a second memorial at the Gate of Supreme Unity. This Wei suppressed, and though Yang sent in a third memorial it never reached the Throne. For three days no audiences were held, and when finally the Monarch emerged he was surrounded by a guard of several hundred eunuchs, all of whom had weapons concealed on their persons. Orders were issued that no memorials would be received, and Yang was compelled to desist.

Nevertheless, other memorials of impeachment poured in; the Censor Huang Tsun-su asked: "Can a Government be pure with eunuchs at its head who usurp the authority of the Throne? Can Your Majesty employ as your right-hand man a creature whose flesh the whole Empire desires to eat? You think him loyal, but you stand alone and in a perilous position. All upright men have left your side, while you lean upon this eunuch as on a pillar. Unless you now act swiftly, Wei Chung-hsien will never cleanse his heart. He began by destroying officials and scholars, but now he aims at higher quarry. If his position is allowed to become stronger not even armed force will dislodge him."

Next, Wei Ta-chung put in a pregnant memorial: "When honest men advise the Throne at risk of their lives and their words remain unheeded the situation is parlous indeed. Yang Lien has not shrunk from the peril of dismemberment, concerned only with the dangers that threaten the State, and hoping to arouse Your Majesty to a knowledge of the truth. Your Majesty has just issued a decree assuming to yourself all the misdeeds with which he is charged, but I fear the author of this laudatory edict is not Your Majesty but Wei himself. It has come to this, that you, the Son of Heaven, have surrendered yourself and your consorts to the keeping of Wei and K'o. The peril of our State makes my blood run cold. Those who surround the Throne are tools and creatures of Wei and K'o and no true servants of Your Majesty. You are become like unto an orphan in a friendless world."

Another impeachment, endorsed by over a thousand academy students, accused Wei of suppressing all attacks upon himself, of inducing the Emperor to ignore the word of the officials who, kneeling at the gate, had begged for Wei's dismissal, and of designs on the Throne itself. Finally, a Board Secretary named Wan Ching denounced the Chief Eunuch fiercely. This official had charge of the building and equipment of the late Emperor's mausoleum; a large amount of copper was needed for its sacrificial vessels, and as there were vast supplies of the metal lying unused in the Imperial precincts, he asked the eunuch Comptroller to issue what he needed for the tomb. This Wei not only refused to do, but he issued a forged decree concerning the application.

Hereat Wan, greatly enraged, impeached Wei. He wrote: "Sovereign power cannot be delegated, and least of all to an emasculated minion. This Wei is practically become Emperor and the fountain of all honour; his friends secure well-feathered nests, whilst the bodies of his enemies are covered with boils and sores. At his asking, hereditary titles are granted; his household servants receive bribes in thousands of taels. Your Majesty favours him with unbounded confidence for that he served your father; yet he refuses to issue copper for your father's shrine. His own grave at Pi Yün-ssü, in the Western hills, is as large as an Imperial mausoleum; in the provinces, stately shrines have been erected in his honour, emblazoned with inscriptions and gaudy ornaments. On his own tomb he has spent a million taels, while His late Majesty's sepulchre is denied even the necessary fittings. Your Majesty's existence is ignored; Wei Chung-hsien fills all men's minds."

Wei, having recovered from his alarm and made sure that the Emperor's favour would not be taken from him, now determined to make an example of Wan, so as to put fear into his other enemies. He forged a decree sentencing him to a flogging of one hundred strokes in the Palace, but first he sent a number of eunuchs to Wan's own house and had him unmercifully beaten there. When the wretched man was brought to the Palace he was still alive, but during the official flogging he became unconscious. The eunuchs then kicked and trampled on him so that he died next day. A Censor had the courage to protest against this outrage and to speak well of Wan, who "had perished by the hands of this abominable and sharp-fanged eunuch." The incident, said he, would be recorded in history for all time, and would cover the Emperor's name with eternal discredit. But the besotted Monarch, having made his fatal choice of evil friends, paid no heed to these remonstrances and warnings, so that Wei hardened his heart and became more reckless than ever in his crimes and bloodthirsty revenges.

The brave Censor, Yang Lien, was now thrown into the

Imperial prison, and with him Tso Kuang-tou and Wei Ta-chung, who had joined him in denouncing the Chief Eunuch. This prison was separate and distinct from the Board of Punishments; tortures were freely practised there. Wei issued a decree that these three men were to be tortured every fifth day, and not to be handed over to the Board of Punishments until all their money had been extorted. All three were tortured most horribly, but none of them would confess to having obtained money wrongfully by taking bribes. Finally Tso Kuang-tou, unable to endure his misery, said to his fellow prisoners: "Either they will torture us to death for not confessing, or else they will hire one of the gaolers to kill us. If now we confess, they must hand us to the Board of Punishments for formal trial, and we may then escape." His companions agreed, and they all confessed to false charges of having taken bribes. But the tiger would not release his prey; Wei issued a decree that they were not yet to be taken to the public prison, and the torturing went on. Yang Lien was eventually killed under a torture which consisted of piling great sacks of earth upon his belly and driving nails into his ears. When at last the bodies of the three victims were handed over to their relatives, they were so mutilated as to be unrecognisable. The arrest of Yang Lien created much public indignation; thousands of scholars and respectable people lined the road by which he had to pass, burning incense in his honour and praying for his safe return. Wei's minions seized all his property, but it amounted to less than a thousand taels, for he was as poor as he was honest. Had not the neighbours come to their rescue, his wife and sons would have been reduced to beggary.

Let us now return to tell of the life and death of His Tsung's noble Empress. The facts recited in Yang Lien's memorial, above quoted, give some idea of the grievous wrongs and indignities which, through the miserable weakness of the Emperor, she suffered at the hands of the Chief Eunuch and Madame K'o.

It was in the year 1623 that the Empress became *enceinte*, to the great satisfaction of Hsi Tsung. But the Chief Eunuch and Madame K'o had no desire to see Her Majesty's influence over him and her authority at Court increased by the birth of an heir to the Throne. Two of the Empress's favourite and most faithful serving-maids were, therefore, put to death by means of forged decrees on false charges, and all her other personal attendants were dismissed, except those upon whom Madame K'o could rely. Their places were taken by women selected by the Chief Eunuch, one of whom, employed as a masseuse, so mishandled the Empress that her child was born dead. Shortly afterwards, Her Majesty, goaded to desperation by the Emperor's crass folly, determined on an attempt to rid the Court at last of the woman whose deplorable influence was the chief cause of its wickedness and shame. Taking her seat on the daïs of the Main Hall in the Palace of Feminine Tranquillity, with a number of armed retainers on either side, she summoned Madame K'o to her presence. When the woman came, suspecting nothing serious, the Empress launched straightway into a recital of all her sins and wickedness, and ended by bidding her prepare to die. K'o knelt at her feet and prayed for mercy; meanwhile a eunuch had gone swiftly to inform the Emperor, busy at his carpentering, of what was taking place. He arrived upon the scene just in time to save his foster-mother's life. From this time forward the Chief Eunuch and Madame K'o endeavoured by all possible means to poison the Emperor's mind against his Consort and to deprive her of his protection. She on her side sought strength and consolation in prayer, chanting Buddhist masses daily for the repose of the souls of the murdered Censors and her faithful attendants. She hoped thus to move her husband to remorse. Especially did she reproach him for allowing the murder of Yang Lien.

Wei Chung-hsien made repeated attempts to ruin the Empress in the eyes of the Court and country by securing the disgrace of her adopted father Chang Kuo-chi, against whom he brought criminal charges backed by the false evidence of his creatures. He produced memorials accusing him of plotting against the Emperor's life, of taking bribes, and of a secret liaison with a lady of the Court, but Hsi Tsung, weak as he was in all other matters, remained strongly attached to his beautiful and virtuous wife, and the Empress found another loyal defender in the Grand Secretary Li Kuo-p'u, who succeeded in checking some of the Chief Eunuch's bloodthirsty schemes and in frightening the woman, his accomplice. Finally, in the spring of 1627, upon a false impeachment, the Emperor was induced to deprive the "Earl of Exalted Strength" of all his titles and emoluments and order him into retirement. This he did, weary of the importunities of Madame K'o, but still he would hear no word against his Consort. When she heard of her adopted father's disgrace, the Empress stripped off all her ornaments, and dressing herself as a mourner, without head covering, sought the Emperor's presence, where, on her knees, she thanked him for his clemency.

Shortly after this episode, in the summer of 1627, the Emperor fell sick of an illness from which he never recovered. As his state became worse, his affection for his loyal and devoted wife increased. At this juncture, Wei Chung-hsien had the effrontery to propose to Her Majesty that she should become his confederate in a scheme of treason and dishonour. This devil incarnate had no belief in the constancy of any sort of virtue—in his world all were bought and sold, loyalty being merely a question of price and opportunity. He and Madame K'o had much to fear from the death of the Emperor, the weakling whose name and authority were necessary to their evil purposes. Wei could not hope to wield the power of the Throne unless it were filled by a puppet or by an ally. He therefore proposed to Her Majesty that, upon her husband's death, she should become Chief Regent, accepting as Regent Assessor (practically co-Regent) a creature named Wei Liang-ch'ing, one of the eunuch's adherents. At the same time he desired that the Empress should give out that she was *enceinte*, with the intention of passing off a son of Wei Liang-ch'ing as her own child after the Emperor's death. In this way the house of Wei would attain to the Throne.

This Wei Liang-ch'ing was merely a tool in the hand of the Chief Eunuch, without political ambition of his own. He was a wine-bibber and a profligate, whose one thought, in accepting the rôle assigned to him, was to obtain possession of the beautiful Empress. To his friends he declared, "I care not a jot for the Dragon Throne, but to enjoy the society of such a woman as the Goddess Chang,[1] that were bliss indeed." The Empress knew that, upon Hsi Tsung's passing, it must come to a life and death struggle between the eunuch and herself, but she held her head high and showed no signs of fear. "For many years," she said to him, "I have made me ready for death. If now I obey you, you will kill me sooner or later; if I refuse, you will kill me only a little sooner. But if I die resisting you to the utmost, I can face unashamed the souls of the departed Emperors in the other world."

As the Emperor's end approached, Her Majesty begged him to name as his successor his brother, the Prince Hsin. "But," said the dying Monarch, "Wei Chung-hsien assures me that two of my concubines are with child. If an heir should be born to one of them, he will become our son and should surely succeed to the Throne." Upon

[1] Thus was the Empress familiarly known in the Palace.

this, the Empress spoke to him most earnestly; the attendants never knew what words passed between them, but the Emperor nodded consent, and summoned his brother to receive his dying behests. Prince Hsin was about to plead his incompetency, but his sister-in-law, attired as a widow, hurriedly emerged from behind an alcove and pleaded with him, saying: "My brother, do your duty, obey His Majesty. The situation is desperate, and I fear a rising in the Palace. Thank His Majesty and do as he desires." Prince Hsin then fell upon his knees, and the Monarch bade him govern the Empire wisely, avoiding the errors which he himself had committed. But, blind to the last, he added: " Wei Chung-hsien fully deserves your trust and may be given the highest office with absolute confidence." Finally, he commended the Empress to his brother's tender care. "See to her welfare; she has been a faithful Consort to me these seven years; much do I owe her. Often has she admonished me and urged me to better things. Her influence has ever been for good. She deserves all your pity; a widow, and so young. To your care I commend her." Prince Hsin left the Presence, and the Empress concealed him in an inner apartment of the Palace, for fear lest Wei should assassinate him. The Emperor passed away at 3 p.m. on the 22nd of the 8th Moon. Thereupon the Empress issued his valedictory decree, and commanded the hereditary Duke Chang Wei-hsien and other officials to escort the new Emperor to the Main Hall of Audience, where he should receive obeisance. Wei Chung-hsien was persuaded to bide his time and to refrain from challenging the authority of this decree by setting up a puppet of his own at once. (The eunuchs, as a body, always preferred intrigue and assassination to open defiance of dynastic law.) The dead Emperor was dressed in his robes of longevity, and his widow, weeping at his bier, so exhausted herself by excess of grief that she fainted away.

THE COURT OF PEKING

On recovering consciousness her first thought was to warn the new Emperor against the danger of poison; she begged him to touch no food prepared in the Palace kitchen. She herself dispatched a confidential chamberlain to the market for victuals which she cooked with her own hands. The Emperor thanked her, and as a sign of his gratitude for her devotion recalled her adopted father to Peking and restored all his honours. He was allowed to enter the Palace and return thanks to his daughter. The Emperor conferred upon her the title of Empress Senior,[1] of Feminine Virtue and Tranquillity, and gave her the Palace of Motherly Peace and of Motherly Blessings for her abode.

The new Emperor had abstained from all participation in Palace politics during his brother's occupancy of the Throne, but he soon showed himself to be a man of strong character and noble disposition. The Chief Eunuch's position soon became one of great danger, for his crimes had made him many enemies, who now combined and turned against him. Also, Madame K'o had been sincerely attached to her foster son, though she had abused his confidence, and at his death, stricken with remorse, she ceased to be useful for treasonable purposes. The power of the evil confederacy which had wrought so many and great evils was now broken. Before the late Emperor's coffin, Madame K'o penitently burned pathetic relics of his childhood, which she had treasured—his first tooth, some locks of baby hair, a few broken toys, and the scabs which had peeled off him after smallpox. But her time had come. Shortly afterwards she was arrested, accused of countless crimes on overwhelming evidence, and sentenced to death by the slicing process, every member of her family and household being also condemned to execution. At her death the people rejoiced as at a festival. In her quarters at the Palace there were found

[1] To be distinguished from Empress Dowager.

six Imperial concubines, all with child, and it was proved that she had intended to poison the new Emperor and to make one of these infants of unknown paternity heir to the Throne. All these wretched women were condemned to death, victims of another's evil ambition.

The tide had now turned strongly against Wei Chung-hsien, and realising that his position was desperate he escaped from the Palace and fled to Shantung. Outlawed, and abandoned by all his followers, he committed suicide near the grave of Confucius, but by order of the Throne his body was subsequently dismembered and the head exhibited at his native city (Ho Chien-fu), and many scores of his adherents, especially those who had conspired against the Empress, were put to death.

Throughout the troublous reign of the new Emperor Ch'ung-chen (1627-1644) the Senior Empress lived on terms of happy intimacy and affection with him and with his Consort, respected and beloved of the populace. In 1642, upon the marriage of the Heir Apparent, she took up her residence, as custom prescribed, in the Palace of Benevolent Old Age.

Her death was as meritorious as her life had been. In 1644, when Peking had fallen into the hands of the rebel Li Tzŭ-ch'eng and the city was being ravaged and burned by his troops, the Emperor sent her a message bidding her commit suicide, but in the tumult and confusion the messenger failed to reach her. When she heard that Li Tzŭ-ch'eng was battering at the gates of the Forbidden City, she called for a sword, but was unable to deal herself a fatal blow, and her attendants endeavoured to dissuade her from seeking death. Failing with the sword, she hanged herself with her girdle, but was cut down by her servants and urged to seek safety in flight. Angrily she stamped her foot, saying: "You have disgraced me," and ran to a side room, where again she tried to hang herself, but some of Li Tzŭ-ch'eng's men arrived just in time to cut her down. As she came to her senses the rebels gathered around her, praising her beauty. One of them, who seemed to be a leader, exclaimed : " We are now in the Palace of the late Emperor's widow; this must be she. Never have I seen so beautiful a face. Let no one lay hands on her. She must await our Chief's orders." But some declared that this was not the Goddess Chang —that she had fled in disguise and escaped—whilst others said she was dead.

The rebels were still disputing as to her identity, while she sat silent, when some eunuchs entered with an elderly woman who was Li's personal attendant and who had been ordered by him to arrange the Palace concubines in batches, according to their age and beauty, for his inspection. The eunuchs pointed out the Empress, saying : " That is the Goddess Chang, wife of the late Emperor." She was placed in the care of attendants, who tried to console her. " Lady Chang, do not be afraid," they said. " You are so beautiful that when our great Prince inspects the concubines to-morrow he will surely choose you for his Empress."

In her grief and despair, the Empress felt as if her breast were being pierced by a myriad arrows, and she was wondering how she could contrive to kill herself, when a loud voice called out from the courtyard : " Where is the Empress Dowager, Goddess Chang ? " This was one of the chief commanders of the rebels, named Li Yen. Before Peking had fallen, some of the eunuchs had gone over to the rebels, and had informed them of the whereabouts of the most beautiful women, whom they divided into three classes.

Li Tzŭ-ch'eng had promised thirty concubines to each of his Generals, and a list of all the women in the Palace had been placed in Li Yen's hands. Li Yen was a licentiate of Honan Province who had joined the rebellion, a fluent expounder of moral philosophy. Seeing that the

Senior Empress's name was at the head of the list of women, he sighed deeply and said: " How dare these wretched eunuchs desecrate Her Majesty's name in this way? She stands too high for such disgrace. I, who come from her own province, must save her from this outrage."

So he hurried into the Palace, and on finding her, bade two handmaidens lead her to one of the Throne rooms, where he assisted her to mount the daïs. Li Yen then dressed himself in Court robes and made obeisance before her nine times. Placing her in the charge of attendants, he hurried away to find Li Tzŭ-ch'eng. That same evening she succeeded in killing herself. When they found her body, she was attired in black silk with gold embroidery and full sleeves; her face was veiled with yellow crape and her hair neatly dressed; she looked like a woman of thirty. Those who saw the serenity of her face felt as if some heavenly visitant hovered near them, so happy was she in her death.

Li Yen buried her in the courtyard of her Palace and did homage at her obsequies. Meanwhile, Li Tzŭ-ch'eng had given orders that the late Emperor and his Consort should be buried, but made no public announcement concerning the death of the Senior Empress. It was freely rumoured that she had been taken alive by one of the rebels. On the same day the concubine Jen [1] surrendered to Li Tzŭ-ch'eng, and to increase her own importance told him that she was the Senior Empress, the wife of Hsi Tsung. Li Tzŭ-ch'eng believed her, and later, on his retreat before the Manchus, took her with him. Thus it came to pass that in the Court of the fugitive Mings at Nanking calumnious tongues insulted this noble woman's memory, and it was noised abroad that she had become the mistress of the rebel Chief.

There were still eunuchs and women at that Court who

[1] *Vide supra*, p.

had been of the faction of Wei Chung-hsien and who were only too eager to besmirch her spotless reputation. The new Ming Emperor, Prince Fu, was in the hands of evil advisers and believed these cruel falsehoods, so that no canonisation was conferred upon her until the following year, when her death was undeniably confirmed. A eunuch eye-witness of her death described it to the Manchu Regent, Prince Jui, who gave orders that she should be buried beside her husband, at his mausoleum to the north of Peking. So came she to her honourable rest.

After the dispersion of Li Tzŭ-ch'eng's force by the Manchus, the Jen concubine, who had accumulated great store of treasure from the Palace, moved to Wu T'ai Mountain, west of Peking, and her abode became the resort of many lawless characters. She still claimed to be the Empress Consort of Hsi Tsung, and in that capacity extorted money from the common people. Eventually complaints were lodged at Court, and she was arrested and brought to Peking. On her arrival there she declared she was indeed the Empress, and some there were who believed her. But the eunuchs of the Court had no difficulty in proving her to be a base pretender. The romantic chroniclers aver that she was compelled to try on one of the Goddess Chang's tiny shoes, before which test she failed ignominiously. Be this as it may, she was allowed to commit suicide, and thereafter the memory of " Precious Pearl," the illustrious and virtuous Empress, has shone undimmed throughout the centuries.

CHAPTER III

LI TZU-CH'ENG'S REBELLION AND THE FALL OF PEKING

The swift decline and pitiful end of the Ming dynasty was primarily due to the corruption and incompetence of its later Monarchs and to the licentiousness of their Court, which gave high office and the direction of State affairs to eunuchs. Its doom was plain-writ upon the wall for many years before the great rebellion of Li Tzŭ-ch'eng ended triumphantly in the Throne Hall of the Forbidden City, because, as one historian has put it, " the ruling house had ceased to display those moral qualities without which no power will long be tolerated by a people like the Chinese."

There had been serious uprisings in various parts of the Empire—notably in Kueichou and Shantung—since the beginning of the seventeenth century; in 1622 the Dutch had appeared upon the scene, seizing the Pescadores and adding new terrors to the life of Chinese officials. In 1625, the rising power of Nurhachi and his Manchu armies had been signalised by the establishment of his capital at Moukden. But the position of the dynasty only became desperate when, in 1641, Li Tzu-ch'eng's rebellion (which had been fitfully active for some ten years) assumed formidable proportions and, sweeping northwards, carried all before it.

Li Tzŭ-ch'eng himself stands out as a picturesque

figure against the lurid background of those days, a great soldier and something of a politician. Cruel, with all the ruthless ferocity of the Oriental, unscrupulous in love and war, full of the lust of power and wealth, he possessed, nevertheless, certain redeeming qualities—courage, and a capacity for sudden impulses of generosity. His most notable characteristic, common amongst fighting men of humble origin who have risen to the purple, was his belief in auguries, omens and portents. Many of the most momentous decisions of his career were the outcome of his superstitious beliefs and fears.

He was born in Shensi, about the year 1606. Historians declare that in his early youth he had fore-knowledge of his great destiny. One of them narrates the following story. As a young man he was addicted to hunting and hawking, and would wander far afield with congenial spirits. One day, in the depth of winter, he found himself with two intimate friends in a remote country district. As evening fell they sat under a tree to rest, and refreshed themselves with deep draughts of wine. A dust storm was raging. Suddenly Li turned to his friends and said: " Listen! If the Imperial Throne is destined to be mine, a sign will be given us to-night in the shape of a heavy snowstorm." With this, he planted an arrow in the ground and added: " If Heaven is on my side let the snow be level with the top of this arrow." His friends replied: " If you become the Son of Heaven we are your men till death." Soon after, the sky began to darken and the wind fell. Snow began to fall gently, and gradually increased, until by midnight the top of the arrow could just be seen. Li and his friends, greatly impressed, walked home through the snow, and from that day his mind was fixed on the ambition to overturn the Ming dynasty. He turned brigand, and after eleven year of perilous adventures found himself at the head of a large army.

To give another instance of the superstitions which continually influenced this born leader of men. In an engagement near the strategic pass at T'ung Kuan his left eye was pierced by an arrow. An ancient prophecy had predicted that the Empire would be conquered by a one-eyed man, and Li was therefore tremendously elated at receiving this auspicious wound; indeed, the incident, widely discussed, brought many new followers to his flag.

And again, after the fall of Peking in 1644, Li Tzŭ-ch'eng entered the Forbidden City by the Southern, or Dynastic, Gate. On arriving at the main entrance, the "Gate of Heaven's Grace," as it was then called, he stopped and aimed an arrow at the character signifying "heaven," painted over the gateway, the conviction having suddenly seized him that if his shot were successful in hitting the mark, it would mean that Heaven approved of his mounting the Throne. His arrow lodged just below the character, and he and, those with him took it for an omen that he had been rejected by the Most High, and that his victorious course was run.

In 1641 Li Tzŭ-ch'eng, victoriously advancing, laid siege to Honan-fu. When his troops had completely invested the city, Prince Fu, the Emperor's uncle, whose fief was the province of Honan, summoned his generals to a banquet at his Palace, and they arranged to raise a force of a thousand volunteers, who would let themselves down by ropes from the city wall and make a successful night sortie. Dissolute and drunken as he was, the favourite son of Wan Li made a brave defence, until Li Tzŭ-ch'eng delivered a surprise attack from the north, and overpowering the guards, took the city by assault. When all was confusion, Prince Fu had himself let down from the city wall and escaped in disguise to a neighbouring temple, but he was discovered and brought into the presence of Li Tzŭ-ch'eng. As he entered the camp

THE COURT OF PEKING

he perceived the Commander of the city garrison in chains, who called to him and said: " Prince, a man in your exalted station has a duty to the State to fulfil; he must die bravely. Let not Your Highness bend the knee in submission to these dogs of rebels." Prince Fu made no reply, but when led before Li Tzŭ-ch'eng refused to speak and was promptly dispatched. After killing him, Li mixed a cupful of his blood in a dish of hashed venison, and called it the " Red pottage of fortune and blessing," this being a pun on the Prince's name, which means " good fortune." He was ever a grim jester.

His chief associate and fellow-rebel, almost as famous a guerilla leader as Li himself, was Chang Hsien-chung, a Shensi Mahomedan, also a grim jester in his way. While Li was besieging Honan-fu, Chang possessed himself of the rich city of Hsiang-Yang, in Hupei. He won it by covering a hundred miles with a small force of cavalry in twenty-four hours, and surprising the garrison, whose scouts had reported the country free of rebels. Having taken possession of the city and burned the Prefect's yamên, he seized the person of Prince Hsiang, a cousin of the Emperor, and over-lord of Hupei. He brought him into the audience hall of his own Palace, and setting a beaker of wine before him, said: " I have no grudge against Your Highness, and you are a harmless person enough, but I have a fierce longing to see the head of General Yang separated from his body.[1] But alas, Yang is not available at the moment, being far from here; and so I propose to make use of Your Highness's head instead. For if I now remove it, the Emperor, wrath at the killing of one of his own kinsmen, may see fit to order the death of Yang, who should have been able to prevent this abominable murder. Will Your Highness drink as much of the wine as you can carry?" He then put him to

[1] Yang Ssu-ch'ang was the Ming Commander-in-chief in Hupei, who had defeated Chang on more than one occasion.

death and burned the body. The same ruffian is alleged by Chinese historians to have made a dish of a wife who had ceased to please him, putting into practice the proverb which says, " The favourite of to-day is served up at to-morrow's banquet."

The news of the fall of Hsiang-Yang created dismay at Court. As Chang had foreseen, the Censors, trembling at the prospect of the approaching cataclysm, ordered that General Yang be put to death for failing to stem the rebellion, but he saved them the trouble by committing suicide.

In the same year, 1641, Li Tzŭ-ch'eng laid siege to the great city of K'ai Feng-fu in Honan; but its garrison made such a stout defence, and its fifty-feet wall was so impervious to his mining and artillery that he was obliged to desist from the attempt. Early in 1643. having subjugated all the surrounding country, he made a close investment of the city, determined to take it at all costs. The siege lasted until September, and the garrison, being well supplied with food, showed no signs of yielding to the rebels. When at last the city fell, it brought no rich reward of booty to the conquerors, but only a harvest of death. Enraged by its stubborn resistance, and fearing the advance of a relieving force from Shensi, Li Tzŭ-ch'eng determined to flood the city by cutting the banks of the Yellow River. Curiously enough, the Commander of the garrison had conceived a similar plan for flooding the rebel camp, and had begun to sap the river's embankment at a spot favourable for that purpose. Li Tzŭ-ch'eng's spies warned him of the danger, upon which he moved his camp to higher ground and made large provision of boats and rafts for his army. Having done this, he compelled the country people for miles around to cut away the embankments at Nia Chia-k'ou. Over a hundred thousand of these unfortunates perished when the river, swollen by heavy rains, finally burst its banks, and so fierce was the flood that ten thousand of the rebels were drowned. It entered K'ai Feng-fu by the northern gate and carried swift destruction throughout the city. Of a population estimated at over a million, scarcely a tenth escaped. The Governor and some of the higher officials saved themselves in boats, and several Princes with their wives and concubines took refuge in a tower on the wall, where they nearly died of starvation before rescuing parties reached them. When Li Tzŭ-ch'eng entered the city in a boat, he found no opportunity for plunder or reprisals.

From Honan, Li marched into Shensi, regaling his troops with three days of looting and rapine at Hsi-an. Here, clad in Imperial dragon robes, he reviewed his forces, while the citizens knelt at his passing. Thence he proceeded to his native place and offered sacrifice at his ancestral tombs, which had been desecrated by the Imperial authorities. On the first day of the new year (1644) he assumed the Imperial title of Yung Ch'ang, as the founder of the "Great Obedient" dynasty; he also canonised his ancestors for four generations as Emperors in the realms above. He would have taken this step at a much earlier date had it not been that he had doubts as to the possible rivalry of his old colleague and fellow-rebel, Chang, who was believed to cherish schemes of establishing a kingdom of his own. But Chang now sent rich gifts to Li and a letter acknowledging him as Emperor. So Li took heart of grace and proceeded to make for himself a new nobility and a Court; he appointed six ministries, with presidents and their staffs, and created nine marquises, seventy-two earls, thirty viscounts and fifty-five barons. At this time his army consisted of 600,000 cavalry and 400,000 infantry. He sent Imperial mandates throughout the country denouncing the Ming Emperor, in these terms: "His Majesty, the present Emperor, cannot be called an utter fool. He stands alone, but the oppression of his officials is like unto the heat of a burning fiery furnace. His Ministers serve only their own selfish ends and form conspiracies among themselves. Loyal men are few and far between. The prisons are full of unfortunate captives, and the officials are devoid of gratitude for favours received. The people are so oppressed by their exactions, that in their misery they abandon their homes."

New Year's Day 1644 in Peking dawned darkly under a fierce dust-storm, and an earthquake occurred at Feng Yang in Anhui, near to the birthplace of the founder of the dynasty. The Court was in despair. The Grand Secretary Li Chien-ta'i, a native of Shansi, who had made an enormous fortune as owner of the well-known Ssŭ Tu-heng banking-house (which still exists), came forward at audience and proposed to place his wealth at the service of the Throne and to lead an army in person against the rebels in his native province. The news of Li Tzŭ-ch'eng's assumption of the Imperial title had come as a great shock to the Monarch, who sorrowfully remarked to Li Chien-t'ai: "My conscience is clear. I have not deserved to forfeit the mandate of Heaven; nevertheless, ruin confronts me on all sides, and the Empire is slipping from me. The inheritance which my ancestors won, after being 'combed by the wind and bathed in the rain,' is rapidly being lost. How can I bear to face them in the next world? Gladly would I march to battle at the head of my army and perish on the sandy plain. How can I ever close my eyes in peaceful death while the Empire is in a ferment?" At this the Monarch burst into tears. Thereupon all the Grand Secretaries present asked to be allowed to lead the army into battle in his place (a task which they were no more fitted to undertake than the Sovereign). The Emperor refused, whereupon Li Chien-t'ai again kotowed and said: "I am ready to pay all the expenses of the army and to march on the rebels."

THE COURT OF PEKING

Ch'ung-chen thanked him warmly: "I myself shall see you off on your journey, as ancient custom prescribes." He bestowed upon him an Imperial sword and full powers in the field.

After a few days of preparation, the Emperor repaired to the Temple of Ancestors and informed the august shades of his decision; then he ascended to the top of the tower at the Ch'ien Men facing the Palace. The troops made a brave show, drawn up in line extending from the entrance to the Forbidden City as far as the Temple of Heaven. The whole Court was in attendance and the musicians played martial airs. His Majesty gave a banquet after the review, at which he presided, and passed the wine round seven times. Thrice he pledged the health of Li Chien-ta'i in a golden beaker, and handed to him a patent inscribed: "Acting as Generalissimo on Our Imperial behalf."

The troops then marched off, and the Emperor watched them leave the city. A little way beyond the city gates Li Chien-t'ai's sedan-chair pole broke, which was regarded as an evil omen. The expedition was a dismal failure. Long before it had reached Shansi the rebels had captured Li's native city and had looted most of his family treasure. Many of his troops died of starvation on the way.

Meanwhile, Li Tzŭ-ch'eng was marching northwards through Shansi, had crossed the Yellow River without opposition, and laid siege to T'ai Yuan-fu. The Governor made a gallant resistance, but the city was betrayed to the rebels by one of his staff.

Li Tzŭ-ch'eng entered Prince Chin's Palace and captured the wretched Prince (a descendant of Yung lo). Him he slew, together with forty-six high officials. On hearing the news, the Emperor issued a pitiful decree deploring the calamities inflicted on his people by the rebellion, as well as the inefficiency of his officials and his own lack of virtue in governing. "In the watches of the night," he said, " I mourn over these things and my self-abasement knows no limit. From this time forth I am determined to turn over a new leaf and to avert the consequences of my errors. I mean to strengthen our resources by employing able men in office, and by adherence to time-honoured tradition to depart from evil. By merciful forbearance I intend to win my subjects' love, and by remitting unjust taxation to make good their lack of funds. I command that lists be drawn up of all worthy and honest men who in the past may have been dismissed from office, so that they may be reinstated. To any member of the local gentry who shall re-capture a city from the rebels I will grant hereditary rank. To all who return to their allegiance and repent them of their sins I promise pardon and high rank; while any one who may capture the rebels Li Tzŭ-ch'eng and Chang Hsien-chung will receive from me a marquisate and corresponding official rank."

"The Devil was sick," but the time for issuing such decrees was past; nothing could now save the doomed dynasty. When a first detachment of rebels entered Chihli and captured Ho Chien-fu the Court dispatched the eunuch Tu Hsün to the Chihli frontier at Hsüan-hua to stop their advance from that side. This was a fatal step, for Tu was a coward and a traitor. He had already advised the Emperor to surrender, saying: "You had better abdicate, you and I will have plenty to live upon in retirement." With this powerful eunuch at the head of military affairs, interfering in matters of which he was profoundly ignorant, the situation was desperate, but none dared to oppose him.

A Censor now advised him to send the Heir Apparent to Nanking, and to place his other two sons, the Princes Ting and Yung, in charge of the defence of Ning-kuo and Tai-ping in Anhui, near the birthplace of the ancestors of the dynasty. While perusing this memorial the

THE COURT OF PEKING

Emperor walked nervously round the Palace grounds, sighing and muttering to himself. He had made up his mind to agree, when one of the Grand Secretaries told him that the scheme was bruited abroad and was creating a bad impression. The wretched Emperor again hesitated, and finally said: " It is the duty of the Sovereign and his family to die for the State. I shall order the Princes to remain in Peking." Urgent messages were sent to Wu San-kuei to defend Shan Hai-kuan and to dispatch all the troops he could spare to the metropolis.

On arrival at Ning Wu-fu, a city of Shansi situated just inside the Great Wall, Li Tzŭ-ch'eng sent forward a herald to announce that all its inhabitants would be put to the sword unless the city surrendered within five days. General Chou Yü-chi, who had retreated hither from Ping Yang, made use of cannon which had been cast by the Jesuit priests, and did great execution amongst the rebels. When his gunpowder was almost exhausted, and the assault continued with undiminished vigour, his men tried to persuade him to surrender. The old General angrily replied: " Why such cowards? If you win the day you will gain great glory, as brave and loyal men. When you find you can hold out no longer, all you have to do is to bind me and hand me over to the rebels. You can blame me for holding out so long." His troops were ashamed and proceeded to lay an ambush for the rebels by posting a few men at certain gates and then opening them to the enemy. In marched the rebels, whereupon the defenders closed the barriers at the end of certain streets, caught them in a trap, and slaughtered them in thousands. But Li Tzŭ-ch'eng continued to bombard the city walls with cannon; as one portion collapsed, the breach was hurriedly repaired by the defenders. Four of Li Tzŭ-ch'eng's bravest lieutenants were slain, and Li had almost made up his mind to retreat, when his aide-de-camp protested, saying: " We outnumber them by a hundred to one; if we persist, in spite of our losses, victory is certain. It would be so even if the odds were only ten to one."

Li Tzŭ-ch'eng was only too willing, and urged his men on. As one company was wiped out another pressed forward to take its place. When the corpses were piled ten feet high the garrison was exhausted and the city fell. General Chou Yü-chi refused to yield; he directed the street fighting until his horse was killed, whereupon he rushed headlong among the rebels, killing several before they captured him, pierced through and through with arrows as numerous as the quills on the porcupine. Still he resisted them, so Li Tzŭ-ch'eng had him tied to a lofty beam and shot at with arrows until he died, after which his corpse was decapitated. His wife and hand-maidens fled to a small guard house on the Great Wall and from there shot arrows at the rebels, who set fire to the building. All of them perished in the flames. No one in the city surrendered: all were put to death.

When Li appeared before the gates of Ta T'ung-fu, General Chiang Hsiung and the treacherous eunuch Commander-in-chief, Tu Hsün, agreed to surrender, though the Governor, Wei Ching-yuan, and his army had taken a solemn oath, consecrated, in accordance with ancient custom, by the blood of a sheep smeared on the lips, that they would hold out to the death. When the rebels arrived, Chiang Hsiung's men, some of whom were posted at each gate, treacherously surrendered the city. Governor Wei on horseback rushed forward, but seeing that he had been betrayed allowed himself to be taken. They led him to Li Tzŭ-ch'eng, who offered him official rank. Wei sat down instead of kneeling in his presence, and called out: " May the Emperor live for ever ! " Then he wept. Li praised his loyalty, saying : " I will never slay so brave a man." Governor Wei then rose and dashed his head against the stone balustrade. The blood poured forth, and the rebels took him away. Meeting the traitor, General Chiang, he reviled him, saying: " Accursed rebel, you have violated the solemn oath which you took before the Almighty; God will reward you according to your crime." Then the rebels brought in his mother, who was over eighty years of age, to induce him to yield. He said: " Mother, you are very old and must do as you think best. I, your son, am a Minister of State, and death is the only way for me." His mother was led away, and he said to the bystanders: " I will curse the rebels no more, in the hope that they will spare my mother's life." He hanged himself in a Buddhist shrine, and the rebels praised his loyal courage. They provided shelter for his wife and family and bade his mother join them. Then they put to death all of the Imperial family who were in the city.

When the news reached Peking, Li Chien-t'ai (who had returned from his inglorious expedition) advised the Emperor to flee to Nanking. Ch'ung Chen called his Ministers to an audience on the Palace terrace, and after telling them of this advice said: " The Sovereign must die for the Altars of the Tutelary Dieties; whither should I flee?"

One of the most loyal and upright of his Ministers was the Grand Secretary Chiang Te-ying. In the early stages of the rebellion he had advised an active policy against Li, and had remonstrated with the Emperor for taxing the people so heavily to provide funds for a non-existent army.

At the audience on the terrace, Chiang again advised that the Heir Apparent should be sent to Nanking, and recommended that a decree be issued, beginning as follows: " Of late, evil-minded persons have been collecting unjust taxes on the pretext of providing army funds, so that our subjects have been cruelly oppressed and the interests of our State have been placed in jeopardy." When the

Emperor heard this preamble, he became very angry and said: "I have only raised these taxes in order to pay my troops and not for my own benefit." Chiang replied: "I am aware of this, Your Majesty, but the taxation is very heavy, and I venture to ask you, is the proportionate number of men and horses forthcoming? The Viceroy of Chichou should have 45,000 troops; he has only 25,000. The Viceroy of Pao Ting-fu should have 30,000; he has 2,000. And so it is with the garrisons around the capital; the money has all been wasted and misappropriated."

The Emperor was very wrath, and accused Chiang of conspiring against him, so the Minister tendered his resignation. Ch'ung chen intended to punish him, but he escaped when the city fell. Hoping against hope, the Emperor now conferred an earldom on Wu San-kuei and bade him hurry to the defence of the capital. The eunuch Wang Ch'eng-en was made Commander-in-chief of Peking and placed in charge of its defences.

The Governor of Hsüan-hua, Chu Chih-feng, an Imperial clansman, had prepared to defend the city; but the eunuch Tu Hsün and General Wang Ch'eng-yün sent him word to surrender. Tu went in person to call on Chu Chih-feng and advised him to submit, but Chu refused to listen to him. When the rebels appeared, Tu Hsün donned his Court robes and dragon jacket and went out to meet Li Tzŭ-ch'eng ten miles beyond the city. The garrison dispersed, whereupon Chu mounted the city wall, accompanied only by a few retainers. The rebels entered the gates, which had been opened by the eunuchs. Li had issued notices that no one was to be massacred, and promised remission of taxation and *corvées*, so the people were in high spirits. The streets were decked with bunting and festooned arches had been erected to welcome the conquerors. Incense was burnt as Li Tzŭ-ch'eng entered. General Chu's servants endeavoured to persuade him to seek a place of safety, but he upbraided them and prostrated himself in the direction of Peking in obeisance to the Emperor. Then he hastily wrote out a valedictory memorial, in which he implored His Majesty to stimulate his subjects to patriotism and loyalty; after which he hanged himself on a beam. The rebels flung his corpse into a ditch, but though the dogs devoured the other dead bodies they left his untouched.

Six days later Chü Yen-kuan was taken by the rebels, and that impregnable frontier was successfully passed. Li Tzŭ-ch'eng had now entered the plain north of Peking, and was only thirty miles from the capital. He proceeded to the sacred enclosure containing the ancestral mausolea, plundered their contents, and set many of the stately halls on fire. His spies were all over Peking, and many merchants and officials in his pay sent him daily word of the Ming preparations. Some of his confidential agents were actually serving on the Board of War, and every decision of the Throne was at once communicated to him by special courier. On the other hand, the spies sent out by the Board of War were captured by Li's patrols and none returned to Peking. Thus Li's advance guard reached the central West Gate of the capital before his approach was even suspected.

The Emperor summoned his Council; all were silent and some wept. The bombardment began. Three regiments which had been placed outside the gate fled at the rebels' approach, only a few guards remained to man the walls. Li Tzŭ-ch'eng moved to the Chang-yi Gate, about a mile and a half further South, and established his quarters just outside the *enceinte*. Here he was attended by the eunuch traitor Tu Hsün; the latter shot a message in a quill on to the city wall, where it was picked up by the guard. It was a letter to the Emperor, stating that the rebels must win, and advising His Majesty to commit suicide. This was handed to Ch'ung Chen, who thereupon issued a penitential decree and again ordered that all extra taxation should cease forthwith. He then ordered his son-in-law, Kung Yung-ku, to send a body of retainers with the Heir Apparent to Nanking. Kung kotowed and said: "It is the rule that relations of the Emperor should keep no arms in their residence; alas! I have no retainers for the mission." The two men wept together.

The rebels scaled the wall of the Southern city with ladders, and took possession of the quarter inside the Chang-yi Gate. Other detachments bombarded the three gates of the Tartar city. The guard fled, and the eunuchs in command cravenly surrendered to the rebels. At this critical moment the folly of trusting to these myrmidons was fully proved, and the wisdom justified of the founder of the dynasty who forbade that they should be allowed to meddle in affairs of State. There were between three and four thousand of them in the Forbidden City, ostensibly charged with the duty of defending it and the Emperor, but of these one only, the eunuch Wang Ch'eng-en, was faithful even unto death. The rest spent the last days before the coming of the rebels either in rioting and feasting or in burying their treasures and making ready for flight. On the very day that Li Tzŭ-ch'eng captured the first gate of the outer city, one of the Chief Eunuchs was giving a theatrical entertainment at his residence just outside the Ch'ien Men. As for the officials, the loyal and the good were, for the most part, so indignant at the eunuchs' supremacy in the counsels of the Emperor, and so certain of disaster, that they prepared to perish with the dynasty, as the Confucian traditions prescribe. The licentious and ignoble continued their feastings as before.

On the 4th day of the 3rd Moon, the Court of Astronomers had handed in a memorial, saying that the Emperor's star was being displaced, and His Majesty issued one of his futile decrees, calling upon his officials

THE COURT OF PEKING

to repent them of evil. Yet he took not the brave and loyal into his favour and confidence, the men who later died for him at the post of duty. The spirit of his degenerate Court was fittingly displayed in the words of a couplet which some one wrote upon the Palace wall. "If this dynasty's star has waned, let us hitch our fortunes on to its successor."

The Emperor now realised that the position was hopeless, and that it was too late to strengthen the city's defences. On the 17th of the 3rd Moon, the rebels attacked the North-West Gate. The Palace officials came to report to His Majesty, who summoned all the Grand Council to a secret audience at the Terrace Pavilion. The Emperor asked the advice of Wu Tsao-te, who could make no reply, but hung his head in forlorn silence. Seeing them all helpless, the Emperor, in a rage, flung his dragon chair to the ground and left the Pavilion. He went from the Palace on to the Coal Hill. It was now evening, and the smoke of the rebels' beacon fires was visible on all sides of the city. For a long while the wretched Monarch stood there, lamenting his peoples' sufferings and his own.

Next morning, long before dawn, the rebels attacked the Western Gate of the Southern city, and the eunuch Tsao, who was in charge, surrendered it to the enemy. The rebels poured in, speedily captured the Ch'ien Men, and advanced upon the Forbidden City.

The Emperor ordered that the Heir Apparent and his younger brother be removed to a place of safety. When they came to take leave of their father they were dressed in their usual Court attire. Sorrowfully the Emperor regarded them: "How is it that at a time like this you are arrayed in robes of luxury?" Then he commanded a eunuch to bring two suits of old and shabby clothes, and with his own hands assisted his sons to tie their girdles. "To-day," said he to the elder, "you are Heir to the Throne; to-morrow you will be one of the people, homeless, and a wanderer on the face of the earth. Reveal not your names and dissemble as best you may. Address your elders with respect as " good sir," and call strangers " uncle " or " kind cousin." If, perchance, your lives should be spared, remember in time to come to avenge the wrongs which your parents have suffered. Forget not these my words." He ended, and the lads were led away.

He then commanded them to bring wine, of which he drank a considerable quantity. Summoning his Empress Consort (who was of the Chou family) and the concubines, he addressed them, saying : " All is over. It is time for you to die." The senior concubine, Lady Yüan, on hearing these words, rose in terror from her knees and tried to escape, but His Majesty pursued her with a sword. Shouting : " You too must die," he wounded her in the shoulder. She continued to run, but the Emperor thrust at her a second time, whereat she fell, weltering in blood. The Empress Consort fled to her Palace of Feminine Tranquillity, and there hanged herself.

Next, the Emperor summoned the Princess Imperial from the Palace of Peaceful Old Age. She was only just fifteen years of age. Wildly he glared at her, saying : " By what evil fortune were you born into our ill-starred house ? " Seizing his sword, he hacked off her right arm, and she sank dying to the floor. He then went to the pavilion of Charity Made Manifest and there killed his second daughter, the Princess of Feminine Propriety. Finally, he sent eunuchs to greet in his name the Empress Consort, and to the senior concubines of his late brother, Hsi Tsung, strongly advising both to commit suicide.[1] Entering the Palace of Feminine Tranquillity, he saw his Consort hanging dead from the rafters, whereat he cried aloud : " Death is best, the only way for us all."

[1] *Vide supra*, p.

THE COURT OF PEKING

It was now nearly 5 a.m. and the dawn was breaking. The Emperor changed his apparel and removed his long Imperial robe. The bell rang in the Palace for the morning audience, but none attended. The Emperor donned a short dragon-embroidered tunic and a robe of purple and yellow, and his left foot was bare. Accompanied by the faithful eunuch Wang Ch'eng-en, he left the Palace by the Gate of Divine Military Prowess, and entered the Coal Hill enclosure. Gazing sorrowfully upon the city, he wrote, on the lapel of his robe, a valedictory decree: "I, feeble and of small virtue, have offended against Heaven; the rebels have seized my capital because my Ministers deceived me. Ashamed to face my ancestors, I die. Removing my Imperial cap and with my hair dishevelled about my face, I leave to the rebels the dismemberment of my body. Let them not harm my people!" Then he strangled himself in the pavilion known as the "Imperial Hat and Girdle Department," and the faithful eunuch did likewise.[1]

Before the Emperor had committed suicide, most of the concubines had fled from out the Palace. One of them, the Lady Wei, on reaching the Imperial Canal, cried out: "All who are not cowards will follow my example," and jumped in. Some two hundred women of the Palace committed suicide. A certain handmaiden, named Fei, jumped into a disused well which was dry. The rebels pulled her out, and seeing that she was fair to look upon tried to take her. Haughtily she said: "I am the Princess Imperial." Awed by her words they desisted, and led her to Li Tzŭ-ch'eng. The latter ordered the eunuchs to identify her. As they all said that she was not the Princess, Li presented her to one of his captains, named Lo. Fei had the whip hand of him

[1] The usual account that he hanged himself to a tree is certainly incorrect, though until quite recently the chain which he is supposed to have used was suspended there.

also, saying : " Really and truly I am of Imperial lineage, and too high in rank to enter into an illegal or temporary union with you. Your Excellency must espouse me in lawful wedlock. I beg you to select an auspicious date for the ceremony." Lo was only too delighted, and set wine before her, of which he himself drank heartily. Fei waited until he was completely intoxicated, then took a stiletto and stabbed him fatally in the throat. As he lay dying, she cried out : " I, a weak woman, have slain a rebel leader. I am content." With that she cut her throat, and when Li heard of the deed he ordered that she should have honourable burial.

Meanwhile, Li Tzŭ-ch'eng had entered the Palace. By his order two door panels were brought, and the Emperor's body, with that of his attendant, was carried to a shop inside the Tung-hua Gate. Here the remains were laid for three days, after which eunuchs were ordered to array the Emperor in Imperial robes and to dress his hair, before laying him in his coffin. The people were allowed to pay their respects, and many did so, but few of the official class ventured to do obeisance to their old master, for fear of attracting Li Tzŭ-ch'eng's suspicions. In fact, many made a long detour on their way to the Palace in order to avoid passing the coffin.

On the 3rd of the 4th Moon, the Emperor and his Consort were temporarily buried in the grave of the T'ien concubine, but only eunuchs and peasants witnessed the burial. Later, when Li Tzŭ-ch'eng had been defeated and the Manchus had entered Peking, their Regent, the Prince Jui, ordered the building of an Imperial mausoleum and prescribed three days of general mourning. But, for the present, the last of the Ming Emperors went to his eternal rest unhonoured. An account of the burial ceremony was subsequently made to the Manchu Regent by the minor official who carried it out under orders from the rebel Prefect of Peking, as follows :

THE COURT OF PEKING

" On the 25th of the 3rd Moon [1] I received orders from Li Hsi-chang, styling himself Prefect of the city, that we were to inter their late Majesties in the grave chamber of the late concubine, the Lady T'ien, and that I was to engage labourers to open up the passage leading thereto, whose wages would be paid out of public funds. On the 1st day of the 4th Moon I therefore engaged thirty bearers for the Imperial coffin and sixteen for that of the Empress, and arranged for their conveyance to Ch'ang P'ing-chou. The preliminary obsequies were fixed for three days later, and the actual interment took place on the 5th. The departmental treasury was quite empty, and as the Secretary of Li Tzŭ-ch'eng's Board of Ceremonies (responsible for the due performance of the ceremony) refused to provide any funds, I was obliged to collect subscriptions from charitable persons. Thanks to the generosity of two worthies, I obtained the sum of 340 tiao.[2] So I set to work to open up the grave-tunnel, which was 135 feet long by 20 feet wide and 35 feet high. We worked for three days and nights, and early on the morning of the fourth day we came upon the stone gate opening into a grave ante-chamber. The workmen were obliged to force the lock before we could enter. Inside we found a lofty hall containing sacrificial vessels and many ornaments. In the centre was a stone vessel, whereon stood enormous candles of walrus fat.[3]

" Next, we opened the central tunnel gate, and found ourselves within a much larger hall, in the centre of which stood a stone couch 1 foot 5 inches high and 10 feet broad. On it lay the coffin of the Lady T'ien, covered with silk drapery.

" At 3 p.m., the coffins of their Majesties arrived at the entrance to the mausoleum, and were sheltered for the

---

[1] That is, seven days after the capture of Peking.
[2] At that time about £6.
[3] The so-called " everlasting lamps."

night in a temporary mat-shed which I had erected. We offered sacrifice of a bullock, gold and silver paper, grain and fruits. At the head of the few officials present I proceeded to pay homage to our departed Sovereign, and we wept bitterly at the foot of the Imperial biers.

" Next day, the two coffins were borne through the tunnel and into the grave chamber. We placed them on the stone couch, from which we had first removed the coffin of Lady T'ien. We then deposited the coffin of the Empress on the left of the couch, the Lady T'ien's remains were replaced on the right, and lastly, His Majesty's coffin was lifted into the central place. The Lady T'ien's death had occurred at a time of peace, and her coffin had consequently been provided with the customary outer shell, but there had been no means of preparing one in the present case for His Majesty. So I had the shell of the Lady T'ien's coffin removed and used to cover that of he Emperor.

"The obsequies having ended, we refilled the tunnel, banking up the earth so as to conceal the approach to the door leading into the grave chamber. On the following morning, the 6th, we offered libations of wine, and I had a mound erected over the grave by the peasants from neighbouring hamlets, besides building a clay wall five feet high round the enclosure."

Thus passed the last Ming Sovereign from the Dragon Throne. On the morning of his death (the 19th), just before noon, Li Tzŭ-ch'eng, mounted on a piebald horse, rode in through the Gate of Obedience to Heaven, attended by his Grand Secretary, the rebel Niu Chin-hsing, and Sung Ch'i-chiao, President of the Ministry of Civil Offices. The Chief Eunuchs with a large following had met him outside the city gate and escorted him into the Palace. He took his seat on the Throne in the Hall of Imperial Supremacy, and bade search be made for their Majesties, the news of their death not having yet reached him.

THE COURT OF PEKING

Some of the eunuchs brought forward the Heir Apparent and his two brothers, the Princes Yung and Ting, who had been found concealed with the family of the Lady T'ien. Li announced that on the 21st he would hold a Court reception, at which all the highest Ming officials must attend; on the 20th he busied himself in superintending the provision of quarters for his troops.

At daybreak on the 21st, the Imperial Duke Chu Shun-ch'en (in whom the late Emperor had placed his trust) and the Grand Secretaries Wei Tsao-te and Ch'en Yen led a melancholy procession of officials to the space in front of the Throne Hall. All were wearing their civilian clothes, not daring to don Court dress. Li Tzŭ-ch'eng did not condescend even to notice their congratulations. The rebels crowded round them and jeered, some prodding them playfully in the back with swords, while others made them kneel, and kicked them in the neck or pulled off their hats. The wretched officials dared not protest or resist, and tamely submitted to these insults in silence. The Grand Secretary Ch'en Yen then sought to curry favour by inviting Li Tzŭ-ch'eng to ascend the Imperial Throne.[1]

Li proceeded without delay to establish his authority and reorganise the Government. He gave to the Heir Apparent the title of Prince Sung, released all officials who had been imprisoned by the Mings, and promulgated a new official system. He changed the six Boards into Ministries, altered the constitution of the Censorate, and converted the Hanlin Academy into the " Institution of Elegant Literature." The old name for a Governor of Province was restored, and the division of the provincial administration into prefectures, departments and counties was simplified. All the changes which he made revealed practical wisdom.

[1] He had assumed the Imperial title at Hsi-an, but could not consider himself Emperor *de jure* until he had been enthroned at Peking.

Thereafter he condescended to receive the Ming officials. Sitting with his face to the South, and attended by his two Chief Lieutenants, he bade each advance in answer to the roll call. He divided them into three classes; all the lower officials gladly accepted their new ranks. In the higher ranks, only Hou Hsün was permitted to retain his former position of Vice-president; all the rest were degraded one or more steps. All alike knelt in anxious expectation, eager to receive employment from their new master. He was now to show them something of his quality.

First, he promulgated a code of regulations ordering that every family in Peking should board and lodge one rebel. There was nothing said against looting and rape, so that for the next few days the rebels indulged in a carnival of slaughter, and thousands of the defenceless citizens committed suicide.

Next, he appointed ninety-two of the renegade Ming officials to serve under his henchman Sung Ch'i-chiao, in the Ministry of Civil Offices. But scarcely had they placed themselves at Sung's disposition than they were compelled to give effect to a decree ordering the arrest and imprisonment of eight hundred officials, including members of the late Imperial family and many who had tendered their submission. These unfortunate wretches were sent in batches to the camp of Li's Commander-in-chief, Liu Tsung-min, to undergo torture by the squeezing board and to be severely beaten, until they disclosed the hiding-places of their wealth. One of the proscribed, a libationer of the Confucian Academy, was lying on a bed of sickness, but he was bound in chains and beaten till he died. The squeezing apparatus was then applied to his wife until her fingers were broken. She confessed where their money had been buried; 7000 taels were dug up and handed to Li Tzŭ-ch'eng. He was much impressed by the largeness of the amount and exclaimed : " Fancy a humble literary man being so well-to-do!" The result of the torturing in this case caused him to issue a decree ordering that all these officials should be tortured. The ransoms, which he extracted from the proscribed, were fixed at Tls. 100,000 for a Grand Secretary; Tls. 70,000 for high officers of the Household; Tls. 50,000 from Supervising Censors; Tls. 20,000 for Hanlin Doctors, and so on down the scale to the lowest mandarins. Members of the Imperial family were squeezed of the uttermost farthing and then put to death.

But not all the Ministers and courtiers of the wretched Ch'ung-Chen were cowards and renegades; helpless though they were to serve or to save him, there were many officials and scholars, even in those degenerate times, who loyally upheld the stoic tradition of the Confucian philosophy, and preferred death to dishonour. Many instances might be cited of their splendid courage and dignity in misfortune, but we must content ourselves with selecting two or three of those which chiefly appeal to the admiration of their countrymen.[1]

On hearing of the death of the Emperor, the Board President Yi Yuan-lu, a native of Chekiang, hastened to the Palace in full Court dress and wrote on a desk the following: "The capital should be removed to Nanking; my duty is to die. Do not wrap me in grave clothes; let my corpse be exposed. Those who understand will pity." Then, sitting with his face to the South, he strangled himself with his girdle. Thirteen members of his family committed suicide on that day.

The President of the Censorate, Li Pang-hua, ascended the city wall with some other Censors, but the eunuchs

[1] It is interesting to reflect that the Japanese samurai's *hara-kiri*, with all its noble traditions of chivalry, loyalty, high courage, and solemn ceremonial, owes its origin to the canons of the Chinese Sages, in whose philosophy lies the very soul of the East; and which can still inspire moral heroism in a race generally unwarlike and devoid of loyalty.

drove them back. Hearing that the outer city had fallen he repaired to the shrine of the Patriots of the Dynasty, and when the rebels had entered the inner city he bowed before the tablets of those enshrined in the temple, saying: " In the hour of my country's disaster I here commit suicide, asking permission to attend to you, worthy gentlemen, at the Nine Springs." Then he wrote out some valedictory verses and hanged himself.

Ling Yi-ch'ü, a Director of the Court of Revision, hearing that the Emperor was dead, burst into loud lamentation and dashed his head against a pillar. The blood poured from his wounded face, and a disciple came to urge him that his duty was to live. Ling reproved the young man: " You ought to give me the kind of advice that an honest man might follow. How can you wish me to prolong existence? " He motioned to him to depart; then, gathering round him his favourite books, he burnt them all, saying: " You at least shall not be defiled by the rebels." He dressed himself in his Court robes, put on his badge of office, wrote a last letter to his father, and committed suicide.

The Director of the Court of Sacrificial Worship, Wu Len-cheng, was on duty at the Hsi-chih Gate; a party of rebels advanced and sought admittance, pretending that they were loyal troops. The eunuch commander was for opening the gate, but Wu refused to allow it. He barricaded the *enceinte* with stones and earth, and at night descended from the wall with a party of volunteers, dealing destruction in the rebel ranks. When the city fell he entered a shrine and wrote to his family, bidding them use a common black cloth to cover his remains, and hanged himself. Wu had always advised the Emperor to recall Wu San-kuei from Ning Yüan, as the danger from the rebels was more pressing than from the Manchus. When too late, Ch'ung Chen regretted that he had not followed this good advice.

THE COURT OF PEKING

The Censor, Ch'en Liang-mi, a Ningpo man, was childless, but a concubine whom he had bought only six months before was *enceinte*. He called her to him and said: "I am about to die, but you will soon give birth to a child; get you to your parents' house." The concubine, weeping, made answer: "If you mean to die, is it not my bounden duty to join you in death? At a time like this it were better that my child should not be born." Her husband rejoined: "Must it be so?" The concubine, aged eighteen, then hanged herself, and he followed her.

The Marquis Liu Wen-ping, a nephew of the Empress Dowager, had had a last audience of the Emperor on the evening of the 11th day of the Moon, and he promised the Emperor that he would die. On leaving the Presence, he went with a party of retainers to the Hata Gate and slew several rebels. Thence he returned home and found that his mother, wife and sisters were already dead. They had hanged themselves after setting fire to the house; the fire was still raging, so that he could not enter the chamber. His uncle, second in command at the Palace, returned at this moment from his duties there, and met Liu Wen-ping in his garden. He proposed that both should throw themselves down the well, but his nephew stopped him, saying: "It is not respectful to the Emperor, whom you will shortly meet in Hades, that you should wear a military uniform. Put on your civilian dress." His uncle did so, and then, shouting: "Long live His Majesty," they died together.

Wu Su, President of the Board of Ceremonies, was a renegade. He accepted office under the rebels, and bade his old servant prepare robes of ceremony that he might proceed to pay his congratulations to Li Tzŭ-ch'eng. The man replied: "The Son of Heaven is dead, and instead of hurrying to do obeisance before his bier you would actually kneel before the usurper! Death is a small thing, but loss of honour is a great thing. Please, sir, reconsider this matter." With these words he kotowed until blood flowed from his temples. Wu Su angrily bade him begone: but again the old servant answered and said: "Your Excellency hankers now after wealth and position. You may disregard my words to-day, but the time is at hand when you will regret it. This rebel Li Tzŭ-ch'eng is treacherous and greedy. Your conduct will displease Heaven, and you will be reviled of men. Surely you have not long to live. As for me, I cannot bear to see one whom I have served all these years losing both life and reputation." So he killed himself; and his words came true, for Li made Wu Su hand over all his treasure, which was very large, and then had him beheaded.

To return to Li Tzŭ-ch'eng, now undisputed ruler of Peking. On the 28th day of the 3rd Moon the President of the Ministry of Rites issued a circular notice, calling on all the officials and elders of the people to memorialise Li Tzu-ch'eng and invite him formally to ascend the Imperial Throne. This was done, and Li, graciously assenting, decreed that an auspicious day be appointed for the great ceremony. He intended that the occasion should be celebrated with all possible pomp and circumstance.

But the auguries of evil were not to be gainsaid; the rebel Emperor's star had begun to decline from the moment he assumed the Imperial title at Peking. The magnificent ceremonies which he had planned for his formal installation on the Dragon Throne were never to take place, and in a little while he, the pursuer and plunderer, was to be pursued and plundered.

It will be remembered that a few days before the fall of Peking the Emperor had sent an urgent summons to General Wu San-kuei (who was then holding Ning Yüan, the last of the Ming strongholds, against the Manchus), bidding him come with all speed to Peking. Wu San-kuei started at once, but he had scarcely got beyond the Great Wall when word was brought to him of the fall of Peking and the death of the Emperor. His army of seasoned veterans was evidently a weighty factor in the situation, especially as his evacuation of Ning Yüan had left the road open for the Manchus to march upon Peking. Wu San-kuei's father, General Wu Hsiang, had gone over to the rebels, and for his own safety's sake was most anxious that his son should tender his allegiance to Li Tzŭ-ch'eng. Wu San-kuei would undoubtedly have done so but for the matter of a certain singing-girl (which will be dealt with hereafter). For the present, suffice it to say that Li's overtures to him proved fruitless. He halted his army at Feng-Yün, near the Great Wall, and while keeping up pourparlers with Li. began negotiations with Prince Jui (Dorgun), suggesting a combination of forces against the rebel Emperor.

On the 29th of the 3rd Moon, eleven days after the fall of Peking, Li Tzŭ-ch'eng, fully aware that, with the Manchus behind him, Wu San-kuei would be a formidable foe, sent him a present of Tls. 40,000 for his troops, and addressed to him the following somewhat tactless letter :

" You have been indeed favoured by fortune in rising to so high a position, since you have never rendered any pre-eminent military service to your Sovereign. But as the country was threatened by powerful enemies, the only way to keep you from going over to the other side was to shower rewards upon you. The principle is a sound one, and was originally enunciated by the philosopher Kuan Tzü as a reason for bestowing honours on doubtful loyalty; it was also exemplified by the founder of the Han dynasty, in his employment of Han Hsin.

" At present you have a large army under you, but it has only a spectacular value. If my troops swoop down upon you, you have neither the will to repel their onset nor the available force to defeat them. This is your last opportunity to join me. Your Emperor is dead and may soon be followed to the grave by your own sire. My advice, therefore, to you, if you wish to combine loyalty with filial duty, is to surrender to me and gain the honours which I promise you. If, however, you persist in overweening self-confidence, your army is not strong enough for victory, and will be destroyed in a single morning. Your innocent father will be decapitated, and you will have lost both Sovereign and father. The proverb says: ' It's only the father who knows his own son.' A pressing message."

To this Wu, still temporising and with an eye to the future, replied by requesting that Li Tzŭ-ch'eng should send him the Heir Apparent, the son of the late Ming Emperor. Instead of so doing, Li sent two renegade Ming Generals with a for e of 20,000 men to attack him; but Wu, too wise to waste his forces in this way, beat a hurried retreat, and laid siege to the stronghold of Shan Hai-kuan, then held by a rebel garrison of 8,000 men. He took the city after a fierce assault, whereupon Li Tzŭ-ch'eng, realising that his Throne could never be secure with this enemy on his borders, left Peking with a force of over 100,000 men to attack him. How Wu San-kuei, aided by the Manchus, defeated Li, will be told in a later chapter.

After his defeat, Li Tzŭ-ch'eng entered into a treaty of alliance with Wu San-kuei for the division of the Empire, and handed over to him the person of the Heir Apparent. By this Treaty, Li was to be Emperor and ruler of Shansi, Shensi and all to the West of those provinces. He then hastened back with the remnant of his army to Peking. He re-entered the capital on the 26th day of the 4th Moon, and two days later solemnly assumed the Imperial title in the Wu Yung Palace Hall. He proclaimed his Consort Kao as Empress, and conferred upon his ancestors for seven generations the posthumous title of Emperor. The ceremony of his enthronement was shorn of the magnificence which he had intended; the gold Imperial seal was not ready and the coinage bearing his reign title had not been struck. Nevertheless, he had his hour of triumph—he wore the Dragon robe, and the whole Court made obeisance before him, while his accession was reverently announced at the altars of the Temples of Heaven and Earth. The chroniclers aver that, while he was receiving the congratulations of the Court, the dragon woven on the carpet of the Imperial daïs " seemed to glare at him angrily." No doubt but that Li himself felt that the auguries were unfavourable. Having been acclaimed Emperor and left his name on that high roll of fame, he returned, with undiminished vigour, to the congenial rôle of plunderer. No sooner were the ceremonies at an end, than he set fire to the main halls of the Palace and to the towers on the city wall. Then he took all the gold vessels of the Palace and melted them down into flat " cakes," each weighing about a thousand ounces, suitable for transport. He loaded some ten thousand of these " cakes " on to his transport mules, and prepared to take the long trail towards his new Empire in the South.

Before leaving, however, he proceeded to administer retributive justice to the Palace eunuchs, to the traitors who had betrayed their Sovereign and the Empire to save their purses and their skins. Collecting them all together, he first compelled them to give up all their pearls and valuables; they were then driven out of the Palace with cudgels. Not one was spared; even the eunuch Tu Hsün, who had advised the surrender of the city, reaped the just reward of his treachery, and was forced to disgorge all his ill-gotten gains. After having been stripped of all portable valuables, they were led outside the Gate of Perpetual Peace and bidden to disclose where their other treasure was hidden. Those who refused either had their legs cut off below the knee or underwent the roasting torture. In some cases those who had given up all their worldly goods were made to endure the finger-squeezing torture, and after that were beheaded.

The Earl Li Kuo-chen, who had been amongst the first to surrender, had not handed over enough plunder to satisfy Li Tzŭ-ch'eng, so he was tortured until both his ankles were broken, after which he was allowed to hang himself. His wife was stripped stark naked by the rebels and placed on a horse, amidst much ribaldry. The Grand Secretary Chen Yen had also surrendered, and had made his peace by paying a toll of Tls. 40,000, but Li thought he might possibly give trouble later on, so put him to death before leaving Peking, as well as Lo Yang-tsing, a Minister of the Household who had paid Tls. 30,000.

With the subsequent fortunes of Li Tzu-ch'eng, Emperor of a day, we are not here concerned; they are recorded in many volumes of history. But the time and manner of his death are still invested with the romantic quality which distinguished his eventful life. According to the official Manchu historians, he met an ignoble end at the hands of peasants at T'ung Ch'eng in Hupei, but this story would seem to have originated in the natural desire of the country's new rulers to have it believed that he was dead, if only because, so long as he remained alive, he must continue to be a cause of unrest. It is recorded that a corpse, supposed to be his, was officially exhumed and decapitated, but the truth seems to be that, after the fitful fever of his adventurous career, he ended his days in peaceful seclusion, not without dignity, as a Buddhist priest. There are, at least, good grounds for this belief.

After the capture of Wu ch'ang by the Manchus (1646), which Li had held against them for some time, he appears to have fled into Hunan, accompanied by a remnant of about thirty followers, and sought refuge at a place called Ching Hua. Thence he retreated to Buffalo Mountain

THE COURT OF PEKING

in the An fu district, and there, bidding his retinue leave him, he proceeded alone to Mount Chia. Near the town of Shih men (Stony Gate) he found a temple, in which he took refuge, shaving his head and donning the robes of a priest. In the priests' burial ground of that temple there still stands the dagoba in which Li is said to be buried. Its inscription runs: " The Buddhist priest whose religious designation was the ' Jewel [1] of Heaven's Grace.' " In front of the tomb is a tablet, on which is written: " None can tell the family name or origin of the priest who lies buried here." When Li first became a rebel he had styled himself, " By Heaven's grace leader of righteousness and supreme commander." Subsequently he assumed the title, " Emperor of the Great Obedient Dynasty."

In the reign of K'ang Hsi (about 1695) an old priest of this temple told a scholar of Ch'angsha that he remembered Li's arrival in 1646; he had refused to say from whence he came, but his accent was that of a Shensi man. He seemed to be well read in the Buddhist Works on Ecclesiastical Discipline. Some years later he was joined by another priest, named Yeh Fu, who had formerly been his disciple, and who attended him with the greatest devotion for the rest of his life. He died in the Chia Yin year of K'ang Hsi (1674), when about seventy years of age, after delivering a valedictory message to his disciple Yeu Fu, in which he described himself as an Emperor who had renounced the pomps and vanities of this world. His picture was preserved in the temple, and the priest who told the story produced it for the scholar's inspection. There could be no doubt that it was the portrait of Li Tzŭ-ch'eng: apart from the loss of one eye, his high forehead and sunken jaw were unmistakable. His remaining eye was large and lustrous (so that he was often called " Owl-eyed "), and his nose was strongly aquiline.

[1] In reference to the Imperial patrimony.

CHAPTER IV

WU SAN-KUEI

Chinese historians, as a rule, are given to describing the characters and deeds of their great men with a somewhat crude and uncompromising finality; they are either good or bad, strong or weak, and every succeeding generation of scholars accepts and confirms verdicts which were often rendered in the first instance upon insufficient or false evidence. Classical Chinese history, on the whole, is strangely indifferent to the changing moods and motives of men; it contents itself with recording results, painting the picture of the past without the light and shade of humanity's mutable purposes and irresponsible impulses. And Chinese historians, being generally scholars anxious for official employment or preferment, are wont to describe men and events in a manner conforming either to constituted authority and the political opinions of the day or to their own preconceived prejudices.

Thus it is, no doubt, that Wu San-kuei, the Chinese General who first broke the power of Li Tzŭ-ch'eng, and finally drove him back, repeatedly defeated, beyond the Yangtsze, stands in history to-day as a great soldier, a statesman and a scholar. Great soldier he certainly was: for several years his military genius had held in check the Manchus, and his brilliant defence of Ning Yüan had earned for him the admiration of those good fighting men. But of his principles and patriotism, the less said the better.

THE COURT OF PEKING

After the fall of Peking and the death of the Emperor his army,[1] standing between the forces of the rebel Monarch and those of the Manchu invaders, was in a position to command the situation and to determine the destinies of China, in so far as these depended upon the occupancy of the Throne. It is certain that if he had obeyed his father's wishes and given his adherence to Li Tzŭ-ch'eng, the Manchus would not have been able to establish their rule upon the ruins of the Ming dynasty. If Wu had observed the terms of the treaty of alliance against the Manchus, which Li Tzŭ-ch'eng made with him after the latter's first great defeat near Shan Hai-kuan, the Mings might have continued to rule at Peking. His final decision, to throw in his lot with the Manchus against the rebels and violate his avowed allegiance to the Ming Heir Apparent, was due, not to love of his country, but to his passion for a certain singing-girl, of whom, after the fall of Peking, Li Tzŭ-ch'eng had deprived him.

The following facts of Wu San-kuei's career at this juncture, critical in determining the subsequent history of China, are taken from a diary written at Peking by one of the Palace eunuchs named Wang Yung-chang, who was an eye-witness of the fall of Peking and a close observer of subsequent events. In this diary are transcribed several letters written by Wu San-kuei to his father, General Wu Hsiang, who had sworn allegiance to the usurping Emperor. They prove beyond all doubt that Wu San-kuei's policy was originally influenced by personal ambition, for he was quite ready to serve under either banner; but that, at the critical moment, his actions were determined solely by his desire to regain possession of his favourite concubine. The Manchus owed their dynasty, under Heaven, to the little singing-girl known

[1] The Manchu records state that Wu San-kuei's army at Ning-Yüan consisted of 130,000 infantry and 40,000 cavalry.

to contemporary chroniclers as Lady Ch'en, the Round-faced Beauty.[2]

Four days after the fall of Peking, that is to say on the 22nd of the 3rd Moon (1644), Wu San-kuei wrote from his camp at Feng-Yün to his father in the Palace a letter which the latter handed over to Li Tzŭ-ch'eng. In it he said: "It is rumoured here that Peking has fallen, but of this we have no definite news. No doubt the city is being besieged. If you can manage to escape, do not bring much money with you, but bury your treasure as best you can. Please tell my favourite mistress, the Lady Ch'en, that I am in good health, and bid her keep up her courage."

Another letter followed, saying: "I have now received definite news of the fall of Peking, and propose to move with my forces to a position outside Shan Hai-kuan. If you cannot possibly escape from Peking, try to send me a line by special courier. If all our women have been seized by Li Tzŭ-ch'eng you will be acting wisely in surrendering to him. I am most anxious about the Lady Ch'en."

A third letter is dated the 25th day of the 3rd Moon: "I have your letter of the 20th and note that you have surrendered to the new Emperor (Li Tzŭ-ch'eng). Under the circumstances, it was the only thing to do, so as to save our women from the hands of the rebels. The truly great man will always frame his actions with careful regard for the exigencies of the moment, and trim his sail to the favouring breeze. But your letter goes on to say that the Lady Ch'en has left Peking on horseback on her way to my camp. I have seen and heard nothing of her. Oh, father! how could you thus recklessly allow a delicate girl of her age to start out on so perilous an adventure? I had moved my troops to Shan hai-kuan,

---

[2] This romantic personage had originally been a slave-girl in the household of Earl Chou K'uei. Wu San-kuei met her there at a wine-party, and loved her at first sight.

and was seriously thinking of submitting to Li Tzŭ-ch'eng. But this news has greatly upset me."

A fourth letter is dated the 27th day of the 3rd Moon: " Yesterday I heard definitely that the rebel General Liu Tsung-min has seized the Lady Ch'en. Woe is me! I shall never see her again in this life. I could never have believed that you, father, would have been guilty of such folly. Yesterday I bombarded Shan hai-kuan and caught the rebels unawares. I had planned to make use of some of the Manchu forces and to march straight on Peking, but hesitated to do so because of the possible consequences to the Lady Ch'en. If she is back again in Peking, and the rebels ascertain that she is my concubine, they will probably spare her life, hoping thereby to induce me to surrender. But if once I move my troops they will certainly kill her. Hence, I send you this by special courier, in order that I may learn how matters stand."

The fifth, and last, letter reads: " I have your letter, in which you tell me that the Lady Ch'en has been appointed a concubine in the Palace, and am glad to hear that she is being kindly treated. But you write as if you were not very positive of your facts; who is your informant? You also say that the Ming Heir Apparent, son of the late Emperor, is in the Palace; have you seen him or not? Now that you have submitted to the Shun dynasty [1] you should memorialise the new Emperor in audience and tell him what I say. All I ask is that he hand over to me the Heir Apparent and Lady Ch'en. Let him do this and I will loyally submit to his dynasty at once."

This correspondence proves the absurdity of the generally accepted version of the story, which describes Wu's loyal indignation at Li Tzŭ-ch'eng's capture of Peking as " making his hair to stand on end, so that his hat was lifted from his head."

[1] The title chosen by Li Tzŭ-ch'eng for his new line.

In demanding the person of the Heir Apparent, Wu San-kuei's first intention, as subsequent events proved, was to proclaim him Emperor—a puppet Monarch—for his own purposes. He went so far as to adopt for him a reign title, and dated his official proclamations and despatches " the first year of Yi-Hsing," or " Manifestation of Righteousness." But he abandoned the plan when, to his intense wrath, he heard that his concubine, the " Round-faced Beauty," had been given to the Heir Apparent. This all-important fact is not mentioned either in the official records or in private memoirs, but the statements in Wang Yung-chang's diary, the account of an eye-witness, are fully confirmed by circumstantial evidence, and fit in with all the other known facts of the situation. They may, therefore, be accepted as true. Witness the following extract : " On the day after the fall of Peking the rebels discovered the Heir Apparent concealed in the house of the father of T'ien, the Imperial Concubine. He and his brother, Prince Ting, were handed over to the rebel Emperor, who conferred upon the Heir Apparent the title of Prince Sung and on his brother that of " Duke of Peaceful Abode." On the 6th of the 4th Moon, Li Tzŭ-ch'eng, in truculent mood, wrote to Wu San-kuei as follows : " The Heir Apparent is safely ensconced in the Palace, so you may abandon all hope of using him for the furtherance of your schemes. WE have given him a princedom, and WE have made over to him your wife and women for him to dally with as he pleases."

Three days later, Li Tzŭ-ch'eng issued a decree proclaiming a punitive expedition against Wu San-kuei; he left Peking on the 12th of the 4th Moon with an advance force of over 100,000 men. In his suite were the Heir Apparent, his brother, three other Ming Princes, Wu San-kuei's wife and two sisters, and a number of Palace concubines, amongst whom was the " Round-faced

THE COURT OF PEKING

Beauty." A fortnight later the armies met at a spot known as the "Stony Valley." Li was utterly defeated, and fled into Shan Hai-kuan. Thence, hoping to come to terms with Wu San-kuei, he sent to his camp the Heir Apparent and the "Round-faced Beauty." Wu, still uncertain as to the future, and wavering in his allegiance to the Mings, agreed next day with Li Tzŭ-ch'eng, and signed with him an offensive and defensive alliance against the Manchus. It read: "The Emperor Yi-Hsing,[1] of the great Ming dynasty, hereby deputes Wu San-kuei, his Regent and Grand Secretary, Prince Pacificator of the West, and the General commanding, Earl Tang T'ung; and the Emperor Yung ch'ang,[2] of the Great Obedient Dynasty, deputes the President of his War Department, Wang Tse-yao, acting with Chang Jo-ch'i, to enter upon a sworn treaty of alliance at Shan Hai-kuan—on this 22nd day of the 4th Moon of the Chia Shen year."

"From the date of this agreement each party shall keep its respective territories, and neither shall invade the other. The Great Obedient Dynasty is now in possession of Peking, but hereby agrees to evacuate and restore it to the Great Ming Dynasty on the 1st day of the 5th Moon, to belong to the Mings for ever. The treasure and valuables seized at the sack of Peking are recognised as the property of the Great Obedient Dynasty. It shall be optional for its inhabitants to become subjects of the Great Obedient Dynasty or to remain under the Ming Dynasty. To the Great Obedient Dynasty shall belong the provinces of Shansi and Shensi and all to the West thereof. If the Manchu troops invade China, both parties to this alliance shall unite against them; their mutual relations shall be those of sympathetic allies, for weal or woe. Whoso breaks this treaty, may Heaven and earth combine to destroy him."

[1] The reign title given to the Heir Apparent by Wu San-kuei.
[2] Li Tzŭ-ch'eng's reign title.

After signing this treaty, Li Tzŭ-ch'eng marched back to Peking, where he arrived on the 29th. He was not left long in doubt as to the loyalty of his new ally, for even before he reached the capital, couriers brought him two proclamations which Wu San-kuei had issued; one in his capacity of the " Regent and Grand Secretary, Prince Pacificator of the West," dated the 1st year, 4th Moon, 24th day of the Ming Emperor Yi-Hsing, the other as " Prince of the first rank, Pacificator of the West," headed with the Manchu date of the reign of Shun Chih. After reading the latter proclamation, Li exclaimed : " If I am victorious, this double-faced villain will be on my side; if the Manchus win, he will join them. Having got the Heir Apparent and the women Ch'en into his hands, he breaks without compunction our solemn treaty. Such a creature is more brute than man."

With that he decapitated Wu's father and sixteen female members of his family.

On the 1st day of the 5th Moon a decree was received in the Palace from the Ming Heir Apparent, that he would enter the city within three days and proceed to perform the funeral rites of the late Emperor and his Consort. At the end of this decree he affixed the date of his own year title, " Yi Hsing," proving that he regarded himself as Emperor and trusted to the loyalty of Wu San-kuei. Memorials of welcome were accordingly prepared, and in due course the news reached the Palace that His Majesty had arrived at the Western Gate, so Wang Te-hua made ready the Imperial sedan-chair and the insignia prescribed for an Imperial progress and went forth to meet him at the head of a large body of officials. The eunuchs were very busy with preparations inside the Palace.

The foregoing details of Wu San-kuei's career are taken from the diary of the eunuch Wang Yung-chang. At this point it ends. There are certain discrepancies in matters of detail between the narrative and other accounts of the period, notably in regard to the time and place at which was signed the treaty of alliance for the division of the Empire and the date at which Wu's father was put to death by the vindictive Li. But the main facts and the documents quoted may be taken as reliable.

Wu San-kuei's lack of filial piety, in putting his "Round-faced Beauty" before his father, has been condoned by historians, who quote with approval his own saying: " A disloyal Minister must expect to have an unfilial son." Wu San-kuei himself, evidently with an eye to the verdict of posterity, justified his action in the last letter which he addressed to his undutiful parent. The following extract from this document is interesting : " Your unfilial son, San-kuei, weeps tears of blood and offers his duty at your knee, father mine. Since childhood I have benefited by your teaching, and have striven night and day to perform my duty on the field, in the hope of repaying something of my Emperor's favours. After the loss of Ning Yüan, the key to Peking, I was determined to recover it at all costs, when to my dismay I learned that the capital itself had fallen, owing to the lack of courage displayed by its defenders. You, father mine, were one of the military commanders and had a large force at your disposal. How comes it that you surrendered so quickly and failed to make the stout resistance which duty required? A mighty city like Peking should not have fallen after a single day's siege. I have learned with shame of His Majesty's death and of the massacre of his subjects. You, my father, have enjoyed a reputation for loyalty; if you could not repel the invader, surely it behoved you to cut your throat at the Palace gates and thus to die for your country? Then I should have hastened, in garb of mourning, to avenge your fate or to perish in the attempt. How now can you bear to prolong your disgraceful existence in the rebel ranks? Wang

Ling's mother committed suicide rather than allow her son to surrender to Hsiang Chi. Chao Pao was the cause of his mother's death, because the barbarians placed her in front of their battle line when he attacked them. You used to tell me of these ancient heroines, but your own behaviour suffers sadly in comparison with that of these noble women. You have failed to act as a loyal Minister; why should I be a filial son? Henceforward I disown you. Even though the rebels place you on the sacrificial altar, so as to make me submit, I shall ignore your fate. Respectful greetings from your son."

From all the evidences of contemporary documents and tradition there is reason to believe that, for a time at least, Wu San-kuei meant to support the Heir Apparent in his claims to the Throne at Peking and, possibly, to allow Li Tzŭ-ch'eng to retain dominion over Shansi and the West. According to the generally accepted records, it was from Yung P'ing-fu, after the rout at Shan Hai-kuan, that Li made overtures to treat with Wu for the division of the Empire and sent him the person of the Heir Apparent. It is certain that at this point Wu desisted from pursuing Li's beaten army, and issued proclamations announcing his intention to enter Peking for the restoration of the Ming dynasty at an early date. One of these proclamations, dated the 30th of the 4th Moon, reached Peking on the morning that Li Tzŭ-ch'eng and his loot-laden army left the city. It announced the approach of the Heir Apparent, and directed the people to wear mourning for His late Majesty.

It was at this juncture that the Manchus showed their hand clearly and gave Wu San-kuei no option but to throw in his lot with them, abandoning the Mings, or to fight against hopeless odds. Wu had hoped to be able to keep the Manchus busy with pourparlers while he carried out his plans and took stock of the situation at Peking, but Prince Jui, the Manchu Regent, suspicious of his intentions, hurried on from Shan Hai-kuan to Chin chou. There, hearing of Wu's proclamations, he sent him an urgent message forbidding him to enter Peking in state and saying that no Ming Sovereign would be acknowledged. Wu made his choice, and the Ming dynasty's chances of restoration went with it.

On the morning of the 3rd day of the 5th Moon, the Peking officials assembled outside the Western Gate to meet, as they expected, their new Ming Emperor. But when the palanquin arrived, its occupant was seen to be the Manchu Regent, and Wu San-kuei was with him. Their entry was received in dead silence. At the Tung Hua Gate of the Palace some eunuchs came forward with the Imperial sedan and invited the Regent to enter it. For some time he demurred, but yielding at length proceeded in it to the Palace. As the Court knelt, he said: "I wish to follow the precedent of Duke Chou in acting as Regent for the infant Emperor. I ought not to ride in the Imperial chair." He then entered the Wu-ying Hall and received the Ming officials, bidding them all remain at their former posts. A memorial was handed to him inviting him to as end the Throne, but his Grand Secretary, Fan Wen-ch'eng, rebuked the memorialists, saying: "We have a young Emperor already who succeeded to the Throne last year at Moukden; the Prince Regent cannot possibly accede to your proposal."

The politic Regent, rightly judging that the atmosphere of Peking at this juncture might have a bad effect upon Wu San-kuei and his army, sent him in pursuit of Li Tzŭ-ch'eng. Wu, well knowing that Li's forces were staggering under the weight of their accumulated plunder, accepted the mission, which he carried out with his usual vigour and success. The treaty of alliance cast to the winds, he routed Li in several fierce engagements, relieved him of his ill-gotten booty, and finally drove him into Shansi. From the date of his entry into Peking by the

Regent's side, until in 1674 he rebelled in his turn, he was the Manchus' man and a solid pillar of their State. They rewarded his services with a Princedom, giving him command over the provinces of Kuei chou and Yünnan.

The correspondence which passed between Wu and the Manchu Regent, before their combined forces defeated Li Tzŭ-ch'eng, is not without historical importance, and may fittingly be referred to here. It was when Li Tzŭ-ch'eng's " punitive expedition " had started from Peking, on the 12th of the 3rd Moon, that Wu made up his mind at Ning Yüan to seek an alliance with the Manchus. Accordingly, he wrote to the Regent, who had made overtures to him some time before. After referring to the invasion of Peking by the rebel host of " pilfering dogs," he invoked the assistance of the Manchus to chastise the rebels, in the following terms :

" The accumulated virtues of our dynastic line have inspired feelings of loyal love and devotion in our people; volunteers are flocking to our standard against the foul invaders, and I, who have received such favours from the Throne, have endeavoured to raise an avenging host which shall attain the decisive victory that all men desire. But I regret to say that my forces are insufficient, and therefore, weeping tears of blood, I implore your assistance. For two centuries our States have been allies, and now that we have met with this catastrophe surely it behoves your dynasty to pity us. Surely you will never suffer these bandit traitors to work their evil will? Your duty to Heaven requires you to exterminate these evil-doers; charity to your fellow men must impel you to rescue the distressed and to save them from utter ruin; generosity and justice call upon you to rescue the people from this scourge of fire and flood; you will gain real glory by restoring a fallen State and renewing an extinct lineage; thus shall you display the prestige of your arms and gain new territories."

THE COURT OF PEKING

"Your Highness is endowed with heroic qualities, and the present offers a splendid opportunity to strike home. I beseech you to pay heed to this loyal entreaty of the orphaned servant of a ruined dynasty, and to send your picked troops to invade China, placing them in the centre and right wing, whilst I march with my forces on the left wing. You should move at once on the capital, expel the rebels from the Palace which they profane, and thus prove your magnanimity to the Middle Empire. What limit can there be to the gratitude which it will be our bounden duty to display? By rights I should address His Majesty directly, but being ignorant of the correct etiquette I have not ventured lightly to intrude upon his sacred intelligence with my entreaties. Will Your Highness graciously memorialise him in my stead?"

On receipt of the above letter, the Regent Dorgun (Prince Jui) at once sent Balaikun to Chin-chou to bring up more cannon. He moved his camp on to Tin Valley, and from there sent the following reply to Wu San-kuei:

"We have repeatedly wished to make peace with the Mings and have sent letters offering to negotiate, but the Ming Sovereign and Ministers did not condescend to reply, being blind to the ruin which threatened their dynasty. For this reason we have twice approached their capital with our armies, so as to read a useful lesson to the Ming Emperor, to induce him to make peace with our nation, and to prove our good intentions to his people. To-day the position has completely changed, and our present purpose is to establish the fortunes of your State and to take your people under our protection. The tidings of the capture of Peking and the lamentable death of the Ming Sovereign have caused my hair to stand on end with horror. Therefore, I am now leading an avenging army, which is resolved to succeed or perish in achieving the deliverance of your people. We shall never desist from our task until the rebels are vanquished.

Your letter has greatly gratified me, and I am advancing to the attack forthwith. In refusing to live under the same sky with the usurper you are fulfilling the duty of a loyal Minister; let not any thoughts of past hostility between us cloud your mind with doubt or suspicion. Did not the ruler of the Ch'i State, Duke Hsian, confer high office on his former enemy, Kuan Chung, and thus attained to supremacy over the feudal states? If you will join our army with your troops I will bestow upon you the rank of a feudal Prince, so that on the one hand you will avenge your master's disgrace, and on the other hand you will assure your own fortunes and those of your posterity for all time. Honours and fortunes will be lavished upon you, and your house will stand for ever, immutable as the hills and the Yellow River."

Dorgun moved on to Lien Shan, and there received a further letter from Wu San-kuei: "I am in receipt of your letter and note that your troops are advancing. Your righteous action will bring you eternal fame. My reason for assisting you is solely due to my veneration for His late Majesty Ch'ung chen, and considerations of personal aggrandisement move me not at all. In obedience to your behests I am occupying all strategic points West of Shan Hai-kuan with my picked men, hoping to decoy the rebels to advance. At present they are in full force around Yung-t'ing, as numerous as ants. Of a surety Heaven intends that they shall dig a pit for their own destruction. I am arranging that a large portion of my army shall co-operate with yours. Let Your Highness dispatch your tiger-like levies towards Shan Hai-kuan, that we may attack the rebels in front and rear. They will fall into our hands, so that Peking and all the region round about will soon know the blessings of peace. One word more: an army such as yours, inspired with the loftiest of motives, must desire above all things to win the confidence of the people. You should, therefore, issue stringent orders against looting, and by so doing both territory and all which it contains will be yours. The Empire is won!"

Next day the Regent was within three miles of Shan Hai-kuan. Li Tzŭ-ch'eng's force had been reinforced and now numbered 200,000 men. With him were the Heir Apparent of the Mings, his two brothers and many Ming Princes of the Imperial family, as well as Wu San-kuei's father. He sent a final summons to Wu to surrender, but the message was ignored, so Li advanced to bombard Shan Hai-kuan. Wu sent despatch riders to inform the Manchus, and Prince Jui, the Regent, dispatched a force which met and defeated the rebel General at Yi-pien-shih. On the following morning, Wu and his men came out of Shan Hai-kuan to welcome the Manchus. The Regent warmly welcomed him, gave him a ceremonial reception, and proceeded with him to perform joint obeisance to Heaven. Wu then introduced his officers, and the Regent bade him return and order his troops to fasten white badges on their shoulders, so as to avoid confusion between them and the rebels. Li Tzŭ-ch'eng's forces were drawn up in line between the mountains and the sea, awaiting the order to attack. A furious dust storm was raging; they could hardly see a yard in front of their position. The Manchu troops were drawn up some distance away, and received instructions from the Regent to bide their time and await order, as any premature movement might mean disaster. "If every man does his best," said he, "the Empire is ours."

Wu San-kuei threw his right wing against Li Tzŭ-ch'eng. With a mighty shout they rushed at the rebel lines, but their first onslaught was repulsed. The wind dropped and both sides engaged in a furious *mêlée*. The Manchus supported the attack with an irresistible charge. The rebel ranks broke, and the day ended in their complete rout, a scene of hopeless confusion and great slaughter.

On the following day the inhabitants of Shan Hai-kuan shaved their heads, in obedience to a proclamation by the Regent. The Manchu Princes had hesitated to believe in Wu San-kuei's assurances, but they were reassured when he appeared in their camp with shaven head. The Regent thereupon conferred upon him a Princedom of the first class, together with the robes and emoluments of his rank. His father received the " happy despatch " at the hands of Li Tzǔ-ch'eng on the same day.

With the next thirty years of Wu San-kuei's successful career, spent first in breaking up the forces of Li Tzǔ-ch'eng and later in hunting down the last fugitive claimants to the Throne of the Mings, we are not at present concerned. When the Manchus' dominion had been definitely established over the whole Empire, Wu was rewarded with a satrapy, giving him command over the provinces of Kuei-chou and Yünnan. At his palace in Yünnan-fu he maintained Imperial state. It was built and furnished in regal style, decorated with splendid halls and pavilions. He spent large revenues in beautifying the city, erecting a pleasure house on an island of the lake which he called " Beside the Crystal Wave," and planted a garden in the western suburb known as the " Park of Peaceful Prosperity," in which he kept his large library. But his prosperity was not destined to be permanently peaceful. In 1674, incensed at the Emperor K'ang Hsi's decision to reduce his semi-independent authority, he, the queller of rebellions, raised the standard of revolt against the Manchus, proclaimed the establishment of a new (Chou) dynasty, and fought with all his pristine vigour and success, until, in October 1678, a stroke of paralysis ended his tumultuous career. His proud spirit, accustomed to command, would not brook the thought of exchanging his vassal state for the position of a subject.

THE COURT OF PEKING

Long before his open declaration of revolt, he had been planning to throw off his allegiance on this far-flung frontier of the Empire, and would sit for hours brooding over his grievances and plotting his revenge. He made his preparations carefully, as was his wont, and laid in large stores of provisions and munitions of war. Whilst he was thus engaged, trouble occurred in his *ménage*. A younger brother of his favourite concubine had given him offence, and Wu threatened to behead him. The offender fled from Yünnan, made his way to Peking, and informed the Emperor of Wu's treasonable designs. K'ang Hsi, who had but recently taken over the Government from his Regent (1667) refused to believe the story. Nevertheless, he dispatched a secret messenger to Yünnan-fu to ascertain the truth. Wu had spies of his own in all the inns of the city, who reported to him at once the arrival of any strangers from Peking. He soon heard of K'ang Hsi's agent and realised that the Emperor suspected him. Desiring to ease the Monarch's mind, and thus to prevent the arrival of Imperialist troops before his plans were completed, he hastily restored on official documents the year title K'ang Hsi, (for which he had substituted a new dynastic appellation of his own), and hung outside the gate of his Palace a new pair of scrolls, proclaiming his allegiance to the Manchus :

" How much mightier is the Emperor than I ! "
" The Minister dreads lest his loyalty be doubted."

The envoy remained a month in the city, but could find no proofs of Wu's intention to rebel. He copied the scrolls above quoted and on returning to Peking handed them to the Emperor. The latter laughed heartily, saying : " My old servant is innocent of rebellious plottings and has been the victim of calumny."

When eventually news reached him that Wu had actually rebelled K'ang Hsi, who was at his ablutions at the time, was greatly enraged, and threw the ewer he was using to the ground, shouting: " How that scurvy rogue has fooled me!"

When the decree reached Yünnan by which K'ang Hsi abolished the three semi-independent vassaldoms and replaced them by provincial administration, Wu invited his officials and secretaries to discuss the situation. They proposed various schemes, all of which Wu rejected. He had already made up his mind to rebel, and would hear of no compromise. One of his staff, however, a Chekiang man, named Hu, sat in a corner, silently smiling with a contemptuous expression, as if he guessed what was in Wu's mind. Next day, Wu invited all the staff to a banquet and selected Hu for special honour by handing him a cup of wine, in which was a large dose of poison. Hu died in great agony.

Wu San-kuei had the physical traits which the Chinese associate with intellectual greatness—conspicuously large and long ears and a fierce aquiline nose. He went clean shaven, and the expression of his face was stern and forbidding. Himself a hard worker, he exacted industry from others, and was a strict disciplinarian. Men feared his wrath; luckily for those who served him there was a danger signal on his face that never failed, for on the bridge of his nose (which was misshapen) there was a black birthmark which would swell and turn purple when an outburst of rage was impending. Also, just before the explosion, he was wont to give out ominous snorts, which served to remind those about him that they had engagements elsewhere.

As we have shown in his correspondence with Prince Jui, Wu had a neat and effective literary style, but scholars admire him chiefly for his proclamations and addresses to his troops, in which he displayed much originality and power of invective. His exhortation to the army to exterminate Li Tzŭ-ch'eng is one of his masterpieces in this style of composition. "That puny hobgoblin," it runs, "that petty traitor, Li Tzǔ-ch'eng, has befouled our sacred capital. The light of the sun is obscured, and his poisonous miasma reeks to Heaven. Wolves and jackals infest our citadel, dogs and swine squat in our Palace halls. They have been guilty of the death of their Majesties; they have put to the sword our scholars and our principal men. They have massacred our people and sacked our chief city. High Heaven resounds with the bitter plaint of our dynasty's illustrious ancestors. The Halls of Hades bear witness to the tears of blood shed by our bravest and our best. But Heaven's mandate to the dynasty is not exhausted; the memory of its virtue still lives in every heart. Patriotic sincerity requires its restoration, this traitor must flee before our loyal resolution. Let volunteers arise and smite him, so shall ten thousand be put to flight by one. Yet a little while and we shall see China faithful to her old rulers and the house of Chu [1] restored to power."

Like most of his contemporaries, Wu displayed a tendency (which the Emperor K'ang Hsi was wont to deplore in his elder statesmen) to allow his everyday actions and his decisions at moments of crisis to be guided by the advice of fortune-tellers and astrologers—"by dreams and by Urim and by prophets." This power of seers and soothsayers has ever been a very vital factor in shaping the destinies of the Chinese, as it has been with all the peoples of the Orient, whose instincts and traditions fit them to hear the voices that Europe has silenced with materialism.

Just before raising his standard of rebellion against the Manhcus in 1674, Wu San-kuei decided to consult a certain Taoist priest, famous throughout the province for his uncanny skill in foretelling destiny by the study of physiognomy. Wu invited him to attend at the Palace,

[1] Chu Yüan-chang, founder of the Ming dynasty.

but the priest refused. Then Wu went, incognito, to visit him and asked to be shown the future. After gazing at him for a long time, the priest said: " Your face is that of a man who will attain to great power, but there are lines on your chin which tell me that your posterity will be overtaken by disaster and your line become extinct."

Wu said nothing; but after returning to the Palace and brooding over this prophecy of evil he decided to send one of his trusty servants and put the priest to death. The priest, however, had recognised his visitor, and, being a judge of physiognomy, had left the neighbourhood and was not to be found.

In early manhood, as a relief from the monotony of a military life which consisted largely of long sieges, Wu San-kuei became an excellent amateur actor, and at one time trained a company of players and singers known as " The Swallows," who brought him no little kudos. Chroniclers relate the following story, which throws a pleasing Kaiser-light on this versatile genius. He was travelling incognito in Kiangsu and had reached the town of Huai-an. Happening upon the residence of a wealthy merchant, where theatricals were in progress, he sent in a card under an assumed name, and was invited to come in. The performance was extremely poor; nevertheless, both host and guests applauded it loudly. Wu sadly and silently shook his head. Thereat the host indignantly jeered at him: " How should a rustic boor like yourself appreciate such acting as this? " Wu replied: " I don't profess to be an expert, but I have been a lover of the play for over a generation." This reply only incensed the merchant the more, but one of the guests, seeking an opportunity to insult the stranger, invited Wu to give them a taste of his own quality. Wu, delighted at such an opportunity of displaying his skill, wasted no time in polite refusals, and sang the whole of a well-known piece called "A Journey Eastward." The audience were struck speechless with wonder and admiration. When he had finished, Wu waited until the musicians had ceased playing and quietly withdrew. His identity was never suspected, but he himself always spoke of this adventure as the greatest triumph of his career.

Wu San-kuei was no incorruptible patriot, but he was undoubtedly one of the bravest men of those stirring days, and an extremely picturesque figure. We shall have occasion to refer to him again in narrating the final scene in the history of the last of the Mings, whom Wu San-kuei pursued into Burmah.

CHAPTER V

THE MANCHU DYNASTY ESTABLISHED

It is not within the scope of the present work to trace the origins and ramifications of the Manchu clans back to the prehistoric period when they made love and war in their ancestral homes, which lay between the Long White Mountain and the Amur River. Their early history engaged the scholarly attention of the Emperor Ch'ien hung, who dealt with it in several of his voluminous works; it goes back to the time of the Sushen tribe which, according to the annals, brought tribute to the Court of the Emperor Shun (2230 B.C.) in the form of bows and arrows.

For the purposes of the present narrative, which describes the establishment of the Manchu dynasty in China after the decline and fall of the Mings, it is unnecessary to go further back than the days of Nurhachi (known in history as Tai-tsu, the exalted founder), born in 1559, of the Sukosuhu Clan of the Manchu branch of the Nuchens. At an early period in his career Nurhachi's father and grandfather had been treacherously put to death by the Chinese (Ming) noble who was warden of the marches. Nurhachi, enraged at this outrage, collected his forces and demanded reparation from the Mings and the return of the bodies for burial. The Mings, already in difficulties, agreed with their adversary quickly, apologised, and sent presents of horses and silk, besides conferring on Nurhachi the title of " Dragon and Tiger General " and Warden of the Marches of Chien Chou. But Nurhachi's wrath was not appeased. He demanded the surrender of the tribesmen who had done the deed. This was refused, and from that time forward all his energies were concentrated on revenge. For years he worked, consolidating his forces and organising the tribes to a pitch of military efficiency hitherto unknown, so that he became a constant and serious menace on China's northern frontiers. In 1586 he had become the recognised ruler of the five Manchu tribes, and the Court of China had agreed to pay him an annual "subsidy" of 800 ounces of silver and fifteen dragon robes, besides allowing him freedom of trade at Fushun and other marts.

From 1593 to 1597 Nurhachi's energies were fully engaged in extending his dominion over the Yeho tribe[1] and their allies from Mongolia and the Long White Mountain territory. This inter-tribal warfare, complicated by breaches of neutrality by the Mings, continued until 1618, when Nurhachi finally invaded the Yeho territory, took over twenty of their strongholds by assault, and subjugated the entire country between the mouth of the Amur and the Tumen river. After this campaign he organised the united tribes under four banners, yellow, red, blue and white.[2] His armies were drilled and maintained under a system of rigid discipline. In the front of each banner corps (7500 men) were the armour-clad spearmen; the bowmen were in the rear. Each company, of 300 men, carried two scaling ladders and twenty siege catapults. In storming a city each company was required to advance as a compact unit; individual initiative was discouraged and personal bravery unrewarded. The company which entered the city first received rewards and promotion. In judging between the claims of the several companies the Princes of the Blood were constituted a Court of Appeal, with Nurhachi as final arbiter.

[1] Afterwards famous as the Yehonala Manchu Clan. The Nalas were another tribe, conquered by the Yehos.
[2] The four striped banners were created later.

In 1616 Nurhachi assumed the reign title of T'ien Ming, or "Heaven appointed," and the dynastic name of Manchu. Being then about to deliver his last combined assault on the Yeho tribe, which alone continued to deny his supremacy, he sent an envoy to the Mings, demanding that China should maintain strict neutrality. This the Mings refused. Accordingly, in 1618, having dealt with the Yehos, Nurhachi declared war upon China, taking a solemn oath in the presence of his army that he would exact full reparation for the wrongs and indignities put upon him. These he stated categorically, as follows:

1. The wanton murder of his father and grandfather;
2. Violations of treaty in crossing the frontier and assisting the Yeho tribe;
3. Illegal acts by Chinese subjects, who had crossed the frontier to steal ginseng and timber;

and several other grievances of a similar nature.

In 1619 the Mings made a determined attempt to crush the power growing on their northern frontiers, and sent a large army, with orders to concentrate at Moukden, and thence advance from both sides on Hsing Ching, Nurhachi's capital. The story of that splendid campaign is well told in the annals of the dynasty, but cannot be given here; nor have we space to recount the desultory frontier warfare of the next seventeen years. It was during these years that Nurhachi perfected his famous left wing as an invincible fighting force, certainly the finest the East had seen for many centuries, hardy veterans, war-seasoned, and moving as one man. Nurhachi himself displayed all the qualities of a great leader and of a strategist, and became the idol of his troops. In the campaign of 1619, with forces numbering less than 50,000 men, he defeated and scattered in rapid succession the four armies of the Mings, which, with their Korean levies, numbered over 400,000. He took 30,000 prisoners and much booty, and finally established his supremacy, not only over the Yeho tribe, but throughout the frontier lands previously held by China. Here, then, were laid the firm foundations of the Manchu power.

Such fluctuating successes as fell to the Mings during the next few years were ascribed by Nurhachi himself partly to the superior artillery (foreign cannon which the Mings had received from the Portuguese by the aid of the Jesuits at their Court) and partly to the principles which the best amongst the Chinese Generals had imbibed from the teaching of the Sages. But most of all he attributed his own triumphs and the impending doom of the Chinese dynasty to the eunuch-ridden Court and the pernicious interference of its intriguing officials with its Generals in the field. The best of these were under no illusions as to the cause of their repeated defeats and persistent disorganisation; witness the following pathetic defence offered before the Throne by General Hsiung, one of the ablest and bravest commanders of the Ming forces.

"None of the officials who surround Your Majesty," he said, "has any knowledge of the art of war. If they hear that the enemy is retreating or even delaying his attack they all proceed to clamour against me for not advancing, whether I am ready to do so or not. If, then, in obedience to the Throne, I reluctantly engage the enemy and am defeated, not one of them recalls the fact that the disaster is principally due to his own advice. When, again, after a time, I have rallied and reorganised my forces, the cry goes up at Court for drastic measures, and they blame me for procrastination. I am quite strong enough to hold for Your Majesty the whole of the Liao Tung peninsula, but I am not able to silence the foolish and envious tongues of my detractors. No sooner do I leave Your Majesty's presence and the capital, than the voice of calumny is raised against me. If you do not actually clog and hamper my movements by appointing some incompetent person to watch and advise me, you permit my plans to be ruined by the interference of armchair critics."

Another brave and successful commander of the Ming armies, General Sun, was even more outspoken. "Your Majesty's forces," he observed, "have lately been deprived of their necessary training and often of their pay. Instead of leaving the command in the hands of competent military officers, you dispatch ignorant civilians to train the troops. In battle the supreme command devolves upon some high civil functionary, supported by a large and quite useless staff of literary men. The tactics which your armies are to adopt in the field are discussed at supper by your courtiers, or decided by a party of eunuchs in the intervals of their debauches."

Many were the heart-sick patriots and valiant soldiers on the Chinese side who perished, like General Yuan at the fall of Liao Yang,[1] cursing the besotted folly of their Sovereign and the name of the infamous Chief Eunuch, Wei Chung-hsien. A Commander-in-chief like General Hsiung, who refused to placate this notorious favourite, was foredoomed to failure and defeat.

In April 1625, Nurhachi, steadily advancing in strength, established his capital at Moukden, choosing that city because, as he said, "it is a position from which the Liao river may speedily be crossed in the event of trouble arising on the Chinese frontier; the road to Korea lies conveniently near, and if we wish to invade Mongolia, it is within two days' march." At this period General Sun (above referred to) had been given a fairly free hand for two or three years, and had succeeded in recovering from Nurhachi's forces practically all China's territory west of

[1] This brave man, seeing that the city was lost, hanged himself in the city tower, from which he had directed the defence, with his sword buckled on and in his hand the seal of his office. The Censor Chang Ch'üan and many other officers followed his example.

the Liao. But Wei Chung-hsien, failing to secure largesse from Sun, persuaded the Emperor to supersede him. His successor, Kao Ti, evacuated all the important strategic points which Sun had held beyond the Great Wall, and fell back on Shan Hai-kuan.

In 1626 Nurhachi, rightly despising Kao Ti, decided to cross the Liao and invade China and attack the stronghold of Ning Yüan. Kao Ti was for abandoning the place, but General Yüan, in command of the garrison, wrote with his own blood an oath, to which his officers subscribed, that they would defend it to the end. Yüan did deadly execution with his European artillery, and for the first time in his forty years of warfare Nurhachi was repulsed. He returned to Moukden, much chagrined and shaken by this reverse; and on the 30th of September this warrior-monarch died, in the sixty-eighth year of his age, and Huang Taiki, his fourth son, reigned in his stead.

Huang Taiki reigned under the title of T'ien Tsung ("Heaven-obeying") and was posthumously canonised as T'ai Tsung, " the Illustrious Ancestor." A great soldier and an empire builder like his father, he was also a farseeing statesman. Looking forward with certainty to the day when his forces would be able to seize the Throne of the degenerate Mings, he perceived the political and strategic necessity of establishing his dominion over Korea on his eastern, and Mongolia on his north-western, borders, since the rulers of both countries were feudatories of China. Therefore, after the death of his father, he welcomed the overtures made by General Yüan, who sent priests to Moukden to present condolences and incidentally to discusst he preliminaries for a treaty of peace. Neither side dsired peace, but both wished to gain time; T'ai Tsung for his conquest of Korea, and the Chinese General for the rebuilding of the fortresses at Chin chou, Ta Ling-ho and other points west of the Liao. The treaty negotiations were interesting but abortive.

The Manchu expedition to Korea, under Prince Amin, was completely successful, but the final conquest of the country was not undertaken at this period, because, after the conclusion of a treaty which fixed the frontier at the Yalu river, T'ai Tsung ordered the army to return. Hearing that General Yüan was making rapid progress with the rebuilding of his fortresses, he desired to take the field against him in force. The army from Korea returned in triumph in May 1627, and a month later T'ai Tsung once more crossed the Liao river; but again the garrison of Ning Yüan, making good use of their cannon, repelled the invaders. Once more, for several years, the tide of war ebbed and flowed over a region which seems destined ever to be the cockpit of furthest Asia. Despairing of taking the city so long as General Yüan was in command of its defences, the Manchus planned and executed a successful raid through Mongolia into Chihli, when the future conquerors of China first set eyes upon the yellow roofs of the Forbidden City. T'ai Tsung led his raiders in force from the North-West Gate of the capital round to the Hunting Park on the South, where he encamped. Here, coming up by forced marches in response to the Court's urgent summons, General Yüan found him; at this juncture the Mings might have recovered their territory and their prestige had the wretched Ch'ung Chen but trusted the ablest and bravest defender of his Empire. T'ai Tsung saw himself caught in a tight place, and, while avoiding a decisive battle, bethought him of a stratagem which he had learned from Chinese history, a ruse which seems to have been applied frequently with success to the undoing of a Court infested with cowardly traitors. He arranged that two of the Palace eunuchs, who were captives in his camp, should overhear a conversation between his Generals and himself in which they spoke of Yüan as a traitor about to come over to the Manchu side. Next day the eunuchs were allowed to escape, and hastened to Court with their evil tidings. The scheme worked. Yüan was arrested and thrown into prison, and the General appointed to his command was routed by T'ai Tsung after a battle fought outside the Yung-Ting Gate of the city. After this victory, as Peking lay paralysed with terror before the invaders, T'ai Tsung's brothers and his son, Prince Su, begged him to finish his work then and there by seizing the capital and the Throne of the Mings. But T'ai Tsung was a far-seeing and prudent ruler. "To take the city would be easy enough," he replied, "but the time is not yet. Their outlying defences are still untaken, we have established no terror in the heart of China proper. If we took Peking to-day we should not be strong enough to hold it. It will take some years to dissipate the remaining forces of the Mings. No; let us return to our own place and prepare for the hour of destiny, when God shall deliver the whole Empire into our hands." So the Manchu army withdrew, fighting several rearguard actions on their homeward way, and returned to Moukden. There the Emperor gave serious attention to the manufacture of cannon of the European type, and engaged the services of several experts to manufacture guns of the kind which the Red Barbarians (Portuguese) had supplied in large numbers to the Mings. The first of these, known as the "Great General," was cast at Moukden in 1631.

In 1633 T'ai Tsung took Port Arthur and the islands off the Liao-tung coast. In the same year he decided on opening up a new path of invasion into China by the subjugation of the Chahar Mongols. This he did, and henceforward the road to Peking lay open through the pass of Kalgan. By this road his cavalry made frequent raids into Shansi and Chihli, until the name and fame of the Manchus were known beyond the Yellow River.

The subjugation of the Chahar Mongols was followed in 1635 by the submission of all the remaining tribes south of the Gobi, whose chief Eje,[1] handed over to T'ai Tsung the great State-seal of China, which had formerly been that of the Mongol (Yüan) dynasty (1206–1333). In commemoration of this great event, the Prince of the Khorchin Mongols came, at the head of all the tribes which inhabit the region South of the Gobi desert, and begged T'ai Tsung to assume the Imperial title. From this time forward the dynasty was established under the title of Ta Ching ("Great Pure"). In return for their allegiance, the Manchu Emperor conferred upon the leading Mongol Khans princely rank and dignities in the Manchu hierarchy. Also, he appointed chieftains over their banners and guaranteed them annual subsidies for war service. Thenceforward the Khorchin and other tribes intermarried freely with the Manchus.

Meanwhile, Korea, believing T'ai Tsung's hands to be full with the Mongols and the Mings, refused to recognise the new Empire and treated its envoys with truculent rudeness. Desiring to consolidate his Empire on its eastern borders before proceeding to the conquest of China, T'ai Tsung determined to chastise the ruler of the hermit kingdom. But first, in order to keep the attention of the Mings engaged within their own borders, he organised a raiding expedition into China, which started in the winter of 1635. It revealed the utter defencelessness of the Chinese provinces, and created a thirst for loot amongst the Manchus and their Mongol levies which was to bear bitter fruit in days to come. Thirteen cities in Chihli were taken and sacked before the raiders, staggering under their booty, returned to Manchuria.

In January 1637, the Mongol Princes with their levies assembled at Moukden to follow T'ai Tsung in the invasion of Korea. The Emperor led his main force in person; commanding the famous left wing was his brother

[1] Eje was a direct descendant of Dayeri whose ancestor was the last Mongol Emperor.

THE COURT OF PEKING

Dorgun (Prince Jui), while to another brother, Prince Yü, he gave command of a picked body of cavalry whose orders were to make straight for Seoul. When this force drew rein at the gates of his capital and demanded its surrender, the Korean King, an arrant coward, forgot his truculence, and sent a herald expressing his hope that the invaders were not tired after their long journey. Thereafter he fled to a refuge in the neighbouring hills, whence he sent abject apologies to T'ai Tsung, without avail. By the end of February T'ai Tsung and his army were encamped close to Seoul. The Emperor declined to discuss conditions, and sternly bade the wretched King come down and present himself for audience at the camp. Eventually, his followers having dispersed, he came in, made obeisance, and handed over to T'ai Tsung the patent of kingship, which he had received from the Mings. His two sons were taken as hostages to Moukden, and he was permitted to retain the Throne as a vassal of the Manchu Empire, in which condition the Kings of Korea remained, more or less loyally, until 1894, when the Manchu power was challenged and upset by Japan.

After his return from Korea in 1638, T'ai Tsung sent an army under Dorgun to make another raid upon China. The Ming Throne was visibly tottering; but its forces were gathered to resist the invasion and might have succeeded had it not been for the intrigues of the Court against General Lu, the Commander-in-chief. The Manchus, marching southwards and east, took city after city, from the neighbourhood of Peking to Chi-Nan fu, the capital of Shantung, where they got much plunder and captured Prince Tê, a cousin of the Ming Emperor, who was taken in triumph to Moukden.

But none of these military operations were intended to effect a permanent occupation of Chinese territory, nor could Peking itself be safely held so long as the Chinese armies continued to hold the various fortresses and walled cities along the Liao River. The operations against Chinchou, Sungshan, Shan Hai-kuan, and Ning Yüan had been dragging on, amidst more or less desultory warfare, for several years, and still three of China's most capable soldiers (of whom one was Wu San-kuei) continued to hold their own. Early in 1641, Prince Cheng, T'ai Tsung's first cousin, took command of the Manchu forces in this region and put heart into their attacks. By the spring of 1642 only Ning Yüan, defended by Wu San-kuei, remained untaken.

The Ming dynasty was now nearing the end of its resources. The military operations against the Manchus were draining the impoverished treasury of more than 17,000,000 taels a year, more than half the military purposes' taxation of the Empire. Nevertheless, despite the increasing urgency of the danger created by Li Tzŭ-ch'eng's rebellion, the eunuchs and household officials were all for an aggressive policy against the Manchus and half-hearted operations against the rebels. The war party at Peking had induced the vacillating Emperor to put to death two high officials who had advised him to make peace with T'ai Tsung, and the latter's despatch to Ch'ung Chen, suggesting friendly negotiations, had been suppressed.

Nevertheless, when the situation at Shan Hai-kuan was becoming desperate, the President of the Board of War in Peking succeeded in persuading Ch'ung Chen to sanction the sending of emissaries to Moukden with a letter asking for a cessation of hostilities. But even now the arrogant folly of the intractable mandarins ruined a wise policy. The Emperor's letter was written in the form of a decree, and couched accordingly in haughty terms. "A Decree to Our Minister of War, Ch'en Hsin-chia. You inform Us that a wish prevails in Moukden to put an end to the calamities of war. We have hesitated to believe this report, inasmuch as Our provincial authorities have said nothing on the subject to Us, but since you assure Us of its absolute accuracy, and guarantee that the Manchus are acting in good faith, We feel that, so far as We are concerned, there need be no difficulty in agreeing thereto, animated as We are by feelings of indulgence towards all strangers from afar. We shall thus be acting in respectful accordance with the merciful principles of the Almighty, and shall restore the immemorial relations of generous condescension shown by Our ancestors towards the Manchu tribes. We empower you to dispatch duly qualified persons to notify Our wishes in the matter, and you are to report to Us on receipt of definite information in regard thereto."

On receipt of this communication the Emperor T'ai Tsung issued the following decree in reply: "The letter brought me by your envoys is not satisfactory in form. If it is meant to be a communication to Us, why does your Sovereign call it a Decree to Ch'en Hsin-chia? If it is a decree from your Sovereign to Ch'en Hsin-chia, why does he seal it with the Imperial seal? Besides, the shape of the seal is oblong and not, as custom requires, square. In a matter of this kind it is impossible to sanction any deviation from usage. It is clear to me from the shape of the seal that the letter is not genuine or, if genuine, that it is sealed in this way for purposes of subsequent repudiation. The letter fails to suggest to my mind any sincere desire for peace. The sentence, " Animated as we are by feelings of indulgence towards strangers from afar," and that which ends with the words " generous condescension . . . towards the Manchu tribes," betray a spirit of haughty contempt for my nation which contradicts the idea of a desire for peace on the part of the Mings. Disregarding these cunning evasions, I will now set forth the plain facts of the case: Hostilities were originally commenced by my people with extreme reluctance, caused solely by the unbearable insults heaped upon us by you Mings, and by your flagrant disregard of right and wrong.

Whenever I have made overtures of peace you have flouted them. To-day, it would seem, you Mings are anxious for peace, but it is impossible to be sure of your *bona fides*. In any case, desirous as I am for peace, I am not to be coerced into making it. By the abundant favour of the Almighty, I now possess all the territory which formerly belonged to the Chin Tartars; the descendants of the Yüan dynasty and Korea have accepted my suzerainty. Several millions of Ming subjects have submitted to me; everywhere my arms have triumphed. In the interests of the people of both nations I desire peace, but only on a footing of absolute equality between the contracting parties. There must be no question of " central " and " outside " nations, nor of great and small kingdoms. Trade shall be conducted on equal terms between our respective subjects, and each nation shall make annual gifts to the other. In this way great happiness may accrue both to rulers and ruled, and we shall enjoy the blessings of peace. My dynasty, in spite of its martial prowess and the prosperity which it enjoys, longs ardently for peace, but you Mings ignore my communications, and your Sovereign, in the fond belief that he is the Son of Heaven, displays contemptuous arrogance towards his equals, and indulges in vain boasting; surely his desire for peace can only be skin-deep. Know you that Heaven has no favourites; the Almighty giveth dominion to the just and overwhelmeth the evil-doer. Look you now: has China been governed by one and the same dynasty from time immemorial? Are you not aware that none has ever enjoyed a perpetual mandate from on high? But you Mings, Emperor and Ministers together, reck not of these things. You, Emperor and Ministers, are guilty of the deaths of millions of your subjects; at your hands have they perished, because you have persisted in warring against me. What I now tell you is the truth, and I desire that it be transmitted to your Emperor."

THE COURT OF PEKING

At this juncture a Censor,[1] Tsu Ko-fa, advised T'ai Tsung to make a proposal to the Mings for the partition of the Empire, with the Yellow River (which at that time entered the sea in Kiangsu) as boundary, on condition that the Mings should send annual tribute to the Manchus. T'ai Tsung declined the suggestion, and gave a final audience to the Ming representatives, at which he presented them with sables and silver ingots, and ordered that a banquet be given in their honour. He commanded that they should be safely escorted over the frontier, and handed to them the following autograph letter for their Sovereign, which shows that he was sincerely desirous of peace with honour.

" The first cause of my war against your nation lay in the unprovoked murder of my two ancestors by you Mings, but my Imperial father, while always ready to defend his frontiers, was ever desirous of keeping the peace. He would have kept it, but that you Mings committed acts of wanton violence and interfered in our country's affairs. You demanded that we should restore the territory which we had wrested from the Hata tribe in battle, and you sent troops to garrison against us strong places in the Yeho region. You have violated our territory, interfered with our business of husbandry, burned our villages, and scattered their inhabitants. For these reasons my father found it necessary to establish supremacy over the various tribes, and solemnly declared to Heaven and earth his purpose to make war upon you Mings.

" Frequently he attempted to negotiate with you, but you ignored his letters. Thanks to the mistakes committed by your predecessor and his Ministers matters have now dragged on for years without hope of settle-

[1] One of the numerous Chinese who already then had gone over to the winning side, and who, after the conquest became, " tribute-eating " bannermen.

ment. I do not blame Your Majesty for these things; I am merely stating the plain rights of the case.

"If now I am prepared to make peace, it is of my own free will, no man coercing me. Since my accession to the Throne Heaven has plentifully blessed my endeavours, and all the territory of the coast has been won by my arms. The population of the northern regions is nomadic, and not addicted to husbandry. Their domestic animals are the dog and the deer; their occupations, hunting and fishing. All North Manchuria has submitted to me; nay, even the descendants of the Mongol Emperors and Korea have owned my supremacy.

"In response to the request of my Mongol vassals and of the Princes of my family I have announced to Heaven and earth that We have assumed the dynastic title of Ta Ching, "Great Pure," and changed my reign title to that of "Consummate Virtue."

"We have vanquished your troops on every occasion that we have invaded your territory. There would not be the slightest difficulty in advancing still further and in making our occupation permanent. At our approach your cities fall; your battle line breaks in disarray.

"But, in the interests of our subjects, my mind is still set on peace. Sooner or later, retribution is visited by Heaven on him who lusts after conquest, while the humane receive their just reward. If our two States can only realise where true happiness lies, and establish relations of cordial and confident friendship, all the ill-feeling of the past may easily be buried in oblivion. What cause is there for either party to arrogate to itself superiority over the other? The adage says: 'To understand everything is to forgive, but a lack of comprehension breeds hatred.'

"I am ready to receive your embassies in audience, and it behoves you to grant equal favours to mine. In this way peace between us may be perpetual. But should you persist in asserting these exaggerated ideas of your own importance, and refuse to meet my envoys face to face, as if they were unworthy to enter your sacred presence, it is useless to hope for any good understanding between us, and nothing but disaster will accrue to your State.

"Do you imagine, forsooth, that your majestic dignity is in any way enhanced by a discourteous refusal to receive my envoys? Have not our peoples always been wont to exchange ambassadorial visits on occasions of ceremony or Court mourning, to convey congratulations or condolences, and has it not been your custom to send us annual gifts, 10,000 taels of gold, 100,000 of silver, in exchange for which we have presented to you 1000 lbs. of ginseng and 1000 sable skins? In future, should any fugitives from our justice, Manchu, Mongol, Chinese or Korean, escape into your territory, it shall be your duty to hand them over to us; we for our part will do the same with your fugitives. Your boundary shall be the range of mountains between Ning Yüan and Shuang-shu p'i, while our frontier shall be Pagoda Mountain. Lien Shan Bay shall be neutral territory, and subjects of both nations shall be permitted to trade there. Any one violating these respective boundaries shall be punished with death. Coastal fishing shall be similarly confined within certain boundaries to Manchus and Chinese respectively. If you approve of the above conditions and are ready to make peace, we can either proceed ourselves in person to announce the solemn compact to the Most High or depute officials to represent us and exchange the respective treaties. If you refuse peace on these terms, pray send us no more envoys, and hereafter whatsoever misfortunes may befall your people will be no fault of mine. I now hand this letter to your emissaries, and have arranged for their safe convoy through my territory, past my outposts at Chinchou, as far as Lien Shan."

The Ming envoys knelt once and kotowed thrice on entering and leaving the Presence; they handed in a further decree from the Ming Emperor addressed, like the last, to his Board of War, in which the Monarch asked for news of the negotiations, and gave the mission full powers to enter into a treaty at Moukden, but there was still no direct communication from Ch'ung-chen to his brother Sovereign.

Unfortunately for the possible success of this mission, the Ming Emperor's instructions to keep its results strictly secret were disregarded. When the envoys returned to Peking they handed in T'ai Tsung's letter and the other documents to Ch'en Hsin-chia, the President of the Board of War, who was proceeding to draft a favourable report to the Throne when, through the error (possibly intentional) of a servant, copies of the Ming Emperor's decrees and a full account of the negotiations were published in the official *Peking Gazette*. Ch'ung Chen had specially enjoined Ch'en to maintain rigid secrecy, and was, therefore, exceedingly wrath at these disclosures. As he had expected, the Censors poured in violent memorials of impeachment, denouncing Ch'en as a traitor for endeavouring to make peace with the Manchus. Ch'ung-chen issued a decree ordering Ch'en to explain his action; but the Minister declined to accept any blame for his conduct, and sent in a memorial asserting boldly that by these negotiations he had rendered a great service to the Throne. Ch'ung Chen felt that he had lost much face, and as usual recovered it by ordering the luckless Minister's public decapitation. So the mission was a failure, and the war went on. *Quos Deus vult perdere prius dementat.*

An interesting memorial by one of the Manchu Court's Censors at this date observed, " Wu San-kuei is still holding out at Ning Yüan, but the garrison are in piteous straits and the city must soon fall. Wu is exceedingly suspicious of our intentions, it therefore behoves Your Majesty to capture him by strategy. Once Ning Yüan and Shan Hai-kuan have fallen, Peking is ours. The Court will flee to Nanking, and the Manchus will be masters of China."

Another Chinese adherent of the Manchus memorialised, advising T'ai Tsung to march on Peking through Mongolia, leaving Shan Hai-kuan isolated. To this he replied: "The capture of Peking may be likened to the cutting down of a great tree. First dig up all the wide-spreading roots and the trunk will fall of itself. Each day lessens the power of the Mings and increases ours. Before long Peking will fall like a ripe apple into our lap."

The apple was ripening fast. T'ai Tsung, to hasten the inevitable end, now dispatched a large army into China under his elder brother, Prince Abtai. In an address to this force he said: "We are no lovers of prolonged war, but our attempts to secure peace have been brought to nought by the purblind obstinacy of the Mings. We now, therefore, command you to invade China and smite them hip and thigh. Take no innocent life, carry off no man's wife and family, nor any wearing apparel. Loot not to excess. Plunder no stores of grain except when it is needed for your use. During the last expedition to Shantung there were instances of people being beaten to death in order to make them give up treasure. Such atrocities are a violation of the humane principles by which we are inspired. Bring back all your captives uninjured, that they may join our ranks." The Emperor accompanied the army as far as the suburbs of Moukden and then bade it farewell. In a few parting words he warned them against the pride which precedes a fall, and advised that if they should fall in with any of the forces of the rebels, then approaching Peking, they should endeavour by soft words to win them over to the Manchu side.

He handed to Abtai his seal of office. Three salvoes of artillery were fired, and the army, in three divisions, set forth. This was in November 1642. The expedition proved a brilliant success. The invaders broke through the Great Wall near the spot where now stand the Manchu dynasty's Eastern Tombs,[1] and from Chichou marched southwards. In South Chihli and Shantung they captured eighty-eight walled cities, and advanced as far as Yenchou-fu in Southern Shantung. In March of the following year they re-entered Chihli. T'ai Tsung's orders about looting had not been taken too literally, for their train of camels and baggage wagons extended over a length of near a hundred miles. To cut them off from Manchuria a large body of Ming troops had collected at Tien-chen under the Grand Secretary Chou Yen-ju, but he feared to give battle, contenting himself with dispatching to Peking bombastic reports of a glorious victory. The only engagement which took place was at Shell Mountain, some thirty miles north of Peking, where the Mings, under the Viceroy of Chihli and Liaotung, were badly defeated. At this time the Mings had no fewer than four Viceroys in command of their territory surrounding the Great Wall, six Governors, eight Generals-in-chief, not to mention a eunuch Commander-in-chief, who tried to concentrate all authority in his own hands and tyrannised over his colleagues. There was thus no attempt at co-ordination, and Li Tzŭ-ch'eng's rebels were daily advancing nearer to Peking.

In July 1643, the Manchu armies returned to Moukden, where they were cordially welcomed by T'ai Tsung, who went to meet them beyond the walls. The expedition had put to death the Ming Prince Lu and five other Princes of the Imperial family, as well as a thousand of the Imperial clan. They had taken possession of three prefectures, eighteen departments and sixty-seven district

[1] Where K'anghsi, Ch'ien Lung and Tzŭ Hsi lie buried.

cities, and routed the enemy in thirty-seven engagements. They had secured booty to the amount of 12,250 ounces of gold, 12,250,277 ounces of silver, 4,440 ounces of pearls, 52,234 rolls of satin and silks, 33,720 suits of raiment, 111 fur coats, 500 sable skins, 1,600 deer horns, and had taken 369,000 captives, besides 551,312 beasts of burden, camels and oxen. One-third of this booty was divided among the officers and men; immense quantities of private loot were also secreted by individuals.

The Emperor T'ai Tsung sacrificed at his father's tomb on the Buddhist All Souls' Day (the 15th of the 7th Moon), when the Mongol Tushetu Khan came to present his congratulations at the head of his tribe. He then went on a hunting trip, on returning from which he had to undergo a long and fatiguing day of audiences in the Moukden Palace. At 11 p.m. on the 9th of the 8th Moon (Sept. 21, 1643) he repaired to his bed-chamber, and there, sitting bolt upright in his chair of state, expired without a word, doubtless from heart failure. He was then in his fifty-first year. He had prepared no valedictory decree nor any instructions regarding the succession. By the laws of the dynasty his eldest son, Meng Ko, Prince Su, then in his twenty-ninth year, should have succeeded him, but this would have thwarted the ambitions of the surviving sons of Nurhachi, especially those of his fourteenth son Dorgun (Prince Jui), who had designs on the Regency, since he could not legally aspire to the Throne. T'ai Tsung's eldest surviving brother, Taishan (Prince Li), was crippled with rheumatism, and was, therefore, incapable of advancing his claims. So T'ai Tsung's ninth son, Fu Lin, a child of five and a half, was placed on the Throne by his ambitious uncle, Prince Jui, who, secure in the Regency, could look forward to many years of power.

Although T'ai Tsung's other brothers were jealous of Dorgun's assumption of the Regency, his claims as a military leader were indisputable, and their assertion was justified by the approval of the bannermen. The young Emperor was a child of splendid physique; he had delighted his father by his promise of athletic prowess, and had accompanied him on the hunting expedition of the previous spring. His mother, a Mongol Princess of the Khorchin tribe, was a very remarkable woman, and exercised great influence over her son, and later in life over her grandson, K'ang Hsi. It was thought strange at the time that she acquiesced so readily in Dorgun's usurpation of power during the Emperor's minority, but she decided, no doubt, that the consolidation and extension of the Empire were more important than any internal or domestic questions.

The new reign opened auspiciously : the King of Korea sent a mission with tribute, and received in reply a graciously condescending message. Prince Cheng, Co-Regent with Dorgun, was dispatched from Moukden to attack the Ming stronghold at Chung Hou-so. He took with him a large number of European guns which had been captured from the Mings. The city was bombarded and taken by assault, some 4,000 men being killed and as many captured. The Manchus now held every important point, except Ning Yüan, outside the Great Wall. The expedition returned into winter quarters at Moukden, and spent that season in casting a number of guns for the next campaign in China.

By the spring of 1644 all was ready for the final overthrow of the Mings; Prince Jui appointed himself Generalissimo of the army, and no doubt cherished ambitions of eventually securing the Throne after the fall of Peking. Suddenly news reached Moukden that Wu San-kuei had evacuated Ning Yüan, which had so long defied all attacks, and that his force was retreating towards the capital. The Manchus were unaware that Li Tzŭ-ch'eng and his rebel hordes were already at Peking, and that the dynasty had collapsed. The Regent was urged to march without delay upon the capital and to effect its permanent occupation. His Grand Secretary, Fan Wen-ch'eng, pointed out that the Manchus had frequently overrun Chihli; thrice already they had put to the sword the inhabitants of Yung-ping, and had evacuated Tsun-hua after holding it for several months. Such tactics created an impression that they were merely raiders and marauders of the marches. They should now establish strict discipline and forbid all looting; the Ming officials should be retained in their posts, so as to mark clearly the difference between Manchu rule and the brigandage of Li Tzŭ-ch'eng. The rebels would assuredly consolidate their power unless the Manchus struck promptly. If they could but secure the region north of the Yellow River, all China must be theirs, sooner or later. Before the army left, a solemn sacrifice was offered to the *manes* of Nurhachi and his son; thereafter the boy Emperor himself presented Dorgun with the seal and patent of his office. The edict issued on this occasion declared, in the best classical manner, that while Korea and Mongolia had acknowledged his dynasty's sovereignty, the Chinese still remained stubborn. His Majesty, unfortunately, was too young to lead his armies in person and had, therefore, entrusted this duty to his uncle, on whom he now bestowed a canopy of Imperial yellow, two dragon banners, a cap of fox-skin, sable robes, a sable rug and dragon robes. The Throne—which meant the power of the pens behind it—retained its prerogatives as regards directing the conduct of the campaign. The edict concluded: " Let there be complete harmony among you, so that success may be achieved, and the august Shades of the mighty dead be comforted. Be reverent."

Prince Jui bowed the knee thrice and kotowed nine times. His army, which was to establish the Manchu rulers upon the Dragon Throne, comprised two-thirds of the Manchu and Mongol banners;[1] and all the Chinese (Hanchün) levies. The other third of the Manchus and Mongols remained to guard the young Emperor and his capital.

The rest of the story has already been told. As soon as Wu San-kuei had been dispatched by the Regent to occupy and exhaust his formidable army in the congenial task of pursuing the booty-laden rebels, the Regent settled down to consolidate the Manchu power against all possible attacks, and to re-organise the Government upon just and liberal principles. With the courage of a great soldier and the skill of a great statesman he laid the foundations of the dynastic rule, which the young Emperor Shun Chih and his immediate descendants were destined to carry to an eminence of fame rarely equalled in the history of China.

We have thought it advisable to narrate thus fully the origin and history of the warlike clansmen who replaced the Mings, and thereafter ruled over the world's largest Empire for 270 years, because some knowledge of the antecedents and traditions of the Imperial Clans is necessary to a proper appreciation of many later events in the

---

[1] The Manchu dynasty instituted three superior and five inferior banners, to one of which every Manchu belonged, as well as all the Mongols and Chinese who had assisted in the conquest of China. The three superior banners are: Bordered yellow, plain yellow, and plain white. The five inferior: Bordered white, plain red, bordered red, plain blue and bordered blue. After the conquest, the inner city of Peking was assigned to the several banners by districts, strating from the North. The colours were supposed to represent the five elements: earth, metal, wood, fire and water. The yellow banners, which were quartered in the North of the city, represented earth, supposed by the Chinese to subdue the element of water. The white banners held the North-East and North-West of the city, immediately to the South of the yellow banners; they represented metal, which is supposed to subdue the element of wood. The red banners occupied the quarter in the centre, from the Ch'i hua Gate to the "P'ing tse" Gate; they represented the element fire, which subdues metal. Lastly, the blue banners were stationed at the extreme South of the Tartar City; they represented water, which subdues fire.

THE COURT OF PEKING

history of the dynasty, and of the causes of its subsequent falling away from the grace that distinguished Nurhachi and his immediate posterity. For the same reason the following genealogical tree should be of interest, even though to-day that interest has become historical and chiefly academic.

GENEALOGY OF THE HOUSE OF GIORO
(Founder of the Manchu Dynasty in China)

Takoshi: killed by officers of the Ming Emperor Wanli in 1583.

His issue :

1. *Murhachi*.
2. *Shurhachi*: whose son Chirhalang (Prince Cheng) was Co-Regent with Prince Jui at Peking in 1643. Founder of the hereditary princedom of Cheng.
3. *Nurhachi*: whose mother was Sitala; born 1559, died 1626. Known in history as Taitsu, "Exalted Founder." Nurhachi married a daughter of Prince Yangkunu, Yehonala, who was the mother of T'ai Tsung, his successor. She died in 1603.

Nurhachi had issue :

1. *Arhhatutumen*: sentenced to death in 1615; his son, Prince Chingchin, was a distinguished soldier, who died about 1650.
2. *Taishan*: Prince Li, founder of the senior princely house of Li; died in 1648. (The title of Sun was taken by the successors of Prince Li for five generations, after which the present title of Li was resumed.)
3. *Abai*: ennobled as Duke.
4. *Tangkutai*.
5. *Mangkurtai*: allowed to commit suicide in 1633.
6. *Tapai*.
7. *Abtai*: Prince Jaoyü, who died in 1646.
8. *Huangtaiki*: who succeeded his father as Emperor.
9. *Baptai*.
10. *Deklei*: cashiered and removed from the Imperial Clan.
11. *Babuhai*.
12. *Achiko*: Prince Ying, who was privileged to commit suicide by Imperial order in 1651.
13. *Laimpu*.
14. *Dorgun*: Prince Jui, the Regent; founder of the House of Jui. Died in 1650, aged 39. Posthumously accused of rebellion against the State, and name removed from the

Imperial Clan. In 1778 his honours were restored to him, when he was given the posthumous name of " Loyal," and his descendants were allowed to resume their former title.

15 *Toto* : Prince Yü, own brother of Dorgun, and founder of the House of Yü. Died in 1649. His son, Toni, succeeded as Prince Hsin.

Huangtaiki : known in history as T'ai Tsung or the Illustrious Ancestor. Born in 1592. Married Bochito, daughter of the Khorchin Prince Sesang, mother of Shunchih, Kang Hsi's Empress Grand Dowager, who died in 1688. Succeeded in 1626. In 1636 adopted the title of Ta Hsing, " Great Pure," for his dynasty. Died in 1643.

His issue were :
2. *Mengko* : Prince Su, ancestor of the princely family of Su. Imprisoned on a charge of treason in 1648 by the Regent. Posthumously canonised with restoration of all his honours and titles.
2. *Shosai* : Prince Ch'eng Tse; his son Bokoto was the founder of the princely family of Chuang, and ancestor of the Boxer Prince of that name who committed suicide.
3. *Kaosai.*
4. *Fulin* : reigned as Shunchih.
5. *Bomubokorh* : Prince Hsiang; died in 1656.

Emperor Shunchih : born 1638; succeeded 1643; assumed government in 1651, and died in 1661. Married (1) Borchichin of the Khorchin Mongol tribe in 1651. She disagreed with her sovereign lord, and was reduced to the position of concubine of the third rank by the Empress Dowager. (2) A daughter of Prince Chorji of the Khorchins, K'ang Hsi's Empress Dowager, died in 1718.

Shun Chih had issue :
1. *Fuchuan* : Prince Yu; died 1703. Referred to by the first Russian ambassador to the Court of Peking as the most prominent subject of K'ang Hsi.
2. *Hsuanyeh* : who became Emperor with reign title of K'ang Hsi.
3. *Changning* : Prince Kung; died 1703. His son, Mantuhu, joined the rebellious brothers of Yung Cheng.

K'ang Hsi : born 1654; assumed the government in 1667; died 1722. His first Empress was a daughter of Gobla of the Hashli Clan, who died in 1674. His second was of the Niuhulu Clan, a daughter of Duke Obilung—died 1678. His third was of the Tungchia Clan—died in 1689. His fourth was of the Wuya Clan; she was the mother of Yung Cheng and by him exalted to the rank of Empress on his accession to the Throne.[1]

[1] K'ang Hsi's sons are enumerated elsewhere : *vide* p.

THE COURT OF PEKING

Yung Cheng: born 1678; died 1735; married the Lady Niuhulu, who became the mother of Ch'ien Lung and Empress Dowager during his reign. A woman of great strength of character; she accompanied her son in many of his journeys all over China. Died in 1777, aged 88, the possessor of eighteen honorific characters in her title.

Yung Cheng had issue:
1. *Hungli:* who succeeded his father as Ch'ien Lung. During his father's lifetime known as Prince Jewel.
2. *Hung-chou:* or Prince Ho; died 1770.
3. *Hungchan:* Prince Kuo. As a lad he was called Yuanmingyuan or Round Bright Garden (the name of the Summer Palace). Was reduced to the rank of Beileh, or Prince of the third order, but Ch'ien Lung visited him on his death-bed, restored his original princedom, and had him canonised. Died in 1765.

Ch'ien Lung: born in 1711; abdicated in 1796; died February 7, 1799. His first Empress was of the Fucha Clan; the second of the Yehonala Clan. The latter accompanied her husband and mother-in-law on an excursion to the South in 1765. She misbehaved herself during this journey, treating her mother-in-law with flagrant disrespect and flippancy, and was sent back in disgrace to Peking from Hangchou, shut up in the "Cold Palace," and subsequently deposed.

Ch'ien Lung had issue:
1. *Tunghuang:* Prince Ting, son of a concubine, and ancestor of Prince Jü Lang, one of Tzŭ Hsi's Grand Councillors. This Prince Ting was debarred from the succession, owing to his being the son of a subordinate concubine.
2. *Yung Lien:* created Heir Apparent, but died in 1738, aged 13.
3. *Yung Chang:* Prince Hsun, died 1760.
4. *Yung Ch'eng:* Prince Li, who became heir to his uncle, Yun Tao, one of Yung Cheng's rebellious brothers. Died in 1777.
5. *Yung Ch'i:* Prince Jung. The Emperor intended him to be Heir Apparent on the death of the seventh son, Prince Che. He died in 1766, aged 25.
6. *Yung Jung:* Prince Chih, made heir to his uncle, Prince Yun Hsi. Died in 1790, aged 46.
7. *Yung Tsung:* Prince Che. Died 1748, aged 3.
8. *Yung Hsüan:* Prince Yi; held many Government posts as adviser to his brother, the Emperor Chia Ch'ing. Died in 1732, aged 86. His son, Mien Chih, succeeded to the Princedom of Yi which was, however, reduced by one grade. Yi Tsai, son of Mien Chih, was declared heir to Prince Ching, but was afterwards deprived of the title when the succession to the house of Ch'ing went to Mien Ti, adopted father of the present Prince Ch'ing.

9. *Yung Hsing:* Prince Ch'eng, a great scholar, and one of the most famous caligraphists of the dynasty. Was adviser to his brother Chia Ch'ing. Died in 1823, aged 71. Great grandfather of Prince Tsai Hsiao.
10. *Yung Ch'i:* died in 1776, aged 25.
11. *Yung Yen:* succeeded his father as the Emperor Chia Ch'ing.
12. *Yung Lin:* Prince Ch'ing, died 1720, aged 53. Grandfather (by adoption) of Yi Kiang, the present Prince Ch'ing, who was originally an impoverished Imperial clansman, adopted into the nearer branch of the Imperial family.

Emperor Chia Ch'ing: born 1760; created Prince Chia (Admirable); took over the reins of government in February 1796; killed by lightning near Jehol, September 1820. Married Hsitala, daughter of Horchingo, the mother of Taokuang, who died in 1797, and, *en secondes noces,* the Lady Niuhulu, who was promoted to be Empress shortly after Ch'ien Lung's death. She was Taokuang's Empress Dowager, and died in 1850, pre-deceasing Taokuang by one month.

Chia Ch'ing had issue :
1. *Mienning:* succeeded his father as Emperor Taokuang.
2. *Mienkai:* Prince Tun, died 1839.
3. *Mien Hsin:* Prince Jui, died 1828; succeeded by Yi Yo, or Yichih, as he was subsequently named. Yichih died in 1850, and Prince Tuan, the Boxer Prince, was adopted as his heir.
4. *Mien Yu:* Prince Hui, died in 1865. His sons were : Yihsiang, Yihsün and Yimo. Yihsün was father of the Duke Tsai Tse, Finance Minister towards the end of Tzü Hsi's reign.

Taokuang: born 1782, succeeded 1820 and died 1850. Married (1) the Lady Niuhulu, who died before his accession but was posthumously made Empress; (2) Lady Tungchia, who died in 1833, and (3) Lady Niuhulu, daughter of Yiling, mother of the Emperor Hsien Feng; created Empress in 1834, died in 1840; (4) Lady Borjikit, who was instrumental in selecting Tzü Hsi for the Palace. She was elevated to be Empress Dowager a week before she died, in 1855.

Taokuang had issue :
1. *Yiwei:* son of the concubine Yehonala; born 1808, died 1831. Tasichung (or Tsai Chih, as he was afterwards called), son of an Imperial clansman, was adopted as his heir. Tsai Chih's son is P'ulun, who very nearly became Emperor in 1875.
2. *Yikang:* died in infancy.
3. *Yichi:* died in infancy.
4 *Yichu:* who reigned as Hsien Feng.
5 *Yitsung:* Prince Tun, was adopted as heir to Mienkai (see above). His sons were : (*a*) Tsai Lien, born 1856, one of the Boxer Princes. (*b*) Tsai Yi, Prince Tuan, born December

1856. His son, P'uchün, was the Boxer Heir Apparent (whom Tzü Hsi spanked). He married a daughter of the Mongol Prince Lo. (c) Tsailan, the Boxer Prince, exiled to Urumchi; born in 1857. (d) Tsaiying. (e) Tsaiching. (f) Tsaihao.

6 *Yihsin*: Prince Kung, born 1833, died in 1898. His eldest son (a) Tsaich'eng, born in 1857, predeceased his father; (b) Tsai Ying, born in 1861, adopted as heir to his uncle, Prince Chung, the eighth Prince. P'uwei, the present Prince Kung, is his son. P'uwei considers he was wrongfully ousted from the Throne on the death of Kuang Hsü.

7. *Yihuan*: Prince Ch'un, born 1840, died 1891. Married Yehonala, sister of Tzü Hsi, by whom he had issue: (1) Tsai Han. (2) Tsai Tien, Emperor Kuang Hsü (some Chinese assert that Tzü Hsi was really the mother of Kuang Hsü). By another wife of low origin, named Tsui (she was the daughter of a groom), he also had issue; Tsai Feng, the Ex-Regent, born 1882, married a daughter of Jung Lu; father of the Emperor Hsüan Tung (Pu'yi), born 1906, and Pukuang. By the same concubine Tsai Tao was born: his elder brother, Tsai Hsün, is by another concubine.

8. *Yiho*: Prince Chung, born 1844, died 1868.

9. *Yihui*: Prince Fu, married a niece of Tzü Hsi, and was dismissed by her from office in 1898 because of his sympathy towards Kuanghsü. He was pardoned in January 1908, on the day of Yuan Shih-k'ai's dismissal.

Hsien Feng: born in 1831, died in 1861. Married (1) Sakota, daughter of Muyanga, in 1848, who died in 1850, one month before his accession. She was posthumously raised to the rank of Empress, and was the "centre" of the three Empresses, Tzu An being the "eastern" and Tzü Hsi the "western." (2) Niuhulu, also daughter of Muyanga, who was made concubine in 1852; afterwards Empress Dowager; died April 1881. (3) Yehonala, afterwards Tzü Hsi

Hsien Feng had issue:
1. *Tsai Ch'un*, born 1856, died 1875, reigned as Tung Chih.
2. An infant son, who died a few days after birth.

Tung Chih: married Alute, daughter of Chungchi, who died in 1875.
Kuang Hsü: born August 1871; married Yehonala 1899, died November 22, 1908. Was practically deposed by Tzü Hsi, after the *coup d'état* of September 1908.
Hsüan Tung: (P'uyi) son of Tsai Feng, succeeded November 1898, abdicated February 12, 1912.

CHAPTER VI

THE MINGS AT NANKING

DEBAUCHED and cowardly as they were, the Princes and courtiers of the Mings were not disposed to relinquish without a struggle their rights to the Dragon Throne, or their claims to the long-suffering allegiance of the Chinese people. After the fall of Peking and the desecration of its high places by the rebel hordes of Li Tzŭ-ch'eng, for a time there was nothing but a *sauve qui peut*, without purpose or direction; but when they saw their fierce harrier [1] himself driven forth by new conquerors and pursued by one who, until then, had been their dynasty's mainstay against the Manchus, small wonder that the more energetic members of the Imperial family took heart of grace and endeavoured to rally their scattered forces upon a new centre.[2] The sybarite retains to the end his

[1] Li Tzŭ-ch'eng's nickname was "Prince Harrier."
[2] An initial cause of their disorganisation lay in the fact that the Heir Apparent had disappeared after the fall of the city, and that none knew if he were alive or dead. Several months after the Manchu Emperor had been proclaimed in Peking this Prince's whereabouts were unknown, but eventually he was brought secretly by a eunuch to the house of one who had had high office under the Mings, and with whom the Ming Princess Imperial was residing. The meeting between brother and sister was most affecting; he had been in hiding at a Buddhist monastery since his escape from the city, but was weary of the suspense and grief of his existence, and came to seek his relatives. The Princess and his host begged him to change his name and adopt a disguise, but he refused. Shortly afterwards he was recognised by several renegade officials and eunuchs and thrown into prison by order of the Regent. The merchants and gentry of Peking petitioned that his young life might be spared, but the Regent had no desire to leave a rallying point for the conspiracies of legitimists, and the unfortunate youth was put to death by poison in the Board of Punishments.

THE COURT OF PEKING

habits and ambitions of luxury, and with the degenerate Mings the lust of perquisites and power, of pomp and circumstance, was not killed by their cataclysmic disasters. For eighteen years, harried from one short-lived capital to another, four successive claimants to the Throne of their dynasty retained some semblance of their regal state and a place in the minds, if not the hearts, of their people. During these years there were times when, had there been a strong man amongst them, their dominion might well have been restored and the Manchus driven back, for the Confucian virtues of faithfulness and loyal devotion (which have generally characterised the relations between the *literati* and their Sovereign in Chinese history) were not lacking at this period; many a brave soldier, many a stoic philosopher of the mandarins, upheld the proud traditions of their caste, and died rather than submit to the rule of the alien, and many millions of the " stupid people " went to their graves like beds because of that loyalty to the central idea of the Confucian doctrine. But the Mings were all unworthy, even in adversity. As they had been before the threatening storm, so they remained when its passing had left their dynasty a tempest-driven wreck—invertebrate, irresolute to the end. Four years after the flight from Peking, when the adherents of Kuei Wang, the last of the Mings, were making a successful stand in the Kuang provinces, when Coxinja was beginning to organise new forces of resistance to the Manchus, and when several rebel forces had taken the field on their own account, a little statesmanship, a little courage, might have won the day. But it was not to be. The little Court in exile kept up its tinsel state, grateful to its loyal adherents only so long as they replenished the Privy purse which paid for its revels; leaving its armies unvictualled whilst it rehearsed some new play,[1] or sent the

---

[1] It is recorded of Hung Kuang, the first of the fugitive Emperors of the Mings, that on a certain occasion, while the Regent's forces

eunuchs through the country in search of new favourites for the harem of the "Palace," that was now a moving tent.

Under these circumstances, the wretched end of the Ming claimants, pursued and slain each in his turn, does not excite our sympathies so much as the calamities which the miserable people were doomed to bear because of the Mings' last struggle for the Throne. History as usual says but little of the widespread and awful devastation created by that struggle, of the pitiful sufferings of the masses; that tale was told (as it is being told again in China to-day) by cities of the dead, by roofless villages and homeless wanderers throughout all the land. In the next chapter, which narrates the sack of Yang Chou-fu, the reader will find a plain, dispassionate account by an eye-witness of the fate which overtook one city because a gallant soldier refused to renounce his principles and his allegiance. That soldier was General Shih K'o-fa, a staunch loyalist, a distinguished scholar, and a man of bravery so rare that it won for him the sincere respect and goodwill of the Manchu Regent. When the Mings had gathered at Nanking and established there, under a grandson of Wan Li, the semblance of a Government and a Court, it was to Shih K'o-fa that the eyes of all men were turned to prevent the Manchu invasion from coming South.

Had he not been handicapped by the jealous intrigues of his rivals at Court, led by one Ma Shih-ying (who had been one of the faction of the notorious eunuch Wei Chung-hsien), Shih K'o-fa might have been able to hold the Manchus in check at the Huai River. Before the Regent's forces began their advance towards the Yangtsze he had collected and organised an effective army of 60,000

---

were advancing to the siege of Yang Chou-fu, his eunuchs, seeing him greatly depressed, inquired the cause of his grief. "What distresses me," he replied, "is that there is not in all my Court an actor worthy of the name."

THE COURT OF PEKING

Shensi troops. Besides these, the Mings had four divisions, of about 10,000 men each, encamped at strategic points in the provinces of Anhui and Kiangsu. Shih asked only to be given a free hand and independent control over these forces, to be relieved of all vexatious interference by the courtiers and civil officials at Nanking; but the new Emperor, foredoomed to vacillation and folly, gave ear to the counsels of Ma Shih-ying, and ordered that the Commander-in-chief should act only upon orders from Nanking. Meanwhile, he continued to squander money on revels and banquets, while the troops in the field were left insufficiently fed and clad.

In the spring of 1645, the dissensions between the rival parties at Court prevented the Commander-in-chief from carrying out any definite plan of campaign. In an eloquent and plain-spoken memorial he placed the facts before the Emperor. " Whilst Your Majesty is banqueting on choice viands," he wrote, " and quaffing wine from beakers of jade, it behoves you to remember your starving servants in the North. If, in spite of all his efforts, the late Emperor was unable to ward off disaster, how much more should you, inferior to him in ability, tremble as one who stands on the brink of a precipice. If you perform your duties with zeal and vigilance, it may be that your ancestors' spirits in Heaven will intercede with the Almighty on your behalf, and that your heritage may be regained. But if you remain in idle dalliance in Nanking, lavishing favours on sycophants and forgetful of the welfare of your troops, if you proclaim our secret plans from the housetops and fail to distinguish between loyal devotion and treason, if you show yourself so lacking in dignity that the worthy men about you are constrained to retire from official life, and the brave hesitate to serve you, then assuredly your ancestors will regard you as unworthy of their aid, and destruction, inevitable and final, will come upon you."

Just at this critical juncture the Court received word

that the people of Honan and Shantung had risen against the officials placed over them by Li Tzŭ-ch'eng, and were sending deputies to beg the Mings to restore their authority. Once more Shih pleaded with the Emperor: " Send now a message of sympathy to your subjects," he said, " that they may know that there is still a ruler in China. The people will then turn to you, and in time you will recover the lost North." The Emperor was pleased to follow this advice, and as a result General Yi, at the head of the Shensi troops, marched into Honan and recovered K'ai Feng-fu and Kuei Te-fu for the Mings. But the cabal against Shih, fearing to see him attain to power through such successes, were able, by their evil intrigues, to cut off his supplies. His supporters at Nanking were actively persecuted by Ma Shih-ying's party, and many were beheaded or banished, while the General's memorials were suppressed. Meanwhile, the Manchus were pressing down through Shantung, under the command of Prince Yü, a younger brother of the Regent and uncle of the boy Emperor Shun-chih.

Anxiously Shih K'o-fa waited, on the banks of the Huai, for the provisions and munitions of war which never came. At last, in despair, he sent a final memorial: " Since the catastrophe of last spring (1664) your ancestors' graves have been left untended, and chaos reigns throughout your Empire. Not a blow has Your Majesty struck in its defence. You forget that Nanking is but a temporary capital, and that it should be regarded only as a base from which to direct far-reaching operations against the Manchus. It is absurd to suppose that unless you take the offensive you will be suffered to remain there in peace. When you came to the Throne your troops were filled with martial spirit, but to-day all is changed. The army is starved, while your Court revels in luxury. Of a surety doom awaits you. My spies report that the flower of the Manchu army is advancing and that their fleets are speeding down the Grand Canal. All North of the Yellow River has been irrevocably lost, and here I sit by the Huai, disabled for want of provisions. Is our avenging army not to move a step? Will you leave the chastisement of the rebels to the Manchus? The Manchu Prince has dared to insult you, branding you with the name of usurper. He has treated your envoys with contumely. Between these invaders and us there can be no peace; we must meet them on the field of battle. I doubt whether we should be certain of victory even if we were to sink our ships in the stream and destroy our camps, determined to crush the foe or die in the attempt. How much more, then, is our case hopeless when those who should lead us stand idly by? A Sovereign must show resolution if the army is to show spirit. Let the Sovereign be lacking in decision and the army must needs be lacking in courage. Let not the flatterers who surround Your Majesty delude you further with fair words. It behoves you to issue orders that the troops shall be properly equipped for a long campaign, and that for bravery high rewards will be bestowed. Is this a time for lavishing honours on unworthy favourites, who should count themselves lucky that they have escaped execution? Fawning eunuchs intrigue to secure high office for themselves and for their *protégés*, while good men and true are forced out into obscurity.

"How can we march without food? You cannot stimulate men to brave deeds by words alone. Let the money in your treasury be now devoted to your army, and let your Palace festivities cease. Refuse all gifts of tribute and exercise thrift, even in your sacrificial rites. Until you have regained your capital, dalliance in the seraglio and at the banquet will bring no contentment to your jaded appetite. Our Manchu foes are watching your every action; if you amend not your ways the allegiance of your subjects will surely be forfeited. You should rise early and not till late seek rest, mindful ever of your forbears' achievements, and eager to avenge your predecessor's death. Only summon good men around you, and Heaven, relenting, may yet aid your cause. I, as a soldier, have no right to meddle in Court affairs, but where the Court is not pure, the army will surely fail in its duty."

This protest proved as unavailing as the rest; Ma Shih-ying's party was too busy persecuting and slaying its opponents to give heed to the dangers of the military situation. Feasts and theatricals were still the order of the day at Court; the Emperor abandoned himself to drinking and profligacy. The Manchu armies advanced in four divisions, and in April 1645 only the Yellow River separated their advance guard from Shih K'o-fa's outposts. His ablest lieutenant, General Yi, was treacherously murdered by a brother officer who deserted to the enemy; on all sides the Manchus were harrying the country. When at last the Throne gave Shih a free hand, it was too late. Then, as a rising broke out in Nanking itself, Shih was hurriedly summoned to come back to the rescue. He obeyed, leaving the road open to the Manchus to enter Kiangsu and Anhui.

So swiftly moved the Manchu cavalry that Shih had only just time to return from Nanking and Sochow and prepare Yang Chou-fu (the key to Nanking) against a siege. No sooner were his dispositions complete than Prince Yü's forces appeared upon the scene. A herald from the Prince came to demand his surrender. Shih cursed the messenger from the city wall. The envoy replied: "The fame of Your Excellency's loyal and eminent services is spread throughout China, yet the Ming Emperor does not give you his confidence. Why, then, not gain a name and a reward by joining the Manchus?" Shih angrily drew a bow upon him, but the shot missed its aim. Prince Yü was most sincerely anxious that so brave a man should not die in so bad a cause; he therefore delayed the bombardment of the city and made repeated efforts to get him to parley. All his efforts having proved futile, he ordered the assault.

Shih, foreseeing the inevitable end, gave orders that his body should be buried near to the mausoleum of the founder of the dynasty at Nanking. For eight days he maintained a splendid defence, doing great execution amongst the Manchus with his superior artillery of Jesuit manufacture. Finally the Manchus effected a breach in the north-west wall of the city and all was over. Shih called one of his officers and said: "The city is lost. Take, I pray you, your sword and kill me." This officer (named Chuang) obeyed, but his heart failed him, and the blow miscarried, so Shih seized the weapon and wounded himself with it in the throat. Here some of his men forcibly intervened, and putting him on a horse made to escape with him by the South Gate of the city. On reaching it they met a party of Manchus. Shih K'o-fa shouted: "I am the Grand Secretary Shih. Lead me to your Commander-in-chief." He was brought before Prince Yü, who said: "You have made a gallant defence. Before the siege I sent several letters to Your Excellency and you refused to negotiate. Now that you have done all that duty could dictate I would be glad to give you a high post. You shall be our Imperial Commissioner for the pacification of Nanking Province." Shih replied: "I ask of you no favour except death." The Prince persevered: "Do not you see," he said, "your former colleague, the Grand Secretary Hung Ch'eng-chou? He made his peace with us and now stands high in our councils." Shih answered with a smile: "Howsoever well you may treat Hung Ch'eng-chou, your kindness cannot outweigh the favours which he received from his late Emperor and mine. In failing to die with his master and in serving a new one he has proved himself disloyal. Such a man will never be loyal to any cause he serves. How can you expect me to imitate his behaviour? Sooner or later he will betray you."

Sadly the Prince bade them lead him away, to hold in custody. Repeated efforts were made to induce him to give in, but as he firmly refused, Prince Yü ordered his decapitation on the third day. He was hurriedly coffined by General Yi, but to this day no one knows the place of his burial. The story was current for many years amongst the dwindling remnants of the Mings that Shih was not beheaded, and that another was put to death in his place. Many years afterwards it was rumoured that he had taken the field against the Manchus in Anhui, but there was no truth in this.

Thus, faithful to the traditions of his caste, died a great soldier and an honest man. How strong were the temptations held out to him to betray his unworthy Sovereign, how many the arguments, which must even have appealed to him, against continuance of the struggle, may be gathered from the correspondence which took place between the Manchu Regent and General Shih in the autumn of the previous year, four months after the fall of Peking.

The Regent's first letter was as follows: "Long ago, at Moukden, I had heard of your high reputation in Peking as a scholar,[1] and since our victories over the rebels I have taken occasion to find out all about you in the literary circles of the metropolis. Some little time ago I sent you a letter of kindly inquiry and sympathy by the hand of your brother, but I know not if you received it. Reports have now reached us that the Ming dynasty has re-established itself at Nanking, and that a new Emperor has been chosen. Now, we are taught that a man may not live under the same sky with the murderer of his father or Sovereign. Furthermore, the "Spring and Autumn

[1] Shih was a native of Peking.

Annals" state that a Sovereign's obsequies may not be recorded so long as his murderer remains unpunished, neither can the new ruler's accession be considered to have taken place. The principle involved is vital, since its object is to minimise the frequency of rebellions.

"That traitor, Li Tzŭ-ch'eng, the 'Prince Harrier,' captured Peking and caused the death of your Emperor and of his kinsmen, whilst scarcely one of his Chinese subjects ventured to draw bow in his defence. One man alone, Wu San-kuei, on your eastern boundary, came in loyal indignation to entreat our succour. In recognition of long-subsisting friendship between our States, and regardless of outstanding differences, we arrayed a host of gallant warriors, and the rebel horde of dogs and rats was swept before us in a panic-stricken rout.

"After capturing Peking we proceeded forthwith to canonise your late Sovereigns, and arranged for their burial in due accordance with the rites of ceremonial observance. We left to your surviving Princes and high officials their original ranks, treating them all with the utmost commiseration and generosity. Our troops were not allowed to loot; the markets remained open as usual, and the husbandman continued to till his fields in peace.

"We had planned, now that the cool weather of autumn has come upon us, to send a punitive expedition, composed of levies from all parts, to pursue Li Tzŭ-ch'eng into his western retreat, and to pay off your accumulated grudges against him—thus displaying our dynasty's magnanimity. Who could have dreamed that you, worthy gentleman, should be so short-sighted as to seek the temporary continuance of your dynasty in Nanking? I greatly deplore that you should be thus blind to visible dangers, and permit yourself to cherish vain and deceptive illusions.

"When our dynasty captured Peking it was not the Ming dynasty which was defeated by our armies, but the rebel Prince Li Tzŭ-ch'eng, who had violated your ancestral temple and desecrated your Emperor's remains. To avenge *your* disgrace we spared no expense, and even imposed heavy taxes on our own subjects. Surely it behoves all good men and true to be grateful and repay this our benevolence! Nevertheless, you have taken advantage of the respite which we have granted to our war-weary hosts, before continuing the pursuit of the rebels, to establish your forces at Nanking. No doubt you hope to follow the example of the fisherman in the fable, who, seeing the oyster-catcher with the oyster fastened on its beak, rushed forward, hoping to seize both bird and oyster. Can such conduct be deemed reasonable or just? Perchance, forsooth, you fondly imagine that the Yangtsze is a natural barrier which will prove insuperable to our forces; you hope that we shall not succeed in 'stemming its current, even though we block it with our whips.'[1] The rebel 'Prince Harrier' had given no offence to our dynasty; it was the Ming dynasty which he had scourged and overthrown. When we smote him it was because of our sense of humanity and our natural longing to avenge a universal wrong.

"But if to-day a rival Emperor enthrones himself at Nanking, there will be two suns in the firmament. This must not be. Do you not see, moreover, that you are playing into 'Prince Harrier's' hands? Is it not clear that we shall have to recall our levies from their expedition against him and dispatch them instead against yourselves? In this way he will escape his well-deserved chastisement, while you will become the victims of our wrath.

"It needs no diviner's skill in augury to foretell that the destruction of your poor remnant by the hands of our victorious armies is sure and inevitable, seeing that, whilst still masters of China, you were forced to bow the knee before a rebel horde. You should face the situation and

[1] A classical reference to Fu Chien, who in the fourth century A.D. uttered a bombastic boast to this effect.

yield to the fortune of war. Your best **way of showing** loyalty to your late master and devotion to the Prince his successor is to advise the latter to renounce his Imperial title, and, as Prince of the Ming blood royal, continue to enjoy our perpetual favour. Our dynasty proposes to assign to him suitable revenues and residence, and will treat him as an honoured descendant of the dispossessed dynasty. I undertake that the highest honours shall be lavished upon him by our Imperial bounty, that precedence shall be accorded to him over all Princes at our Court, and that his posterity shall be accorded similar hereditary privileges until the Yellow River shrinks to the width of a girdle and Mount T'ai to the size of a whetstone. Our dynasty desires to be faithful to the motive which inspired us in subduing the rebels, and to act in harmony with the spirit which saves the fallen from destruction and renews a lineage extinct.

"As for yourself and other distinguished worthies of the South, if you will repair to our Court and do obeisance before the Manchu Throne you will be rewarded with the highest hereditary ranks and rich fiefs. Is not our treatment of Wu San-kuei an earnest of our good intentions towards you?

"Only let Your Excellency consider wherein lies the way of advantage. Now-a-days, many scholars and statesmen are apt to forget their duty to the people in their desire to win for themselves fame as men of unwavering principles. When a catastrophe occurs they are paralysed, and resemble the man who sought to build a house by asking the casual advice of unknown passers-by. Remember the example of the Sung dynasty, whose rulers were busy arguing academic points even when the Mongol invaders had crossed the Yangtsze and were knocking at the gates of their capital. You, Sir, are the wisest of your contemporaries and must know full well in what direction the dictates of prudence should lead you.

Rather than allow yourself to be carried away by the current, or influenced by those who trim their sails to the passing breeze, surely you will determine on a consistant and statesmanlike course, and then stick to it without swerving a hair's breadth.

"Our troops are ready to march against you if needs must be; everything now depends on your decision. I hope that you will share my desire to complete the destruction of Li Tzǔ-ch'eng, and that you will not cling stubbornly to the fleeting emoluments which you now enjoy, so as to involve your old dynasty in irretrievable disaster. I beseech you to avoid becoming the laughing-stock of rebels and traitors. This is my earnest prayer. In the Book of Rites it is written : 'Only the superior man can fully appreciate good advice.' Therefore I lay bare my inmost heart and respectfully await your decision. Across the Yangtsze's flood I turn in spirit to Your Excellency and entreat your early reply. There is still much which remains unsaid."

To this dignified appeal Shih K'o-fa replied, in words no less eloquent, as follows: " Shih K'o-fa, Commander-in-chief of the great Ming dynasty, President of the Board of War and a Grand Secretary of the Eastern Throne-hall, prostrating himself respectfully before Your Highness, the Regent of the great Manchu dynasty, has the honour to reply as follows : On receipt of your valued favour, I sent it at once to General Wu in order that I might take his opinion. I hesitated to indite an immediate reply, not because I failed to appreciate your kindness in writing to me, but out of regard for the principle enunciated in the " Spring and Autumn " classic, that a Minister of one State ought not to carry on secret correspondence with the representative of another.

"At a time of urgent military preparation like the present, your elegantly worded composition is indeed a godsend, and I have perused it again and again, full of admiration for the sentiments which it conveys. It fills me with gratitude and at the same time with shame that your great nation should have occasion to deplore the delays which have occurred in destroying that parricide and rebel, Li Tzŭ-ch'eng. But I desire to make a few remarks regarding your lightly-uttered statement that we, officials and people of the great Ming dynasty, are forgetful of the outrages inflicted on the late Emperor, and have sinned against his memory in proclaiming His present Majesty at our 'temporary retreat,' south of the Yangtsze.

"His departed Majesty was a wise and just ruler who obeyed Heaven and followed the behests of his ancestors, in constant affection for his subjects and in the faithful performance of his duty. The disaster of the 19th day of the 3rd Moon, when Peking fell, was due to the infatuate errors of his Ministers, and I was too far away at my post in the south to bring up reinforcements to his succour. The sorrowful tidings of his death reached me at my camp on the Huai, whilst I was hurrying north. Heaven was rent and the earth shaken by this monstrous catastrophe; the waves of the sea wept in unison, and the trees withered on the hills. Breathes there the man who does not love his Sovereign? Though my body were hacked to pieces in the market place, still, because of this disaster, my soul must bear its heavy burden of guilt, and never can I dare to look His late Majesty in the face in the realms below.

"The grief of his officials and people in the South was like that of orphans mourning for their parents, and we burned to avenge our Emperor by drawing sword against the traitor who had caused his death. But it seemed good to our eldest and wisest statesman to place a new Emperor on the Throne, not only for the sake of the ancestral shrines and the tutelary deities, but to satisfy the desire of the nation. His present Majesty is the grandson of Wan Li, the nephew of that Monarch's successor, and cousin to His late Majesty. He is of the direct line, his accession is meet and proper, and he has found favour with Heaven and with his people. When he entered Nanking, on the 1st of the 5th Moon, his subjects lined the roads and welcomed the Imperial chariot with thunderous acclaim. His Ministers besought him to mount the Imperial Throne, but he hesitated at first to comply, and assumed the title of Regent. It was only in response to repeated petitions from his subjects that at last he declared himself Emperor. On that eventful day nature wore a garb of joy, and prestiges were not wanting of an auspicious reign. As the smoke of the incense ascended to Heaven at the ancestral sacrifice the worshippers felt that the Almighty had vouchsafed His approval.

"A few days after His Majesty's accession he bade me take up my command North of the Yangtsze and prepare to march against Li Tzŭ-ch'eng. It was then that the tidings reached us that our Generalissimo, Wu San-kuei, had borrowed aid from your great nation, and that the rebel host had been completely routed. We learned that you had given fitting burial to the remains of Their Majesties, and that you had purged the Palace of the polluting presence of the usurper. By pacifying the people's alarms and by cancelling the edict which had enjoined the shaving of the head[1] you showed a respect for our dynastic usages, and your generosity will be enshrined for all time in our history. Not a subject of the great Ming dynasty but kneels in gratitude, rendering willing obeisance from a full heart for this kind deed. Surely your letter errs grievously when you remind us of our duty ' to cherish gratitude, and thus to repay your benevolence.'

"So little do we need this reminder that on the 8th Moon of this year I dispatched an envoy bearing a number of trifling gifts to be distributed as largesse to your victorious forces, and I directed him to submit to you proposals for

[1] This cancellation was only temporary.

a joint expedition westward against the rebels. I waited with my troops on the banks of the River Huai, solely because I wished to learn your intentions in the matter.

"The letter which I have had the honour to receive takes me to task for violating the principles laid down by Confucius concerning succession to the Throne. I admire the aptness of your allusion, but Confucius was only referring to the deaths of feudal Princes who had perished by assassination. In such cases it was deemed unseemly for the son and successor to announce his accession, either to his suzerain or to his fellow Princes, until his father's murder had been avenged. But the Sage never meant this to apply to a case in which the Sovereign Lord of the whole Empire had committed suicide for the sake of the altars of his gods, his family having already come to a cruel end. In such a case, slavish adherence to the letter of the principle in question would show callous indifference to the interests of the Empire as a whole, and would assuredly plunge our ancient State in the horrors of anarchy and civil war. For a supreme ruler is needed to inspire the nation with courage and patriotism; without one no national spirit could exist, nor could the army be rallied to fresh efforts. Historical instances of the truth of this will readily occur to Your Highness; I need scarcely quote them here. When the Sung Emperor Ch'en Tsung (A.D. 1126) was carried into captivity by the Chen Tartars, together with his father, the ex-Emperor, his brother was at once elected to the Throne, because it was felt that it could not safely stand empty for a single day. History has approved of this principle, and has recognised that in no other way can the fortunes of the State be preserved.

The sixteen Emperors of our Ming dynasty have, each in his turn, exercised a civilising influence, and have enabled the remotest nations to benefit by their self-sacrificing magnanimity. They have restored princedoms and treated their vassals with unfailing generosity. You Manchus, who have for generations figured on the roll of our feudatories, can scarcely fail to be aware of these facts, since you, too, have been nurtured by our Throne's wide-embracing and enfolding protection. The fact that our two nations had been at enmity for a generation was brought about by wicked plotters, whom His late Majesty visited with condign punishment.

"You may well be proud of your action in hastening so loyally to suppress the rebel invasion, and in coming to the rescue of our dynasty. It has been worthy of the principles of Confucius, and deserves to be remembered for all time.

"In olden days, when the Ketans made peace with the Sungs, annual gifts of gold and silks were sent by the latter, but that did not mean that the Ketans acquired any territorial advantages from the Sungs. How much more, then, should this be the case with your great nation, which has loudly proclaimed its altruistic intentions, and which has moved with troops to our succour simply and solely (for so you have assured us) out of regard for the friendly feeling existing between our States from time immemorial.

"If now, taking advantage of our misfortunes, you covet our territory and hope to benefit yourselves by annexing portions of our dominions, you will be open to the reproach that your good intentions were but transient, and that your actions, which began in good feeling, have ended in unrighteous cupidity. Then may the rebels even despise you, as being no better than themselves! I am reluctant to believe this of you Manchus.

"His late Majesty was far too tender-hearted in dealing with the rebellion; he could not bear to employ drastic methods in suppressing it. It is because of his adoption of this lenient policy that the Mings have been brought to their present evil pass. The present Emperor's one thought is to avenge the wrongs of his predecessor, and all our statesmen are of the same mind, while thousands of volunteers have rallied to the flag, burning to wipe out this national disgrace.

"It is my confident hope that 'Prince Harrier's' tether is a short one. The proverb says: 'Let your good actions breed successors, but pull up evil by the root.' At this moment, however, the traitor has escaped to his Shensi lair and still awaits Heaven-sent retribution. Nay, my spies tell me that he still hopes to regain the territory he has lost, and is even now preparing to strike a fresh blow. This is not only a disgrace to our dynasty, but is scarcely calculated to give your nation satisfaction, since your efforts have only met with partial success.

"I beg, therefore, that you will now complete what you have so well begun, and arrange with us plans for a joint punitive campaign into Shensi, where we may have the joy of seeing the traitor's head roll in the dust. In this way you Manchus will have set the crowning achievement on your glorious work, and we shall do what in us lies to reward you. Hereafter, our two nations shall dwell together as neighbours, in perpetual amity. How splendid to think that peace can never again be broken between Chinese and Manchu!

"Our dynasty's ambassador is now on his way, and should soon reach Peking, where the terms of a treaty may be negotiated at leisure. Looking northward towards the mausolea of our mighty ancestors my eyes can weep no more, for lack of tears, and I feel that I deserve to die the death. My only reason for not following my late master to the other world was that I still hoped to render some service to the State. It is written: 'Strain every energy for your country whilst life lasts; be loyal and fear not.' My one desire is to be privileged to lose my life in the performance of my duty. May this aspiration be fulfilled.

THE COURT OF PEKING

I would beg Your Highness to be pleased to peruse the above. Hung Kuang,[1] 9th Moon, 15th day.

"*Postcriptum.*—If I do not hear from you, I intend to cross the Huai with my whole force and expel the rebel horde of dogs and rats from their lairs, that the glories of old may be restored to our Empire, and that the benefits bestowed upon me by His late Majesty, now in Heaven, may in some measure be requited. Finally, I would observe that it is unseemly for the Minister of one State to have private intercourse with the ruler of another, and I treat with the contempt of silence your ignoble endeavour to lure me with promises of rewards and dignities."

This correspondence between the Manchu Regent and the loyalist General is cited to this day by Chinese scholars as a model of the best classical traditions; even for those who read it in another language it carries conviction and an irresistible appeal, telling its own story of the dignity and wisdom which underlie the weather-beaten but unconquered philosophy of China's Sages.

But for the humanitarian, admiration of this stoic philosophy halts before its consequences, as we see them reflected in the unspeakable misery of the masses. The Regent's shrewd indictment of Shih K'o-fa's attitude was justified by every humane instinct, when he said that "scholars and statesmen were apt to forget their duty to the people in their desire to win for themselves fame as men of unswerving principles." Both he and Shih K'o-fa were sincerely anxious for peace, anxious to avert from the innocent community of toilers the awful calamities of war; but neither was prepared to buy immunity for the people by the surrender of his own rigid principles. Let us turn now from the arguments of the leaders to contemplate the consequences of their differences as reflected in the lives and deaths of the "stupid people."

[1] The Ming dynastic title of the new Emperor, "Distinguished Glory."

CHAPTER VII

THE SACK OF YANG CHOU-FU

The history of China, ancient and modern, is a series of paroxysms; its keynote is bloodshed and famine, periods of peace and prosperity purchased by the slaughter of countless innocents. Its splendid civilisation, based on an unassailable moral philosophy and the canons of the Sages, has ever proved powerless against the inexorable laws of nature, against the pitiless cruelty of the struggle for life, intensified by a social system which inculcates procreative recklessness and passive fatalism. Under Mongols, Mings and Manchus the stern retributive law and its fulfilment have ever been the same, history always repeating itself, at the passing of dynasties, with fearful monotony of wholesale massacres.

The following narrative of the sack of Yang Chou-fu by the Manchus in 1645 was written by one (his name is unknown) who was himself a victim and an eye-witness of those fearful days of slaughter, and of events which may be taken as normal at times of conquest and civil strife in Far Eastern lands. The blood lust of the victorious Manchus was no more fierce than that of the Mongols before them, or, for that matter, of the Chinese of to-day. Throughout all the recorded history of the Empire, these ruthless massacres of non-combatants have been an accepted feature of the sorry scheme of things; a deliberate, cold-blooded, almost instinctive fulfilment of the law which prescribes the survival of the fittest, amongst a people with whom the problem of daily bread is ever insistently insoluble. Compared with the most merciless butcheries of ancient and modern times in Europe, with the worst excesses of " Kirke's lambs " or Alva's butchers, the slaughter of Orientals by Orientals lacks the factors of religious and political hatred which often explain the extermination of whole communities. Yet another feature, common to these pitiful records of Chinese cities left desolate, is the complete lack of resistance on the part of their inhabitants—a few thousands of savage soldiery let loose, without discipline or military cohesion, upon a walled city of a million inhabitants, will convert it almost methodically into a shambles, their terror-stricken victims awaiting death with abject helplessness.

Yang Chou-fu, on the Grand Canal in Kiangsu, has always been an important city. Strategically, before the days of railways, it was the gate of the southern capital, Nanking, for invaders from the north.[1] Its ancient walls are some four miles in circumference, and in olden days, when the Grand Canal was the great artery of trade between the Yangtsze and North China, it boasted great wealth and a large population. Before the Manchu invasion, it had suffered, as all Central China had suffered, from the disorders of Li Tzŭ-ch'eng's rebellion and the general unrest brought about by the chaotic condition of affairs in Peking; but until 1644 the tide of civil war had flowed northwards, and though the cities of the plain had paid for it in silver, there had been but little bloodshed in their streets. After the fall of Peking and the collapse of the Mings before the rebel forces of Li Tzŭ-ch'eng, came the swift turning of the tide; Li's great army, routed by Wu San-kuei and the Manchus, fled southwards and west, while the fugitive Mings established their Court at Nanking, and gathered together their shattered forces to prevent the Manchus crossing the Yangtsze.

In 1644, when the Manchu armies began their invasion

[1] In 1282 Kublai Khan conferred upon Marco Polo the governorship of the city.

and subjugation of the South, the population of Yang Chou-fu was estimated at over a million. Lying on the direct route of the invaders to Nanking, it was held for the Mings by their ablest General, Shih K'o-fa, and garrisoned with an army of about 40,000 men. If Prince Fu, heir to the throne of the Mings, had not been hopelessly dissolute and incapable, if he and his advisers at the Court of Nanking had given General Shih the loyal support he deserved, the Manchus would probably never have reached the Yangtsze. But (as we have shown elsewhere) the Court was wholly engrossed in licentious pleasures, its scanty revenues wasted in wine-bibbing and play acting, its forces in the field unprovided with the necessaries of life and materials of war. Shih K'o-fa had been obliged to detach part of the garrison of Yang Chou-fu at a most critical moment to protect a store of ammunition and equipment, which he had been compelled to leave behind him on his forced march from Soochow. Even so, he might have destroyed the army of the invaders before the investment of the city, had he been willing to cut the banks of the Huai River and flood the country. But Shih was a scholar and a humane man, and preferred the risks of war to the infliction of enduring misery on vast numbers of his fellow countrymen. He might have saved himself, his army and the city had he been willing to entertain the advances made to him by the Manchu Regent and forsake the cause of the Mings. But hoping against hope for reinforcements and final victory he remained at his post, and met with a dignified refusal the Regent's offers to confer wealth and honour upon him as the price of disloyalty. He took a terrible responsibility, and he paid the price of high failure, and with him more than half a million men, women and children, " went to their graves like beds."

The diary from which the following narrative is taken is dated the 4th Moon of the " Yi Yu " year (1645):

"On the 14th day of the Yi Yu year it was reported to General Shih K'o-fa, the Commander-in-chief, by his staff, that Yang Ho (on the Huai River) had fallen, and our garrison prepared for a siege. Soldiers were quartered in every house; a certain Colonel Yang and his men were billeted on me. Their discipline was very bad; we had to supply them with everything, and their keep cost us several strings of cash per day. As their demands became ever more importunate, I invited Colonel Yang to a banquet, and seized the opportunity to beg him to keep his men in better order. After this we were somewhat less disturbed. The Colonel enjoyed listening to the flute, and we called in some singing-girls to entertain his men.

"There was fierce fighting on the walls and around the city for ten days and nights,[1] and we all hoped that the garrison would repel the enemy. But one evening, while we were having quite a lively party at our house, orders from the Commander-in-chief were suddenly brought to Colonel Yang. He read the note, turned deathly pale and hurried out on to the city wall. Our party broke up, every one wondering what evil tidings were in store for us. Next morning all the walls of the city were placarded with a proclamation from General Shih K'o-fa, saying: 'I alone will bear the brunt; none of you blameless people shall pay the penalty.'

"I felt quite reassured and touched by these good words. Later in the day every one's spirits rose, for news came in that our men had been victorious in a heavy skirmish outside the city. That afternoon my married cousin came in from Kua-chou in order to escape from the lawlessness of General Li's dispersed troops. My wife was delighted to see her, and the two women were chatting away, when suddenly rumours began to circulate that the Manchus were in the city. I made immediate inquiries, and at first came to the conclusion that the troops who had

---

[1] Other chronicles say that the siege lasted seven days.

come in were those of the Marquis Huang Te-kung, our own General, the more so as our guards on the city wall showed no signs of panic. On reaching the main street, however, I met crowds of men, women and children, many of them barefooted and half naked, all rushing wildly along. To my inquiries they could make no clear replies, all muttering and gibbering incoherently. Next I observed a small party of horsemen desperately galloping towards the South Gate of the city. They passed like a torrent in flood, but I had time to notice that the person they were escorting was none other than General Shih K'o-fa himself. They had tried to leave by the East Gate, but finding that the Manchus held it already outside, were hoping to escape by the South. The General was wounded,[1] and had been forced to leave by his bodyguard.

"Next I saw another of the Ming Generals riding northwards, evidently intending to surrender to the enemy. His face wore a look of misery such as I never wish to behold again. By this time the troops on the wall had begun to throw away their weapons and were tearing off the badges from their uniforms. Many of them were severely hurt in the crush and confusion as they rushed from the wall; soon the section adjoining my house was quite deserted. General Shih had erected gun-platforms on a level with the wall, because it was too narrow for artillery purposes; these platforms were reached from the roofs below by a sloping gangway of planks lashed together. The Manchus gained the wall near the North Gate, and came rushing along it, sword in hand, driving our men before them. On reaching the gun-platform adjoining my house, crowds of them, pursuers and pursued, came down it helter-skelter; the gangway collapsed beneath them, and a score or more were killed. Those who succeeded in reaching the roofs engaged in fierce hand-to-hand fighting, making a din most terrifying to the

[1] He had endeavoured to commit suicide by cutting his throat.

occupants of the house, cowering in the rooms beneath. My courtyard was filled with routed soldiery and panic-stricken refugees, who listened in terror to the fierce yells of the Manchus. I had no means of preventing these fugitives from entering my premises; even the women's quarters were full of them. From a window at the back of my house I observed a body of troops marching towards the south-west of the city. They seemed well disciplined, and at first I hoped they were some of our own men. At this moment there came a sound of knocking at my gate. A few neighbours had come to suggest that we should join them in preparing a welcome to the Manchu invaders, and that we should burn incense in token of allegiance to our new Emperor. As matters stood I dared not refuse to join in these preparations, so hurriedly we put on our ceremonial robes and shaved our heads in the Manchu fashion. This done, we waited a long while, but no Manchu Prince put in an appearance. The fight in my courtyard was now over, and about a dozen soldiers lay dead upon the ground. The Manchus had passed on to other parts of the city.

" As I looked out from my window I saw a few soldiers coming and going; in a little while there came a troop of them escorting a bevy of gaudily clad women—women belonging to this city, of evil repute. At the spectacle a sudden thought struck me, and I went to my women-folk and said: 'The city has fallen; you must be ready to commit suicide and thus escape outrage.' All the women agreed, and handed me their ornaments and their money, saying: 'Keep them; we don't expect to live more than a few hours at most.'

" Next I saw a small party of horsemen riding slowly from the North; every person whom they met they stopped, demanding money. These men were not extravagant in their demands, and if they were refused they would prod their captive with swords, but not so as to hurt him seriously. (I heard afterwards that a Yang-chou man had treacherously conducted this party to the house of a rich merchant, who had paid ten thousand taels as ransom, but had nevertheless been murdered.)

"When they came near to my house one of the horsemen pointed to me (I had come out and was standing in the court); 'Search that fellow in the blue gown,' he shouted to one of his comrades, who at once dismounted; but I was too quick for him and rushed inside. The men rode away laughing. I wondered why they should wish to search me, as I was clad in the garments of a rustic. At this moment my two brothers came up and, discussing the point, we concluded that, as this part of the city was chiefly inhabited by wealthy merchants, they had suspected my disguise. I therefore decided to remove all the family from my house and take refuge in that of my second eldest brother. My two brothers and the women all made their way thither by unfrequented alleys. Just at the back of my brother's house were some of the slums of the city, a quarter known as the 'Graveyard of the Ho family.' Meantime, I remained behind in my own house to see what would happen. All of a sudden my eldest brother came running back to tell me that the main street was running with blood, and that if I stayed where I was I should surely be murdered. 'Come with us; we can at least all die together in our brother's house.' At that, I took the ancestral tablets from their shrine and went with my brother. We were all together in his house, a party of ten: four of us brothers (two older and one younger than myself) my wife and little son, my sister-in-law, my nephew and my wife's brother and sister.

"As evening drew on we could hear more and more clearly the shouts of the Manchus at their hellish work of butchery. It was pouring with rain, but that did not stop them. Hoping to escape detection we all lay out on the flat roof of an outhouse under the heavy rain, covered with a large felt plaid, which soon became soaked. The death-cries of wounded and dying men, of women and children, rang in our ears and made our blood run cold. Not till midnight did we dare to come from our hiding-place and make for the kitchen, where we managed to kindle a fire and boil a little rice. By this time flames were bursting out all over the city; several of our neighbours' houses had been burnt to the ground; the total number thus destroyed must have run into thousands. The night was as light as day; the tumult and the shouting were incessant. Every now and then we could hear curses in Manchu, blended with some woman's frantic appeal for mercy. We tried to eat, but our chopsticks refused to carry the food to our mouths. We could think of no way of escape; my wife took some ingots of silver and divided them amongst us four brothers. We hid them in our top-knots, in our boots and loin-cloths. My wife also found for me an old robe and a pair of frayed shoes, which she bade me wear.

" All night we sat desperate, awaiting the end, and dared not close our eyes. A bird in the room sang without ceasing; its notes sounded like a clarion. Close at hand I heard a child sobbing, but could not locate it. As dawn broke, the conflagrations seemed to die down. I mounted a ladder and concealed myself in the loft. We all crouched on some boards by the ceiling, when suddenly, from the eastern side, a man's head appeared. He climbed in by one ladder and rushed down another, but the Manchu trooper who followed him, paused when he saw us and gave over his pursuit, coming towards me instead. In my terror I too rushed down the ladder and out into the street, followed by my two brothers. We ran at least a hundred yards, but stopped on finding we were not being pursued. For the time being I lost sight of my wife, and knew not whether she lived or died.

" The cruel soldiery, to save themselves the trouble

of hunting for their victims, posted notices telling the people that if they surrendered they would be given badges guaranteeing them their lives, but if they hid themselves and were caught they would be killed. Many people gave themselves up in consequence. As my brother and I were standing in the street we saw a group of fifty or sixty persons, half of them women, a little further on, and my brother said : ' If we hide and are discovered we shall certainly be killed. We are only four helpless men, so we had better surrender and join that group over there. By so doing we may possibly find a means of escape, and if not, at least we shall have the satisfaction of perishing in a general massacre.'

" I was far too terrified to suggest any better course, so we went and joined the group, expecting to receive our badges of safety. The Manchus searched my brothers and took away all their money, but oddly enough they left me alone. At this moment some women came up, and one of them spoke to me. I recognised her at once; the second concubine of my old friend Chu Shu, but I begged her not to draw attention to me. She was in a pitiable condition, her hair all dishevelled, her breasts exposed, and her legs besmeared to the knees with mud. Another concubine had a girl baby in arms, but the troops first flogged her and then threw her down in the mud. Then some more soldiers came forward, collected the women and began tying them together at the knees, like a string of pearls. We were then marched off in a body, one man with a sword leading the way and another on either side to prevent any one escaping, just as if they were driving sheep to market. At every step we took we saw dead bodies lying in agonised attitudes, babies who had been crushed to shapelessness beneath the hoofs of horses, women with their new-born babes by the roadside all beaten to a pulp. The streets reeked like a shambles, here and there one heard the groans of a few dying wretches. Arms and legs protruded from every ditch, inextricably mingled.

"We were taken to the house of Colonel Yao Yung-yen, entering it by the back door. Every room that I saw was full of corpses, and I said to myself that mine would surely be added to their number. However, there were no Manchu butchers at work there for the time being, and after passing through several courtyards we were brought out through the front of the building. Thence we were led to the house of a Shansi merchant, one Ch'iao Cheng-wang, the headquarters of the men who were our captors. As we entered I noticed a soldier mounting guard over three comely females. The floor was strewn deep with valuable silks and furs. Our three guards laughed loudly at the sight and then drove us, a party of fifty, into the back room, while they placed the women in an inner apartment. In the room into which we were driven three seamstresses were sitting at work. One of them was about thirty-five, and very smartly dressed. She was a native of Yang-chou, and seemed perfectly happy, chaffing the soldiers merrily. Her behaviour was wanton in the extreme; as I watched her making eyes at the men I heard one of the Manchus say: 'During the Korean campaign hardly a woman bought her life at the price of her virtue. Who would have believed that the inhabitants of this great Empire of China could be as shameless as this wench?'

"Then the soldiers began undressing the women who had accompanied us; they stripped them of their wet apparel and made them stand up stark naked before us all. The seamstress was called in and told to measure them for fresh clothes. The women were too much afraid of the soldiers to attempt to hide their nakedness with their hands. When they had all been dressed in new clothes they were supplied with meat and drink, and the soldiers began making love to them. Most of them yielded readily enough to the solicitations of their captors.

"Next one of the Manchus began brandishing his sword and shouted: 'Come here, you Chinese savages.' They then bound all of us who were in the front row with cords, including my eldest brother. My second brother called out to me: 'It's all up with us; what's the use of talking?' He seized my hand and led me forward; my younger brother followed. We were bound, some fifty of us in all, and the Manchus led us out into the courtyard, yelling like savages. Then the butchery began: Every one was struck dumb with terror, and I stood there and watched it for a few moments, awaiting my turn. At first I looked forward to death calmly enough, but suddenly I felt as if aid had been vouchsafed to me from some supernatural power. Bound as I was, I managed to creep away unnoticed, and reached one of the back rooms of the house, where I freed myself from my bonds. I found that I was in the women's quarters, where there were still some of the older women who had been unable to escape.

"At the back of this part of the house the Manchu horses and pack camels were stabled, completely blocking all chance of egress. Creeping on hands and knees, I managed to crawl under the beasts, any one of which might have trampled me to a jelly. After getting past them I found the walls too high for escape in that direction, but to my left there was a passage leading to a postern door. This door—half way down the passage—was nailed securely, so I went some distance up the passage, where I could distinctly hear the groans of my dying comrades and the shouts of their executioners. Passing the kitchen, I saw four men at work there. They had been pressed into the job by the Manchus, and I implored them to let me join them as hewer of wood or drawer of water. They angrily refused, saying: 'We four have been specially assigned to this duty; if the Manchus find an extra hand here they will suspect us of conspiracy, and we shall all be killed.' As I continued to beseech them they pushed me out, driving me forth with a carving knife.

"I then rushed back to the door leading out of the passage and pulled at it with all my might. I seized the support in the socket of which the door was inserted, and with a stupendous effort managed to pull it out. With bleeding fingers I tried to push the door open, but it was still effectually closed from the outside by a heavy beam. The long spell of wet weather had caused it to stick fast in its socket, and I could not move it. But as I pushed and pulled, by great good luck the top hinge of the door gave way, and it fell outwards with a heavy crash.

"Again some unseen power seemed to aid me, and I was through the postern door in a flash. The spot at which I emerged was at the foot of the city wall, and some scouts made signs to me to advance no further, so I made my way into a house just beyond the one I had left. Every room in it was full of refugees in hiding, except the gate-house, which looked out on to the main street, and which was so often visited by soldiers that no one had ventured to go there.

"There was a corner in this gate-house behind a very high cupboard, into which I managed to climb. As I waited, scarcely daring to breathe, I heard an agonised voice, which I recognised all too well, the voice of my younger brother begging for mercy. A sound of blows followed, and then I heard my second eldest brother cry: 'I have money buried in my cellar at home. Let me go and I will bring it to you.' After that all was silence, and my heart seemed to cease beating. I felt as if my brain were on fire; the tears refused to well from my eyes, and my bowels were rent asunder. My tongue clove to my mouth, and I think I lost consciousness. Shortly afterwards a soldier came in, dragging a woman with him.

THE COURT OF PEKING

He ordered her to lie with him on the couch; when she refused, he forced her until she was compelled to yield.

"My own position was now one of extreme peril. Seizing the first opportunity, I managed to climb from the cupboard, which was open at the top, on to the cross-beam of the loft above. It was as black as pitch up there; and every now and then soldiers passing by would look in and prod the loft matting above their heads with their long spears. Hearing no sound, they concluded it was empty. I lay up there all that day; during that time about a score of persons were murdered in the room beneath me. Out in the street I could hear sounds of horsemen riding by, with shrieking women in their train. There was no rain that day, but the sky was overcast.

"As the day drew to its close there were fewer soldiers about, but the wailing of homeless refugees served to remind me of my two brothers' pitiful deaths. I wondered if my wife and son still lived and if so, where they might be hiding. As the night fell I crept down from my loft and went out into the street. The road was full of people crouching in attitudes of despair, some stooping over corpses and calling them by name. Seeing torches moving towards me, I hurriedly made down a side lane towards the city wall. Here the piles of corpses made progress difficult, and I stumbled over them again and again. It took me three hours, from eight o'clock to eleven, to reach my eldest brother's house. He, with my wife and child, were there before me; I could not bear to tell them of the death of our two brothers.

"I asked my wife how she had escaped. She replied: 'When the soldiers were driving us along, I was ahead of the rest and somehow or other escaped attention. Carrying Peng'rh in my arms I got away and hid myself in a cellar. My sister could not come with me; she had sprained her ankle, and a soldier was carrying her in his arms. My hiding-place was soon discovered, and we were taken to a room in which there were some thirty or forty men and women, all bound. My captor gave me into the charge of one of the women jailers. In the meantime, my sister had been carried away and I saw her no more. After a while, as the soldiers did not come back, I persuaded the women jailers to allow me to escape. They did so, and outside I met Mrs. Hung (a relative of her brother's), who brought me here.'

" I then told them my experiences. While I was speaking Mrs. Hung came in and brought some rice, but none of us could eat. Fires were again breaking out all over the city; by their light one could see a long distance. Back of the Ho family's graveyard there were groups of people lying about under the trees, and the sound of wailing mothers and children was most pitiful to hear. My wife said she wished to kill herself; we talked together all through the night, and I dissuaded her for the present. In the morning she led me to the end of a winding passage, where there was a room full of coffins awaiting burial. Here I crouched down in some straw and hid, after placing the child in one of the coffins and covering him with matting. My wife concealed herself in front. I dared not move hand or foot, and soon my limbs were completely numbed. All day we could hear the voices of soldiers cursing, and the pitiful entreaties of their victims. A southerner before a Manchu was like a sheep in the hands of the butcher; hardly any attempted even to escape. Towards evening I peeped out and counted over a hundred dead bodies in that one courtyard.

" Little Peng'rh slept on the top of the coffin right through that terrible day, and never stirred but once, when I wetted his lips with water which I brought in a hollow tile from the ditch outside. As evening came on Mrs. Hung came again, and with her we returned to the room in which we had passed the night. She told me that my sister-in-law had been carried off, together with my little nephew, an infant in arms. We counted them both for dead, which made four deaths in my family in two days.

"I tried to procure a little rice, but without success. My brother and I talked together all that night. Thrice my wife attempted suicide, but each time Mrs. Hung prevented her. Then my brother said: 'We are not all likely to survive another day. I am still unhurt. Give me the child now and let me try to escape with him.' I agreed, and my brother left us.

"Mrs. Hung advised my wife to hide in her cupboard, proposing to change places with her. However, we went back to our coffin room. A party of Manchu soldiers entered the house shortly afterwards, and discovering Mrs. Hung's hiding-place they beat her cruelly; but she told them nothing of our whereabouts, thereby earning my undying gratitude. Then more troops appeared on the scene, but as soon as they saw the coffins came no further in our direction. At last a party of ten ruffianly-looking Manchus entered the room, and one of them seized a pole and began poking at my feet. I rose and showed myself. Their guide was a Yang-chou man whom I knew by sight, and I begged him to ask them to spare me. They asked for money, and I gave them some. One of the soldiers shouted: 'Let's spare this fellow's life for the present,' and they all went away. Then a young fellow in red clothes with a long sword entered, and began brandishing it in my direction. He, too, wanted money, and I gave him some. He was not satisfied, and pointed at my wife. She was expecting her confinement very shortly, and now lay motionless on the ground. I deceived him by telling him that she had been injured: 'My wife is near her time,' I said, 'and yesterday she fell from a roof and injured herself. She cannot sit up, and has to remain lying down.' The red-clothed man did not believe me, but pulled open my wife's dress to examine her person. He noticed that her lower garments were caked in blood (she had previously daubed it on), and so believed my story. He had with him a young woman and two little children: one of them, a boy, cried to his mother for food. This enraged the soldier, who brained the poor child on the stone floor. He then departed with the mother and her little girl.

"After this I made for a neighbour's house, and implored him to let us take shelter there. He said he had no room. My wife again begged to commit suicide, and as I felt there was no longer any hope I agreed; so we proceeded to hang ourselves with one rope to the rafter. But the noose had been clumsily adjusted, and we both fell with a crash to the ground. More soldiers entered the premises, but they marched straight through and went their ways. My wife rushed out from the chamber into an outhouse, which was full of straw; here there were a number of country women, who allowed her to enter, but they had no room for me. I ran as quickly as I could towards some straw which was piled in a heap in the southern corner, climbed up to the top of the stack, and covered myself completely with the straw. I thought I should be safe there, but in a little while there came a soldier, who jumped up and began poking about with a long spear. I came forth from the straw and offered him money to spare my life. He searched about and discovered several other refugees, who all escaped by likewise tendering him silver. After he had withdrawn we all crept back into our hiding-place. Down in the middle of the straw I noticed a couple of long tables, which seemed to offer an excellent refuge for several persons. Unfortunately for my idea, part of the adjoining wall had collapsed, and there was a wide chink, through which our movements could be seen from without. I had not noticed this, and had just lain down when a soldier began prodding at me with a spear; he succeeded in wounding me and my companions in misery. The lower part of my back received a nasty gash. We all scrambled out as best we could, and again I went to my wife's new quarters. All the women there were crouching on piles of firewood; they had smeared their faces and hair with blood and mud and cinders, so that they looked more like demons than women, and I only recognised my wife by her voice.

"I implored them to allow me to get in amongst them, and they managed to find me a place right at the bottom of the straw, with the women all lying on top of me. I was nearly stifled, but my wife procured a long hollow bamboo, which I placed in my mouth, and through it inhaled a little fresh air from above. A soldier came to the door, murdered two women whom he had dragged thither, and then went off.

"The day wore on; it grew dark, and the women got up. I then came out of my hiding-place, soaking with perspiration, and my wife and I went back to the Hung's house, where we found not only Mrs. Hung and her husband but also my brother and little Peng'rh. He said he had been forced by some Manchus to load carts all day, but they had been kind to little Peng'rh. They had given him a string of cash at the end of his day's work besides a safe conduct flag. The streets were piled high with corpses and all the ditches choked with blood. A report was current that a certain Colonel Wang Shao-yang, on good terms with the Manchus, was providing relief for the homeless and destitute, and that his intercession had saved many from being murdered. In spite of all our misery I slept soundly that night; when morning broke we had entered upon our ninth day of tribulation.

"So far we had marvellously escaped, but rumours were being noised abroad that all the survivors were to be massacred that day, so that many, at the risk of their lives, fled from the city by means of ropes let down from the wall. Meantime, outlaws and cut-throats from the country had begun to make their way into the city, plundering whatever was left, or else, lying in wait outside, they would intercept the escaping town people and despoil them. Under these circumstances I dared not make the attempt to quit Yang-chou, and my brother was unwilling to start forth alone. So that evening I concealed myself again under some straw; my wife and the child lay on top. Many times did my wife owe her safety to her advanced pregnancy. Soldiers often came in, but we were able to buy them off with bribes. Finally a wolf-eyed, lantern-faced Manchu entered and glared at my wife ferociously. He pulled her about violently, but she lay still, and told him the same story about having fallen from a height. He did not believe her and compelled her to rise. She sank again immediately, whereupon the soldier took his sword and cut at her back, blood gushing from each stroke. My wife had previously begged me not to betray my presence, even to save her life, as there was a chance of their sparing the child even if they killed her, and if I discovered myself the child would surely starve, for both its parents would be dead. So I remained hidden in the straw and said nothing, expecting that each moment would be my wife's last. The soldier finally caught her by the hair, twisted her long tresses round his arm and brutally pulled her along, belabouring her all the while. He dragged her from the pile of straw down the street for about fifty yards, pausing after every few paces to slash at her with his sword. At this moment a party of cavalry came up, and one of the horsemen spoke to the soldier in Manchu. He at once desisted, and left my wife, who managed to crawl back, bleeding in seven or eight places, and covered with the marks of her terrible ill-treatment. She continued moaning all the rest of that day.

"More fires were started and several stacks of straw in the Hos' graveyard blazed up. It is impossible to estimate the number of those who were either burned to death that night or, escaping from the flames, were butchered in the streets. The safest course, which we adopted, was to lie by the roadside concealed amongst the festering corpses, but even then there was no certainty of escaping destruction.

" Towards dawn we crept out and lay awhile at the back of a gravemound. We were caked all over with mud and excrement, and looked like any thing but human beings. A fire close by spread to the trees by the graveside, and, what with the roaring of the flames and the howling of the wind, we felt as if we were already in the infernal regions. Ghastly was the spectacle as the dawn broke and a pallid sun appeared. On all sides we beheld gaunt fleeting spectres of men and women, our fellow countrymen, while the Manchus, like so many Rakchas,[1] chased them up and down as if they were already denizens of the nethermost hell. If we closed our eyes our fevered brains conjured up visions of tortures worse than those we had already undergone. Suddenly I heard the sound of rushing feet. Looking up, I was horrified to see that my brother had been seized by a Manchu soldier and was making desperate efforts to escape from his hold. At last he broke away, but the soldier was after him. For a few breathless moments I gazed in horror; in the end my brother came tottering back, stark naked and with dishevelled hair, in the firm grasp of the Manchu. He implored me to offer the man money to save his life. I had only one silver ingot left and this I offered to the man, but he seized his sword furiously and stabbed my brother in the neck. He fell to earth, blood gushing from his wounds. Poor little Peng'rh (aged five years) seized the soldier's knees and begged him with tears to spare his uncle's life. The soldier calmly wiped his blade on Peng'rh's coat and then stabbed my brother again, this time in the head, and as it seemed to me, mortally. Then

[1] Demons of the Buddhist inferno which devour men.

he caught me by the hair and demanded money, belabouring me the while with the blunt side of his sword.

"I told him that my money was all gone, but offered to get him other articles. So he dragged me to the Hungs' house, where I showed him my wife's silk clothes and jewellery, which we had hidden in two water-jars. Everything was turned out on the doorstep, and he helped himself to whatever took his fancy. He removed all the pearls and gold ornaments, made a selection of the best clothes, and observing that little Peng'rh had a silver locket round his neck, wrenched it off with his knife. Then he turned to me and said: 'I won't kill you, but don't rejoice too soon; others will kill you before very long.' This showed me that a general massacre was afoot, and I felt that our last hour had come. But my wife and I hurried back to see how it fared with our brother. The wound in his neck was fearful—a gaping hole, several inches deep—and from the gash in his head a portion of the brain was protruding. He had also a terrible wound in the breast. We took him to the Hungs' house and asked how he felt. 'No pain,' he replied, 'just drowsy. I want to sleep.' He was only half conscious when we left him there to go and hide ourselves close to a neighbour's house amidst a pile of corpses. As we lay there, suddenly we heard a voice cry: 'The general massacre is fixed for to-morrow. All who can escape had better do so.'

"My wife urged me to fly the city, but I reflected that my brother was desperately wounded, and could not find it in my heart to leave him. Besides, we had now no money, and if we left the city we should only be facing the certainty of death from starvation. We discussed our position miserably for a long time. By this time the fires had burned themselves out, and we could hear the booming of distant guns. There were not so many soldiers about, so I moved with my wife and child to an outhouse, in which dry dung was kept. Mrs. Hung soon joined us.

"As we sat there some Manchus came by with five women, two of whom were stricken with years. The youngest one laughed gaily and seemed quite happy. Two more soldiers came up and tried to snatch the younger women away. A fight ensued, and one of the original party, speaking in Manchu, pleaded with the newcomers to desist. The last two men managed, however, to carry off the youngest woman, and bore her underneath a large tree, where they assaulted her, while their comrades did the same with the other females. The older women pleaded for mercy, but the younger did not seem in the least ashamed. Later on I saw that the youngest woman was in a state of collapse. I recognised her as the wife of an acquaintance named Chia, and thought that her wanton behaviour had met with its just reward. Frailty in a woman is paid for, sooner or later.

"At this moment a young man of about thirty, wearing a Manchu hat, clad in red clothes and wearing black satin boots, came riding by. He had a breastplate of the finest mail; his steed was beautifully caparisoned and he was attended by a large suite. His features, though Tartar, were exceedingly handsome; he had a long protruding chin and a lofty forehead. Amongst his retinue there were many Yang chou people. This was Prince Yü, the Manchu Commander-in-chief, and uncle of their Emperor.

"He looked closely at me, saying: 'You don't look like a common person; who and what are you?' I reflected that some of our people had escaped by saying that they were scholars by profession, while others of the *literati* had been murdered on suspicion of anti-Manchu proclivities. I did not, therefore, reveal my identity, but concocted a plausible story. Then he asked about my wife, and I told him the truth. He then said: 'I have given orders that all killing shall cease from to-morrow, so you will be quite safe.' He bade some of his retinue give me clothes and an ingot of silver. 'How long,' he asked, 'is it since you have had a good meal?' I answered: 'Five days.' He commanded us to follow him; my wife and I dared not disobey, though suspicious of his intentions. We reached a mansion where preparations for a banquet were laid out on a most lavish scale. Victuals of all kinds were there in abundance. He called a woman, saying: 'Treat these people well,' and then departed. It was now twilight. My wife's younger brother had been carried off and we knew nothing of his fate; my wife was very sad at his loss. The woman soon came out with bowls of fish and rice, and as this mansion was quite near to the Hungs' house, I carried some food to my brother; but he could not eat it. I combed his hair and washed away the blood from his face, feeling all the time as though a sword were at my own heart. People's minds were more composed on hearing that the massacres were to cease.

"Next day was the 1st of the 5th Moon; although the situation was much improved, looting and murder did not cease entirely. All the well-to-do families had been stripped bare of everything; hardly any females over ten years of age had escaped violation. To-day one of the Manchu Generals, the Earl of Established Peace, re-entered Yang-chou and distributed some food to the people, over which they fought like ravenous tigers. On the second day proclamations were issued that the Manchus had established local officials in Yang-chou and the surrounding districts. The magistrates were sending out runners to tranquillise the people. The Buddhist temples received orders to burn all corpses; there were still many women hiding in their shrines, and many had died there of starvation. According to the official records of bodies found, the total number of persons who perished during these days was eight hundred thousand, but this does not include those who perished in the flames or who drowned themselves in the river.

"On the third day a notice was circulated that relief offices were distributing grain and rice. I went with Mrs. Hung to the place, which was the former commissariat department of General Shih K'o-fa. There were tons of rice and grain stored in bins, but in a very short space of time the whole of it had been distributed to the famishing crowd. They presented a pitiful spectacle, most of them with maimed limbs and broken heads, and all in filthy apparel. But when the grain was distributed each and all fought like wolves; children even forgot to consider their parents, and struggled only for themselves. Many aged and infirm persons waited all day without securing a mouthful.

"On the fourth day the sky cleared and the heat of the sun was great. The stench of the corpses was over-powering, and thousands were burned during the day. A mighty smoke was raised, and the smell of the burning bodies filled the air, tainting it for miles around. I burned some cotton wool and human bone, and with the calcined ashes prepared ointment for my brother's wounds. He accepted it gratefully, but could not utter a word.

"On the fifth day many people who had remained in hiding began to come forth; people's hearts were too full for speech. We five, including the Hungs, were still alive, but as yet we did not dare to spend the day in our own house. After breakfast we went out and sat by the roadside. No one dared to wash or dress his hair, for there were still robbers about, but these were only common footpads; they had no swords, only cudgels, with which they frightened people into giving them money. But even so they beat several people to death and outraged many women. We could not tell if these wretches were

Manchus or Chinese soldiers or merely local ruffians. To-day my brother died of his grievous wounds, which had mortified. My loss is not to be described. At the beginning of the trouble we were a party of eight brothers and sisters and their issue; now only three remained, I, my wife and Peng'rh.

"In all I have described the events of ten days, from the 25th of the 5th to the 5th of the 4th Moon. I have only told of my own experiences and the things of which I have been an eye-witness. In all my story there is not one word of hearsay or rumour, and I have refrained from mentioning events which did not come under my own observation. Hence I know that this record is true. Perchance posterity, born in a happier age, may be interested in perusing this diary, and it may serve to point a moral for the unreflecting. It may even cause vindictive and cruel-minded men to reflect on the error of their ways, and thus be of some value, as a solemn warning."

Thus it was in China in the year 1645. For 265 years thereafter the Manchus ruled over the Empire which they had won by the sword. Under the wise government of their earlier Emperors the country rapidly recovered, as it always does, from the abomination of desolation wrought first by Li Tzŭ-cheng's rebellion and then by the Manchus' ruthless war of conquest. New cities sprang up where no stone had been left upon another to tell the story of the dead; once more the wilderness was made to blossom as the rose, until, in the fulness of time, the Manchus' course of Empire was run and, as they lost their prestige as rulers, rebellion and anarchy once more laid waste the land.

In the events which have marked the passing of this once Imperial race, none display more vividly the pitiless irony of Fate and the innate savagery of Orientals in their crises of battle and sudden death than the slaughter of the Manchu garrisons at cities like Sianfu during the recent revolution. Describing the sack of the Tartar city at Sianfu in October 1911, one who passed through it shortly afterwards wrote : [1]

"Once the Chinese set about this business of destruction, the lust of blood, the madness of killing, possessed them. Old and young, men and women, little children, were alike butchered. The Tartar General, old, hopeless, cut off from his people at the critical juncture, was unable to face the situation. The safety he had won for the moment he felt not worth the keeping; he ended his life by throwing himself down a well. Houses were plundered and then burnt; those who would fain have laid hidden till the storm was past were forced to come out into the open. The revolutionaries, protected by a parapet of the wall, poured a heavy, unceasing, relentless fire into the doomed Tartar city. Those who tried to escape thence into the Chinese city were cut down as they emerged from the gates. At the western gates the Mohammedans cynically received them for their own purpose. In the darkness some managed to scale the city wall, and descend the other side, wade through the moat and escape to the open country. But not all who attempted this succeeded. The wall is thirty-six feet in height and at the top is some sixteen yards wide, and on it at various points clustered the Chinese soldiers. The fugitives to escape had to slip between these, avoid the flashing lanterns and find a means of affixing their ropes safely before descending. Some possibly escaped by venturing to leap from the height.

"In despair, many Manchus themselves set fire to their houses; at least they might cheat their murderers of the loot they sought. Into the English Hospital, days afterwards, when the first fury was passed, men were brought in a shocking condition; men who had attempted to cut

[1] *The Passing of the Dragon.* By J. C. Keyte. (Hodder and Stoughton.) 1913.

their throats. Asked why they had done so they answered simply: 'The wells were full.' And the Shensi wells are not the shallow ones of some parts of China; they are thirty-six feet deep. There is such a man in that hospital to-day. All his family, wife, daughters, sons, were slain or destroyed themselves; he lives because the well was choked with dead or dying, and he failed in his attempt to end his life by other means.

"There were many Manchus in the Chinese city at the time of the outbreak. Some escaped for the moment through taking shelter with friends. But even twenty days after the outbreak, a Manchu detected on the street would be dragged off to instant execution. Hundreds were thus hunted through the streets and lanes of the city. They were known by their clothing, by their cast of countenance, by their speech....

"When the Manchus found that further resistance was useless, they in many cases knelt on the ground, laying down their weapons and begged the soldiers for life. They were shot as they knelt. Sometimes there was a whole line of them. In one doorway a group of between ten and twenty were thus killed in cold blood.

"A girl came down the street; a girl of twenty, with hands bound. She had been hastily dragged before the 'judges!' in the Magazine, temporary headquarters of the Revolution, and was now being taken out a hundred yards or so to be beheaded. And in her face was that which once seen—by the passer-by at least—was never to be forgotten. It was not despair. Ah no! That anodyne had had no time in which to reach her. It was the full young life cheated of its days, going out into the dark, the path before her littered by fearful reminders of the fate in front. From the pallid lips no sound issued; they were held, as the girl's whole being was held, by utter terror. The shaking limbs, the stumbling gait, proclaimed it, but more than all the awful haunting eyes. Along the route where the reek of blood made the very air bitter, acrid in the brilliant sunshine, where curses and sobs mingled with groans and derisive raucous cries rent the air, they went. A woman, a very girl, caught within the enemy's gates, not dying with her own people, not able to save herself with them if only in a death she saw and chose; but hurried along thus, as to a shambles. And her crime? Her birth. A Manchu. The soldier muttered impatiently. He had other affairs to attend to when this was over. Time meant money, meant sport, in those days. He stalked along behind her with naked sword held up. 'Hurry,' he snarled, 'Hurry.'

"Days after the outbreak an Englishman, passing down a side street, heard groans, heard the cry of pain, coming up with hollow sound from the depths. At the mouth of a well stood some Chinese. It was their day. The pitiful cries went on, the feeble moaning varied with the sharp cries. A Manchu, who had thrown himself, or been thrown down this well, had lain there with broken limbs; lay there in agony, appealing almost unconsciously for pity.

"The men at the well mouth picked up lumps of earth, stones, picked up what came to hand. There came up from the well's depths the thud of missiles on human flesh."

And so the whirlgig of Time brings in its merciless revenges; the butchers of to-day are the victims of to-morrow. Europe, with its reserves of inherited wealth, with outlets overseas for its surplus millions, its organised philanthropy and scientific economics, has no conception of the realities of life in furthest Asia, the same now as they were in the days when " the Lord commanded Moses to war against the Midianites, and they slew all the males, and burnt all their cities wherein they dwelt." It is not possible for us, in our well-ordered materialism, to sympathise with the forces of atavism, the instinctive terrors and cruelties that dwell for ever in the soul of this people. The sack of Yang Chou-fu and that of the Tartar city at Sianfu are in reality insignificant incidents, normal features in the life history of a race which since the beginning of recorded time has learned " to eat its bread with quaking and to drink its water with trembling."

CHAPTER VIII

THE LAST OF THE MINGS

KUEI WANG (Prince Kuei), the last and the longest-lived of the four fugitive claimants to the Dragon Throne, kept up a semblance of sovereignty from 1646 (when his predecessor was executed by the Manchus at Foochow) till 1659, when he was compelled to flee over the Yünnan frontier into Burmah. When he succeeded to the Great Inheritance, under the reign title of "Yung Li," the harried Court of the Mings, shorn now of all its regal pomp and revenues, was in Kuang tung, but in the following year, closely pursued by the ever-victorious Manchus, it fled into Kuangsi. There a stand was made, and for a time the fortunes of the Mings seemed to be in the ascendant. In 1648 three provinces owned their allegiance, and a force of over 200,000 men still held in check the alien invaders. The death of the Regent, Prince Jui, (1649) put new heart into the cause, and the serious rebellions which broke out against the Manchus in Hunan, Chêkiang and other provinces, all justified the Mings in hoping for a restoration of their House. But it was not to be. By the year 1650 the rank and file of the Mings' adherents consisted chiefly of freebooters and recruits drawn from Li Tzŭ-ch'eng's scattered armies, and the small remnant of respectable men who continued to follow their fallen fortunes were influenced as much by hopes of perquisites and power as by patriotic dislike of a foreign ruler. Gradually the flag of the old dynasty became nothing more than a rallying point for political adventurers, and the Court a cave of Adullam, to which gathered themselves all those that were in distress or debt or bitterness of soul. In 1651 the wretched Yung Li had been forced to flee further and further West, until at last we find him, a refugee and a pensioner, under the protection of a leader of desperadoes, one who had taken an active part in Li Tzŭ-ch'eng's rebellion, and who now used the Ming claimant and his few faithful Ministers to give to his own ambitious schemes a reasonable pretext and some semblance of patriotism. From 1655 to 1659 Kuei Wang, with a remnant of troops commanded by another famous freebooter named Li Ting-kuo, was closely pursued by the Manchu forces, which then stamped out the flickering flames of rebellion in Kueichow and Yünnan. Finally, his last battle fought and lost, he fled for his life, with a poor handful of followers, across the Burmese frontier, near Teng-yueh; there, for a time, he found a refuge from the fierce pursuit of Wu San-kuei. This General, now all-powerful ruler of two provinces under the Manchus, but once the chief hope and defence of the Mings at Peking, showed himself brutally pitiless in his treatment of the unfortunate Kuei Wang, a broken fugitive who could no longer threaten the power of the Ta Ching dynasty. The pathetic figure of the last of the Mings in exile was, indeed, something to arouse sympathy in the mind of any magnanimous man, and Wu's implacable cruelty towards him is only explained and condoned by Chinese scholars by the fact that his education was not that of a literary man. A military training, they declare, does not inculcate the canons of the Sages.

From his retreat in Burmah the last of the Mings wrote to Wu San-kuei, endeavouring to placate him, or at least to dissuade him from further relentless pursuing. The letter was written in December 1662.

THE COURT OF PEKING

"Your Excellency has deserved right well of the present dynasty, but once you were a bulwark of our own. Under it you received hereditary rank and a provincial satrapy, so that His late Majesty Ch'ung Chen may be said to have conferred exceptional favours on Your Excellency.

"Unhappily, our dynasty fell upon evil days; the rebel bandit, Li Tzŭ-ch'eng, laid waste the land and marched on our capital. Our tutelary altars were destroyed, so that His late Majesty felt that suicide was his duty, and thousands of our subjects were put to the sword.

"At that time Your Excellency had not lost all right and natural feeling; you wept at the thought of the dynasty's plight, and marched to its aid clad in mourning, at the head of an avenging host.

"How comes it then that, since that day, you have staked your fortunes upon those of the Manchus, like the fox which relied on the prestige of the tiger to lord it over the beasts of the forest? You pretended a loyal desire to wreak vengeance on our enemies, and all the time you were the very humble and obedient servant of the new dynasty.

"Since then, Li Tzŭ-ch'eng's rebellion has been suppressed and its leader has met with the fate he deserved, but our dynasty had already lost the whole of the northern portion of the Empire. Our Ministers in the South could not bear to see the dynastic altars bare and untended, so they raised up the Emperor Hung Kuang at Nanking to succeed Ch'ung Chen. Was it to be expected or believed that even then the attacks of the Manchus would continue, unrelenting and unceasing? Hung Kuang perished in battle, and his successor, Lung Wu, was put to death at Foochow. Facing these swift-footed disasters, I, all unworthy, had but little desire to live; what thought had I to spare for our dynastic altars? Nevertheless, my Ministers forced the Throne upon me, and I was reluctantly induced to take up the burden of inheritance.

"Since then fifteen years have passed; the first campaign of my reign lost us Hupei, and after that, further disasters followed in Kuang tung. Again and again have I had to flee, in panic-stricken confusion, before the advancing Manchus. Fortunately, at a moment of great peril, Li Ting-kuo came to my aid in Kuei-chou and brought me safe to Nan-an in Yünnan. There I had hoped to be left in peace by my ruthless enemies, to be allowed to remain in possession of that remote and worthless corner of my ancestors' patrimony.

"But Your Excellency has forgotten the benefits which my ancestors bestowed upon you; evidently you hope to go down to history as one of the founders of this new dynasty. You led your armies into Yünnan, destroying my nest of peaceful retreat. Again I had to cross a desert barrier, and now I look for my protection to Burmese hospitality. In this remote region joy and I have long been strangers; tears are my daily meat and drink. Although I have lost the glorious heritage, won by my ancestors at the cost of so many and great hardships, no doubt but that I should count myself lucky in that I still draw the breath of pain among these people of the barbarian South!

"But Your Excellency, not to be appeased, desists not from pursuing me to the end. You have now asked your Sovereign's permission to invade Burmah at the head of a mighty army, in order ruthlessly to hunt me down, me, a sad and solitary dweller in the land. Is not the whole Empire wide enough for your ambitions? Is there then to be no resting-place for me, 'neath heaven's vault upon the bosom of earth? Or is it, perchance, that your insatiate ambition is not content with the princedom which you have received, and that you seek my destruction in order that you may be crowned with fresh honours? Is it that you are jealous of our founder, T'ai Tsu, who won the Empire by deeds of glorious merit, after being 'combed by the wind and bathed in the sun,' and that you feel it hard that you have not been left one inch of ground which you could boast of having won by yourself? In despite, you must needs first destroy our ancestral altars, and now follow up that brave deed by slaughtering T'ai Tsu's descendants! Can you, I wonder, bear to peruse the ode, 'Oh! owl, oh! owl, you have robbed me of my young; destroy not also my nest; with love and care I nurtured them; truly I deserve to be pitied without shame'?

"Your Excellency's ancestors won a glorious place in our annals; it may be that you refuse to show to me an atom of pity, but can it be that you are lost to all remembrance of His late Majesty, who gave you high rank? Even if you reck nothing for him, surely you cannot forget the merits of my great ancestor T'ai Tsu and of his son Yung Lo (Cheng Tsu) and their successors! It may be that you have also forgotten their names; but even so, you cannot be so devoid of filial piety as to forget the example of your own forefathers!

"What has the Great Pure Manchu dynasty done for Your Excellency to win such loyal devotion and service at your hands? What crime, what act of unjust oppression, have I committed towards Your Excellency that you thus evilly intreat me? Thinking to be wise, you are become as a fool; believing yourself loyal to your new masters, you are at heart a traitor both to old and new. Ten thousand generations hence, what name will Your Excellency leave in history? what manner of man will posterity call you? To-day I make appeal to Your Excellency. I am left with scarcely a soldier to defend me; I stand alone, like one bereft of his parents, against a hostile world. My life, humble and worthless, is in Your Excellency's hands. If you must have my head, it is forfeit to you. I shrink not from death, though the undergrowth be soaked with my blood and my scattered bones lie whitening the plain. Far be it from me to expect Your Excellency to spare my life, or to plead with you to grant me a narrow plot of ground on which I, the descendant of the glorious Ming dynasty, may still eke out an existence. Yet why should you not allow me to benefit by the nurturing protection of the Manchu dynasty, under which even the grass of the field is watered by timely dew and rain from above? If I had a million men-at-arms, cheerfully would I place them all under your banner. It is now for Your Excellency to decide. Faithful servant of the new dynasty though you be, it remains for Your Excellency to show that you have not forgotten past benefits heaped upon you by His late Majesty, and that you still cherish the memory of my predecessors' glorious achievements. I must leave Your Excellency to think out and decide this matter for yourself."

To this pathetic letter Wu San-kuei made no reply, but proceeded to threaten the Burmese King with dire penalties unless the fugitive were promptly surrendered.

About three months after Yung Li's vain attempt to placate Wu San-kuei, the Burmese invited the remnant of the Emperor's Court to meet one of their chieftains on a small island for the purpose of arranging the terms of a treaty. Here they treacherously seized them all, and slew Prince Sung with forty-two high officials. Many women of the Imperial and princely households committed suicide. Only a few of the Emperor's followers escaped, among them a General named Teng. He subsequently declared that the Burmese would have killed the Emperor also, but a message arrived from the Burmese King (who had just succeeded to the Throne) that he was to be held as a prisoner and handed over to Wu San-kuei. Early in the 12th Moon the Manchus arrived upon the scene and carried off Yung Li to Yünnan.

A certain Chi T'an-jan, native of Nanking, and his

THE COURT OF PEKING

father accompanied the escort which brought the ex-Emperor back to China. The following account is in Chi T'an-jan's own words, as recorded in a contemporary memoir: "When His Majesty crossed the Yünnan boundary he was met by Wu San-kuei, who had prepared a sedan-chair for his use. All along the route the people crowded to see him, saying: "This is the former Son of Heaven," and hardly a man but shed tears as he gazed on so pitiful a sight. The Emperor was round of countenance, with a protuberant forehead; his beard was long and full, and he looked every inch a King. A number of the Manchu bodyguard joined in a plot to rescue and defend him, so moved were they at the thought of his wrongs and so wrath with Wu San-kuei for his treachery. But the plot miscarried, and over forty of them were executed. I myself witnessed their deaths; one of them was of immense stature, nigh seven feet in height, and broad in proportion. It was said that he was the champion archer and rider in the Manchu army, as well as a great wrestler."

This conspiracy made Yung Li's plight all the more desperate. Wu San-kuei sent couriers to Peking for instructions, and in the 3rd Moon of the following year, 1663, he received a secret decree from the Regent Ao Pai, in the name of the Emperor K'ang Hsi, ordering him to put Yung Li to death. So Wu invited the ex-Emperor to a chess tourney at the Treasury building, just outside the northern gate of Yünnan-fu, and there had him strangled. A Chinese author, himself a descendant of the Mings, has the following note on Yung Li's death: " No one knew that his death had been decided upon for that day, but, at about the eleventh hour, the sky, which had been clear and calm, became suddenly overcast, and there arose a terrible storm, darkening the air with dust. Peasants at work near the Temple of Buddhist Conversion, close to the Chin-chih lake, half-a-mile from the city, beheld a shooting star fall from Heaven, and it was afterwards found that the hour at which they saw it was that in which Yung Li was murdered. His remains were buried in Yünnan-fu. His wife and mother were both sent to Peking, where they were kindly treated, but soon afterwards the ex-Empress Dowager committed suicide. Yung Li was thirty-eight years of age at the time of his death. He resembled the Emperor Wan Li, his grandfather, in face, and also in his hatred of extravagance. He was a man of simple tastes, and drank but little wine. Although not a great scholar, he was a keen reader, an eager student of the classics. Great grief and indignation were felt in Yünnan at his cruel death. Surely, a happier day is dawning; let us hope that China may soon see the descendants of her old hero, Chu Yüan-chang,[1] restored once more to their own, and the alien barbarians driven back to their Gobi desert."

One of Yung Li's most devoted adherents was Kung Yi, who was President of his Board of Rites; he followed his master to Yünnan, and when that province was lost fled with him to Burmah. Here he set to work to induce the local tribesmen to rally to his succour, but before he had had time to achieve any results, Yung Li was treacherously captured by the Burmese, who handed him over to Wu San-kuei. Kung Yi followed the captive to Yünnan-fu. One day soon after his arrival he prepared food and wine and bore them to the place where Yung Li was confined. The guards sought to prevent him from entering, but he persisted, saying : " Your prisoner is our Chinese Emperor, and I am his Minister; all I ask is to be allowed to see him once more. Why do you prevent me ? " So the guards reported the matter to Wu San-kuei, who permitted Kung Yi to enter. He prepared his little feast in the main room, and then invited the Emperor to take his place facing the South in the seat of honour on the daïs, as if he were

[1] The founder of the Ming dynasty.

presiding at a Court banquet, while he knelt dutifully below.

Having made obeisance, he presented the wine. The Emperor wept bitterly and put the cup down untouched. Kung Yi prostrated himself in the dust, utterly overcome with grief. Once more he besought His Majesty to drink, and Yung Li forced himself at last to swallow a little. Then the Emperor handed a cup to Kung Yi, who drank it, and in a few moments he expired. The Emperor raised him in his arms and wept bitterly when he saw that his faithful servant was dead. Not long after this Yung Li was strangled, as above stated, and with him ended the last attempt of the Mings to recover their Throne. Two centuries later the Taiping rebels raised the cry, "Restore the Mings," but it was a battle-cry only, just as much lacking in political significance and genuine loyalty to the departed dynasty as Sun Yat-sen's melodramatic performance at the shrine of Chu Yüan-chang on the 15th of February, 1912.

An interesting and little-known result of the tribulations and vicissitudes of the fugitive Ming Court, was that many of the Imperial clanswomen sought consolation, and probably hoped to find practical benefits of European intervention, from the practice of the Roman Catholic religion. When we remember how great had been the influence of the Jesuit fathers (Schall, Ricci, Verbiest and others) under the last of the Ming Emperors at Peking —an influence which made itself felt, as we have seen, in secular and military matters—it is not remarkable that their immediate posterity should have founded some hopes on a continuance of cordial relations with the Roman Catholic priests, who at that time were zealously propagating their faith, not only at Peking, but in the southern provinces. The Portuguese colony of Macao was a very important headquarters of Jesuit missionary work, and during the earlier years of Yung Li's struggle for the recovery of the Throne, while his forces were endeavouring to hold Kuangtung, a German Jesuit, named Andrew Xavier Koffler, was attached to the Ming Court. As the result of the labours of this earnest worker in a truly grateful soil, Yung Li's wife and mother embraced, and openly professed, the faith, and their example was followed not only by many of the secondary consorts, but by several eunuchs, by over a hundred members of the Imperial Clan and forty high officials. All these, as was duly reported to the Vatican, were baptised. Yung Li's titular Empress Dowager received the baptismal name of Helen, the Heir Apparent that of Constantine, the Empress Mother that of Mary, and his Consort that of Anne. Yung Li himself never became a convert, because, like his ancestors, he was a confirmed polygamist, and could not be persuaded to give up his harem.

In the year 1649, the Empress Helen, acting upon the advice of Father Koffler and her Chief Eunuch, "P'an Achilles" (who appears to have been a sincerely devout Catholic), sent an envoy to the head of the Church at Macao desiring that a special mass should be celebrated in thanksgiving for the restoration to health of the Heir Apparent, and incidentally to pray for the restoration of the Ming dynasty. On this interesting occasion the Governor of Macao gave a banquet in honour of the Imperial envoy and made him a present, useful and significant, of a hundred muskets.

In November of the following year it was decided to send a mission *viâ* Goa to the Vatican. The Empress Helen addressed a letter to Pope Innocent X in her own very indifferent handwriting, announcing her conversion to the true faith and that of the mother and wife of the Emperor. The text of this interesting document was first published in a work by the Jesuit Athanasius Kirchner at Amsterdam in 1666. (*China monumentis, qua sacris, qua profanis*, etc.) Father Dominic and another Jesuit priest and two Chinese Christians were entrusted with this mission to the Vatican; they also bore letters addressed to the Society of Jesus at Rome. Owing to many difficulties and delays they did not reach Italy, travelling overland *via* Persia and the Levant, until the summer of 1652. In Rome, too, they met with unexpected obstacles, and it was not until 1655, that Pope Alexander VII consented to receive the mission in audience and gave them replies in the form of letters addressed to the Empress Helen and the eunuch P'an. With these the envoys returned in due course to China. The Empress's letter to Pope Innocent and another from the eunuch are still preserved in the archives at the Vatican.[1]

The Empress Helen's letter contains little beyond general expressions of piety and goodwill, but that of P'an Achilles records the interesting fact that this eunuch, then sixty-two years of age, was in command of all the land and sea forces of the Mings in the provinces of Fukhien and Kuangtung; commander also of the Imperial Guard, with full powers over the financial and commissariat departments, Master of the Ceremonies, and Guardian of the State Seal. Which proves that the last of the Mings had learned little wisdom from adversity.

With the death of Yung Li, bowstringed at the furthest frontiers of the Empire, the Manchu dynasty's rights to rule China were no longer disputed by any legitimate claimant, and the splendid recuperative powers of the Chinese people, fostered and guided by the wise government of the Emperor K'ang Hsi, speedily brought about an era of great prosperity and a widespread revival of art, literature and commerce. We shall now proceed to consider some of the most notable events and principal motive forces in the lives of the Manchu Sovereigns, elucidating as far as possible the causes of the dynasty's

[1] An English translation of both documents was published by Mr. E. H. Parker in the *Contemporary Review* of January 1912.

gradual decline in virility and statesmanship; endeavouring, by means of the documents at our disposal, to throw new light on the personal relations, human equations and domestic affairs which affected the policies of China's rulers in the first instance, and eventually the destinies of the nation.

But before concluding this review of the last years of the Ming dynasty, we would refer once again to the part which the superstitious belief of the Chinese in prophecies and omens has always played, and still plays, in every national crisis. A proverb or a prophecy, current in the market places and tea-shops of the provinces, carries far greater weight than Imperial edicts in determining the popular attitude in any great emergency. For this reason certain prophecies which foretold long ago, in language very similar to that of Old Moore, the collapse of the Ming dynasty and the destinies of the Manchus, have always stirred the popular imagination, and affected public opinion, to a degree which Europeans of the present day can hardly imagine.

One of the most widely spread of these prophecies has long been known in China as "The Song of the Cakes." It is generally believed to have been composed by Chu Yüan-chang, the founder of the Ming dynasty, shortly after his accession to the Throne, and it is supposed to foretell the fate of the dynasty, the coming of the eight Manchu banners, and the final overthrow of the Manchu power. The last lines of this effusion run as follows:

"Ten-mouthed women,[1] with grass on their heads, once more carry a babe in their arms to be lord over the Empire.

"The eight banner flags find it hard to escape from the Japanese devils.

[1] Ten-mouthed women: *i. e.* Yehonala—(meaning Tzŭ Hsi and Lung Yü). The first character of the name Yehonala having the sign for "grass" at the top, and below it the signs for "ten" and "a mouth."

THE COURT OF PEKING

"In the provinces of Hunan-Hupei, a wondrous being shall arise.

"A red pear tree, with a round hole in the middle of its fruit, shall startle the slave-son's descendants.

"A monkey shall stand in the central place and drive forth the little child.

"A woman shall enter the room, bearing a son in her arms; another woman shall leave the room, bearing a son in her arms.

"The grandson's reign shall be brief. In the sky a yellow star shall shine."

To understand the manner in which such prophecies appeal to the Chinese, scholars and common people alike, it is necessary to possess a knowledge of the written language, for all the hidden meanings of such utterances, actual or alleged, depend upon an ingenious and often far-fetched play upon words. The pundits, who claim that the above prophecy refers to the overthrow of the Manchus by the recent revolutionary movement, aver, for instance, that the "red pear tree with the round hole in the middle of the fruit," etc., can only refer to Li Yuan-hung, the present Vice-president of the Republic, because the "Li" in his name is identical in sound with the word "Li" for a pear, while Hung is "red" and Yuan is identical in sound with "round." And the slave-son is Nurhachi, because the first two Chinese characters in his name (nu erh) mean "slave-son." To Western minds this sort of thing may seem fantastic gibberish, but to the Chinese it is extraordinarily convincing. For a similar reason "a monkey" is Yuan Shih-k'ai; the "driving out of the infant" refers to the Manchu abdication; the "grandson" is Sun Yat-sen, the "yellow star" is Huang Hsing, and "the woman leaving the room" is the Empress Lung Yü with the baby Hsüan T'ung, the woman entering the room being Shun Chih's mother.[1]

[1] Cf. Dr. Arthur Smith's *Chinese Proverbs*, new edition, p. 325.

THE COURT OF PEKING

The importance of prophecies like this lies not in the interpretation which scholars or journalists may choose to give to them, but to the indisputable fact that the common people know and vaguely believe in them. If, on the authority of "The Song of the Cakes," the man in the street persuades himself that Huang Hsing's appearance on the scene is an event fraught with vast issues, that unscrupulous adventurer starts with an advantage which neither wealth nor personal merit could confer. Readers of *China under the Empress Dowager* may remember that Tzŭ Hsi herself often displayed superstition as gross as that of the commonest coolie in the land, and that many a vital step in her career was determined upon the advice of charlatan soothsayers and astrologers. In studying the lives of China's rulers, whether Ming or Manchu, it is necessary to bear in mind this deep-rooted characteristic of the race.

END OF PART I

PART II
THE MANCHU DYNASTY

CHAPTER IX

THE EMPEROR SHUN CHIH

THERE is comparatively little material in contemporary annals and memoirs which bears upon the life of the Sovereign and his Court during the first reign of the Manchu dynasty, that of the Emperor Shun Chih. The fact is readily explicable in several ways. In the first place, although the history of Shun Chih's reign covers a period of seventeen years from the date of his accession to the Throne of China, he was only twenty-three years of age when he passed from the scene. During the Regency of his uncle, Prince Jui, and until the latter's death in December 1650, the Lord of Heaven was only a little lad, interested in hunting and in hearing the day's news of the Manchu army's victorious progress through the central and southern provinces, carefully tended by his mother and the Imperial tutors. When, three months after the death of the Regent, he assumed nominal control of the business of the State, he was an intelligent youth of twelve, but the high spirits which had marked his childhood had already given place to the contemplative and serious temperament which became intensified with each succeeding year. One of his first edicts, after assuming the actual direction of the Government, prescribed certain regulations for controlling entrance to the priesthood and supervising the training of candidates. He concerned himself actively, too, with public education and the revision of the system of examinations for degrees. The

Court was eminently respectable, and perhaps even a little dull, under the first of the Manchus, but no doubt the citizens of Peking were glad enough to be rid of the wild extravagance and debauches which had disgraced it under the Mings.

An essay, published since the abdication of the Manchu dynasty by a Chinese historical writer who signs himself "Born out of time," sets out to prove that Shun Chih was illegitimate, and that the rulers of the House of Gioro, beginning with Shun Chih and ending with Kuang Hsü, had no better claim to pure blood than those of the House of Romanov. He asserts that the father of Shun Chih was not the Emperor T'ai Tsung, but a Chinese hunter, named Wang. The evidence with which he supports this statement can scarcely be called even circumstantial. The writings of "Born out of time" prove him to be one of those typical products of Young China, in whom self-interest and an emotional kind of patriotism combine to produce a blind hatred of the Manchus. His work is marked by the same quality of reckless vituperation as that of Wen Ch'ing and K'ang Yu-wei, and contains more evidence of constructive memory than of historical research. Nevertheless, the fact is important that many Chinese write and many more believe, fantastic legends of the kind upon which "Born out of time" bases his assertion that the Emperors Shun Chih, Yung Cheng, Ch'ien Lung and Kuang Hsü were all illegitimate, and born of Chinese fathers. We reproduce his account of the birth of Shun Chih not, as the Imperial edicts say, "for purposes of historical accuracy," but as an illustration of Young China's historical methods.

"Shortly after the capture of Moukden by the Manchus," he says, " there arrived in the thinly populated district of Fu Chou a family of settlers named Wang, driven from their native province of Shantung by poverty. Their son Wang Kao became a mighty hunter. One day, in

THE COURT OF PEKING

1637, the Lady Borjikitu, a favourite concubine of T'ai Tsung, was with her maids in the forest, hunting the stag; like most Mongol women, she was an expert horsewoman and huntress. She had shot three times at a magnificent stag and missed, when Wang Kao appeared upon the scene, and with him a comrade called Teng, nicknamed the 'large-thighed.' The deer rushed through the forest straight towards Wang, who promptly shot it dead. When Lady Borjikitu reached the spot she was greatly impressed by Wang's fine figure and pleasing features and, after asking him a few questions as to his origin, engaged both him and 'Large-thighed' Teng, and took them back with her to Moukden, appointing them to her special bodyguard. Thereafter Wang was her constant attendant on hunting expeditions. Soon an intimacy sprang up between them, and when in March of the following year she gave birth to Fulin (who reigned later as Shun Chih) most people believed that Wang was the father. Shun Chih was an exceptionally robust youngster, and could lift heavy weights when only four years old. T'ai Tsung, well aware of his origin, had Teng assassinated for fear of his betraying the secret. He was murdered by hired bravos on the road leading out of Moukden towards Liao yang. To this day there is a popular phrase in Moukden which refers to the murder of Teng. They say to 'Send Large-thighed Teng about his business,' meaning to get rid of any kind of incubus by giving it the 'happy dispatch.' A little later Wang Kao himself was assassinated by T'ai Tsung's order, and legend avers that his ghost walked in the Moukden Palace until appeased by the young Prince Fulin kneeling before his coffin and acknowledging him as his father. After this filial recognition, they say, T'ai Tsung was troubled no more. He gave orders for Wang Kao's burial in the family mausoleum of Nurhachi, and the saying goes that he is included to this day among the family heroes worshipped in the Manchu dynasty's private [1] shrine at Peking, where the Emperor used to make obeisance on the morning of the second day of the year. Common rumour also alleges that on the occasion of Imperial visits to the Moukden mausolea, where Nurhachi and his son are buried, a special sacrifice has always been offered to the memory of Wang Kao. An adage in Moukden itself says: 'The Emperor first pays obeisance to Wang Kao and then to the Imperial tombs.' On the Long White Mountain there is a memorial tablet recounting Wang's history, though naturally it contains no reference to his relations with the proud house of Gioro."

So much for the latest annalists. Nevertheless, the fact remains that there is nothing in contemporary history or literature which gives colour to these attempts to besmirch the founders of the dynasty, and that the reign of Shun Chih himself was singularly free from all sorts of *chroniques scandaleuses* and evil report.

The personal character of the Emperor and his youth go far to account for the absence of scandal and intrigue at Peking during the reign of Shun Chih, but the factor which undoubtedly contributed more than all others to give the Court its happy immunity from treasons, stratagems and spoils, lay in the relegation of the Palace eunuchs to their proper position as menials, and in the dynastic house-laws, instituted by the Regent shortly after the Manchu accession, which sternly forbade their employment in any official capacity. After the fall of Peking, many of the " rats and foxes " who had debauched and degraded the Court of the Mings, and battened on the vices of the licentious Clansmen, had either fled to their homes at Ho Chien-fu, or had followed the fortunes of the Chinese dynasty to Nanking and further South. Those who remained, to take service under the new

[1] The site of the shrine has been occupied since 1900 by the Italian Legation.

THE COURT OF PEKING

régime, found their influence and their perquisites lamentably reduced; and with them vanished the intrigues and the insolences which had distinguished the followers of Wei Chung-hsien. For a breathing space the Forbidden City was cleansed of its chief source of evil.

The Regent, Prince Jui, fourteenth son of Nurhachi, died, as we have shown, in December 1650, killed, near Kalgan, by an accident whilst engaged in his favourite sport of hunting, at the early age of thirty-nine. The boy Emperor was sincerely grieved at the loss of his uncle, who for seven years had been the guiding spirit in the counsels of the Manchus. He issued an edict, in which the many virtues of the deceased were eloquently recorded, and went out to meet the body when it was brought back to Peking. But no sooner was the masterful Prince dead, than certain of the Manchu Princes and nobles, who had always been opposed to his usurpation of the Regency, denounced him on charges amounting to high treason, and demanded the rescindment of the posthumous honours conferred upon him by the Throne. They accused him, not only of having habitually assumed Imperial prerogatives, but of having plotted with his immediate followers to depose his nephew-ward and to seize the Throne for himself. Later on, further accusations were brought against him; he was charged with having appropriated rich jewels belonging to the Throne, and it was said that a certain necklace which had belonged to Nurhachi had been buried with him, by his orders. Upon formal investigation these grave charges proved to be substantially true, and the young Emperor was compelled, much to his regret, to record a solemn decree of censure and degradation against his illustrious relative. The name of Prince Jui and that of his mother, the Concubine Wala-nala, were removed from the roll of the Imperial clans, and all their titles and dignities were posthumously cancelled. Thus early came the canker of personal ambition to breed disruption in the fine flower of the Manchu aristocracy. The disgrace that fell upon the Regent's memory was keenly felt, not only by his contemporaries, but by the descendants of Nurhachi, so much so, that more than a hundred years afterwards we find the Emperor Ch'ien Lung taking steps to restore Prince Jui's name and fame. In the forty-third year of his reign (1778) this Monarch issued an edict intended "to attain historical accuracy," much in the same way as the great Tzü Hsi attained it, by retrospectively cancelling all her Boxer edicts, in February 1901. Ch'ien Lung came to the conclusion, after carefully considering the case, that Prince Jui had been unjustly accused, and he therefore made full restitution of his honours and dignities, restored his tablet to its place in the temple of ancestors and re-established the Princedom of Jui in the person of Ch'un Ying, his descendant in the fifth generation. This princedom is now the second in rank of the hereditary nobles.[1]

Shun Chih was married at the age of fifteen to the Empress Tung Chia, mother of K'ang Hsi, who died two years after her son's accession. Of this lady's virtues or failings the chroniclers record little that is of interest. This may be due to the fact that, during the few years of the Sovereign's married life, he was completely under the influence of his favourite concubine, the Lady Tung, a woman who seems to have combined unusual physical attractions with literary accomplishments of a high order and a very masterful disposition. A Chinese commentator goes so far as to describe her as meddlesome (which he considers a peculiarly feminine failing), and declares that she was wont to admonish the whole Court on festive occasions to spare the drink, to dine wisely and not too well. She considered it her duty to keep

[1] The present holder of the title is a typically degenerate specimen of the latter day Manchu aristocracy, whose opium-smoking proclivities recently formed the subject of official investigation.

the Emperor up to the mark in his public and private life; she insisted upon his reading the whole text of routine business memorials without skipping, and the Emperor himself recorded (in an epitaph which partakes of the nature of a full obituary notice) that she was accustomed, before retiring for the night, to see for herself that the Imperial bedchamber was not overheated.

The Lady Tung was evidently good, and she died young, in the autumn of 1661. Her death affected Shun Chih with uncontrollable grief, from which he never recovered. The chronicler above mentioned naïvely remarks that His Majesty's regret for her loss seems to have been perfectly genuine, whereby he is greatly distinguished amongst Imperial husbands, " who generally rejoice at the death of their consorts." In the epitaph to which we have referred, Shun Chih indicates the breadth and depth of his lady's virtue by citing the fact that she invariably declined his invitations to supper, but would urge him to allow his chief Ministers to join him at the table; a statement which tends to show that the Court etiquette of the Manchus in those days was far less strict than it became at a later period, when they had assimilated the punctilious formalities of the classical Chinese code of manners.

According to the official annals of the dynasty, Shun Chih died and was buried in the winter of 1661, that is to say, only a few months before the last of the Mings was bowstringed at Yünnan-fu. The Lady Tung had " gone before " in the autumn of that year. But there appears to be good reason for doubting the dynastic annals in this matter of his death, and for sharing the belief, widely held by Chinese scholars, that the young Emperor, pining for his lost mistress and weary of the dull routine of statecraft, voluntarily handed over the Government to four of his Ministers (acting as joint Regents for his youthful son, K'ang Hsi) and retired to the contemplative life of the priesthood. This story, naturally enough, is not to be found in the dynastic records, since the priesthood is held in little reverence by the *literati*, and its admission would have cast a slur on the Emperor and the Imperial Clan; but the circumstantial evidence which supports it, in the writings of contemporary poets and others, is very strong. One, who is frequently quoted, wrote, " He threw away the Empire as one who casts away a worn-out shoe; he rejected the sovereignty thrust upon him in this incarnation, and, following the example of the Lord Buddha, preferred to seek the mystic solitudes." There is no doubt that the Emperor became imbued in his early youth with strong leanings towards the Buddhistic ideal of renunciation, and that he is known to have written, amongst other things, the following antithetical couplets:

" The future is as dark to me as the past out of which I have come;

" Vainly have I lived through one existence in this world of men;

" I have yearned to become a devoted follower of the Lord Buddha;

" Why, then, do I still hanker after the vanities of the Imperial Throne?"

It is also recorded that, shortly before his disappearance from the scene, he told Ao Pai, one of the four Ministers subsequently appointed to act as Regents for his successor, that he hoped to kneel amongst the crowd which should witness the ceremonial procession of the new Emperor, his son; much in the same way that Alexander I of Russia told his sister-in-law, the wife of his successor, Nicholas I, that he hoped, after his abdication and taking of religious vows, to witness their coronation procession in Moscow.[1]

---

[1] Vide *The Legend concerning the decease of Alexander I, in Siberia, in the guise of the monk Theodore.* By the Grand Duke Nicholas. (Petersburg, 1907.)

THE COURT OF PEKING

It is certainly the common belief amongst Chinese students of history that the Emperor Shun Chih did not die in 1661, as the annals have it, but that he arranged with his Ministers that he should vacate the Throne and conceal his identity in that of the Abbot of the T'ien T'ai temple, which lies amongst the hills, fourteen miles to the west of Peking. It was said by contemporary writers that the Abbot bore an extraordinary resemblance to the Emperor, and to this day the temple contains a life-sized gilt mummy statue of a priest, some thirty years of age, whose features are unmistakably of the Manchu type.

The illustration on page   reproduces a photograph of this mummy statue. It differs from the ordinary mummies of Buddhist bonzes in that it is clad in yellow Dragon robes instead of the usual red Kachâya vestments. It is alleged by tradition that the Dragon robes were sent by K'ang Hsi. The priests of the shrine also show the large vat in which the body was dried. The features of this mummy are covered with dark brown lacquer, whereas the usual procedure is to gild them. Finally, tradition declares that the Emperor K'ang Hsi visited the temple on three occasions, and paid his respects to the Abbot, who did not kneel to the Sovereign as custom would have required in the case of an ordinary priest. When, in 1670, the Abbot passed away, K'ang Hsi had a life-sized presentment of him cast in bronze, and sent presents of pearls and jewels to be buried in his tomb.

The stone dagoba under which he is said to lie is still standing, and every year the temple is opened to the faithful, who come to prostrate themselves at the shrine in the full belief that here a Lord of Heaven lies buried. Those who have compared the image of the Abbot of T'ien T'ai-ssü with the picture of Shun Chih in the collection of dynastic portraits in the Hall of Imperial Longevity

THE COURT OF PEKING

(which adjoins the Coal Hill of the Forbidden City) have testified to the remarkable resemblance.

But whether he departed this life, or only died as Emperor, Shun Chih vacated the Throne at the age of twenty-three, leaving his son, a boy of seven, to the care of four of his Ministers. This child was destined to reign over China for sixty-one years, and to confer enduring fame on the Manchu dynasty.

CHAPTER X

K'ANG HSI AS A FATHER

THE character of this famous Emperor, his wise government, his prowess in war and sport, his deep learning, multitudinous paternity and kind eart, all these have been described in the works of the Jesuit fathers, who until towards the end of his reign, held positions of dignity and influence at the Court of Peking. Naturally enough, many of these descriptions suffer from the theological bias of class, but, generally speaking, they are the work of broad-minded and sympathetic men, and show the Emperor K'ang Hsi in a kindlier light than that which usually beats upon a Throne. Indeed, kindness of heart seems to have been his most prominent quality, combined with a very clear perception of the truth that China's ruler must be firm. From the account of five voyages into Tartary,[1] on which the French Jesuit Gerbillon (mandarin of the third class) travelled in the suite of the Emperor between the years 1691 and 1697, the student of history may gather much to explain the revival of art and literature which distinguished this period, and learn to admire, at close range, the character of a Monarch truly great. Jean François Gerbillon, mathematician and writer, shared with the Portuguese, Anthoine Péreira, a degree of Imperial favour as high as that which His Majesty had previously given to Verbiest, the astronomer

---

[1] See *Histoire Generale de la Chine*, par le Père Mailla de la Société de Jésus, Vol. XI. (Paris, 1780.)

and reviser of the calendar. In 1693, they had introduced quinine to the notice of the Court physicians, when K'ang Hsi was dangerously ill of a fever, and he had shown his gratitude by granting them permission and money to build a church, and had given them a house inside the Palace enclosure. Even before this, however, greatly impressed by the virtue and learning of priests like Philippe Grimaldi, Jean de Fontaney, Joachim Bouvet, Louis le Comte and Claude de Visdelon, he had issued his famous Edict of Toleration (1692), which gave so great an impetus to the spread of Christianity in China, until the internal dissensions between the Jesuits and Dominicans led him to rescind it and to withdraw his favour from the missionaries.

The efforts of the Jesuits to convert K'ang Hsi and the Heir Apparent were discreet but unceasing. They endeavoured to convince him and to win him to the true faith by appeals to his intelligence, by continual demonstration of the Europeans' superiority in the arts and sciences; and for a time it seemed as if they might eventually be successful. In 1693, we find Father Fontaney sending a letter to his Abbé by the hand of Father Bouvet, in which he describes K'ang Hsi as " ce merveilleux Prince, à qui rien ne manque que d'être Chrétien pour être un des plus accomplis monarques de la terre."[1] He adds the following significant reference to the Heir Apparent: " Le Prince Héritier, que nous appelons ici Hoang-Tai-Tie, âgé de 21 ans, nous a marqué aussi qu'il désiroit quelque bel horloge de France,[2] qui sonne les heures et les quarts.

[1] *Lettres sur les Progres de la Réligion à la Chine.* (Paris, 1698.)
[2] Many clocks, watches and musical-boxes of French manufacture, decorated with ormulu and Limoges enamel, found their way to Peking in the seventeenth century, after the first specimens had been presented to the Throne and Court by the Jesuit fathers. Many of them were brought back to Europe, after the looting of the Summer Palace by the British and French armies in 1860, and more again after the looting of the city in 1900.

THE COURT OF PEKING

Ce Prince régnera un jour, et il est déjà bien intentionné pour nous; et il est important de le gagner tout à fait."

News of this kind, sent to Europe from the Court of Peking, was likely to create hopes of the ultimate conversion of the Emperor and his heir, and rumours to that effect were widely circulated shortly after the issue of the Edict of Toleration. In 1697, however, a letter from Peking[1] expresses doubts on this subject: " Je ne sais si le bruit de la conversion de l'Empereur de la Chine au Christianisme, qui se répandit il y a quelque temps, parvint jusqu'à vous, mais je sçay bien que je ne voulus pas vous en écrire parce que je n'en étois pas fort persuadé." Other letters, written in 1695, had announced the conversion and baptism of a Prince at the Court, " whose mother was a sister of the late Empress," and again of another Prince, aged thirteen. But the Imperial author of the " Sacred Edict," for all his tolerant goodwill towards them, was not likely to take anything from the Christian missionaries which could shake his own implicit faith in the Canons of the Sages. His subsequent persecution of Christianity in China was directly due to the excessive zeal of the Jesuit fathers, who presumed upon the place they had won in the confidence of this liberal-minded Emperor.

With the history of K'ang Hsi's wars, of the revival of literature and learning under his direction, and the political relations of China with her neighbours and vassals during his long reign, the present work does not profess to deal. We have referred to the writings and other activities of the Jesuit fathers at Peking for the reason that students of history will find in them much that is of interest and importance.

For five years after his succession to the Throne, in 1662, the lad K'ang Hsi was under the charge of the Board

---

[1] Quatrième lettre historique de Hollande, imprimée à la Haye au mois Fevrier de l'année, 1697.

of Regents appointed by his father to administer the Government, but from the outset he was influenced against them (and particularly against Duke Ao Pai, the most masterful of the four) by his grandmother, the strong-minded Mongol Empress of T'ai Tsung, and by Shun Chih's Empress, Borjikin. The Regents also incurred his youthful displeasure by their harsh treatment of the Roman Catholic fathers,—towards whom Shun Chih had shown himself well and kindly disposed—and particularly by their imprisonment of Adam Schaal, who had been appointed special tutor to K'ang Hsi. It was largely because of this persecution of the worthy Father Adam [1] and other Christians that, in 1667, the young Monarch, aided and abetted by his grandmother and the moral support of his Court, dismissed the Regents and assumed control of the Government at the age of thirteen.

It is interesting, at this point, to observe that the whole history of the Manchu dynasty illustrates the quality which Mill has described as peculiarly characteristic of Orientals, the quality of inveterate jealousy, which successive Emperors and their advisers displayed towards high officials who had attained to influence in the councils of their predecessors. Thus, in Shun Chih's reign, we have the posthumous deposition of the Regent, Prince Jui: K'ang Hsi dismisses his Board of Regents; Chia Ch'ing orders the death of his father's chief favourite; Tao Kuang dismisses his father's all-powerful eunuch; Hsien Feng orders Mu Yang-a into retirement; T'ung Chih (under the influence of Tzŭ Hsi) rids himself of the usurping Regents; and finally, to come to our own day, the Emperor Lung Yü, in the name of His Majesty Hsüan T'ung, dismisses Yüan Shih-k'ai.

To return to K'ang Hsi. After his assumption of the Government, the Regents, who retained office as Ministers,

[1] *Vide* Du Halde, *Description de l'Empire de la Chine et de la Tartare Chinoise*, 1735, Vol. IV, p. 286.

continued for some time to be a thorn in his side; the Duke Ao Pai, in particular, treating him with studied arrogance, which his proud spirit could ill brook. But the ex-Regents commanded a powerful following, and the old Empress Dowager therefore advised the young Monarch to go warily. The following account of the way in which these Ministers were finally removed, is interesting, if only because it reveals in the aged consort of T'ai Tsung the naïve credulity and superstition which, to the end, remained characteristic of the notable women of the dynasty.

On New Year's Day 1669, the Duke Ao Pai appeared as usual, at the head of the Court, to offer the season's congratulations. He wore an Imperial state robe, the only difference between his attire and that of the Sovereign being that, instead of the great Imperial pearl which the Emperor wore on the front of his official hat, he contented himself with a knot of red velvet. K'ang Hsi made no comment at the time, but on returning to his private apartments asked his grandmother to advise him by what means they could get rid of the haughty Minister. At that moment the old lady's favourite eunuch was by her side, throwing dice out of a cup for luck. In throwing Chinese dice, of which there are usually six, the best throw occurs when the six different numbers all turn up. K'ang Hsi seized the cup, paused an instant as if invoking supernatural aid, and made a cast. The numbers came out all different, whereupon the Empress Grand Dowager, delighted, exclaimed: "You need not be afraid of him any longer" (referring to Ao Pai). A few days later, a decree was issued by the Emperor dismissing the ex-Regents from their offices, and inviting his Princes and Ministers to consider their offences and advise as to the proper penalty. They recommended that Ao Pai should be sentenced to the lingering death, but as the Empress Grand Dowager did not consider it expedient to take such extreme measures, the sentence was commuted to permission to commit suicide and the forfeiture of his estates and titles, except the hereditary dukedom. Before the sentence could be carried out, a Buku (palace wrestler), strangled him in prison.

In commemoration of this happy release, K'ang Hsi subsequently issued a decree establishing as a house-law, to be observed by his posterity, that, on every New Year's Day, the Emperor should throw the dice, to learn the omens for the coming year. And so, until the abdication of the dynasty, it was done; but, like all good uses, it became corrupted in later years at the hands of the eunuchs. On New Year's Day, after the Court had done obeisance and the Emperor had retired to his apartments, it was the invariable custom for the Chief Eunuch to hand him a golden plate with six dice on it. The eunuch would kneel while the Emperor cast the dice. Invariably they turned up all different, and the eunuch, congratulating the Sovereign on the continued favour of Heaven, would then hurriedly remove them. But Heaven had nothing to say to this invariably auspicious result, because these Imperial dice were carefully made, so as to ensure favourable omens, with a different number, and one only, on each.[1]

Concerning Ao Pai, the chroniclers also aver that a week before his dismissal, he had applied for sick leave, and the Emperor went to pay him a visit. He found him lying on the stove-bed, covered with a sable robe. While K'ang Hsi was talking to him, one of the suite suddenly drew the sable robe slightly aside, and a dagger was dis-

[1] In the record of Father Gerbillon's first journey in the suite of K'ang Hsi to Tartary (1691), he states that the Emperor (then thirty-seven years of age), discussing with him affairs connected with the Board of Astronomy, expressed the utmost contempt for those who superstitiously believed in good and evil hours and auspicious days. Not only did he regard these beliefs as false and vain, but he held that they did great injury to the State, when the rulers of the country are obsessed by them.

THE COURT OF PEKING

covered. It is treason for a subject to have arms on his person in the presence of the Emperor, but K'ang Hsi only smiled at the sight and said: "Ao Pai is indeed a true Manchu warrior; he keeps his weapon ready by his side, even when on a bed of sickness, that he may rise at any moment to defend his Emperor." From these words the courtiers knew that the days of Ao Pai's power were numbered.

Towards the end of his long reign, K'ang Hsi's life was made a burden to him and his health undermined by the undutiful and lawless conduct of several of his sons. He was a great ruler and a wise man, but he resembled many other great men in the history of the East, from Solomon down to the statesmen and scholars of to-day, in that his philosophy was not proof against the vicissitudes of polygamy and the penalties of excessive paternity. His sons, like the sons of Eli, dealt evilly with the people, and brought their father's grey hairs in sorrow to the grave, a result by no means uncommon under China's patriarchal system. K'ang Hsi's edicts and exhortations concerning his domestic broils reveal the fact that, firmly convinced of his own virtues and intelligence, he took pride in his procreative capacity, and hoped to confer on his dynasty and on China an abundant posterity, imbued with his own moral and intellectual qualities. In this, he was grievously disappointed, and the incessant broils created by his sons when they had reached years of discretion embittered his declining years and dimmed the prestige of his reign.

K'ang Hsi had thirty-five sons; of these twenty-four attained to manhood. The following is a list of those who by good or evil report, figured prominently in the annals of his reign and that of his successor, Yung Cheng:

*Yün Ch'ih : born in 1672, son of the concubine Hui, who was of rank too low to permit of her offspring being eligible to the Throne. He was created Prince Chih (Upright), and was cashiered and confined to his residence in 1708. Obiit 1734.

Yün Jeng: Prince Li (Principled), son of the senior Empress Consort Hoshli, who died in 1674. He was made Heir Apparent when two years old; deprived of his title and confined to one of the palaces in the rear of the Coal Hill in October 1708, reinstated in April 1709, again degraded and imprisoned in October 1712. Died in prison in the second year of Yung Cheng's reign, 1725.

*Yün Chih: Prince Ch'eng (Sincere). Born in 1677, imprisoned by his brother Yung Cheng in 1730 at the Coal Hill, and poisoned (officially stated to have died of a sudden disease) in July 1732.

Yin Chen: created Prince Yung (Just), succeeded his father as Emperor Yung Cheng. Born 1678, died 1735.

Yün Ch'i: Prince Heng (Steadfast), born 1680, died 1732.

Yün Yu: Prince Shun (Pure), born 1680, died 1730.

*Yün Ssŭ: Prince Lien (Conscientious), usually called the eighth Prince. Born of " a woman of poor origin, named Hinyeku," in 1681, deprived of his title and imprisoned by Yung Cheng in 1726. Expelled from the Imperial Clan and given the opprobrious title of " That unspeakable person." Died (poisoned) six months later. Posthumously restored to the Imperial Clan in 1778 by the Emperor Ch'ien Lung.

**Yün T'ang*: born in 1680, deprived of his title and name erased from the Imperial Clan in June 1726. Given the name of " Full of black thoughts." By a strange coincidence his death (in prison at Pao Ting-fu in September 1726) occurred within a few days of that of the eighth Prince, Yün Ssŭ.

*Yün O: born in 1683, given the title of Prince Tun

THE COURT OF PEKING

 (Solid) in 1709; imprisoned by his brother Yung Cheng in 1726; set free by Ch'ien Lung.

Yün T'ao: Prince "Walking in Righteousness," born 1685, died 1763.

Yün Hsiang: Prince Yi (Harmonious), born 1686, died 1730. Ancestor of Tsai Yuan, the usurping Regent of T'ung Chih's reign.

Yün Ti: Prince Trustworthy, born in 1688, imprisoned in 1726 in a side court of the Palace of Imperial Longevity, where his father's coffin had reposed. Restored to liberty by Ch'ien Lung.

Yün Lu: Prince Chuang (Sedate), born in 1695. K'ang Hsi's favourite son; a friend of the Jesuit fathers and a good astronomer and mathematician. Died in 1767.

 Of these the five marked (*) conspired to have the Heir Apparent, Yün Jeng, put aside and to set Yün Ssŭ on the Throne. The latter was undoubtedly an able man, but became an object of suspicion at Court, owing to the general belief that he had become a Christian. K'ang Hsi had originally been very well disposed towards the Roman Catholics, but, weary of their disputes, turned against them in later years and opposed his sons' intimacy with the Jesuit fathers. The objections of the five Princes to the Heir Apparent were not entirely unreasonable (though their methods were unfilial), as Yün Jeng was certainly possessed of an evil spirit.

 In the autumn of 1708, K'ang Hsi went on a hunting trip to the country around Jehol. He was sick at heart, for the unseemly conduct of his sons had latterly given extreme offence to the Ministers of his Court. News of their continued misdeeds reached the Emperor at his hunting, whereupon he addressed his Court Chamberlain as follows: "I hear that my sons frequently assault and insult the Ministers of my Court and the Imperial bodyguard, besides picking quarrels with other Princes of my house and ill-treating them. Now I wish it to be clearly understood that my sons are only authorised to inflict summary chastisement on their own servants; in all other cases they are bound to report to me and await my decision. How can they be permitted to run riot and flog whomsoever they please? I am the lord of the world, and I myself conform in all things to correct principles. Every innocent man is by right exempt from punishment. There can only be one Head of the State, and my daily prayer is to secure universal happiness and peace. The rule which forbids summary decapitation or strangling, without due reference to me, by nobles or high officials, was framed in the interests of the State, and not solely for the protection of the individual. It is an insult to my dignity that my sons should treat officials, high and low, with outrageous contumely, and these practices must be stopped. If they break the law of the land by abusing their power and putting my officials in terror of their lives they are guilty of usurping Imperial prerogatives, which belong to me alone. Are they not aware that sovereign authority cannot be delegated to another? There is but one ruler—myself. Not even my brothers, the Princes Yü and Kung, would venture to take such a liberty as to flog my Ministers and members of my bodyguard! However guilty any of these might have been, I would never have allowed my brothers to take the law into their own hands and to put my officials to death. In any case, however, they never perpetrated any such offences, and my sons cannot be allowed to commit them.

"The founder of my dynasty and his son issued wise precepts concerning these matters, expressly forbidding that the Princes of the Imperial house should scourge or maltreat their inferiors, and I never could have believed that such unlawful practices would sully my reign. If, in future, my sons disregard my injunctions and flog or insult any Minister of the Court, the injured parties are hereby specially enjoined to report the facts to me with full details. I shall not fail to hear the case and to give impartial judgment, without visiting any punishment on the plaintiff. If things continue in their present course, the next thing will be massacres perpetrated without my knowledge. If this my mandate be not transmitted verbatim I shall order the decapitation of those responsible for its due transmission."

A few days later, at Bur-hastai, the Emperor bade the Court assemble and order the Heir Apparent (Yün Jeng) to kneel before him. With tears in his eyes he addressed him as follows: "It is now forty-eight years since I received the Great Inheritance; during the whole of that time I have aspired to rule over a contented people with compassionate affection. But my son, Yün Jeng, constantly violates the ancestral precepts and my own admonitions. His wanton cruelty and vindictive oppression have been allowed to continue unreproved, and I have borne with him for the past twenty years. His wickedness has waxed more and more flagrant; he has insulted or beaten the Princes and Ministers of the Court; he has presumed on his position to collect a lawless band around him for the purpose of keeping watch on my movements and of reporting to him my every action.[1]

"As I see it, the Empire can only have one ruler; by what right, then, does Yün Jeng ill-treat and beat my Princes and Ministers? Prince P'ing and the Beileh Hai-shan have both been flogged by his orders, and few of my officials, few even of my bodyguard and personal servants, have escaped his wrath.

"I am fully aware of all that has been going on. If any official reports his conduct to me, Yün Jeng regards him as a mortal enemy and treats him with cruel vindic-

[1] K'ang Hsi suspected his son of a design to assassinate him.

tiveness. Knowing this, I have refrained from making inquiries from my Court as to his behaviour. In the course of my numerous journeys in the provinces of the Empire, by road or river, I myself have never transgressed the path of decorum by a single step, nor injured any of my subjects. But Yün Jeng and his band of ruffians stop at nothing; they violate every right principle. His behaviour makes me blush; I am ashamed to speak of it. When the Mongol Princes sent tribute horses to me as a present, Yün Jeng dispatched his servants to seize them on the road to Peking, and kept them for his own use. The Mongols naturally resented this and they blamed me.

"His misdeeds are innumerable, but I have kept on hoping that he would repent him of his errors and return to the right way. So I have borne with him in silence and shown foolish leniency until to-day. I was well aware long ago of Yün Jeng's extravagant habits and, with the object of meeting his exorbitant requirements, I made his foster-mother's husband, Ling P'u, Comptroller of the Imperial Household, so as to give him every opportunity. To my amazement, I find that Ling P'u is even more corrupt and greedy than Yün Jeng, and the consequence is that the retainers of my household all hate him. When Yün Jeng was a child, I used to teach him that the needs of my privy purse are provided out of the people's life-blood, and that wise economy was essential to good government. But he has disregarded my teaching, and has given the rein to his shameless extravagance and savage violence. If he continues in this way he will surely end by killing off all his brothers.

" A few days ago, when my eighteenth son was mortally sick, every one sympathised with me in this grief, afflicting my old age. But Yün Jeng was quite callously indifferent to his brother's fate and, when I reproved him, had the audacity to lose his temper. Stranger still, his foster-mother incited him to tear a hole in the cloth of the travelling pavilion in which I had retired for the night and to peep through at me with insolent scrutiny.

"On a previous occasion So-e-tu aided and abetted him in a conspiracy against my life. I discovered the plot and put So-e-tu to death. In revenge for this, Yün Jeng has now collected a band of desperate villains, planning to put an end to me. At times they seek to poison my food, and again they plot to assassinate me. I have to be perpetually on guard and never enjoy a peaceful moment.

"How can I permit such a man to succeed to the august Inheritance? Let us not forget also that Yün Jeng's mother, the late Empress, died in giving birth to him. The ancients always regarded such conduct as unfilial. Ever since my accession I have practised scrupulous parsimony; my bed quilt is shabby and my hose are made of commonest cloth. Yün Jeng's household is on a scale infinitely grander than mine. Yet still he is not satisfied and must needs appropriate money from the Imperial Treasury, besides interfering in State affairs. Unless prompt measures are taken, the result will be disaster to the State and ruin to my subjects. If I allow so unfilial a son and so evil a man to become Emperor, how shall I face my ancestors, and how will it fare with their heritage?"

At this point the Emperor paused and burst into a paroxysm of noisy sobbing. He collapsed and grovelled on the ground, from which undignified posture he was raised by his Ministers.

With an effort he proceeded: "I cannot allow such a man to succeed to the inheritance won by my ancestors and consolidated by myself. On my return to Peking I shall announce my decision to the Almighty and the spirits of my ancestors, and inform them of Yün Jeng's deposition.

"On a previous occasion I bade my eldest son, Yün Ch'ih, to give good heed to my personal safety, but I never contemplated making him Heir Apparent. He is quite impossible, being of excitable temperament and obstinate in the extreme.

"I shall inflict no punishment on such of Yün's Jeng's followers as were forced through fear into joining him. I hereby order the immediate decapitation of So-e-tu's sons and of Erh-ko-su-erh and Te-ha-shih-t'ai. This matter vitally concerns the whole Empire. I have taken care to deal with it while still in the enjoyment of good health and in the possession of all my faculties. Yün Jeng is to be placed under arrest at once, and the Princes, Ministers and common people are all at liberty to memorialise me on the subject, giving their views as to the justice of my sentence."

The Court kotowed and burst into lamentations. The Ministers replied: "Your Majesty is indeed sage and enlightened. Every word you have uttered about Yün Jeng is true. There is no need for us to memorialise in reply."

To the Ministers of the Presence, K'ang Hsi delivered a separate homily: "When Yün Jeng was Heir Apparent you naturally had to obey his orders, but I suspect that some among you were guilty of intrigue and flattery. Now that you have been witnesses of his deposition I can imagine that you are passing days and nights of abject terror lest I should discover your relations with Yün Jeng and punish you with decapitation. Yün Jeng's wicked behaviour has forced me to take this action in his regard, but if I began instituting a wholesale proscription of all his faction, not one of my Court would escape punishment. I should be left to reign in solitary state. I have already dealt out a measure of punishment to the guilty, and there let the matter rest. Even if you are denounced I shall ignore the impeachment, so pray you, be at ease.

"My reason for summoning my third son, Yün Chih,

to private audience to-day was due to his great intimacy with Yün Jeng, and I had certain questions to put to him. It is not my intention to order his arrest, since, notwithstanding his close relations with his elder brother, he has not encouraged or abetted his pernicious designs. In fact, he assures me that he has frequently admonished the ex-Heir Apparent to forbear, but without success. I believe he is telling the truth, and I am fully acquainted with the facts. I have been greatly upset by these events, and my heart is disquieted within me; hence my omission in the previous decree to reassure your panic-stricken minds and to bid you be at peace for the future."

On the following morning K'ang Hsi, who was now on his way back to the capital, summoned his Court and the Manchu Grand Secretaries to his travelling tent, and thus addressed them : . " I have always been guided by my historical studies and the lessons which past dynasties afford, and have refused to allow pretty women to have free access to the Palace. In the same way I have never allowed good-looking youths to minister to my wants and attend my table, because I wished there to be no flaw in the jade of my good name, and to keep my body in subjection. Among my hearers at this moment are Kuan Pao and Wu Shih, both of whom have attended me since my childhood; they know all my goings out and comings in, and are aware that what I say is true. But this business of the ex-Heir Apparent has come as a terrible blow, and I have not slept for six nights." At this point the Emperor burst into loud weeping, and the courtiers, affecting an equal distress, responded : " Pray control yourself and be pleased to consider the sacred duty Your Majesty owes to the State and to your ancestors. It is essential that you take care of your health."

K'ang Hsi then proceeded : " I have now reigned for nigh fifty years, and have won many new territories for my Empire. I brought the Eleuths to their knees, although they had never before acknowledged allegiance. I may be getting old, but if I may say so without boasting, I am still thoroughly capable of ruling with a statesman-like mien. Your love and loyalty for my person are, I am convinced, sincere; I have always treated my officials with kindness and have never unjustly inflicted corporal punishment on my attendants.

"But this year I had have to deplore the loss by death of many trusted officials. You do not know of the tears which I have shed in secret. Now you beg me to take care of my health, and I naturally feel bound to comply with your request. Ever since the beginning of the year I have had an apprehension of coming calamity, and I have mentioned my fears to the ex-Heir Apparent. When the incident of the mad priest, who claimed to have found the Ming descendant, occurred th other day, Yün Jeng remarked that my prophecy had come true. But at the time I told him that there was further trouble ahead, though I never anticipated the present misfortune.

"You remember when my grandfather defeated the Ming armies, in the third year of T'ien Ts-ang (1629), and appeared in person outside the gates of Peking? His Generals then urged him to seize his opportunity and take the city. 'Now is your time,' said they, 'to found a dynasty. The city is yours; why not take it at once?' My grandsire replied: "Peking, it is true, can easily be captured, but it behoves us to wait for the mandate of Heaven. The time is not yet ripe.' Fifteen years later, as you know, the capital fell into the hands of rebels, and the Princes and clansmen captured it for my father without trouble. The Empire became ours and in due course descended to me. Our dynasty has now ruled for two generations, and if the people are at peace it is due to my obedience to ancestral tradition and my ceaseless labours.

"On occasions of drought I have fasted three days in

the Palace, burning incense and praying to the Almighty without ceasing. As soon as I proceeded to the Temple of Heaven to sacrifice, my prayers were heard and abundant rain fell. Does not this prove that I have found favour in the sight of Heaven? But I have never indulged in vain boasting nor fancied that Heaven was bound to hearken to my prayers. Henceforth it is your duty to help me and to labour more earnestly."

Yün Jeng went with the Court on the return journey to Peking, and K'ang Hsi observed him closely. The result of his diagnosis was given to his Ministers, as follows: " Yün Jeng is not a normal being. He sleeps the livelong day and breaks his fast at midnight. He indulges in deep potations, and can carry thirty or forty cups of strong spirit without becoming intoxicated. When I used to send him to perform sacrifice, he would become very nervous on reaching the altar and fail in the performance of the ceremonial. He is in terror of thunder and lightning, and even heavy rain alarms him. His behaviour is most eccentric, and he talks a lunatic gibberish. There can be no doubt that he is mad and sore vexed by demoniac possession. I have come to the conclusion that the Palace in Peking occupied by Yün Jeng, that of 'Picked Fragrance,' is haunted. Its situation is low and unhealthy, and many deaths have occurred there. Through constant residence there Yün Jeng has fallen a victim to an evil spirit, which has taken up its habitation in his body. It is a most extraordinary circumstance, but his conduct can only be due to demoniacal influence."

On the following day the cortège reached Peking; during the journey the ex-Heir Apparent had been in the custody of his elder brother, Yün Ch'ih. On reaching the city, K'ang Hsi ordered a felt tent to be prepared for his reception in the Imperial equipage department, and placed Yün Jeng in charge of Yün Ch'ih and of his fourth brother (who reigned later as Yung Cheng).

The first thing to be done was to inform the Empress Dowager.[1] After Her Majesty had signified her approval of the ex-Heir Apparent's deposition, K'ang Hsi ascended the Throne of the T'ui ho (Exalted Peace) Palace and read his decree:

"The position of heir to the Throne is of the greatest importance to the State, and I, who am a keen student of history, could never regard the question of succession with indifference. During Yün Jeng's childhood I taught him myself, and afterwards nominated competent preceptors to instruct him in philosophy. It cannot be said that he did not show progress in his studies, while in horsemanship, archery, caligraphy and composition he was quite up to the average. But lately his mind has become clouded through demoniac possession: he fidgets incessantly, and talks and acts in the most peculiar fashion. He is always seeing visions; his sleeping and waking hours are full of terror. He keeps changing his abode, and will devour seven or eight bowls of rice at a meal without satisfying his appetite. He can carry thirty beakers of wine without inconvenience.

"My inquiries have elicited several other interesting and surprising facts: of all his multitude of attendants not one speaks well of him. This is proof conclusive that his mind is deranged. I had intended to wait until my arrival in Peking before putting him under arrest, but circumstances rendered prompt action necessary. What is your opinion of his case?" The Court remained on its knees, and Prince K'ang, the senior Prince present, answered: "Your Majesty nurtured the Heir Apparent with benevolence and trained him in the path of duty. But of late years he has become demented, and is possessed

---

[1] The consort of Shun Chih, by name Borjikin, a daughter of Duke Chorchi, of the Mongol Khorchia tribe. Now in her seventy-third year, she was a remarkable old lady, who took an active part in the Government. K'ang Hsi was devoted to her. She died in 1718, aged eighty-three.

by a devil. Your decision to disinherit him is warranted by circumstances; our opinion is unanimous."

K'ang Hsi replied: "I have made up my mind, and shall inform Heaven and earth and the Temple of Ancestors. The Heir Apparent is sentenced to confinement in prison. He was son of my Empress Consort, and has received the most loving care at my hands. I used to teach him that he must obey the precepts of our ancestors, and would point the moral which the classics and history teach—how that the success or ruin of a dynasty depends upon its retention of the confidence of the people. However ignorant he may be, surely he must be aware that no one can afford to forfeit the people's trust. But, in spite of the careful training which he has received, his conduct has left him without a single friend. Can it be doubted that he is a victim to demoniac possession, irresponsible for his actions?

"Yün Jeng's case is disposed of. If my other sons make it a pretext for forming cabals and for endeavouring to ruin Yün Jeng's former partisans, I shall show them no mercy.

"My great grandfather, our founder, decapitated his eldest son Ch'u Yen on charges brought against him by the other Princes; my grandsire visited punishment on one of the Princesses in connection with the charge against Prince Mang-ku-erh-tai; in my father's time Prince Li accused his son Sheto and his grandson At-a-li of breaking the law, and both were beheaded; the former Regent, my uncle, Prince Jui, put Princes to death for flattery and intrigue; in my own childhood, soon after my accession, Ao Pai paid off grudges against his colleague in the Regency, Su-ko-sa-ha, by exterminating him and all his family, in spite of my remonstrances. Such cases are common, and in our family it seems inevitable that these fratricidal quarrels should occur, owing to its inveterate tendency to form cabals. Will not this be a warning to you all? I have now reigned forty-eight years, a period longer than all (save a few exceptions) of my predecessors in history. This is a sure sign that the Almighty regards me with affection, and in return am I not bound to do my best for the Empire and my subjects?"

Upon the deposition of the Heir Apparent, two high officials of the Court, partisans of the eighth Prince, Yün Ssŭ, hoping to gain credit and the succession for their patron, circulated fresh charges against Yün Jeng for the purpose of poisoning the Emperor's mind and inducing him to have the wretched Yün Jeng put to death. On perusing the memorial which they put in the Emperor was very wrath, and decided to order his son's execution. But he was turned from this purpose by Lou Te-na, a Chamberlain of the Presence, an aged official who had great influence over him. He had fixed on the day of his return to the Palace from the western hills to issue his death decree, but before the cortège started for the city Lou asked for audience. After speaking of routine details he said: "A strange thing has happened: the commandant of the guards at the city gate, who used to be excessively fat, has been suddenly smitten with sickness, and is now as thin as a lathe." When K'ang Hsi reached Peking, he saw the commandant standing at the head of his men, and noticed that he was as fat as usual, whereupon he rebuked Lou with making a false report. Lou laughingly answered: "This may show Your Majesty how unreliable are these reports about the former Heir Apparent. If false rumours can get about concerning your commandant's loss of flesh, how much more so in the case of a Prince who is naturally a target for the calumnies of jealous persons!" K'ang Hsi nodded and tore up the decree which would have consigned his son to the scaffold.

The Hanlin Academy drew up a form of liturgy for the Emperor to use in informing Heaven, earth, the tutelary deities, and the ancestral spirits of the Heir Apparent's deposition. But its form was not modest enough to please K'ang Hsi, who substituted one of his own, and ordered that it be rendered into Manchu without the alteration of a character, " to show the depth of his sincerity." On the translation being completed the Emperor was still dissatisfied, and administered the following rebuke to all concerned. " In my draft of the proposed service I used the words : ' Bending my body and exhausting my energies, ceasing only with death.' I was quoting the words of Chu-ko Liang (a famous General) in his memorial on taking the field. You are, no doubt, under the impression that such language can only be appropriately used by a Minister, and should not proceed from the Sovereign. You therefore altered the meaning in the Manchu version. Now I consider that these words are worthy of a loyal and good Minister like Chu-ko Liang, but if such devotion be fitting in the statesman, how much more is it so in the Sovereign ? Let me explain my meaning to you Ministers. The statesman can always lay the blame for his mistakes on the Sovereign, but on whom is the Sovereign to shuffle off his responsibility ? It is his bounden duty to ' bend his body and exhaust his energies ' in reverence to God and diligent care for the people. I am the son of Almighty God, and God is my only stay; the Heir Apparent was formerly the object on which my hope and trust centred. But his conduct has rendered his deposition inevitable; how. then, could I omit to inform God Almighty ? The ceremony is fixed for to-morrow."

The Heir Apparent had intrigued with the various Ministries and frequently interfered in Government appointments, doubtless for a tangible consideration. K'ang Hsi ordered an investigation, as the result of which the Cabinet reported that there was no proof of his having actually altered or cancelled any orders issued by the Throne. K'ang Hsi replied : " Naturally he would **not** have had the effrontery to make changes in rescripts and decrees issued by my vermilion pencil; nevertheless, he was always seeking to usurp the supreme power. It is certain that in many instances he secured the shelving of measures of which he disapproved, and conversely the expediting of those in which he was interested, besides having exerted illicit influence for venal objects. I hereby command that every appointment or measure which has been recently promulgated, and about which there is the least taint of suspicion, shall be cancelled forthwith."

The following is the text of his Decree to the Nation: " By God's grace I succeeded to my ancestors' patrimony, forty-eight years ago. Throughout my reign I have reverenced the Almighty and striven to meet my subjects' wishes. I do not forget that God created the people, and appointed a ruler to govern them in order that their needs might be studied. I have ever made careful inquiries as to the condition of my subjects all over the Empire; in no single instance have I shown slackness; I have made grants from my privy purse amounting to scores of millions of taels. I have relieved their distress by reducing the land tax, and have saved thousands of lives by amnesties to offenders, because it is the duty of a Sovereign to cherish his people, and this principle was inculcated by my ancestors as a behest to their posterity.

" But in spite of all my careful training, the Heir Apparent, Yün Jeng, is vicious by nature, and has disobeyed my instructions. Although his conduct steadily deteriorated, I was in hopes of his amendment, and allowed him to accompany me on my numerous journeys to the southern and western provinces, in the hope that he might thus acquire a knowledge of local conditions and of the people over whom he would one day rule.

" But he blackmailed the Viceroys and Governors, and extorted bribes from local officials. His retinue was composed of bad characters, who levied tribute on the countryside and committed acts of violence and robbery. I would often urge him to be more economical, as it is the people who have to provide for all our requirements, but he gave full play to his wicked lusts, and showed no signs of amendment. He has made away with articles of tribute which were destined for my use, and has appropriated huge sums from the Imperial treasury. There are no bounds to his oppression of the people. Of late his fiendish cruelty and unholy lust have become still more flagrant; the Princes and Ministers have all been victims of his overbearing insults, and have even suffered beatings at his hands. When I found out that So-e-tu and Ch'ang-t'ai were plotting against me on his initiative I put them to death at once; in consequence of which Yün Jeng has harboured resentment against me, and has even dared to spy on my movements in the privacy of the Imperial tent. Beyond all doubt, he intended to assassinate me, and his whole behaviour indicates demoniac possession. The classic of history says: 'Heaven sees as my people see; Heaven hears as my people hear. Heaven will surely detest the man whom the people hate.'

"How can such a man be permitted to perform the ancestral sacrifice or worship the tutelary dieties as Emperor? I have given most careful thought to this matter, and feel that my bounden duty leaves no alternative. I have received the gracious orders of the Empress Dowager to announce Yün Jeng's deposition and arrest at the several shrines, in order to propitiate the ancestral spirits and to comfort my people.

"I have now stated all the circumstances, and as a special grace bestow exemption on my subjects in remitting taxation, out of sympathy for the exactions which they have endured at Yün Jeng's hands. By purifying the fountain of national life, the stability of my dynasty will be enhanced; by this act of clemency the bounty of the Throne will everywhere be manifested."

On the following morning K'ang Hsi thus addressed his sons: "At the time of Yün Jeng's arrest, my eldest son, Yün Ch'ih, said to me: 'Yün Jeng's behaviour is utterly base and abominable, he is scarcely to be called a human being. Not long ago a fortune-teller named Chang Ming-ti examined Yün Ssŭ (the eighth son's) physiognomy, and declared that he would eventually inherit the Throne. If you desire Yün Jeng's death it can be arranged by us, and there is no need for Your Majesty, my father, to lay hands on him.' When I heard the above speech I was completely dumbfounded. I am well aware that my eldest son is violent by nature and of a besotted ignorance, for whom duty and principle mean nothing. If he and his brother, Yün Ssŭ, were really hatching a plot to assassinate Yün Jeng they are quite capable of carrying it out, regardess of the possible consequences to myself. Such men are no better than traitors or parricides, since they transgress every tie of loyalty and filial duty. They will reap their reward either in the judgment of Heaven or the punishment of man."

K'ang Hsi compelled his eldest son, Yün Ch'ih, to hand over the physiognomist Chang Ming-ti (who had foretold that his eighth son would be Emperor), and commanded his trial by a commission. The Emperor remarked: "I am acquainted with the circumstances of the case, which are most grave and involve a large number of persons. This man, Chang Ming-ti, has been sending notices round to many officials, but he alone is to be punished, and no general proscription will be permitted."

By this time K'ang Hsi was thoroughly uneasy about his domestic affairs, and evidently in abject terror of assassination. Again he summoned his sons to the Palace, and thus addressed them: "You must really keep your retainers in better order and prevent them from creating disturbances. The husbands of your foster-nurses are of thoroughly disreputable antecedents; indeed, your households are mainly composed of scheming and illiterate persons who misbehave and ill-treat the people. Take Yün Ch'ih's four eunuchs, for example, or his two body-servants. They are always spying on my movements and endeavouring to get hold of Palace gossip. I know all about the origin of these men, in fact I have had to banish several of Yün Ch'ih's servants before now, while others have been killed in brawls. You, Yün Ch'ih, really ought to have some little self-respect. I have not spared Yün Jeng, and shall certainly not be more lenient with the rest of you. When, on a previous occasion, I called you all to my presence, Yün Ch'ih replied as follows: 'Hereafter all of us brothers will dwell together in unity. We shall spend our days happily in the light of your presence, O Imperial father.'

"Now, I regard the above remark as far from satisfactory: suppose that among your number there be one bad character, who conducts himself lawlessly, are all you brothers going to 'dwell together in unity' with him? Besides, Yün Ch'ih's own record is very bad; he uttered slanders against the ex-Heir Apparent and tried to induce me to put him to death. Who can believe a word he says, when he talks so glibly about unity in future? In the past Yün Ch'ih has had the effrontery to lay violent hands on my guardsmen and major domos; these men can be produced as witnesses. When Yün Jeng was in his custody he carried off several of the workmen and labourers at his brother's residence and had them cruelly flogged. The result was that some committed suicide and others ran away. No wonder that every one thinks badly of you, Yün Ch'ih.

"My troubles come thick and fast: first my eighteenth son died suddenly, and now I have had to bear Yün Jeng's deposition. You ought to consider your poor father a little and conduct yourselves with decency. Does not the classic say : 'He who loves his father will never dare to incur the hatred of others; he who respects his father will never allow himself to deserve contempt.' You set a bad example and are breaking my heart; how can you have the heart to treat me so? Kindly inform your respective households of this decree."

Yün Ssŭ was at this time Comptroller of the Household, and had been ordered to assess the value of a disgraced official's property, who was an ex-Comptroller. The amount was far less than the Emperor had anticipated, as the official in question was noted for his vast wealth. K'ang Hsi, enraged at this, summoned Yün Ssŭ to his Palace : " Your report is inaccurate," he said. " If you try to hoodwink me like this I shall cut your head off. You are always trying to make a good impression on people by pretending to be lenient and generous. The result is that you assume all the credit for my acts of generosity and clemency. Every one praises you, while I am blamed for severity. The fact is you are following in the wake of Yün Jeng; hereafter, if any one says a word in your favour to me I shall decapitate him. How can I allow my sovereign authority to be delegated to such as you? "

K'ang Hsi's rages were fast becoming hysterical. His sons were kept in constant attendance. Again he addressed them : " When I deposed Yün Jeng, I made it quite clear to all of you that if you intrigued for the position of Heir Apparent you would be treated as rebels against the State, and would be subject to decapitation without further warning. How can the succession to the jewelled Inheritance be made the object of your vulgar scheming and intrigues? I am well aware that Yün Ssŭ is cunning and treacherous, and that he cherishes ambitions for the Throne. In the past he and his partisans have tried to assassinate Yün Jeng. Their plot now stands revealed. I command that Yün Ssŭ be placed under arrest at once, and that he be examined by the Council of Government. When I deposed Yün Jeng, my eldest son Yün Ch'ih dared to say: 'Yün Ssŭ is a good man.' Now it is a principle laid down in the Spring and Autumn Annals that when a subject plans treason the Sovereign is bound to put him to death."

At this point Yün T'ang, the ninth Prince, interposed, and, disregarding their sire's presence, rudely shouted out to his younger brother, Yün Ti: " If we don't speak now we shall never have a better opportunity." Yün Ti then loudly exclaimed: " The eighth prince, Yün Ssŭ, never plotted against Yün Jeng; my brother and I will guarantee his innocence."

At this K'ang Hsi burst into one of his frantic rages (he was subject to epilepsy), and seized the sword which he was wearing with the intention of slaying Yün Ti there and then. But the fifth prince, Yün Ch'i, knelt and implored mercy, while the remainder kotowed. K'ang Hsi became calmer, and ordered the other Princes to administer a sound whipping on Yün Ti's person, after which Yün Ti and Yün T'ang were forcibly expelled from the Palace.

After this serio-comic episode, the commissioners presented their report of the examination of the physiognomist. They said: " The physiognomist, Chang Ming-ti, under examination, has confessed that he was recommended by Prince Shun's major domo to Prince Chih (Yün Ssŭ). He says: 'I had the audacity to speak random words, and ventured to accuse the Heir Apparent of committing cruel deeds. I even said I would slay him if I got the chance. I also made a vague boast that I was endowed with supernatural power. I gained access to the Prince, Yün Ssŭ, and tempted him, in order to make money. When I was presented to him and told his fortune I said: 'Your Highness is highly intellectual, kind-hearted and brilliant; you will have a long life, enjoy high honours, and, indeed, your face is that of a future Emperor.' This is the whole truth." The Commission recommended his decapitation.

This report did not serve to improve the Emperor's temper; he summoned the whole Court to audience, and said: " Yün Ssŭ is a traitor. I shall not permit you to ask for any remission of his punishment on the ground that he is my son or that he has been the tool of others. Heaven is above me and I am just in all things; how could I show favouritism to my sons? My father ascended the Throne at five years of age, and I at eight. We both had to depend on our officials' assistance. Regarding my successor, I have made up my mind long ago, but do not choose to make the selection public. When the time comes, do you all conform to my wishes."

Referring to the physiognomist Chang Ming-ti, the Emperor issued the following decree: " Before the deposition of the Heir Apparent, Chang Ming-ti planned to assassinate both him and myself. He declared that he was able to summon at will sixteen magicians who could fly, and that two of these had already arrived. But all the good men and true in the Empire were now drawing the Emperor's pay, and success would be impossible unless one or two of these could be enticed from their allegiance. He also said that nothing could be accomplished until at least half of the young Princes had been won over. Language of this kind is indeed revolutionary. It is fortunate for me that my personal bodyguard is composed of men of determined loyalty, who refused to listen to his insidious suggestions. My eldest son heard of the plot and informed me, but Prince Shun and others were responsible for the physiognomist's introduction at Court, and are extremely guilty. Yün Ssŭ knew of the design, yet he never said a word to me. Is this fitting conduct in a son or Minister of State? Supposing Chang Ming-ti had only told Yün Ssŭ's fortune and made no treasonable proposals, what made him speak to his two younger brothers about the conspiracy? Yün Ssŭ is now in custody; Prince Shun is also to be arrested. As to Chang Ming-ti, his guilt is too great for simple decapitation; he is sentenced to dismemberment."

At the examination Prince Shun confessed that Chang Ming-ti had tried to induce him to join his plot against the Heir Apparent, but that he had at once informed the eldest Prince. The two younger Princes, Yün T'ang and Yün ti declared under examination that they had remonstrated with the physiognomist for his mad suggestions and refused to have any dealings with him. Yün Ssŭ admitted having told his younger brothers of the physiognomist's wild remarks. K'ang Hsi accordingly degraded Yün Ssŭ to the rank of an unemployed Imperial Clansman, and ordered all the parties concerned in the case to be present at Chang Ming-ti's dismemberment. All these troubles were affecting the Emperor's health, and his Court begged him to take more care. In reply he issued a long decree recounting his sorrow at his sons' unfilial behaviour. Now that his years were advancing, he was more than ever afraid of making a false step, lest he should dim the glory of his reign and diminish the veneration with which the Empire regarded him.

The Emperor's refusal to make any announcement concerning the succession was undoubtedly due to his fear of creating fresh dissensions and precipitating a crisis in the Palace. There was, in fact, not one of his sons in whom he could place absolute confidence, not one to whom he had transmitted the qualities of wisdom and virtue on which he so frankly prided himself. The sheep in his domestic flock were all black, and the son upon whom, on his deathbed, he conferred the Throne, in the belief that he came nearest to the paternal model, was little better, though more prudent, than the rest. K'ang

THE COURT OF PEKING

Hsi enlarged the borders and increased the prosperity and culture of his Empire, but he left to China in his unrighteous posterity a legacy of evil that was destined to create increasing trouble with every generation, and eventually to bring about the downfall of the dynasty. The only important difference between the sons of K'ang Hsi and the dissolute Princes of the Imperial Clan of the present day, lies in the fact that the former were comparatively virile and physically active, and that they were not subject, like their effete descendants, to the dominations of Palace eunuchs, the last and most powerful of the enervating influences which finally demoralised the Court of Peking.

CHAPTER XI

THE TRIBULATIONS OF YUNG CHENG

In December 1722, being then in his sixty-eighth year, the Emperor K'ang Hsi was seized of a sudden illness whilst engaged in a hunting expedition in the Imperial Park to the south of Peking. He made haste to return to his favourite retreat, the Garden of Bright Spring, close to the Yuan-Ming-yuan Palace. At first he seemed to be getting better, but was unable to perform the winter solstice sacrifice at the Temple of Heaven, and therefore deputed his son Yin Chen (Prince Yung) to officiate in his stead. The Prince proceeded to the Hall of Fasting to prepare for the solemn ceremony, but had scarcely arrived there when there came urgent messengers to inform him that the Emperor was dying, and that he must hasten to his bedside. When he came to his father's presence, he found there assembled, by the Emperor's command, seven of his brothers, and K'ang Hsi's brother-in-law, Lung Ko-to. The dying Monarch, without wasting many words, communicated to them his last mandate, that Prince Yung was to succeed to the Throne. " My fourth son is very like me," he said, " and ought to make a good Emperor." At these words, Yün Ssŭ (unquestionably the ablest of all K'ang Hsi's sons), who until then had never abandoned hope of securing the Throne, was so overcome with mortification and wrath, that, simulating intense grief, he left the bedchamber. The Heir-designate proceeded, as custom required, to array his dying father in his "robes of longevity," and after witnessing his decease (20th December, 1722) accompanied the remains to the Forbidden City, where they were temporarily laid to rest in the Chien-Ching-kung.

It was no bed of roses to which the new Emperor succeeded. He was then forty-four years of age, and had distinguished himself chiefly amongst his turbulent and treasonable brethren by prudently abstaining from their plots against the first Heir Apparent and against K'ang Hsi himself. But judged in the light of his own record as Emperor, and of his writings and decrees, his only claim to the admiration of posterity lies in his literary attainments and in his painstaking attention to the routine business of government. In his domestic life, as in his relations with his Ministers and Court, he has written himself down, beyond all possibility of doubt, as a suspicious, querulous and savagely vindictive individual. Indeed, the dynastic annals of his reign are so burdened with the long-winded homilies and lachrymose complainings of his domestic infelicities, that, were they the only sources of our knowledge of the period, one might be led to the belief that the discussion and settlement of the Imperial Clan's unseemly wranglings constituted the entire business of government. Nevertheless, these edicts and homilies of Yung Cheng (to give him his reign-title) are replete with a deep human interest, and help greatly to explain the causes of the Manchu decline, which (though arrested during the sixty years of Ch'ien Lung's reign) may be said to have commenced with the sons of K'ang Hsi. We have thought it advisable to reproduce the most important of these documents, because, taken as a whole, they afford a very striking indictment of the results of polygamy, as practised by Oriental Courts, and partially explain the failure of the East's patriarchal system as an integrating social force.

Yung Cheng ascended the Throne with the unpleasant

certainty in his mind that all his brothers, with the one exception of Yün Hsiang,[1] were hostile to him. His first act was characteristic of the Oriental diplomat. He appointed a council of four to administer the government, so as to leave him free to observe the ceremonial ritual of mourning for the full three years enjoined by the Sage. This Council consisted of his two brothers, Yün Ssŭ and Yün Hsiang (the bad boy of the family and the good) together with the Grand Secretary Ma Chi and his uncle Lung Ko-to. His object in appointing Yün Ssŭ, whom he feared and hated, to this responsible post, was to keep him under his eye, as he knew him for a arch plotter, and believed that none of his other brothers were strong enough to carry out a successful conspiracy without the masterful Yün Ssŭ's directions. At the same time, as the rebellion in the north-west was causing much anxiety, the Emperor took an early opportunity to recall Yün Ti (K'ang Hsi's fourteenth son), then in supreme command of the Imperial forces, for the reason that this Prince was one of Yün Ssŭ's party, and Yung Cheng feared that he might be induced to proclaim Yun Ssŭ Emperor, and support him with his army.

Yün Ssŭ showed plainly enough his dislike and distrust of his brother, the Emperor; when congratulated on his own new title, he remarked that the Emperor evidently meant to have his head, so that condolences would be more in order. This was duly reported to Yung Sheng by eunuch spies; not an auspicious opening.

Yung Cheng, following in his father's footsteps, began at an early date to administer long-winded homilies to his family and Court; a habit which seems to have been inveterate in all the Emperors and, for that matter, the

[1] For whom the grateful Emperor created the Yi princedom. A direct descendant of the house of Yi, in the person of Tsai yuan, conspired against the Old Buddha in 1861 (vide *China under the Empress Dowager*).

Empresses, of the Manchu dynasty. Only in the case of the Old Buddha were these Pecksniffian utterances redeemed by the saving grace of humour; even when dealing out unctuous platitudes with a lavish hand, that great woman always gave the impression that, in performing this congenial duty, she was chuckling to herself. As a specimen of one of Yung Cheng's earlier efforts the following tirade is worth quoting: "The habit of forming cabals and parties is thoroughly objectionable. It prevailed to an appalling extent under the Ming dynasty and, alas, it still continues. The late Emperor erred ever on the side of leniency and was loth to put any offenders to death. Even you, members of my own family, it seems, are not above this abominable tendency, but if you imagine that you are going to enjoy the same immunity as you enjoyed during my father's lifetime, you do err most grievously. Human nature is always the same; those in office naturally desire to retain the right to make private friends wheresoever they will. But the business of State requires that all personal predilections must be rigorously set aside. You all remember when I was a Prince and went about among you. When did I ever try to promote my own interests or to intrigue on behalf of my *protégés?* You never knew me to pay clandestine visits for unlawful purposes; my father recognised my unswerving rectitude, and therefore made me his heir. Since then, it seems to me that I have displayed an admirable leniency in not venting past grudges on those who are against me. It is my earnest hope that if any of you are in the habit of fomenting conspiracies, you will now desist. If I err in thus accusing you, see to it that you never merit charges of the kind in future."

As may be supposed, this sort of thing was not calculated to induce brotherly love, and the plots continued as before. It was unfortunate for the reputation and influence of the Roman Catholic Church that several of the conspiring Princes were known to be on friendly terms with the fathers at Court, and some, it was believed, had even been baptised into the faith.

In the first year of Yung Cheng's reign it was decided by the Board of Rites, upon a memorial of the provincial *literati*, that the foreign priests should be excluded from all parts of China (except Peking) and that their churches should be destroyed. The priests were accordingly compelled to leave their then flourishing missions in the interior and seek refuge at Macao and Canton. Over three hundred churches were destroyed. The intrigues of the fathers at Peking and their interference in the domestic broils of the Court were no doubt to some extent responsible for the attitude of the Emperor; but the trouble had been brewing all through the later years of K'ang Hsi.

Yün Ssŭ's principal aiders and abettors were the Princes Yün O and Yün Tang, but all the brothers, except Prince Yi, were more or less implicated. Yung Cheng decided to get Yün O out of the way for a time by sending him on a mission to Mongolia, but he refused to proceed any further than Kalgan, and threatened to return thence without leave. Yung Cheng met this insubordination with characteristic Manchu wiliness by ordering his brother, the chief plotter, Yün Ssŭ, to recommend a suitable penalty for the offence. Yün Ssŭ cheerfully proposed that Yün O be deprived of his princedom, shorn of his estates and confined for all time in the Court of the Imperial Clan. Thereupon Yung Cheng issued the following decree:

"Yün O is a mean and contemptible person, whose conduct is that of a wild and insensate fool. Although he had the benefit of my father's training, both in literary pursuits and martial exercises, for over thirty years, yet he has completely failed to derive any profit therefrom. His conduct was a constant source of grief to His late Majesty. So infatuate is he, and so bereft of reason, that he does not realise his own utter stupidity and worthlessness; instead of retiring into private life and thinking over his misdeeds, he lets his evil designs be noised abroad. Yün Ssŭ's recommendations in this matter meet the case. All the world knows that I have displayed the fullest measure of frank sympathy for my brothers all these thirty years. All the world likewise knows how they have requited my father and me. I shall now be glad to be favoured with the candid opinion of my Court in regard to Yün O's case; but I warn you all not to imitate Yün Ssŭ in uttering high-sounding but specious catchwords, for in so doing you would not only be doing yourselves an injustice, but would insult the memory of your late Sovereign. It is, of course, conceivable that Yün Ssŭ, in giving his decision, has spoken from honest conviction, concealing no sinister motive; but of this I have grave doubts."

The Princes and courtiers debated the case, and finally advised that Yün O should be cashiered and imprisoned, as Yün Ssŭ had recommended. To their memorial Yung Cheng replied: "When first I handed over Yün O's case to Yün Ssŭ I was curious to see how he would deal with it. It is to be borne in mind, that Yün O, Yŭn Tang and Yün Ti have always been entirely under the influence of Yün Ssŭ, whose duty it was to train them in the right way. Far from so doing, he has invariably encouraged them to disobey my mandates. And now, behold, he urges me to inflict a severe penalty on an offender who has acted at his instigation, in the hope that, if I adopt his advice, public opinion may blame me for excessive cruelty to my brother. He does not appear to realise that no penalty, however severe, could be excessive in a case of such flagrant disobedience to the orders of a Sovereign and an elder brother. Leniency would be misapplied in Yün O's case, because he would fail to appreciate it; admonitions have no effect on one who fears not the law. You will, therefore, prepare for me a full report of Yün O's past and present record. I myself have no thought of sparing my brother, but you are at liberty to recommend either a milder or a severer penalty than that advised by Yün Ssŭ, as you may think fit." This inquiry, as was to be expected, resulted in Yün O's being stripped of his princedom and sentenced to imprisonment for life.

In 1724, Yün Tang, another of the disloyal brothers, incited by Yün Ssŭ, was impeached for having speculated in land belonging to nomad Mongols while on a mission to Hsining, and for having caused the people in that region to rebel by flagrant abuse of power. He was deprived of his princedom, and the Emperor, whose morbid fear of a plot against his life increased with every fresh evidence of his brothers' evil doings, seized the occasion to deliver himself of the following irrelevant remarks: " Yün Ssŭ hates me because I will not allow myself to be influenced by personal prejudices. He endeavours to excite my wrath and to induce me to embark on a general proscription against my enemies. In this way he hopes to make me hated by my people and to bring about a rebellion. But his wish will never be gratified. The ancient adage has it: ' Any one is at liberty to slay a rebellious Minister and a bad son.' My father often quoted this wise saying with special reference to Yün Ssŭ."

Yung Cheng even took the trouble to compose a long-winded pamphlet setting forth the evil results of parties in the State working against the Throne's advisers, and denouncing the conduct of certain of the Princes who had bestowed parting gifts upon one of Yün Ssŭ's party, condemned to banishment at the post roads. " Yün Ssŭ," he wrote, " is a traitor ever conspiring against me, who, since my accession, has always tried to counteract my orders. I have had occasion to refer his conduct to the Court of the Imperial Clan on more than a score of counts, but have hitherto refrained from punishing him as he deserves. In spite of this leniency many of my courtiers blame me for undue severity towards him; the fact being that Yün Ssŭ has befooled them. I can read in their faces their resentment, yet how many Ministers have suffered punishment for Yün Ssŭ's misdeeds while he has gone scot-free! But no cabal can be formed by one man, and unless Yün Ssŭ found sympathisers he would be powerless. He wins adherents by a fictitious display of generosity, which is meant as a foil to my meanness. He gains a cheap reputation at my expense, but his motives are plain enough. It seems perfectly hopeless to expect any amendment from Yün Ssŭ, but I repeat my solemn warnings to the Princes and Ministers."

Yün Ssŭ certainly displayed great ingenuity in winning popularity; he managed to obtain credit for all the Emperor's acts of generosity and to place him in a bad light. When head of the Li Fan-pu, he disallowed, on behalf of the Throne, the Khorchin Princes' travelling allowance after their yearly appearance at Court. As head of the Board of Works he granted exemption from certain dues without reference to the Emperor, and so on.

Yün Jeng, the former Heir Apparent, whom K'ang Hsi had deprived of all his titles and imprisoned for life, was reported to be dying in his prison at the Coal Hill. Yung Cheng sent physicians to attend him, but they pronounced his case hopeless. The Emperor dispensed with the formality of paying the sick man a personal visit, on the ground that the patient would be obliged to make obeisance before his Sovereign, which was contrary to etiquette, as he was the elder brother. Accordingly, he sent a message to say that, instead of seeing him, he would perform libations to his spirit after decease, which was doubtless very gratifying to Yün Jeng. His title of Prince Li was formally restored to him.

On the completion of the orthodox twenty-seven months of mourning for K'ang Hsi, the Emperor excused his

THE COURT OF PEKING

Council of Four from further duties and bestowed rewards on Yün Hsiang. Of Yün Ssŭ he said: "Ever since I bestowed this appointment upon him he has neglected all his duties and shifted responsibility on to his colleagues. He has never spoken a helpful word nor performed one useful act. He has done his utmost to poison men's minds against me, to put obstacles in my path and to confuse my judgment. For instance, when head of the Board of Works he was responsible for the arrangements at my father's obsequies. Custom required that twenty thousand bearers should be engaged to convey the catafalque to its last resting-place (ninety miles away) at the Eastern Tombs. He actually dared to memorialise me, saying that, on the ground of expense, the number might well be reduced by one half. Unaware of the established precedents, I weakly agreed. Had not the Grand Secretaries come to my rescue and explained the demands of etiquette, a terrible blunder would have been committed. Also, in his capacity as head of the Mongolian Superintendency, he tried to prevent the Mongol Princes from coming to Peking to pay their respects to my father's coffin, on the plea of unnecessary expenditure; they were moved to tears in the extremity of their grief, and had the matter not been brought to my notice, their loyalty to my House might have been seriously affected. He took it upon himself to weed out more than half the horses in the Imperial stables, pretending to economise, but his real object was to call attention to my father's extravagance in maintaining so large a stud. The result was that there were not horses enough for my needs. He was wont to use dirty bits of the commonest paper on which to memorialise the Throne. When it fell to him to prepare the pavilion adjoining the sacrificial temples, where I changed my robes in the intervals of the liturgy, the smell of new paint on the various utensils was so nauseating that while robing I could scarcely breathe. The tables were all in a very rickety condition, and it was unsafe to sit on the chairs. He showed gross disrespect in the arrangements made for reciting the prayers at this solemn ceremony. Every one knows the levity of his behaviour. I have no time to recount all the instances of his careless sloth and malevolent vulgarity. Yet have I borne with them all! Yün Ssŭ is no fool, and knows full well what he is about. Who can guess his motives? In connection with the supply of red earth required at Moukden for the mausoleum of our great founder, Yün Ssu had the effrontery to purchase all the supplies available and then to sell it to the department concerned at a handsome profit to himself. He deserves my sternest censure, and I must decline to bestow any reward or honour upon him for his work on my Council."

Next came the case of Yün Tang. At a conclave of all the courtiers Yung Cheng delivered himself of a characteristic sermon: "Owing to the abominable conduct of Yün Tang, I sent him to Hsining. There he connived at the lawless acts of his personal staff, and arrogated to himself rank higher than he possessed. Accordingly, I sent General Ch'u Tsung to remonstrate with him and to urge him to amend his ways. Ch'u now informs me that Yün Tang did not take the trouble to come from his residence to meet him with the respect due to an Imperial envoy; he omitted to bend the knee, and when at last he did condescend to summon Ch'u to his presence he showed no signs of shame or regret. On the contrary, he seemed thoroughly self-satisfied and displayed contumelious arrogance. Ch'u's report says: 'Your servant commanded him to come out into the courtyard and to kneel while I read to him your Imperial mandate. He came out, but flatly declined to kotow, rose rudely from his knees after hearing your decree and remarked: "What the Emperor says is no doubt true enough; what need for me to answer? I shall take the vows of the Buddhist priest-

THE COURT OF PEKING

hood. When I am become a bonze, perhaps His Majesty will believe that I no longer am a rebel against the Throne." Even his servants seemed quite callous and undisturbed.' My object in sending Ch'u to Hsining was simply that he might tell my brother to keep his people in order. I fully expected him to amend his ways and lead a new life. It was surely to his own interest to obey the law, but his nature is both base and proud, and he knows not the respect due to a Sovereign from a subject. When he talks of intending to become a bonze and to forsake the world, does he really imagine that if he did so it would be the end of his duty to his elder brother, and that thenceforth he would part company from his Emperor? These are wild and wanton words indeed. During my father's lifetime these brothers of mine, Yün Ssŭ, Yün Chih, Yün Tang, Yün O and Yün Ti, by their wicked behaviour and heartless conspiracies, made His Majesty's life a burden to him, so that he never knew a moment's peace. After he had passed away, Yün Tang, on arriving here from the west, did not even take the trouble to salute the Empress Dowager or myself. Instead of proceeding at once to the Palace to inquire after my health, he wrote to the Board of Ceremonies and asked them to inform him of the prescribed etiquette. On entering the Palace of Imperial Longevity to do obeisance before his father's coffin, he saw that I was kneeling before it in worship, but he kept carefully out of my way, and his face showed no signs of sorrow, nor of affection for myself. When I went forward to meet him, he remained unmoved. La Hsi, who was standing by his side, pulled him forward towards me. Yün Tang turned and reviled La Hsi, after which he advanced in my direction, saying: ' I was trying to show you all possible respect, when La Hsi began dragging me forward. I am the Emperor's own brother, yet this fellow La Hsi treats me like a menial. If I have misbehaved, let Your Majesty punish me. If I have done no wrong, then you ought to behead La Hsi in order to vindicate the law.' He had lost his temper and behaved in my presence like a common brawler. I could hardly believe my eyes.

"On the occasion of my father's funeral Yün Ti also showed gross disrespect for the solemn ceremonial and engaged in altercations with La Hsi and Fo Lun. On my issuing a decree to rebuke him Yün Ssŭ came forward from out the tent and called out: 'Kneel down there,' showing plainly that Yün Ti obeyed Yün Ssŭ in all things, and that his word was law.

"As for Yün O, he had received an Imperial mission to proceed to Urga with a message from me to the Taranatha pontiff; on reaching Kalgan he feigned sickness and declined to proceed. To Yün Tang he sent private letters with a gift of horses. Yün Tang wrote in reply: 'Alas! the opportunity has gone by, and we can now only regret that we have missed the chance.' What could this be but treason? Moreover, I know that Yün O has uttered incantations against my life.

"Yün Ssŭ's conduct is quite incorrigible; he and his brothers wilfully persist in treasonable and perfidious conduct. If I were to subject them all to a criminal trial death would be the only possible penalty. But I am too tender-hearted to adopt such a course; I desire my brothers to continue to draw the breath of life, so I shall not proceed further, in deference to what my father's wishes would have been."

It seems certain that Yün Ssŭ, aided by his brothers, came within an ace of seizing the person of Yung Cheng and the Throne. Yung Cheng feared to take any strong measures against the conspirators, because he felt that there was much discontent against his rule. A vigorous political campaign was being carried on in the south by Yün Ssŭ's party, and it was not leniency which led the Emperor to spare his brother. A little later Yün Ssŭ was

THE COURT OF PEKING

again impeached for not repairing the ancestral temple in a seemly manner, and for not constructing the ancestral tablet of K'ang Hsi with due reverence. On this occasion Yung Cheng hysterically complained that these cares were rapidly driving him to distraction. He followed up this complaint with a decree attributing the inclemency of the weather to Heaven's dissatisfaction with his erring brethren.

Yung Cheng now learned that his Commander-in-chief, Nien Keng-yao, who had deserved well of the State for his many victories over the Eleuths, was conspiring in the interests of Yün Ssŭ. Gratitude was never characteristic of the Manchu rulers, except possibly in the case of the Old Buddha. The Emperor, greatly perturbed, decided that Nien Keng-yao must be removed at all costs. He was therefore charged with " indulging in wicked behaviour," with having ill-treated the inhabitants of Kokonor, and suppressed all reference to a famine which had raged there; he had shown " excessive zeal in slaughtering," and generally misled the Throne. Yung Cheng first transferred him to the sinecure of Tartar General at Hangchow, but every one knew this step was merely preliminary, and that his final despatch was only delayed because the Emperor feared to act precipitately, lest he should bring about a revolt of the troops. But the wretched Commander lost nothing by waiting, and, meanwhile, the fact that the armour of his troops was reported to be falling to pieces, afforded an opportunity for more criticism of the unlucky Yün Ssŭ who, as head of the Board of Works, was responsible for its condition. " It is only too plain," wrote the Emperor, " that Yün Ssŭ acts deliberately in not providing my army with proper armour. Our relations are like those of fire and water, or like two countries at war. His fixed idea is to be in the right himself and to put me in the wrong. My father knew his real nature as well as I do. When his foster-mother's husband, Yachi-pu, was beheaded for flagrant misconduct, my father issued a decree to all of us brothers, in which he said : ' Henceforward I disown Yün Ssŭ, let him no more be called my son.' At that time Yün Ssŭ appealed to me to stop the publication of the decree, saying that he would ' lose face ' if people knew our father's opinion of him. Accordingly, I put it away under seal, so as to spare my brother's feelings. But he is a monster utterly incapable of gratitude."

On receiving the Imperial mandate, Nien Keng-yao flatly declined to leave his former post. " I am informed," says His Majesty, " that he consented to have his luggage sent on ahead, but has refused to depart himself, although the people were delighted on hearing of their persecutor's impending removal. He is now trying to pose as a meritorious officer and thus to make me appear in an unbecoming light for unjustifiably dismissing my old advisers. Let him hand over his charge to his successor forthwith."

Yung Cheng's maternal uncle, Lung Ko-to, was also dismissed at this time for being concerned in the conspiracy. " I have treated both Nien Keng-yao and Lung Ko-to with absolute trust and regarded them as my right-hand men. But they have harboured rebellious thoughts and have rewarded my favour by conspiring against me, and have besides attacked my reputation. I refrain from inflicting the severest penalties because I feel that I myself am to blame for having been over trustful."

With the contemptible meanness and lack of generosity which seems inseparable from Chinese mandarins in the mass, the Board of Appointments memorialised the Emperor as follows concerning Nien Keng-yao's case : " Your Majesty has shown this wicked sinner all possible benevolence, but the measure of his offences is full to the brim. Instead of proceeding straight to his new post he has had the effrontery to linger at Yi Cheng-hsien in Kiangsu, on the ground that ' its situation is central,' and he has dared to address you, saying: 'I shall await your further instructions here.' It is difficult to guess his real motives, but his abominable wickedness awakens universal detestation and exposes him to the sudden visitation of Heaven. We ask that he be cashiered, deprived of the Dragon robes and decorations conferred upon him in times past, and of the purple reins.[1] We request that he be summarily arrested and brought to Peking in chains, there to undergo the severest examination (under torture) and then to be decapitated, as a warning to disloyal and ungrateful Ministers." To this the Emperor made reply: " I previously asked Nien Keng-yao for an explanation of his outrageous conduct, and his answer was: 'I have acted in everything in accordance with precedent and with my position as Commander-in-chief.' In times past, various Princes of my house have held this post, but, with the exception of Yün Ti (who is a bad example to follow), none of them has ever dared to act with the lawless arrogance displayed by Nien Keng-yao. He has even gone beyond Yün Ti's atrocities, and has slaughtered vast numbers of people. He ventures to adduce Yün Ti as a precedent, as if Yün Ti's treasonable conduct were justifiable. I now order Nien Keng-yao immediately to send in proper replies to my previous questions. Why is he delaying at Yi Cheng-hsien and neglecting his duties in this perfunctory way? On the receipt of his explicit reply I shall proceed to issue a decree in reply to the request of my Ministers for his arrest and decapitation."

Nien Keng-yao had enjoyed almost unlimited power in the provinces, and his *protégés* held the most important posts throughout the country. All of these were now removed from their lucrative offices and their places taken by nominees of the opposing factions. It was ever thus with the Manchu dynasty; each reign witnessed the

---

[1] Usually bestowed only on Princes.

downfall of its predecessor's favourites; and the Court, anxious to share in the plunder of their estates, invariably acquiesced.

Yung Cheng was very sensitive to public opinion and did not wish it to be said that " the bow was put away in obscurity after the birds had been shot," or, in other words, that he was ungrateful for services rendered to the State. Accordingly, he invited the high provincial authorities to memorialise as to what penalty should be inflicted on Nien; and he was careful to ask them to treat the case with complete impartiality.

Still hesitating to deal with Yün Ssŭ, for fear of precipitating a rebellion, it was Yung Cheng's policy gradually to rid himself of his brother's most prominent confederates. Two of his first cousins, sons of Prince Kung (a younger brother of K'ang Hsi), were sentenced to imprisonment, one for abetting Yün Ssŭ and the other nominally for " making rude noises " in the Emperor's presence on the steps of the Palace of " the Peaceful Mean." In the same manner, Yung Cheng dealt with Yün T'ang's case, on the pretext that one of his servants had beaten a graduate in Shansi. " During my father's lifetime," said the Emperor, " Yun T'ang was often admonished for unfilial conduct, and once he had the effrontery to reply : ' The worst you can do to me is to strip me of my paltry fourth class princedom.' Whenever he was given any fatiguing duty to perform he would say to my father : ' If you would only put me in prison in the company of my two eldest brothers, I should have a much easier life than I lead at present." We were all shocked to hear such language from his lips. When the late Emperor died there was no vestige of tears in Yün T'ang's eyes. Since my accession he has behaved with incurable haughtiness, and has always disobeyed my orders. From Hsining he sent a letter to Yün O, couched in treasonable language. When I sent a messenger with a decree to rebuke him, he showed no fear and had the insolence to receive my envoy in his bedchamber, instead of kneeling to greet him in the outer court. He has squandered huge sums in Hsining, hoping to make friends for his treasonable designs; the people call him the ninth Prince of the blood, although he is not entitled to any such rank, being only a Beitze. I order, therefore, that he be stripped at once of his title and emoluments, and give warning that any one addressing him hereafter as Prince will do so at his peril."

Lung Ko-to, Yung Cheng's maternal uncle, was the next victim; all the Imperial gifts and honours were taken from him, which he had received from K'ang Hsi and from Yung Cheng himself.

The chief conspirator against Yung Cheng's authority, his brother Yün Ssŭ, appears to have been convinced that the Emperor would not dare to take extreme measures against him, for notwithstanding His Majesty's outspoken complaints and warnings, he continued to go his own unlawful ways. His next move was to send in a memorial recommending that the pay and allowances of the Imperial bannermen, and more particularly those of the three superior banners, should be raised, his evident object being to ingratiate himself with the Manchus nearest to the Throne. His Majesty's chief cause of complaint on this occasion was that Yün Ssŭ, in private audience, had advised against increasing their emoluments. The Imperial edict referring to this matter plaintively observes: " All the disorderly and disreputable members of the Household Banner Corps recently assembled at Yün Ssŭ's house and started a most unseemly brawl. Yet Yün Ssŭ never reported the occurrence, and it was only on the following day that I heard of it from my Ministers of the Household. Forthwith I issued a decree stating that no strangers could be permitted to enter this part of the Palace where an Imperial concubine resides (Yün Ssŭ's mother lived with him, by special permission of the

Emperor). Furthermore, Yün Ssŭ, on one of his drunken bouts, recently put to death one of his body-guard and failed to report the incident. The family of the murdered man brought complaint, but Yün Ssŭ sent a eunuch to bid them hush the matter up. When I cross-questioned him about it he prevaricated, and it was only after confronting him with the facts that he hung his head and ceased to argue. This incident clearly reveals the man's hypocritical nature and his inveterate desire to earn golden opinions from every one while perpetrating acts of cold-blooded cruelty. I command the Court to recommend an appropriate penalty." The Court recommended that Yün Ssŭ be deprived of his Imperial princedom and reduced to the level of a Mongol Prince; but for the moment Yung Cheng took no action on this advice.

The Board of Punishments now brought in its final memorial respecting Nien Keng-yao, who had been brought in chains to Peking. They declared that the number of accusations against him made a pile higher than Mount Tai, while his offences reached depths lower than ever plummet sounded. He had committed five distinct acts of treason and sixteen acts of usurpation, one of which was to have the roads sprinkled with yellow earth in his honour and to have the streets cleared as for an Imperial procession. He had allowed the green audience tally (which is only used in the presence of the Son of Heaven) to be employed by officials seeking an interview with him. He had the audacity to seat himself before the dragon tablet of the Emperor, instead of meekly kneeling upon his knees. He had worn the Dragon robes and seated himself in the position of the Emperor, facing south, when receiving the congratulations of his subordinates, who were made to kneel and prostrate themselves in the dust. He had committed thirteen distinct offences of gross presumption (one of which was the omission to publish an Imperial amnesty) and eighteen of greedy covetousness. There were twelve cases of arbitary action, fifteen of appropriating Government funds; nine cases of deceiving his Imperial master; six cases of unjust suspicion of subordinates, and five of wanton cruelty. The penalty for the gravest of these offences, committed singly, was the lingering death, and decapitation for many of the others. The memorial asked for his immediate execution by dismemberment; his father, brothers, sons, grandsons, uncles, nephews and cousins above the age of sixteen to be decapitated. All below that age, and all the female members of the family, to be given as slaves to the families of meritorious officers. The whole of his property to be confiscate to the Throne and his crimes published for the information of all men, as a solemn warning for ages to come, so that traitors and disloyal Ministers should hesitate to abuse their master's confidence and display atrocious cruelty.

To this bloodthirsty indictment the Emperor replied: "Nien Keng-yao's treason is manifest to all men; it is the inevitable consequence of a nature made up of reckless presumption and gross depravity. But I call to mind his earlier services to my House during the Kokonor campaign, and am loth to inflict upon him the extreme penalty. I command that he be given over to the charge of Achitu, Prefect of the city, and be allowed to commit suicide. I have long been aware of his obstinate disposition and evil hardness of heart. He has always ignored his father's admonitions and treated him and his elder brother with callous contempt. I content myself with cashiering his father and brothers. The various Imperial gifts bestowed upon the family are to be returned to me. His sons are very numerous; one of them, Nien Fu, resembles his father in character and deeds; let him be decapitated forthwith. Let the rest of his sons over fifteen years of age be banished for life to a malarious region on the remotest frontiers of Yünnan. His wife was a member of the Imperial Clan; let her be sent back to her father's household. The million or more of his confiscated wealth is to be handed to the Viceroy of Hsian to cover the sums which Nien has embezzled from time to time. Property belonging to the remainder of his family is hereby exempted from confiscation, as an act of grace. Every member of his clan now holding office is to be cashiered, and as each of his sons or grandsons reaches the age of fifteen years he shall be banished for life and be exempt from all benefits of Imperial amnesties. Any one privily adopting one of his sons or grandsons shall be subject to the same penalty as Nien has incurred. His accomplice Tsou Lu is to be beheaded, and his family banished as slaves to the Amur."

Having persuaded and frightened the Imperial Clan Court into a state of subservience and removed from his path the most powerful adherents of the rebellious brothers who had incurred his bitter enmity, the Emperor now proceeded to take his long-cherished vengeance upon Yün Ssŭ. At the same time, he continued to keep a watchful eye upon public opinion in Peking and in the provinces, ever careful to put upon his actions a gloss of the utmost orthodoxy and flawless justice, to go down to posterity as the Superior Man. Before administering his justice, therefore, he proceeded to put a good complexion on his actions in advance and to prepare the public mind.

CHAPTER XII

YUNG CHENG DISPENSES JUSTICE

The Imperial Clan Court, having been purged of all injudicious sympathy for the Emperor's seditious brethren, dutifully memorialised him with a request that he should punish Yün T'ang, "as a warning to all unfilial and disloyal persons." Yung Cheng, ingenuously enough, adopted his usual tactics for killing two birds with one stone, and ordered Yün Ssŭ and Yün Ti to consider the case of their accused brother and to recommend a suitable penalty for his offences. Their report was naturally not of a nature to satisfy the Court (which understood full well what was expected of it), and it proceeded to urge the Emperor to sentence Yün Ssŭ to death by decapitation. Its members were, no doubt, anxious to make an end of these eternal wranglings and inquiries in a matter which, as they knew, could only end with the legal murder of the Emperor's brothers.

On receiving this latest memorial of the Court, Yung Cheng delivered himself of a typical address to an audience convened at the Lake Palace, at which Yün Ssŭ was present:

"If, on your demand, I put Yün Ssŭ to death," said he, "and he should hereafter be proved to have been innocent, you will by your act have murdered a descendant of our founder and thus place me in the position of an unjust Sovereign. If any of you feel in his heart that this man does not deserve death, let him now step out from his place and kneel on my right hand." Naturally enough, no one was anxious to accept this invitation, and all shouted unanimously: " He deserves to die." Yung Cheng then continued: " I fully endorse your opinion; the guilt of Yün Ssŭ makes him worthy of death; nevertheless, I have no intention of beheading him. I remove him from my Clan because of the imprecations which he dared to utter in the presence of the whole Court, when he said that he hoped that I and my family would come to a bad end. I may deal with his wife on a further occasion."

If the Emperor was sincere about lenient measures, he soon had cause to change his mind; it came to light that a Prince of the clan, named Lu Pin, had been a member of Yün Ti's party at Hsining and had been employed by that Prince to convey certain letters to Yün Ssŭ at Peking. These letters spoke definitely of a plot for the killing of Yung Cheng, and added disrespectful references to the Emperor's alleged illegitimacy, respecting which matter Yung Cheng was peculiarly sensitive. Worse than all, when Yung Cheng demanded an explanation, Lu Pin spoke gratefully of Yün Ssŭ as his benefactor. The result was perpetual imprisonment for Lu Pin, while Yün Ssŭ was confined in the Forbidden City in a high-walled courtyard, two " respectable eunuchs " being told off to guard him.

At this point of the tragic business, Yung Cheng displayed his vindictiveness in a form so derogatory to the dynasty of a great State that his edicts read like the utterances of a petulant child reviling its playmates, rather than the decrees of the world's most ancient Throne. First of all, he formally prescribed for Yün Ssŭ and Yün T'ang titles of reproach, by which they were to be known officially, namely, " That disreputable person " for the one, and " Black-hearted monster " for the other. As for Yün Ti, the third and least serious offender, he was dealt with at once, to clear the ground for the principal culprits, in the following decree:

"Recently I sent Yün Ti to live near my father's sepulchre in the fond hope that the contemplation of that holy spot might move him to remorse. But he has shown no contrite spirit; on the contrary he becomes daily more incorrigible. Lately an attempt at rebellion has been fomented in the neighbourhood of the Imperial tombs, and most abominable statements have been circulated about my moral character. I therefore order that Yün Ti be sent back at once to Peking. He will hereafter be confined in the Palace at the back of the Coal Hill, close to the hall of Imperial Longevity, where rest the portraits of my parents. Perchance he may be moved to repentance by their august proximity. His son Pai Chi is thoroughly evil and will be imprisoned with his father."

The Emperor goes on: "'That disreputable person' and 'Black-hearted monster,' with Yün Ti, have been wont to form friendships with the lowest classes of society in the fomenting of their conspiracy against me; they consorted with bonzes, lamas, physicians, soothsayers, astrologers, physiognomists and even with mimes, barbers and Europeans. The bond-slaves of the highest officials were invited into their houses and treated as honoured guests, to be used as auxiliaries to their malevolent designs. If they wanted to ruin any member of the opposite party they would invent the most wicked and preposterous stories about him, and have them circulated by these creatures. In this way they expected to mislead the foolish and unthinking mob. My father was exposed to their calumnies and had always to be on his guard against their base plots. On my accession a common tea-house report was in circulation to the effect that I was a confirmed drunkard. I was accused of habitually passing the livelong night in carousing with Lung K'o-to, our revels ending with both of us completely in our cups. As the result of our alleged orgies, Lung K'o-to was said to be reduced to such a state of blind intoxication as to require bearers to carry him out from the Forbidden City. It was even alleged that he was so completely oblivious to decorum as to refuse to quit my Palace, and that he and I, both tipsy, would indulge in common brawls. I was accused of sleeping off my debauch in my clothes on the spot where I finally collapsed. When Tsai Ting came to Peking from Szechuan and was summoned to audience he soon perceived me to be a man of most temperate habits. One day, naïvely enough, he memorialised me as follows: 'In Szechuan it was common gossip that Your Majesty was usually intoxicated, but since I have come to Peking I have observed, after constant attendance on Your Majesty's person day and night, that you never touch a drop of liquor.' So, too, Li Chen-yang on arriving here was received in audience several times; before finally taking leave he said to me: 'I have repeatedly heard that since your accession you have indulged habitually in Bacchanalian orgies; but after having had several opportunities of seeing you at audience, I notice that Your Majesty is always at work and your breath betrays no indication of the liquor habit.' Many other officials have written or spoken in the same sense, the fact, of course, being that 'That disreputable person' and his brother were habitual wine-bibbers themselves and have been often reproved by me for their shameless drunkenness. Therefore they callously invented this accusation, and caused it to be rumoured and believed all over the Empire that I was a hopeless drunkard. The whole of my Court knows well that I cannot stomach wine at all.[1] Of a truth, men who will invent such falsehoods about me are capable of anything.

[1] Nevertheless, the charge was true enough; Yung Cheng was addicted to drinking bouts, as was K'ang Hsi before him.

THE COURT OF PEKING

"In yesterday's *Court Gazette* I note the following: 'On the occasion of the Dragon Festival the Princes and Court all paid their respects to His Majesty at Yuan-ming-yuan, after which the Emperor left the Palace and entered the dragon barge, while the Court followed him in thirty other boats. Music was played and His Majesty presented every one with 'rush wine' in honour of the festival. After an excursion lasting some hours the Emperor returned.'

"Now, if the Lord of the Universe, who receives tribute from every region under Heaven, were pleased to take a boating excursion on a holiday and to invite his Court to partake of wine, it would only be the perpetuation of an ancient ceremony and in accordance with the example set by sage Sovereigns of antiquity. But, as it happens, I issued special instructions that none of my Court were to come out from Peking to pay their respects, and I confined myself to receiving the Princes actually resident at the Summer Palace. It is highly improper of the *Gazette* to insert such false news, and I direct the Board of Punishments to investigate the matter and to find out whence the statement emanated. It is necessary to issue this as a warning to those who calumniate their Emperor."

The time was now come for less "lenient" measures. Yung Cheng therefore proceeded to address his servile Court in a long and bitter harangue recounting his brothers' misdeeds, evidently intended as a preliminary to their happy despatch. The report of this speech is too long to give in full, but a few of its choicest passages will serve to show the ingenuous puerilities in which the Son of Heaven saw fit to indulge. "None of you know my brothers' characters as I do," he said; "I have had the misfortune to live with them for thirty years. By bribery and corruption they have built up around themselves a solid phalanx of debauched and treacherous criminals. There was not a depraved priest, physician, soothsayer, rowdy, actor or European, who was not of their gang. There is no doubt at all that these wicked minions shortened my father's life by their misdeeds, and for this ' That disreputable person ' and his brothers are chiefly to blame. . . . It is very certain that if such a man were to ascend the Throne he would involve the ancestral shrines in dire peril. As for the ' Black-hearted monster,' he is only a fat fool, who combines flabbiness with clumsy forms of deceit and a shameless wallowing in debauch. His late Majesty regarded him as more brute than man, while all of us, his brothers, looked upon him as a buffoon and a common butt. No one realised more clearly his blear-eyed stupidity than ' That disreputable person '; nevertheless, he used him persistently to forward his evil designs.

"These things being so, how came it about that, in my father's lifetime, the people all acclaimed ' That disreputable person ' as a Buddha, when he took no part in Government affairs and had earned no title to fame ? It was because his evil associates never wearied of singing his praises and thus induced the unthinking mob to make an idol of him. If he were really a good man, no words of mine could affect the popular judgment. My criticism would be wasted. Now that I have exposed his real character I shall be much interested to hear what resemblance any of you can trace between him and the Buddha ! In my father's reign it would have been an easy matter for me to have gained popularity by cheap displays of patronage; I preferred, however, to remain in honourable obscurity and to minister to my father's wants. I never schemed for the Throne, and whenever any of my brothers offended my father I always intervened to shield the culprit. This was not so much in the interest of my brothers, as because I dreaded the effect of excessive wrath on my venerable parent. Had

THE COURT OF PEKING

I ever coveted the Throne there would have been no occasion for me to cherish resentment against my brothers, once my ambition had been gratified and I had become the Sovereign. My quarrel with them rests on other and broader grounds. During my father's reign lavish fortune emptied her horn upon me, and it would have been beneath my dignity to associate, still less to quarrel, with men of my brothers' low type.

"If they have hoped to turn me from my duty and to make me cease from my merciless campaign against corruption in high places they must indeed take me for a coward. When the people presume to call 'That disreputable person' a Buddha, which of his devilish qualities, I wonder, appeals to their imagination? Is a monster of impiety and disloyalty worthy of the title of saint? If *he* be a Buddha, he is the first of the type in history! Why is it that baseless rumours are circulated of the nation's hatred towards me? Am I to suppose it is because I have punished those who plot against my life and Throne?

"Our Manchu house has now held its Imperial sway for a century, and the clans have basked in the benevolence of my four predecessors. In due course I succeeded to this goodly heritage, and even as one sun reigns in Heaven, so only one Sovereign may rule the Empire. It is incredible that my loyal Manchus should swerve from their devotion to their sovereign lord and allow themselves to be misled by the seditious arguments of evil traitors and fratricidal monsters. I am convinced that my present decree will come to them as a great shock, and that the wickedness of 'That disreputable person' and his brothers will be like the revelation of a lightning flash.

"The former memorial of the Princes and Court, which urged the immediate decapitation of my three pernicious brothers, was absolutely warranted by the facts. Death is the penalty which they merit, and if I decide to execute them no one can possibly blame me. But for the present, I am willing that they should draw the breath of life yet a while longer."

The Court next advised that the two offending Princes should be dismembered and that the whole of their estates be confiscated. It recounted the crimes of "That disreputable person" under forty headings, of which two may be quoted as fair samples:

"(1) On the occasion of his mother's death he showed disgraceful disregard of etiquette, by affecting excess of grief; even after the hundred days of mourning were over, he needed to be assisted as he walked. At the same time, while professing to observe thrifty simplicity in his diet, he was having luxurious fare brought him privily to his chamber (which adjoined his mother's coffin), through the connivance of his brothers. On this he regaled himself in epicurean style, his table groaning under its weight of viands. When the days of mourning were over he had actually put on weight, and his face indicated every symptom of gross living. (2) His wife has always behaved in a most unwomanlike manner, and the late Emperor issued orders that she was to betake herself back to her own family. One of Yün Ssŭ's concubines recommended him to apologise to the Emperor on her behalf, but he angrily replied: 'I am her husband. Who ever heard of a husband interceding with another man about his own womenkind?' This same concubine was so greatly distressed by his habitual and gross debauchery that she hanged herself."

After preferring a number of equally puerile charges against the "Black-hearted monster" and Yün Ti, and quoting the dictum of K'ang Hsi that rebellious sons deserved death as public enemies, the Court requested Yung Cheng to order the decapitation of the three offending Princes, "as a warning to traitors for ten thousand generations." To this the Emperor replied that he found himself in a position of extreme embarrassment; evidently, brothers like these were not to be moved by advice nor to be reformed by example. Many details had been omitted in the memorial, and their conduct was even blacker than his Court was aware. If he refrained from putting them to death he would be guilty of irreverence to his ancestors. He could not allow any pain he might feel to prevent him from carrying out a disagreeable duty. Yün Ti's guilt was less than that of his brothers', and perhaps he might yet repent if granted a reprieve. As to the other two, he was in an awkward position and needed time for further reflection. He hoped that the Empire would appreciate the difficulties under which he laboured, and would believe that he was acting solely so as to secure law and order for the country and the tranquillity of the ancestral shrines and tutelary deities.

No one knew better than Yung Cheng that a public execution of his brothers would create a strong public opinion against him; he knew full well the strength of their party, and had to be wary, if he wished to avoid a rebellion. His illegitimacy [1] was matter of common report, and he was hated for his tyranny and greed, so

---

[1] The Chinese annalist "Born out of Time," already referred to (*vide supra*, p.   ), gives the following explanation of the much-discussed illegitimacy of Yung Cheng. The Emperor K'ang Hsi, not content with the multitudinous domesticity of the Palace, had a roving eye and a highly susceptible nature. In one of his excursions to a temple fair, he was struck by the beauty of a young married woman, and having sent a eunuch to discover her identity, invited the lady to take up her residence in the Palace, and conferred upon her husband (named Wei) a lucrative post. Six months after her installation as an Imperial concubine of the fifth rank, the Lady Wuya (as she was called) gave birth to a son, who was recognised as K'ang Hsi's fourth born, but who (as His Majesty well knew) was no son of his. The Monarch remained devoted to Lady Wuya, and eventually conferred the succession upon her son, who became the Emperor Yung Cheng. The conspiracy of Yung Cheng's brothers against him is explained and justified by this annalist, on the grounds of his illegitimacy and usurpation, but his narrative contains much internal evidence to show that he relies upon a fertile imagination for most of his facts.

he hastened slowly. About two months after the issue of his decree postponing judgment in his brother's case, the Viceroy of Chihli sent word from Pao Ting-fu, where " Black-hearted monster " was imprisoned, that the Prince had died of dysentery. The fact was that he had been strangled by the Emperor's order. In his decree, rejoicing over tne victim's death as a judgment of offended Heaven, he alludes again to the tale of his offences : " Many years ago there was a disreputable and impecunious native of Shansi in Peking, who became ' Black-hearted monster's ' chosen friend. This man had received presents of money from the Prince and was so grateful that, when his patron was banished to Hsining, he, too, proceeded thither and handed him a letter in which he had written : ' I should like to devote myself to the cause of a virtuous Emperor, and do not wish to be the subject of a cruel and unjust Sovereign. I mean to stir up rebellion among the troops and people of Shansi and Ssuchuan in order to overthrow the present Emperor and to deliver my good master from bondage.' Yet when ' Black-hearted monster ' heard these terrible utterances of rankest treason, he merely remarked : ' Oh ! we brothers cannot expect to secure the Throne.' Then, too, when he was at Hsining, he sent back some of his eunuch staff to Peking and gave them as parting gifts expensive articles, such as European watches and other curios. It was plain that he wished to curry favour so as to further his designs on the Throne. When I heard of his sickness some time ago I ordered the officials to send a competent physician to treat the dysentery from which he was suffering.

"But the cup of his offences was full to the very brim; Heaven and my ancestors, against whom he had so grievously sinned, were about to visit him with death. Truly, the way of the wicked does not prosper; the wages of sin is as certain as death, or as the reverberations of an echo. He has escaped punishment at the hands of man, but was not fated to escape the wrath of offended Heaven. The Viceroy is to arrange for his burial, and his family is to be brought back from Hsining. I am to be informed when their arrival may be expected. When I summoned 'Black-hearted monster' here from Hsining, I was much astonished to learn that he had been placed in shackles, although I had given no orders to this effect. The persons who adjusted the shackles fastened them very loosely, so that he was able to remove them from his limbs. I said nothing about this informality at the time, because I did not wish it to be thought that I was dealing over harshly with my brother. But the offence is unpardonable, and the parties responsible are to be placed in chains and subjected to severe examination."

One brother having died, Yung Cheng thought to deceive posterity (his own Court were too well aware of the facts to be thus hoodwinked) by asking the Ministers whether they thought he could safely pardon "Disreputable person" now that one of the conspirators was dead. Officials from all parts of the Empire were asked to report on this delicate question.

Yung Cheng next ordered the arrest and trial of Ch'u Tsung, the Viceroy of Kan-su and former gaoler of his dead brother, on the ground that he had not reported " Black-hearted monster's " dealings with the European Mu Ching-yuan, and had even memorialised the Emperor, saying that the Prince's popularity was a source of danger to the Throne, and that it would be best to bring him back to Peking, where he could be more carefully guarded. The Emperor observed that the Viceroy was evidently trying to frighten him with empty threats. " Knowing that he was guilty of gross disrespect in thus memorialising, he has tried to cover up his fault in a cheap attempt to win my favour by placing my brother in shackles on the journey from Kansu. His conduct was calculated to turn public opinion against me for undue cruelty, and if he meant the man to be in shackles he should at least have seen that they were not loosely fastened.

A month later "That disreputable person" was reported to be dying of blood-spitting in his prison at the Coal Hill, near the Palace. He, too, was put to death by the Emperor's orders. The Court asked that his corpse might be decapitated, a punishment which the merciful Monarch graciously remitted.

Of the third brother, Yün Ti, who was still confined near "the august portraits of his father and mother," in the Hall of Imperial Longevity, Yung Cheng said: "Yün Ti's guilt is less than that of the two prime offenders. On a previous occasion he was furious with my father for placing Yün Ssŭ under arrest, and even threatened me for not pleading on his behalf. It was then that he expressed a desire to die. I am, therefore, sending to ask if he is still of the same mind." The message was "When our father was living you said you would like to die with Yün Ssŭ; now he is dead, and if you so desire, you are welcome to take a look at his remains. You are also at liberty to kill yourself by his side if you see fit." To this Yün Ti replied: "I was befooled by 'That disreputable person,' and have no desire whatever to see him again, now that Heaven has punished him as he deserved." On this the Emperor observed: "The above reply would indicate that Yün Ti is inclining towards a better mind, but it is not improbable that he only adopts this attitude in order to save his neck, and still hopes to be revenged against me by and by. It is hard to say, but for the moment I commute his sentence of decapitation, and shall watch him carefully in future. If he does not amend, the sentence will be duly carried out. As to my brother Yün O, he is only half-witted, and it would be unfair to sentence him to the same penalty as the two chief criminals. He will be confined in prison for life, and for him the extreme penalty is hereby remitted."

Some years later the Emperor imprisoned his third elder brother, Yün Chih, Prince Ch'eng, on the Coal Hill (that favourite site for princely offenders), and he, too, died by violence. The eldest brother, Yün Ch'ih, was still confined in his own residence, and died in 1734. On Ch'ien Lung's accession the surviving Princes were all released and their titles were restored to them. In 1778, that Sovereign re-opened the process against Yün Ssŭ and Yün T'ang, and posthumously restored their original titles, replacing them on the Imperial Clan register.

The remainder of Yung Cheng's reign was disturbed by sedition all over the Empire, notably in Hunan and Ssŭchuan. Repressive measures of the sternest kind were carried out and many thousands were beheaded; nevertheless, scholars and patriots wrote violently against the Manchu dynasty, pointing out that the clan's internal dissensions and the Emperor's vindictive policy were a source of unrest to the whole country. Hundreds of seditious pamphlets were seized by the authorities, but they served their purpose in sowing in the minds of the people seeds of distrust, forerunners of rebellion against the Tartar rule. The Emperor, who had a keen sense of the need of moral qualities on the Throne and the value of popular endorsement of its government, issued many long explanations intended to reassure the public mind concerning the death of his brothers. Edicts, in the form of *apologiæ* for the Manchu dynasty, were promulgated throughout all the land; they ran into hundreds of thousands of words. Yung Cheng realised that the people, and especially the *literati*, who had prospered and rejoiced under the wise and dignified rule of K'ang Hsi, were already becoming restive under his own, and that the ominous word " alien " was again in men's mouths. He made it, therefore, his special business to defend the Manchu's alien origin, quoting Mencius to show that some of the best Monarchs of China's revered antiquity (such as the sage Emperor Shun) had come of a foreign stock.[1] But the fact was patent that his misrule was rapidly undermining the prestige of the house of Nurhachi, and it may safely be said that, had it continued, the dynasty would soon have gone under. His death came as a great relief to Peking and to the provinces alike.

A modern Chinese commentator, referring to the cruelty and base ingratitude of the treatment meted out to General Nien Keng-yao by his Sovereign,[2] observes: " How can a dynasty which produces Emperors of this type hope to retain the mandate of Heaven? and where, throughout all its annals, do we find instances of loyalty and generous sympathy for those who have sacrificed all in its cause? All the Sovereigns of the dynasty—K'ang Hsi, Yung Cheng, Chia Ch'ing and the rest—are alike in this respect. Only in the edicts and actions of the great Tzŭ Hsi do we find occasional gleams of nobler impulses, qualities of generosity and loyalty which evoke the more admiration when we compare them with the record of her predecessors, face-saving hypocrites and literary humbugs all."

[1] Precisely the same arguments were used by the last Regent, when terrified by the advance of the revolutionary movement in 1911.

[2] At the conclusion of a long and very literary farewell message to this old and trusted servant of the State, when conveying to him the Throne's permission to commit suicide, Yung Cheng observed: " As I peruse the State paper, I weep bitterly; but as Lord of the universe, I am bound to display unswerving justice in the matter of rewards and punishments. I remit the penalty of decapitation and grant you the privilege of suicide. With lavish generosity and merciful forbearance I have spared the lives of the rest of your family, with one exception. You must be stock or stone, if, even at the moment of death, you fail to shed tears of joy and gratitude for the benefits conferred upon you by the Imperial master whom you have so foully betrayed.

THE COURT OF PEKING

Nevertheless, beyond the turbid atmosphere of his domestic circle and fratricidal activities, Yung Cheng was a painstaking and earnest worker, with a good literary style and scholarly ambition, virtues which have done much to preserve his memory from utter contempt. He had a marked penchant for writing annotations on memorials and impromptu rescripts, and to do him justice he did it very well. Yung Cheng's rescripts were published by his successor, the Emperor Ch'ien Lung; together with the memorials to which they were appended, they fill some sixty large volumes, a monumental witness to His Majesty's industry.[1] In certain cases he was wont to append caustic or ironical comments; in others he would dismiss the memorialist's statement with a laconic " Ridiculous " or " Quite absurd." In one instance his marginal note says : " You evidently take me for a fool, but you forget that I was over forty when I came to the Throne, and that I know quite well how my officials make their money. Before I came to the Throne I had heard your name connected with a discreditable case of bribery. In fact, if I mistake not, you then endeavoured to secure my influence with His late Majesty by offering me presents. Have a care; my eye is upon you." To another memorialist he writes : " I do not know you by sight, but your reputation is well known to me, and I admire the efforts you are making to govern your

[1] The Regent, Prince Ch'un (appointed by Tzŭ Hsi in November 1908, to administer the Government during the minority of the child Emperor, his son, Hsüan T'ung) imitated this example during the brief period of his singularly ineffective Regency. A remarkably stupid man, and timid withal, he realised the Chinese people's innate reverence for a scholar, and so endeavoured to gain fame from literary rescripts to memorials. But having no scholarship of his own, he took the wise precaution of getting these written by Chang Chih-tung, the ablest pen in the Empire, and hoped for some share of the credit for their excellence. Unfortunately, Chang Chih-tung died, and thereafter the Regent abandoned his habit of literary rescripts, contenting himself with an occasional " Good," in an infantine hand, as a marginal note to some platitude which pleased his fancy.

province." Again, a certain official, on being rebuked by Yung Cheng, replied that shame and fear had combined in his mind, so that he knew not how to bear his remorse. Yung Cheng replied: "I fully believe in your fears, but I have my doubts as to your shame and remorse. Of these I shall judge by your future conduct rather than by your present protestations." In criminal cases he was apt to assume the rôle of counsel for the defence, or rather of a friendly judge of appeal. In one instance the provincial authorities recommended decapitation for a wife who had murdered her husband. After reviewing the evidence, as presented in the memorial, Yung Cheng observed: "I have no doubt but that this woman murdered her husband for proposing to her that she should earn money for him by prostitution; her conduct was wholly admirable, and deserves no punishment whatsoever. On the contrary, I order that a memorial arch be erected in her honour." In all cases where he suspected treasonable writing, he showed great harshness. Scholars frequently criticised his unpopular government by innuendo, and on them he invariably inflicted the death penalty. For instance, when a certain poet wrote: "To-morrow at dawn I shall enter the bright capital" (Ming chao ju ching tu), the Emperor's attention was drawn to the verses and to the fact that these characters might also mean (and probably were intended to mean) "The Ming dynasty enters the Ching, or Manchu, capital." At any rate, this was the interpretation which Yung Cheng chose to place on the line, and the poet expiated his *double-entendre* on the scaffold.

Yung Cheng was by nature suspicious and inconstant; but certain of his favourite Ministers enjoyed his goodwill to the end, and it is possible that, but for his unfortunate family troubles, he might have left a better record. Despite his persecution of the Christian religion, more than one of the Roman Catholic fathers then living at

THE COURT OF PEKING

Peking has written of his public and private life in terms that imply certain good qualities in his character.[1] Also his handling of affairs, outside those of his family circle, seems to indicate a certain sense of humour. For instance, one of his favourite Ministers, named T'ien Wen-ching, was a good administrator, but a poor scholar. T'ien, aware of his own shortcomings, relied for the performance of the literary part of his duties on the services of a notable scholar, named Wu, whose work is quoted and admired to this day. When T'ien was serving as Director-General of the Yellow River Conservancy, it was Wu who advised him to impeach Yung Cheng's uncle, the Duke Lung K'o-to, brother of the Empress Dowager, an act which secured for him high promotion and Imperial favour. Mr. Secretary Wu, who had sources of private information about the Court, had learned that His Majesty was growing weary of his uncle's presence and patronising ways,[2] and therefore advised his employer to indite this memorial of impeachment, at a moment when the Emperor was seeking a pretext for ridding himself of his uncle. T'ien's fortune was made, but he failed to display the kind of gratitude that his secretary expected, and Wu, greatly offended, resigned from his service. From that day, T'ien's memorials and despatches lost the literary quality which Yung Cheng expected in his high officials, and drew from the fastidious Monarch sarcastic rescripts and criticisms as to their contents and style. Finally, T'ien was compelled to implore Wu to return to him, which the secretary consented to do only on condition that he was to be paid a " shoe " of silver (50 taels) every morning before the day's work began. By his aid, T'ien recovered and

---

[1] Vide *Histoire Générale de la Chine*, Mailla, Vol. XI, p. 370.
[2] Lung K'o-to had been very intimate with Yung Cheng before his accession, and had been instrumental in persuading K'ang Hsi to appoint him to the Throne.

retained the Imperial favour; but Yung Cheng was well aware of the authorship of the literary gems in T'ien's official documents, for on one occasion, when the Minister had sent in a memorial inquiring after his health, the Emperor's rescript read: " Our health is good; how goes that of Mr. Secretary Wu? " Eventually, after T'ien's death, the Emperor engaged Wu's services for the Palace.

Whatever Yung Cheng's defects, however bad his rule, he was, at least, not guilty of the ignominious folly which led a later generation of his dynasty to give their confidence, and delegate their authority, to the eunuch servants of the Palace, that crime against the State to which Tzu Hsi (guilty of it herself) ascribed the downfall of the Manchu power. Yung Cheng kept his eunuchs in their proper place, employing them as servants and actors, but allowing them no voice in the administration of the Government nor any recognised opportunities for levying blackmail on the official class. Of his attitude towards the eunuchs of his own household it is recorded that, on a certain occasion, one of them, an admirable actor and *raconteur*, had delighted the Court by an unusually excellent performance. Upon the conclusion of the play the Emperor summoned the man to his own table, gave him food and wine, and ordered him to tell some theatrical stories. Elated by his master's favour the eunuch chatted away, and eventually made allusion to the part of Cheng Tan, which he had just been olaying (in a famous piece called " Cheng Tan slaying his son "). At last he made bold to remark : " In olden times this Cheng Tan was Department Magistrate of Ch'ang Chou-fu in Kiangsu. Can Your Majesty [1] tell me who is now the Department Magistrate at Ch'ang Chou ? " (This he meant as a delicate hint that the Emperor should bestow upon him the post of magistrate, a thing strictly

[1] He used the colloquial expression " Yeh " (Master) employed by eunuchs in addressing the Emperor.

forbidden by the dynastic house-law). The Emperor's countenance darkened, says the chronicler, till it became black as thunder. "How dare you, a eunuch minion, ask Us about Our officials? What have you to do with such matters?" He then called to his bodyguard: "Have the creature beaten with the heavy bamboo here and now; We will witness his chastisement." The eunuch whined for mercy, but Yung Cheng was obdurate. After a few strokes of the bamboo the culprit fainted; the Emperor then ordered that he be ejected from the Palace and banished to a pestilential part of Yünnan, as a slave to the Manchu garrison troops of that frontier province.

Despite his proscription of the Roman Catholic mission and the expulsion of the priests to Macao and Canton, Yung Cheng's attitude towards the head of this religion was courteous and even friendly.[1] This may have been due to recollection of the benefits derived by his father's and grandfather's intercourse with the Jesuit fathers, or to a vague sense that the spiritual Chief of men, so devoted and so learned, deserved the respect of scholars, even though, for political reasons, the activities of the missions had to be suppressed throughout his Empire. At all events, the annals of his reign record more than one instance of a courteous and conciliatory attitude towards the Vatican. Witness the following letter addressed to Pope Benedict XIII in the year 1725.

"A decree to the religious Prince of the West. I have perused your memorial and have examined the tribute which you have forwarded. Your evident sincerity pleases me. His Majesty the late Emperor showered

[1] Chinese chroniclers aver that many letters written to each other by the conspiring Princes were in the Portuguese language, which they had learned from the priests at Court. One of Yung Cheng's decrees refers to letters written to Yun T'ang by "his secretary, Maotai tungpao," and found sewed into the socks of a groom-messenger, which were "amazingly like the European characters," but which none of the Europeans then in Peking could (or would) recognise.

his bountiful protection on all alike; his love knew no limits. At this death every one was smitten with unspeakable grief. On my accession to the Great Inheritance I strove earnestly to follow my father's good example in all things. You, oh Prince, reside in a far land; nevertheless, you have sent your special envoy with a memorial expressing gratitude for the late Emperor's benefits and with best wishes for my own prosperity. Your language betokens a dutiful sincerity and respect. I highly applaud your devotion and have shown every courtesy to your envoy. Regarding the Europeans resident in China, I fully recognise that all mankind are members of one family and have frequently told them that if they behave themselves with becoming circumspection, practising a wise aloofness and virtue, and obeying the laws of the land, I shall ever bestow upon them my compassionate favour. In addition to conferring this decree upon yourself, I am forwarding by the hand of your envoy sundry gifts of silks and rolls of satin. Do you, oh Prince, receive them reverently and appreciate my friendliness towards you."

And again, when the Pope wrote asking for the release of two priests who had been imprisoned at Canton for several years, His Majesty replied, graciously enough, that, after investigation of their cases, he found they were not too serious to benefit by the general amnesty published in honour of his accession to the Throne. He therefore willingly acceded to the Pope's request, and added that, even if His Holiness had taken no steps in the matter, he would have set the prisoners free " to give proof of his sense of the common brotherhood of the human race and of his own far-reaching compassion."

There is no doubt that this fussy, terror-ridden Monarch often meant well enough. One of his favourite Ministers has left it on record that in his youth he made for himself two rules (which fittingly illustrate the nature and value

THE COURT OF PEKING

of his " far-reaching compassion "). One was, always to avoid stepping on the shadow of anybody's head, since that would bring misfortune to the substance. The other, never to tread upon an insect.

According to many Chinese chroniclers, Yung Cheng was murdered by the widow of a Hunanese named Lu, who had been dismembered on a charge of treasonable conspiracy. The story, which finds no place in the dynastic annals, goes to show that this woman succeeded in getting access to the pleasure-garden at Yuan-ming-yuan and, concealing herself there, lay in wait for the Emperor and stabbed him to the heart; after which she committed suicide.

CHAPTER XIII

HIS MAJESTY CH'IEN LUNG

CH'IEN LUNG ascended the Dragon Throne at the age of twenty-five, in 1736, and reigned over China for sixty years, at the end of which cycle he abdicated in favour of his son Chia Ch'ing. Judged by the verdict of his contemporaries and of posterity in his own country, as well as by the evidence of European observers, he was beyond question the ablest administrator and the wisest ruler that China had known for several centuries. By his good government, as well as by his successful wars in Sungaria, Central Asia, Burmah and Tibet, he completely restored the prestige of the Manchus, which his predecessor had seriously undermined. In his private life, he appears to have been distinguished by qualities of sincerity, broad-mindedness and courage which alone suffice to raise him far above the level of his predecessors and successors. He was impulsive, it is true; intolerant of failure in those upon whom he conferred high authority, especially in military affairs; superstitious and naturally ignorant of China's relative place and power amongst the nations; but gifted nevertheless with clear insight, sweet reasonableness and a highly sympathetic nature. He combined in his person, to a high degree, the best qualities of the soldier and the statesman, but was besides a scholar, a historian and a poet. In his domestic life also he was successful in maintaining his parental authority, while preserving the respect of his sons and grandsons; a polygamous autocrat in his relations with women, he was neither uxorious nor luxurious. After a reign of unexampled success, he left the Empire stronger and more prosperous than it had been for several centuries.

For Englishmen, the reign of this great Emperor is particularly memorable, in that it witnessed the first Embassy from the King of Great Britain to the Court of China—that of the Earl of Macartney, in 1795, undertaken with the object of improving commercial relations between the Chinese authorities and British merchants at Canton. Sir George Staunton's "authentic account" of that Embassy (London 1797) affords instructive reading to this day, besides giving a most interesting and sympathetic description of the aged Monarch and his Court of Jehol and a valuable, because impartial, impression of the personality of the Grand Secretary Ho Shen, to whose hands, for many years, was delegated much of the Sovereign's power, and who was destined, under Chia Ch'ing, to meet the common fate of Imperial favourites.

At the time of Lord Macartney's Embassy the Emperor was eighty-four years of age, and of his numerous sons, only four were then living, namely the eighth, eleventh, fifteenth and seventeenth. (The eleventh son, at that time Governor of Peking, subsequently succeeded to the Throne under the title of Chia Ch'ing). Some years before, in 1784, the question of the succession had been raised, and His Majesty had been urged to appoint his Heir, because several members of the Imperial Clan were afraid of the growing power and ambitions of Ho Shen, to whose son the Emperor had given one of his daughters in marriage. The Imperial Clan were jealous of the powerful favourite, and the orthodox were anxious to prevent a possible breach of the laws of succession. But Ch'ien Lung was not the man to accept advice on such a subject; the zealous memorialist paid for his temerity with his head, the Emperor firmly declining to announce his intentions. In November 1784, he issued a decree carefully explaining his reasons for this decision, a document which reveals much of the character of the Sovereign, and shows that he had read, marked, learned and inwardly digested the lessons taught by the domestic tribulations of his predecessor. Incidentally it throws valuable light on the manners and customs of the Court.

The following is a translation of this decree :

" I have perused the compilation entitled *History of Official Ranks*, prepared under my orders by a Commission of Princes and Ministers, and I observe, in the section : ' Supervisorate of Instruction for the Heir Apparent ' the following note : ' The staff of this office consists of officials ministering to the Heir Apparent, but our dynasty has promulgated a house-law, which is to last for all time, that no Emperor shall nominate an Heir Apparent until the close of his reign. The Supervisorate of Instruction is thus retained merely to provide Academy doctors with stepping-stones for promotion.'

" This note is obviously based on my previous decree, in which I explicitly stated the reasons against a formal selection of an Heir Apparent. The Commission has adopted my identical words, but has omitted to quote their context. The narrow pedantry of a scholar naturally fails to appreciate the larger issues of State, so that my intention has been misconstrued. But should this history be read by later generations, it is probable that the Commission will be calumniated in the belief that they must have acted upon some treasonable motive in drawing up such a note. It therefore behoves me to issue an explicit pronouncement on the subject. Now, in remote antiquity we find the Emperor Yao transmitting the Throne to Shun, a precedent which was followed by his successors. Unfortunately times degenerated, so that under the Han dynasty the nomination of an Heir Apparent frequently resulted in fratricidal strife and civil war. You will recall that the founder of the T'ang dynasty (A.D. 618) selected his eldest son as Heir, with the result that he was murdered by his younger brother, Li Shih-min. In the same way, during the reign of the Ming Emperor Wan Li (circa 1600) the Court begged him to select an Heir, and dire confusion of parties ensued, each official endeavouring to further his own future interests by securing the favour of the probable successor. In Wan Li's reign, when an attempt was made on the Heir Apparent's life by armed men who entered the Forbidden City, the Emperor received his son in audience and tearfully reproached the Court for supposing that he had desired his Heir's death. Such a scene between father and son is enough to make one despair of the State.

"These examples show the evil results of a formal nomination of an Heir Apparent. As regards my own dynasty, my grandfather K'ang Hsi selected Prince Li as Heir Apparent. He was placed under the tutorship of T'ang Pin, an upright man, but his conduct degenerated so woefully after his selection that even T'ang Pin was unable to check and control him. Mean schemers and sycophants implanted seeds of discord in the Prince's mind: endless troubles resulted, and my grandfather's peace of mind was so much disturbed thereby, that he finally cancelled the appointment. But even had Prince Li been a model Heir, his early death would only have given him two years on the Throne. In due course his son Yung Hsi would have succeeded, but he, too, was a reprobate of the worst type and was not destined for a long life. Within a few years there would thus have been two vacancies to the Throne, a result fraught with danger to the destinies of our dynasty and to the welfare of our subjects.

"My grandfather realised this and made no further

public nomination of an Heir. On his demise the Throne passed to my father Yung Ch'eng, and for thirteen years that sage Emperor administered the Government and gave peace to the Empire. In obedience to the precedent established by K'ang Hsi, he made no public choice of an Heir Apparent, although naturally he came to an early decision on the question of the succession, which affects the fortunes of our dynasty. In the first year of his reign he wrote my name and placed it in a sealed casket which he secreted at the back of the Imperial tablet, 'Grandly upright and gloriously bright,' in the main hall of the Palace. He also wrote my name on a paper that he put in a pouch which he always wore.

"When my father departed on his distant journey (in 1735), I reverently opened the casket, in the presence of his Ministers, and we found the mandate which appointed me to the Throne. On our comparing the seal impression on the document with the other half, which had been secreted in the Imperial household, the two portions tallied exactly. The Empire then gave me its allegiance, as is well known to all my subjects. Early in my reign, in accordance with dynastic house-law, I selected my second son as my Heir, both because he was born to my Empress Consort (and not to a concubine) and because of his keen intelligence and correct behaviour. In obedience to my father's example I wrote his name, placed it in the casket, and secreted it behind the tablet of my Palace hall. But the fates were unkind, for he soon left this world. I then commanded my two Grand Secretaries, O-erh-t'ai and Chang T'ing-yü, to remove and destroy the document in the casket, and I bestowed on my deceased son the posthumous appellation of 'Orthodox and Discerning.'

"Thus you will see that I duly nominated the child of my Empress Consort to be Heir to the Throne, but refrained from announcing my choice to the world.

THE COURT OF PEKING

After his death, my seventh son, Prince Che, also born to the Empress, was very dear to me, because of his sincerity and strength of character, but in a little while I had to mourn his untimely death. Thereafter, of all my children, it was my fifth son, Prince Jung, who stood highest in my affection. He was well versed in Chinese literature, could speak both Manchu and Mongol, and was skilled in horsemanship, archery and mathematics. I was strongly inclined to select him as Heir Apparent, but never formally recorded his name. He too is dead, so that, if I had adopted the narrow pedantic view, and following ancient custom publicly declared an Heir, we should have seen three Heir Apparents within a space of thirty years, a state of affairs utterly subversive of dignity! In the thirty-seventh year of my reign (1773) I wrote out the name of my proposed Heir and since then have always carried the document on my person. On the occasion of the New Year sacrifice at the Temple of Heaven this year, I bade all my sons attend me during the ceremony, in the course of which I informed the Almighty of my choice, and reverently prayed, that He might be pleased to shed Divine grace upon my Heir and to regard him with benevolent protection, so that if he found favour in the Divine sight he might reach a good old age. But if he whom I had chosen were displeasing to the Almighty, then might He speedily visit him with destruction, so that I might select another successor, and that the dignity of our dynastic altars and the fortunes of our State might be duly protected.

" Early this year, I made a pilgrimage to the tomb of the founder of my dynasty and that of his son. There, in the presence of my glorious ancestors, I besought their august protection. Think not that I do not love my son! But I love even more the interests of the State. It will be to the eternal happiness of our Manchu dynasty if in this matter my successors will follow my example.

"I have summoned my sons and the members of the Grand Council to audience this day and have made known to them this, my mandate. It corresponds exactly with the words which I uttered in the presence of my ancestors, where no falsehood could find a place. Day and night I toil, performing the heavy duties of the Government, exhausting myself in manifold directions. How then, think you, that I could possibly have failed to make long ago all necessary arrangements in a matter of such importance as the succession to the Throne?

"Last autumn, at Jehol, I was shooting duck by the riverside, when my foot slipped, I fell into the water, and my clothes were wet through. Not only did the Princes and Chamberlains hasten to my assistance with eager inquiries as to my condition, but even the Chinese Grand Councillors came hurrying to the spot. I treated the accident as of no moment, and walked back with them to the Palace, chatting and smiling all the way. No eunuch ventured to stop them from entering the forbidden precincts. In the same way, supposing that I were smitten with a sudden illness, any of you Ministers would be at liberty to make his way even into my bed-chamber, because I have ever treated you as members of my family, and held daily converse with each of you. In my reign, there could be no possibility of happenings such as former dynasties have witnessed, when a eunuch would rush out from the Palace at dead of night, bearing a slip of paper in which the demise of the Throne and the appointment of a successor were mysteriously recorded. He who fears such an event to-day is like the man of the Ch'i State who feared that the sky was going to fall and crush him!

"In short, although the formal selection and investiture of an Heir Apparent must be definitely avoided, my reverent announcement to the Almighty and to my ancestors, in all humility and sincerity of heart, provides

THE COURT OF PEKING

for all emergencies. In this matter, I have avoided following the example of past dynasties, which incurred disasters by their strict observance of the letter of the law. And thus it comes to pass that the staff of the existing 'Supervisorate of Instruction for the Heir Apparent' is maintained in accordance with ancient custom, but has no duties to perform, the office being retained as a stepping-stone to promotion for doctors of the Academy.

"I do hereby solemnly promulgate this my decree, in the earnest hope that my descendants will faithfully observe it for all time, because thereby, in my judgment, the fortunes of our dynasty will be established for generations to come. Lastly, I claim no infallibility for my words : I may be mistaken, and therefore refrain from expressly forbidding my descendants to follow the ancient practice which sanctioned the appointment of an Heir Apparent. But perchance, if they do follow it, and if, as a result, strife shall arise between father and son, and fratricidal dissensions culminate in dire disaster to our dynasty, then will posterity remember the words I have uttered to-day. Let the Commission duly record this decree as a preface to their *History of Official Ranks*, so that my Imperial wishes may be made known to the whole Empire for time everlasting. The words of the Emperor!"

How different this lucid and straightforward utterance of Ch'ien Lung from the insincere phrases and machine-made platitudes of his predecessor! All the recorded writings of Ch'ien Lung are distinguished by the same quality of intellectual independence and disregard for empty or harmful conventions. Take, for example, the edict in which he declares his intention of vacating the Throne upon the completion of sixty years of reign, issued in the 8th Moon of the 59th year of his reign (1795) :

"I have now reigned for fifty-nine years. By the favour of high Heaven and the protection of my ancestors, peace prevails throughout my dominions, and new territories have come to share the blessings of China's civilisation. During all these years, I have striven to alleviate my people's lot and to show myself worthy of Heaven's blessings. Again and again have I granted exemptions of land tax in times of flood and famine and bestowed upon the sufferers over ten million taels from my privy purse.

"Next year will witness the sixtieth anniversary of my succession to this goodly heritage of the Throne: few, indeed, of my predecessors in this and other dynasties, have completed a sixty-year cycle. Those among them who have reigned over sixty years came to the Throne in early childhood, whereas I was twenty-five years of age at my accession. To-day I am eighty-four, and my natural strength is not abated. I rejoice in the possession of perfect health, and my descendants to the fourth generation surround me. Immeasurably thankful as I am to the Almighty for His protection, I feel encouraged to yet further endeavour. On New Year's Day of my sixtieth year an eclipse of the sun is due, and on the Festival of Lanterns (1st Moon, 15th day) there will be a lunar eclipse. Heaven sends these portents as warnings, but a Sovereign's duty is to be guided by his conscience and to be aware of his shortcomings at all times, so that an eclipse is not needed to awaken him to a sense of duty. To find favour in the sight of Heaven he must regulate his conduct. There is no need for empty catchwords and platitudes on the occasion of such natural events.

"During the course of next year, I shall prepare for my impending abdication, and the new Emperor will mount the Throne on New Year's Day of the year following. In recognition of the warning conveyed by these eclipses, I purpose to hold no New Year's Court next year, and the customary banquet to the Princes will be omitted. During the period of the eclipses, I shall array myself in every day raiment and doff my Imperial robes of ceremony.

"These phenomena can be foretold, as Mencius says, a thousand years before they occur, but in the present case, the coincidence of two eclipses is a fresh indication of the favour of Heaven towards me, for had this phenomenon taken place in the following year, it would have signified an inauspicious opening for my son's reign. I feel profoundly grateful to Heaven for its favour, and in return I hereby cancel all birthday celebrations in the capital for next year, and shall content myself with receiving the congratulations of my Court at Jehol."

Ch'ien Lung's instinctive reverence towards Heaven and his ancestors, the good example of his temperate and industrious life, all his precautions of statecraft and military activities, were directed towards the consolidation of the Manchu power and of a government which should confer prosperity upon the Chinese people. Nevertheless, and despite the sincerity of his good intentions, he had established beside the Throne, in the person of his favourite Minister, the Grand Secretary Ho Shen, a source of demoralisation, an initiative of wickedness and greed in high places, which was destined (as we shall show) to destroy the very foundations of the State. Amongst Chinese historians and scholars there is a common saying : " A cycle of virtuous rule was brought to nought by Ho Shen : the disastrous century of rebellion and decline which followed, was due to him and to him alone."

We shall have occasion later to relate the dramatic story of this all-powerful satrap, to whom (as Staunton says) the people looked as to a second Emperor. For the present, suffice it to say that Ch'ien Lung's personal devotion to the highest ideals of government was greatly prejudiced, even during his reign, by his blind belief in

Ho Shen. It was the example of extravagant luxury set by this great Vizier, which led to the rapid deterioration of the Manchu Court's old simple style of living; his nepotism and venality, displayed in the employment of corrupt officials, were fundamental factors in the rebellions which broke out in the reign of Chia Ch'ing. But Ch'ien Lung's devotion to his chief Minister knew no wavering; during the last twenty years of his reign, he allowed Ho Shen to exercise despotic power and to amass a huge fortune. To his son, he gave an Imperial Princess for wife, and to his brother, Ho Lin,[1] he entrusted the command of the Imperial forces and the administration of Tibetan affairs.

This Ho Lin was directly concerned in the affairs of Lord Macartney's Embassy, for in 1790 he was summoned by the Emperor to return from Lhasa to Peking, in anticipation of the British Envoy's probable intention of discussing Great Britain's interests in India, affected by China's successful campaign of the previous year against the marauding Ghoorkas of Nepal. The Emperor's edict concerning China's suzerainty over Tibet and the relations of the Imperial Resident at Lhasa with the Dalai Lama, is of permanent interest.

"We are informed," he wrote, "by Cheng Te, who has just arrived from Lhasa, that Ho Lin is displaying great skill in the management of Tibetan affairs, and does not kneel or kotow to the Dalai Lama, who obeys every order that he may give. We are the more delighted to hear that Ho Lin is thus conscious of the dignity of the State, because of late years Tibet has been steadily sinking into depths of barbarism and its government has degenerated into hopeless inefficiency. Now that Ho Lin has set things on a more stable basis, it will be easier to enforce our control over the country, and the real

[1] Whose attitude towards the British Envoy and his suite is described by Staunton as "formal and repulsive."

power will be vested in our hands. We are now sending Sung Yün to be our Resident at Lhasa: he is a Mongol and is therefore a devout believer in the Buddhism of the Lamas. Should he fail to show due regard for his own dignity, the Dalai will surely put fresh obstacles in his way. We therefore command that he be instructed not to perform any degrading ceremony of obeisance to the Dalai Lama. If he wishes to display his individual respect to the head of his religion, let him wait until his term of office has expired: then, before leaving Lhasa, he may, if he thinks fit, ask the Dalai for his blessing."

Ho Lin returned to Peking and was present at the Emperor's reception of the British Embassy at Jehol. Staunton relates [1] that although Earl Macartney was at pains to reassure the Grand Secretary, Ho Shen, that Great Britain had no intention of interfering in the contests of the countries neighbouring on India, and that the dissolution of the Great Mogul's Empire involved no new dangers to China, nevertheless, Ho Lin accompanied Ho Shen at all his meetings with the Ambassador, " as if fearful that any explanation, relative to the Tibet war, might take place between them." He made no attempt to conceal " the violent prepossession which he had imbibed against the English," both in Tibet and earlier at Canton. Doubtless the influence of this cantankerous individual was to some extent reflected in the attitude of certain members of the Court, but Ho Shen himself took a broad view of the Embassy's objects in coming to China, and remembering the friendly services rendered by the British at the end of the Nepalese campaign, was instrumental in persuading the Emperor to waive the ceremony of the kotow, upon which the more conservative officials and courtiers were disposed to insist.

Ho Lin's influence and advice were undoubtedly factors in the Emperor's refusal to accede to Earl Macartney's

[1] Vol. II, p. 241.

requests for the establishment of a British representative and a trading centre at Peking; for the extension of shipping facilities, and a regular Customs tariff applicable to British traders at Chusan, Ningpo and Tientsin; and for the authorisation of missionary labours in China. It was common report at the time that Ho Shen had advised the Emperor to grant some, at least, of the Ambassador's requests, but that the aged Sovereign was finally dissuaded from this course by his sons, and especially by the opinions of him who subsequently became the Emperor Chia Ch'ing.

The Imperial "mandate" to King George III, issued by His Majesty a few days after his reception of the British Embassy at Jehol makes strange reading to-day. How swift and complete has been the process of the Great Celestial Empire's decline and humiliation, since its Sovereign could describe himself in all sincerity, as "swaying the wide world." In those days, only a brief century ago, China's ignorance of the outer world was bliss indeed.

The following is the text of this historic document:

"You, O King, live beyond the confines of many seas, nevertheless, impelled by your humble desire to partake of the benefits of our civilisation, you have dispatched a mission respectfully bearing your memorial. Your Envoy has crossed the seas and paid his respects at my Court on the anniversary of my birthday. To show your devotion, you have also sent offerings of your country's produce.

"I have perused your memorial: the earnest terms in which it is couched reveal a respectful humility on your part, which is highly praiseworthy. In consideration of the fact that your Ambassador and his deputy have come a long way with your memorial and tribute, I have shown them high favour and have allowed them to be introduced into my presence. To manifest my indulgence,

THE COURT OF PEKING

I have entertained them at a banquet and made them numerous gifts. I have also caused presents to be forwarded to the Naval Commander and six hundred of his officers and men, although they did not come to Peking, so that all may share in my all-embracing kindness.

"As to your entreaty to send one of your nationals to be accredited to my Celestial Court and to be in control of your country's trade with China, this request is contrary to all usage of my dynasty and cannot possibly be entertained. It is true that Europeans, in the service of the dynasty, have been permitted to live at Peking, but they are compelled to adopt Chinese dress, they are strictly confined to their own precincts and are never permitted to return home. You are presumably familiar with our dynastic regulations. Your proposed Envoy to my Court could not be placed in a position similar to that of European officials in Peking who are forbidden to leave China, nor could he, on the other hand, be allowed liberty of movement and the privilege of corresponding with his own country; so that you would gain nothing by his residence in our midst.

"Moreover, our Celestial dynasty possesses vast territories, and tribute missions from the dependencies are provided for by the Department for Tributary States, which ministers to their wants and exercises strict control over their movements. It would be quite impossible to leave them to their own devices. Supposing that your Envoy should come to our Court, his language and national dress differ from that of our people, and there would be no place in which to bestow him. It may be suggested that he might imitate the Europeans permanently resident in Peking and adopt the dress and customs of China, but, it has never been our dynasty's wish to force people to do things unseemly and inconvenient. Besides, supposing I sent an Ambassador to reside in your country, how could you possibly make for him the requisite arrangements? Europe consists of many other nations besides your own: if each and all demanded to be represented at our Court, how could we possibly consent? The thing is utterly impracticable. How can our dynasty alter its whole procedure and system of etiquette, established for more than a century, in order to meet your individual views? If it be said that your object is to exercise control over your country's trade, your nationals have had full liberty to trade at Canton for many a year, and have received the greatest consideration at our hands. Missions have been sent by Portugal and Italy, preferring similar requests. The Throne appreciated their sincerity and loaded them with favours, besides authorising measures to facilitate their trade with China. You are no doubt aware that, when my Canton merchant, Wu Chao-ping, was in debt to the foreign ships, I made the Viceroy advance the monies due, out of the provincial treasury, and ordered him to punish the culprit severely. Why then should foreign nations advance this utterly unreasonable request to be represented at my Court? Peking is nearly two thousand miles from Canton, and at such a distance what possible control could any British representative exercise?

"If you assert that your reverence for Our Celestial dynasty fills you with a desire to acquire our civilisation, our ceremonies and code of laws differ so completely from your own that, even if your Envoy were able to acquire the rudiments of our civilisation, you could not possibly transplant our manners and customs to your alien soil. Therefore, however adept the Envoy might become, nothing would be gained thereby.

"Swaying the wide world, I have but one aim in view, namely, to maintain a perfect governance and to fulfil the duties of the State: strange and costly objects do not interest me. If I have commanded that the tribute offerings sent by you, O King, are to be accepted, this was solely in consideration for the spirit which prompted you to dispatch them from afar. Our dynasty's majestic virtue has penetrated unto every country under Heaven, and Kings of all nations have offered their costly tribute by land and sea. As your Ambassador can see for himself, we possess all things. I set no value on objects strange or ingenious, and have no use for your country's manufactures. This then is my answer to your request to appoint a representative at my Court, a request contrary to our dynastic usage, which would only result in inconvenience to yourself. I have expounded my wishes in detail and have commanded your tribute Envoys to leave in peace on their homeward journey. It behoves you, O King, to respect my sentiments and to display even greater devotion and loyalty in future, so that, by perpetual submission to our Throne, you may secure peace and prosperity for your country hereafter. Besides making gifts (of which I enclose an inventory) to each member of your Mission, I confer upon you, O King, valuable presents in excess of the number usually bestowed on such occasions, including silks and curios—a list of which is likewise enclosed. Do you reverently receive them and take note of my tender goodwill towards you! A special mandate."

A further mandate to King George III dealt in detail with the British Ambassador's proposals and the Emperor's reasons for declining them: " You, O King, from afar have yearned after the blessings of our civilisation, and in your eagerness to come into touch with our converting influence have sent an Embassy across the sea bearing a memorial. I have already taken note of your respectful spirit of submission, have treated your mission with extreme favour and loaded it with gifts, besides issuing a mandate to you, O King, and honouring you with the bestowal of valuable presents. Thus has my indulgence been manifested.

"Yesterday your Ambassador petitioned my Ministers to memorialise me regarding your trade with China, but his proposal is not consistent with our dynastic usage and cannot be entertained. Hitherto, all European nations, including your own country's barbarian merchants, have carried on their trade with our Celestial Empire at Canton. Such has been the procedure for many years, although our Celestial Empire possesses all things in prolific abundance and lacks no product within its own borders. There was therefore no need to import the manufactures of outside barbarians in exchange for our own produce. But as the tea, silk and porcelain which the Celestial Empire produces, are absolute necessities to European nations and to yourselves, we have permitted, as a signal mark of favour, that foreign *hongs* should be established at Canton, so that your wants might be supplied and your country thus participate in our beneficence. But your Ambassador has now put forward new requests which completely fail to recognise the Throne's principle to 'treat strangers from afar with indulgence,' and to exercise a pacifying control over barbarian tribes, the world over. Moreover, our dynasty, swaying the myriad races of the globe, extends the same benevolence towards all. Your England is not the only nation trading at Canton. If other nations, following your bad example, wrongfully importune my ear with further impossible requests, how will it be possible for me to treat them with easy indulgence? Nevertheless, I do not forget the lonely remoteness of your island, cut off from the world by intervening wastes of sea.[1] nor do I overlook your excusable ignorance of the usages of our Celestial Empire. I have consequently commanded my Ministers to enlighten your Ambassador on the subject, and have ordered the departure of the mission. But I have doubts that, after your Envoy's return he may fail

[1] Cf. "Toto divisos orbe Britannos."

to acquaint you with my view in detail or that he may be lacking in lucidity, so that I shall now proceed to take your requests *seriatim* and to issue my mandate on each question separately. In this way you will, I trust, comprehend my meaning.

" (1) Your Ambassador requests facilities for ships of your nation to call at Ningpo, Chusan, Tientsin and other places for purposes of trade. Until now trade with European nations has always been conducted at Aomen, where the foreign *hongs* are established to store and sell foreign merchandise. Your nation has obediently complied with this regulation for years past without raising any objection. In none of the other ports named have *hongs* been established, so that even if your vessels were to proceed thither, they would have no means of disposing of their cargoes. Furthermore, no interpreters are available, so you would have no means of explaining your wants, and nothing but general inconvenience would result. For the future, as in the past, I decree that your request is refused and that the trade shall be limited to Aomen.

" (2) The request that your merchants may establish a repository in the capital of my Empire for the storing and sale of your produce, in accordance with the precedent granted to Russia, is even more impracticable than the last. My capital is the hub and centre about which all quarters of the globe revolve. Its ordinances are most august and its laws are strict in the extreme. The subjects of our dependencies have never been allowed to open places of business in Peking. Foreign trade has hitherto been conducted at Aomen, because it is conveniently near to the sea, and therefore an important gathering place for the ships of all nations sailing to and fro. If warehouses were established in Peking, the remoteness of your country, lying far to the north-west of my capital, would render transport extremely difficult.

Before Kiakhta was opened, the Russians were permitted to trade at Peking, but the accommodation furnished to them was only temporary. As soon as Kiakhta was available, they were compelled to withdraw from Peking, which has been closed to their trade these many years. Their frontier trade at Kiakhta is on all fours with your trade at Aomen. Possessing facilities at the latter place, you now ask for further privileges at Peking, although our dynasty observes the severest restrictions respecting the admission of foreigners within its boundaries, and as never permitted the subjects of dependencies to cross the Empire's barriers and settle at will amongst the Chinese people. This request is also refused.

" (3) Your request for a small island near Chusan, where your merchants may reside and goods be warehoused, arises from your desire to develop trade. As there are neither foreign *hongs* nor interpreters in or near Chusan, where none of your ships have ever called, such an island would be utterly useless for your purposes. Every inch of the territory of our Empire is marked on the map and the strictest vigilance is exercised over it all: even tiny islets and far-lying sand-banks are clearly defined as part of the provinces to which they belong. Consider, moreover, that England is not the only barbarian land which wishes to establish relations with our civilisation and trade with our Empire: supposing that other nations were all to imitate your evil example and beseech me to present them each and all with a site for trading purposes, how could I possibly comply? This also is a flagrant infringement of the usage of my Empire and cannot possibly be entertained.

" (4) The next request, for a small site in the vicinity of Canton city, where your barbarian merchants may lodge or, alternatively, that there be no longer any restrictions over their movements at Aomen, has arisen from the following causes. Hitherto, the barbarian merchants of

THE COURT OF PEKING

Europe have had a definite locality assigned to them at Aomen for residence and trade, and have been forbidden to encroach an inch beyond the limits assigned to that locality. Barbarian merchants having business with the *hongs* have never been allowed to enter the city of Canton; by these measures, disputes between Chinese and barbarians are prevented, and a firm barrier is raised between my subjects and those of other nations. The present request is quite contrary to precedent; furthermore, European nations have been trading with Canton for a number of years and, as they make large profits, the number of traders is constantly increasing. How would it be possible to grant such a site to each country? The merchants of the foreign *hongs* are responsible to the local officials for the proceedings of barbarian merchants and they carry out periodical inspections. If these restrictions were withdrawn, friction would inevitably occur between the Chinese and your barbarian subjects, and the results would militate against the benevolent regard that I feel towards you. From every point of view, therefore, it is best that the regulations now in force should continue unchanged.

" (5) Regarding your request for remission or reduction of duties on merchandise discharged by your British barbarian merchants at Aomen and distributed throughout the interior, there is a regular tariff in force for barbarian merchants' goods, which applies equally to all European nations. It would be as wrong to increase the duty imposed on your nation's merchandise on the ground that the bulk of foreign trade is in your hands, as to make an exception in your case in the shape of specially reduced duties. In future, duties shall be levied equitably without discrimination between your nation and any other, and, in order to manifest my regard, your barbarian merchants shall continue to be shown every consideration at Aomen.

" (6) As to your request that your ships shall pay the duties leviable by tariff, there are regular rules in force at the Canton Custom house respecting the amounts payable, and since I have refused your request to be allowed to trade at other ports, this duty will naturally continue to be paid at Canton as heretofore.

"(7) Regarding your nation's worship of the Lord of Heaven, it is the same religion as that of other European nations. Ever since the beginning of history, sage Emperors and wise rulers have bestowed on China a moral system and inculcated a code, which from time immemorial has been religiously observed by the myriads of my subjects. There has been no hankering after heterodox doctrines. Even the European (missionary) officials in my capital are forbidden to hold intercourse with Chinese subjects; they are restricted within the limits of their appointed residences, and may not go about propagating their religion. The distinction between Chinese and barbarian is most strict, and your Ambassador's request that barbarians shall be given full liberty to disseminate their religion is utterly unreasonable.

"It may be, O King, that the above proposals have been wantonly made by your Ambassador on his own responsibility, or peradventure you yourself are ignorant of our dynastic regulations and had no intention of transgressing them when you expressed these wild ideas and hopes. I have ever shown the greatest condescension to the tribute missions of all States which sincerely yearn after the blessings of civilisation, so as to manifest my kindly indulgence. I have even gone out of my way to grant any requests which were in any way consistent with Chinese usage. Above all, upon you, who live in a remote and inaccessible region, far across the spaces of ocean, but who have shown your submissive loyalty by sending this tribute mission, I have heaped benefits far in access of those accorded to other nations. But the demands presented by your Embassy are not only a contravention of dynastic tradition, but would be utterly unproductive of good result to yourself, besides being quite impracticable. I have accordingly stated the facts to you in detail, and it is your bounden duty reverently to appreciate my feelings and to obey these instructions henceforward for all time, so that you may enjoy the blessings of perpetual peace. If, after the receipt of this explicit decree, you lightly give ear to the representations of your subordinates and allow your barbarian merchants to proceed to Chêkiang and Tientsin, with the object of landing and trading there, the ordinances of my Celestial Empire are strict in the extreme, and the local officials, both civil and military, are bound reverently to obey the law of the land. Should your vessels touch the shore, your merchants will assuredly never be permitted to land or to reside there, but will be subject to instant expulsion. In that event your barbarian merchants will have had a long journey for nothing. Do not say that you were not warned in due time! Tremblingly obey and show no negligence! A special mandate!"

As is well known, the ceremony of the kotow was waived by Ch'ien Lung in deference to Earl Macartney's objections, but the Manchus subsequently declared, and to this day affect to believe, that, when the Ambassador entered His Majesty's presence, he was so overcome with awe and nervousness, that his legs gave way under him, so that he grovelled abjectly on the ground, thus to all intents and purposes performing an involuntary kotow.

Finally, two days before his abdication, in 1796, the Emperor addressed the following letter to King George III:

"Chu Kuei (Viceroy of Canton) memorialises Us that the King of England has forwarded a memorial with tribute. Two years ago, on the occasion of the tribute mission from the King coming to Peking, We conferred upon him many valuable presents, so he has now dispatched a further memorial with offerings of tribute, thus indicating his loyal sincerity. We raise absolutely no objection to the fact of his having omitted to send a mission on this occasion, and are graciously pleased to accept his offerings. In addition, We bestow upon him the following mandate : " Your nation is inaccessible, lying far beyond the dividing seas, but you sent a mission with a memorial and tribute to pay homage at our Court, and We, in recognition of your loyal sincerity, conferred upon you our mandate and valuable gifts, as evidence of our satisfaction. Now, O King, you have again prepared a memorial and offerings, which have been conveyed by your barbarian vessels to Canton and transmitted to Us. Your reverent submission to Our person is manifest. Our Celestial dynasty, which sways the wide world, attaches no value to the costly presents which are offered at Our Court : what We appreciate is the humble spirit of the offerers. We have commanded Our Viceroy to accept your tribute in order that your reverence may be duly recognised.

As regarding Our sending of a punitive expedition to Nepal, Our Commander-in-chief marched at the head of a great army into that country, occupied the chief strategic points, and terrified the Ghoorkas into grovelling submission to Our majestic Empire. Our Commander-in-chief duly memorialised Us, and We, whose Imperial clemency is world-wide, embracing Chinese and foreigners alike, could not endure the thought of exterminating the entire population of the country. Accordingly We accepted their surrender. At that time Our Commander-in-chief duly informed Us of your having dispatched a mission into Tibet, with a petition to Our Resident, stating that you had advised the Nepalese to surrender. But at the time of your petition Our troops had already gained a complete victory and the desired end had been attained.[1] We were not obliged to trouble

[1] The Chinese expedition against Nepal was commanded by Fu K'ang-an, Ch'ien Lung's ablest General. It started from Kokonor in

THE COURT OF PEKING

your troops to render assistance. You allude to this matter in your present memorial, but are doubtless ignorant of the precise course of events in Nepal, as your tribute mission was on its way to Peking at the time of these occurrences. Nevertheless, O King, you entertained a clear perception of your duty towards Us, and your reverent acknowledgment of Our dynasty's supremacy is highly praiseworthy.

"We therefore now bestow upon you various costly gifts. Do you, O King, display even more energetic loyalty in future and endeavour to deserve for ever Our

---

the 2nd Moon of the Emperor's 57th year (1793), and entered Tibet *viâ* the Tant-la Pass (of Abbé Huc's *Travels in Tibet*), where a fierce wind usually blows, but Fu K'ang-an reported that on the occasion of his troops crossing the pass the weather was bright and there was no wind. In gratitude to the spirit of this mountain for having vouchsafed such good weather to the expedition, Ch'ien Lung ordered that the Tant-la should be included amongst the mountains of the Empire which are entitled to receive an Imperial sacrifice.

In July of that year the Chinese forces marched into Nepal, invading it from three sides. The Ghoorkas sent a mission to seek aid from Great Britain, whereupon Cornwallis dispatched an officer to Khatmandu to act as peacemaker. But by the 7th Moon the Imperial troops had defeated Nepal in six battles, and when they were only one day's march from Khatmandu the Nepalese tendered an abject submission. The Chinese did not linger in Nepal, the season being far advanced, but returned to Tibet in the 8th Moon, after exacting an undertaking to bring tribute to Peking once in every five years in the form of tame elephants, horses and musical instruments. The Nepalese had invaded Tibet at the request of the Red Priesthood two years previously (1791) ostensibly on the ground that the duties imposed on salt at the Nepalese frontier were excessive, and that the commodity was adulterated with earth. On this occasion the Commander of the Chinese forces, Pa Chung, had declined battle, and had induced the Tibetans to promise the Nepalese an annual subsidy of 15,000 ounces of silver if they would withdraw. At the same time he reported to the Throne that he had defeated the Nepalese and that they had accepted Manchu suzerainty. In the following year, 1792, the promised subsidy of 15,000 taels not being forthcoming, the Nepalese again invaded Tibet. Pao Tai, the Resident at Lhasa, made no preparations to resist them, but conveyed the Panshen Lama to Lhasa, abandoning Hou Tsang to the invaders, who sacked the sacred city of Tashilhunpo and conveyed its treasures back to Nepal, at the same time leaving a strong force inside the Tibetan frontier.

gracious affection, so that we may conform to Our earnest resolve to pacify distant tribes and to manifest Our Imperial clemency.

"Chu Kuei is to hand this mandate to your Agent, for transmission to yourself, in order that you may be encouraged to display still greater gratitude and reverent submission hereafter, in acknowledgment of Our indulgence.

"It is contrary to Our dynastic ordinances for Our officials to enter into social relations with barbarians, and Chu Kuei acted therefore quite properly in returning the presents which were sent to the former Viceroy and Superintendent of Customs at Canton."

In his private life, and in the administration of his household, Ch'ien Lung combined a high sense of his Imperial dignity with frugal habits. Throughout his long life he retained his devotion to the chase, for the wilds of Manchuria and Mongolia, for the simple, open-air life which had made his forefathers the hardy men they were. It would be interesting to study the coincidence of the decay of the Imperial hunting parks, the decline of manly exercises amongst the Manchu aristocracy, with the gradual ascendancy of the eunuchs that begins definitely to assert itself in the reign of Ch'ien Lung's successor.

As the head of his family and of the Palace household, Ch'ien Lung exercised a very strict supervision over his domestic affairs until old age and the increasing cares of State combined to relax his energies in this direction. In private as in public life, the secret of his success lay in personal attention to detail, indefatigable energy, a broad mind, and a personality in which a strong sense of order and discipline combined with many sympathetic qualities. Ch'ien Lung was essentially a statesman; but he was also a good sportsman, with a touch of the poetic temperament. As the traveller gazes to-day on the melancholy ruins of Yüan Ming-yüan, or the hunting parks at Jehol and Peking, he cannot but wonder that a race which could produce so wise and so virile a ruler, and send its armies half across Asia, should to-day be represented only by the besotted and effeminate creatures who walk so delicately and so uselessly as Manchu Princes.

Ch'ien Lung hated extravagance, and until the close of his reign, when the contagion of Ho Shen's purple and fine linen had begun to breed luxury in the Imperial household, he set the example of thrift and simple fare. At the same time, there was nothing of the Puritan about him, nor of the total abstainer; he loved a pretty woman and a good dinner, but held the Oriental faith that both were gifts of the gods, not to be easily won, nor lightly esteemed. Throughout his sixty years' reign he never once omitted the custom of offering sacrifice of propitiation to the kitchen god, who on the 23rd day of the 10th Moon proceeds heavenwards, to make his annual report on the family's behaviour during the year. The Palace in which the sacrifice used to be performed is the K'un Ning-kang ("Earthly Repose") and the ceremony took place on a brick platform or *k'ang*, in the centre of the hall. Drums were placed in readiness, and it was the custom for the Empress first to proceed thither and await the Emperor's arrival. He himself then beat the drum and sang the ditty known as: "The Emperor's search for worthy officials." The household were drawn up in lines, and on the conclusion of the song, crackers were fired to start the kitchen god on his mission. The custom was discontinued by Chia Ch'ing.

Ch'ien Lung was no ascetic kill-joy. To the east of the Lake of Happiness, at the Summer Palace or Yüan Ming-yüan, in a garden called the "Park of Universal Joy," he was fond of giving theatrical entertainments to his Court. At the New Year he used to have booths erected along the main road of the garden and there organised a market fair for the amusement of the Court. There were curio and porcelain stores, embroidery shops, dealers in silks, as well as restaurants, wine taverns and tea-houses. Even pedlars and hawkers were allowed to come and ply their trade. The shops were managed by eunuchs, and the jade and other articles were supplied from the large establishments in Peking, under arrangements made by the Supervisor of the Octroi, who selected what goods should be sent.[1] High officials and their wives were admitted to this fair, and allowed to make purchases or to order food or tea at the restaurants, just as they pleased. Everything was done exactly as at a real market fair: waiters and shop attendants were brought from the chief restaurants in the city, care being taken to select only those of good appearance and clear pronunciation. As His Majesty passed down the line of booths, the waiters would shout out their menus for the day, the hawkers would cry their goods, and the clerks would be busy calling out the figures which they were entering on the day-books. The bustle and animation of this scene used to delight the Emperor. The fair continued daily till the end of the 1st Moon, when the booths were taken down. This pleasant custom was also abandoned by Chia Chi'ng, whose temperament was morose and opposed to all forms of gaiety.

According to the annalists, Ch'ien Lung displayed in his domestic affairs the same thrifty virtues which distinguished the great Tzŭ Hsi, and some of the same little weaknesses. He was fond of certain dainties, and on his travels loved to experiment with new dishes; for rich, greasy ones he had a particular liking. It is recorded in one of several old diaries in the possession of a Manchu, whose family has held high positions at Peking for several generations, that on one occasion, while journeying through the Yangtsze provinces, His Majesty desired to try a famous Yangchou recipe for beancurd. Finding it to his taste,

[1] Tzŭ Hsi instituted a similar custom at the Summer Palace during the period (before the *coup d'état* of 1898) of her retirement from State affairs.

he asked the cost, and on being told that it was only thirty cash (about a penny) directed that this cheap and excellent fare be added to the menus of the Palace at Peking. After returning to the capital, he discovered, however, that the eunuchs entered the dish in the household kitchen account at twelve taels (then £3). When he asked the reason they informed him that " southern delicacies are not easily prepared in the north."

These housekeeping " squeezes " were a frequent source of worry to Ch'ien Lung, as they were later to Tzŭ Hsi. They contributed to make posts in the Imperial Household amongst the most coveted in the Empire. Such posts were only open to Manchus; in recent years the annual income of a senior Secretary of the Household was estimated at over a million taels. Any attempts to cut down the perquisites of these offices (such as were made by the parsimonious Tao Kuang) naturally made the Emperor unpopular with the Imperial clansmen, many of whom were directly or indirectly beneficiaries in these Palace squeezes.

It is recorded that one cold winter's day, receiving an official named Wang Yu-tun in audience, Ch'ien Lung asked him whether he had had anything to eat before attending Court at dawn, to which Wang replied, " We are very poor. All the breakfast that I can afford consists of two or three eggs." At this the Emperor exclaimed : " You dare to tell me you are poor, yet you confess to eating three eggs at a time ! Eggs cost me 75 cents a-piece —I should never dream of ordering three." Wang did not dare to tell the Emperor the true price of eggs, so he said : " I was speaking of an inferior type of egg, not the sort which would be suitable for Your Majesty's table. My sort can be bought for about a cash apiece." The Emperor understood and gave orders that the Palace eggs were henceforward to be charged at a more reasonable figure.

Where women were concerned, Ch'ien Lung was, naturally polygamous and patriarchal, after the Oriental manner, but ever mindful of the proprieties and jealous of his Consort's dignity, and for the rest, courteous and gentle, and generous. His domestic life was free from bickerings and scandals and his children were well brought up, for he knew how to combine the *suaviter in modo* with the *fortiter in re*. According to the annalists, His Majesty was wont, in the *moments perdus* of his manifold official and domestic duties, to indulge occasionally in emotional adventures and even escapades. There were entr'actes in the dignified drama of his public life. The following story, for instance, is one of several—not necessarily true, but certainly believed at the time.

In the earlier years of his reign the fame of a certain literary courtesan, named San Ku-niang, had penetrated even to the Palace. Her gate was thronged with Princes and high officials : a word from her was esteemed as a high honour. So great was her influence that she was able on more than one occasion to intercede successfully on behalf of scholars and officials who had incurred the Emperor's displeasure.

One night the Commandant of the Peking Gendarmerie summoned one of his Lieutenants and handed him an arrow (the sign of authority for summary arrest), bidding him convey San Ku-niang to prison. The Lieutenant was much alarmed, but dared not disobey. Having effected an entrance to the lady's house, he proceeded upstairs to her bedchamber. At the door he found a handmaid, to whom he communicated his orders. Soon a soft voice was heard from within, saying : " Sir, you are my honoured guest : it would not be seemly for me to appear before you, except clad in my gayest raiment. Pray wait a few minutes whilst I change my dress, and I shall be happy to welcome you."

After a considerable time had elapsed, the Lieutenant

began to fear that the lady had made good her escape by a back door. So he called out, to make sure, whereupon she answered: "Whoever heard of a prisoner escaping from the clutches of the Commandant of Gendarmerie? Wait but a little longer and I shall be ready to go with you."

At last San Ku-niang came forth, and handed to the Lieutenant a pearl in a casket. This he politely declined. She then gave him a small box, covered with Imperial yellow silk. "Take this," she said, "and present it to your chief. It will perhaps make my presence unnecessary." The Lieutenant looked uncomfortable, not knowing what to do, but the lady reassured him. "You can but try; if the Commandant is not satisfied, come back for me. There is plenty of time. This box has travelled all over the Empire" (it was one of the kind used for forwarding Imperial decrees); "there is really no deception about it." The Lieutenant took the box and wrapped it up carefully. "Might I ask," he inquired, "if you had a visitor just now?" "Yes," was the reply, "he was a person of high position, but he has left the house by an underground passage which runs beneath my boudoir." The Lieutenant trembled and turned pale. He returned to the Commandant, gave him the box and told him what had passed.

Next morning, the Commandant was summoned to audience. The Emperor said to him: "I know that you are a zealous official, but you should look at things from a broader aspect and refrain from doing petty detective work. Such behaviour lacks dignity and will get you into trouble."

The Commandant kotowed and expressed his contrition. From that time forward the Peking police refrained from displaying too much zeal in the matter of domiciliary visits.

Travellers who have visited Peking may remember the

beautiful ruins of the Mahomedan Mosque which until last year stood just outside the south wall of the Lake Palace of the Forbidden City. Until five years ago services were still held in this Mosque by a Chinese Mahomedan who had made the pilgrimage to Mecca, an aged man, supported in his ruined shrine, by a handful of the faithful; but he died in 1908, and thereafter, the inner wall and pillars fell in, so that the place became still beautiful in the last stage of ruin—a pathetic monument to the splendours of a by-gone day. It was pulled down in May last, by order of President Yuan Shih-k'ai, ostensibly because it had become unsafe and because the site was required for the erection of barracks, but really because its upper storey dominated the Palace enclosure at the point where the President's residence is located, and might have been used, by mutinous troops, for " sniping " purposes. The history of the building of this Mosque, by the Emperor Ch'ien Lung, is as pathetic in its way as was the ruined shrine, and it has this merit that its main facts are unquestionably true.

During the first campaign in Sungaria, Ch'ien Lung heard rumours of the remarkable beauty of the wife of one of the tribal chiefs, a Mahomedan named Ali Arslan, then in arms against him. She was known all over the western frontier-land as the " Model Beauty "; and celebrated for the softness of her skin, upon which she never used cosmetics. At a farewell audience given to his Commander-in-chief, Chao Hui, Ch'ien Lung casually told him of the reports he had heard of this lady and bade him do his best to secure her for his Court. After the successful end of the war, when the Prince, her husband, had committed suicide, Chao Hui took her prisoner and brought her to Peking. He sent couriers ahead to inform the Emperor of his success. Ch'ien Lung, greatly pleased, gave orders that special honours should be shown to her en route, and that every care be taken lest the hardships of the journey should impair her beauty. Besides this, he ordered Chao Hui to see to it that she did not commit suicide.

On arrival at Peking she was quartered in the western Palace by the southern lake.[1] She was officially known as the Hsiang (Fragrant) Concubine, but more commonly referred to as the Stranger (K'o) Concubine. At first she seemed quite contented, indifferent to her former husband's death and the ruin of her tribe. But when Ch'ien Lung approached her, she remained coldly silent, refusing to utter a word in reply to his questions.

Ch'ien Lung bade some of his concubines, in whose powers of persuasion he had confidence, to tell her of the high destinies which awaited her. Her only reply was to draw a dagger from her sleeve. Asked what this meant, she replied : " My tribe is destroyed and my husband is dead. Long since I have resolved on death, but when I die, it shall not be alone, like any meek peasant girl perishing by the roadside. I mean to avenge my lord's memory by slaying his enemy. If the Emperor forces me to become his concubine, I shall kill him and myself too." The Palace women, horrified, bade her attendants take the dagger from her. She smiled : " Whatever you may do, I shall find a way. As for you, if you do not cease from troubling me, I shall kill one of you first."

Despairing of persuading her they reported what she had said to the Emperor. He saw that for the moment it was hopeless to try to win her, but he often visited her apartments and sat for a short time in her company, believing that time would heal her wound and that she would ultimately come to regard him with favour. At the same time he had her carefully guarded, to prevent her from making any attempt on his life. When she

---

[1] The building in which she lived and mourned is now the main gate-hall of the President's Palace, known as the Hsin Hua-mên, or Gate of New China.

found that she was continually watched, she seemed to abandon the idea of suicide: but one day after she had been in the Palace about two years, her attendants reported that on the occasion of the Moslem New Year, she had been found weeping bitterly. It was then that Ch'ien Lung gave orders for a mosque to be built just outside the Lake Palace, on the south side, which she would be able to see from her residence, the Tower of the Jewelled Moon. Houses and shops were built there exactly like those of her native Sungaria, in the hope of giving comfort to her wounded spirit. The spot was known as the Moslem Encampment.

Now the Empress Dowager, then in her eightieth year, had great influence over her son. She was sorely distressed at Ch'ien Lung's infatuation, and feared for him the risk of assassination. So she said to him: "As the woman is obstinately resolved not to yield to your advances, and as she is sick of life—why not put her to death? Or at least send her back to her own home, and trouble yourself no more about her." But the Emperor could not bear the idea of losing her so, hoping against hope, he continued to wait. At last, on the day of the winter solstice, when he was due to be absent from the Palace and to spend the night in the Hall of Fasting at the Temple of Heaven, the Empress Dowager determined to act.

She waited until the Emperor had quitted the Palace, and then sent a messenger to bid the " Model Beauty " attend her at the Palace of Motherly Tranquillity. When she had come into the presence, the outer gates of the Palace were made fast. " I hear that you will not submit to His Majesty," said the Empress sternly. " What is it that you propose to do? " She replied, " I mean to die." " So be it! I am ready to grant you the privilege of committing suicide, here and now." The unhappy woman expressed her gratitude by kotowing several times. " Your Majesty the Empress Dowager is showing me undeserved kindness in thus meeting my wishes. I submitted to the ignominy of being compelled to make this long journey under escort, in the hope that I should not die alone, that I might be able to avenge my husband's memory by a deed which would stagger the Empire. But this cannot be, for I am too closely guarded. What then is the use of my continuing this useless and aimless existence? Is it not far better that I should re-join my late lord in the other world and close my eyes, satisfied, in death? I thank Your Majesty for your grace in acceding to my wishes, and, in the realms of Hades, shall not forget your benevolence." As she made an end of speaking the tears welled from her eyes. The Empress, greatly touched, bade a eunuch convey her immediately to a room in one of the wings of the Palace, where she hanged herself to a beam.

The Emperor was at the Hall of Fasting, but a confidential eunuch came running to tell him that his beloved concubine had been summoned to the presence of the Empress Dowager. Fearing the worst, in great distress of mind, he set out in all haste for the Palace, although in so doing he violated the rule which required him to remain in the Hall of Fasting till the morrow. On his arrival, finding the doors of the Empress Dowager's Palace barred, he stood there weeping, till the gates were opened and a eunuch said: "Her Majesty desires that you will repair to her presence." He entered, and the Empress took him to the side room where the concubine was hanging from the rafter, quite dead. There was no sign of pain or struggle on her beautiful and placid face. Ch'ien Lung was greatly grieved at her death, and had her buried with the honours of a concubine of the first rank.

During the last decade of Ch'ien Lung's reign, the Government of China was practically concentrated in the hands of the Grand Secretary, Ho Shen, and of his *protégés* and partisans in the provinces. As his power increased, so did his ambition. During the three years which elapsed between the Emperor's abdication and his death (1796–99) his word was law in the land, and his fortune grew to an extent unparalleled in the history of China. He levied a fixed percentage on the pay of the troops and instituted a regular tariff for the sale of offices, so that it was said of him (as of Prince Ch'ing under Kuang Hsü) that his back door was a market-place for peacocks' feathers and buttons. His private residence was far more magnificent in its furnishings than the Emperor's Palace, and he had amassed a wealth of jade and jewels greater than all the Imperial treasure. It was inevitable that in a land where money is the beginning and end of politics, this man's vast fortune should expose him to the gravest dangers so soon as the protection of the Emperor was withdrawn.

Ho Shen's origin was a humble one, though he showed no signs of it, his education and manners being sufficiently good to impress and charm Lord Macartney and his staff at Jehol. He was originally a sergeant of the Palace guards, and being strong and handsome in appearance, was specially selected to escort the Imperial sedan. From one of the diaries of the Manchu clansmen, above referred to, we take the following description of the manner in which he first won Ch'ien Lung's favour. When the Emperor was about fifty years of age, it happened one day that he was leaving the eastern gate of the Forbidden City in his chair, and as he was carried along, he was reading a memorial which had just reached him regarding an outbreak of rebellion in Ssŭ-ch'uan. The Everlasting Lord's face was clouded as he read, and his bearers overheard him saying : " If the tiger or the rhinoceros escapes from its cage, if the gem be injured in the casket, who is to blame ? " This well-known quotation, from the Discourses of Confucius, means that the party responsible for a misfortune must expect to bear the blame. None of the bearers understood the allusion, but Ho Shen who was riding alongside said to them: "'Yeh' (the Master) means that officials holding responsible posts must be made accountable for every dereliction of duty."

Ch'ien Lung heard this reply, and was pleased at the man's quick intelligence. He called to Ho Shen: "You are only a sergeant, but you have evidently read your Four Books to some purpose. Attend for audience after Our return to the Palace." The Emperor was so greatly delighted with his conversation at the audience which followed, that he gave him unparalleled promotion. His ready wit and prompt replies to Ch'ien Lung's epigrams, which he capped with a pointed antithesis, appealed to the Emperor's literary tastes. He rose to be Viceroy, President of a Board and Grand Councillor, until at the last his power was supreme in the Empire. His education, from the scholar's point of view, was superficial, but he concealed his lack of learning under a remarkable talent for epigrams. He was appointed tutor to Prince Chia, who succeeded Ch'ien Lung on the Throne. Ho Shen disliked the young Prince, whose character was surly and generally unsympathetic, and did his best to dissuade Ch'ien Lung from selecting him as his Heir. It is recorded that on one occasion he lost his temper with his pupil and kicked him slightly. The insult was never forgotten or forgiven by Chia Ch'ing and Ho Shen lived to regret that he had not adopted a more conciliatory attitude towards the Heir to the Throne.

Until the death of Ch'ien Lung, however, it was Ho Shen, and not the future Emperor, who dominated the situation. After his abdication, Ch'ien Lung adopted the title of "Tai Shang-huang," or "Exalted Emperor who has vacated the Throne," but he continued to take an active part in State affairs and for the remaining three years of his life was always present at Imperial audiences, besides giving his decision on all decrees. At audience he sat in the Imperial seat, facing the south, while his son, Chia Ch'ing, sat on a small stool facing the west. It is recorded in the diary above mentioned, that one morning, Ho Shen, as doyen of the Council, came in as usual for audience, and knelt in waiting for a long time. His Majesty, the ex-Emperor, sat with closed eyes, as if in deep slumber, but all the while he could be heard muttering to himself.

The Emperor Chia Ch'ing listened intently, but could not catch a word. At last, Ch'ien Lung, opened his eyes, saying: "What are the names of those men?" Ho Shen promptly replied: "Kao T'ien-te and Kou Wen-ming." Ch'ien Lung closed his eyes again and repeated the names several times, after which he motioned to Ho Shen to leave the hall and not another word was uttered. No other audience was held on that day.

Chia Ch'ing was greatly astonished, and a few days later summoned Ho to secret audience. "What was His Majesty saying to himself the other day, and what did those six syllables mean which you uttered in reply?" Ho answered: "His Majesty was reciting a famous Tibetan mystic spell, which means death to the person against whom it is uttered, at what ever distance he may be, even though he be perfectly well at the time. Your slave heard His Majesty uttering this incantation, and knew that the persons whom His Majesty wished to ban were the leaders in the White Lily conspiracy: therefore in answering him, I spoke their names." Chia Ch'ing laid this incident to heart, for Ho's proficiency in Buddhistic arts of incantation struck him as dangerous. After Ch'ien Lung's demise, two years later, this was one of the things which he remembered against Ho Shen.

CHAPTER XIV

THE DOWNFALL OF HO SHEN

As already stated, the old Emperor Ch'ien Lung continued after his abdication to supervise all important business of State, and showed no signs of failing health until the autumn of 1798, when he was attacked by paralysis. He lingered on until February 7, 1799, when he died, at 8 a.m., on the third day of the Chinese new year, in the Hall of Mind Nurture.

The opening of Chia Ch'ing's reign had not been auspicious; it seemed as if the zenith of prosperity had been reached in the sixtieth year of Ch'ien Lung (1795), and with that Monarch's abdication a period of decline set in. Rebellions had broken out in Hunan, Hupei and Kueichou, and the White Lily sect had become a power in the land. Ch'ien Lung had the mortification of feeling that he was leaving a disturbed Empire to his son, who was now in his thirty-ninth year, a man without natural ability, of suspicious and vindictive temperament.

On the day after his father's death, Chia Ch'ing issued a decree complaining that the military operations against the rebels were being dragged on without appreciable result. With good cause he observed: "The Commanders-in-chief do not seem to be in the least anxious to put down the rebellion, since they are able to enrich themselves and wax fat at the expense of the disturbed districts. They report mythical victories, and are lost to all sense of shame. Manchu bodyguardsmen and secretaries are all only too glad to proceed to the seat of trouble, but their zeal is not due to any patriotic motive. Penniless officials come back from service at the front with amply lined pockets. On their return to Peking they apply at once for leave to revisit their family tombs, not from a sense of filial respect, but in order to invest their ill-gotten gains in the purchase of land. All this money comes ultimately from the unfortunate people, plundered to satisfy their insatiable greed. No wonder, then, that more and more recruits join the rebels, and that none can foresee an end to the troubles. Not only are the rebels' numbers as great as ever, but their ranks are steadily increasing.

"My late father lost both sleep and appetite because of his anxiety at the spread of the rebellion, and with his last breath he asked whether there were any news of a victory at the front. In his valedictory mandate he left behind no instructions concerning other matters, presumably because he left me with full authority to deal with them in my discretion. Until these lawless sects have been suppressed I shall feel myself unfilial towards my late father's memory. If my Grand Councillors and Generals in the field are all disloyal to the Throne, how can I comfort the soul of my father in Heaven? Is it the fact that they are indifferent to the fate which is about to visit them, and are content to be disloyal themselves, as well as making their Emperor unfilial?

"I cannot allow further leakages of funds to enrich the official class. Taxation cannot be increased, and the Government revenues should be ample for all needs. My father in his extreme old age became too lenient and bestowed high rewards upon the least report of a success. In the case of a reverse he would merely administer a mild rebuke, and reinstated the offender so soon as he had retrieved his error. During the last few years Yung Pao alone was sent to prison for cowardice, and even he was promptly released. It is very certain that Yung Pao is not the only coward in our ranks! Every trifling success is exaggerated and serious defeats are glossed over. Possibly the idea was to save my father distress, which at his age would have followed upon evil tidings, but in military matters accuracy is essential. There were always reports of terrible carnage on the rebels' side, but the figures were a tissue of falsehoods.

"These abuses cannot be allowed to continue. I insist that I be informed of the true state of affairs. What good can come of representing a disgraceful defeat as a glorious victory? I am Lord of the Empire, and I require the truth above everything. All I care about is peace and plenty, absence of rebellion, and the contentment of my subjects. I shall show no mercy for misconduct in the field; all my commanders will do well, therefore, to purge themselves of error and to clear their minds of cant. Let them exert themselves to restore the halcyon days of peace, otherwise they will be dealt with by martial law. My words will be followed up by action; do not imagine that your new Sovereign can be hoodwinked!"

The above decree was specially directed at Ho Shen and his party, which included the majority of high officials, both civil and military. Four days later a decree was issued, in response to memorials from the ever servile Censorate, which stripped Ho Shen of all his offices and commanded his imprisonment in the Board of Punishments, together with Fu Ch'ang-an, the President of the Board of Revenue. Ho Shen was Comptroller-General of two boards, and held a plurality of offices. Chia Ch'ing placed his elder brother, Prince Ch'eng, on the Council and made him Comptroller of a Board, although this was contrary to dynastic house-law. Further sweeping changes were made, and many of Ch'ien Lung's trusted Ministers were summarily dismissed before he had been dead a week. Such hasty action, while the Court was in deep mourning, was regarded by the orthodox as extremely unfilial. Chia Ch'ing endeavoured to justify his action on the ground that, had his father been alive, he would have cordially endorsed the curt dismissal of those whom he had delighted to honour. We have already alluded to the frequency with which, under the Manchus, the favourites of the old *régime* have been dismissed by the new, but Chia Ch'ing acted with almost indecent haste.[1]

Two days later, on the 9th, he issued the following decree concerning Ho Shen's offences: "Ho Shen received extraordinary favours from His departed Majesty, and was promoted from the low position of Imperial guardsman to the highest offices, which he has held for nigh on twenty years. He has been steeped in the lavish bounty of my late father to an extent unparalleled in the history of the Court. The arduous duties of Government have now devolved on me by inheritance, and my father's demise finds me 'sleeping on a straw mat and pillowed on a clod.'[2] My thoughts dwell ever on the Confucian precept: 'For three years after a parent's death none of his former surroundings should be changed.' But all within and without the wide seas realise my late sire's reverence for Heaven, his obedience to ancestral tradition, his diligence in government, and affection for his people. His example stands out as a shining light for my house and dynasty to follow for all time; how, then, should a period of three years suffice for obedience to his behests? I could not find it in my heart to dismiss from office any of my father's Ministers, even were they guilty of offences. I should take into consideration any extenuating circumstances to mitigate their punishment. I am sure that His Sacred Majesty is at this moment fully conscious of my sincerity and concurs in my sentiments.

[1] When Chia Ch'ing died, struck by lightning, the orthodox regarded it as Heaven's chastisement for his lack of filial piety.
[2] A classical metaphor for a son's mourning.

"But as regards Ho Shen, his crimes are too grave to admit of possible pardon, for he has been impeached on many counts by the Censorate. I therefore placed him under arrest two days ago, and shall now proceed to state his offences *seriatim* for general information.

"On the 3rd day of the 9th Moon of the 60th year of Ch'ien Lung, Ho Shen presented me with a jade sceptre, intending thereby to signify that I had been nominated successor to the Throne. He thus betrayed a State secret, in the hope that I should consider myself beholden to him for advancing my claims with the late Emperor.

"In the spring of last year the late Emperor was at the Summer Palace, and summoned Ho Shen to audience. He actually presumed to ride on horseback through the central gate, past the main Imperial Hall, right up to the entrance of my father's apartments. Could any action equal this in base presumption, as if he had forgotten what was due to his Sovereign and father! Pleading an affection of the leg, he would enter the Forbidden City in a chair borne by bearers. He was the observed of all observers as he passed calmly in and out of the Gate of Divine Military Prowess, without the smallest vestige of shame or compunction.

"He even dared to appropriate to his own use, as secondary wives, women who had been employed as handmaidens in the Palace.

"After the outbreak of the Hupei and Ssuchuan rebellion, propagated by seditious sects, my father used eagerly to await news from the front, sitting up until late into the night, taking neither food nor sleep. But Ho Shen deceived him, deliberately suppressing and even falsifying reports from the field, so that the operations have dragged on and on.

"My father appointed him Comptroller-General of the Board of Civil Offices and Punishments, and at the same time, because of his knowledge of finance, appointed him to supervise and direct the proceedings of the Board of Revenue. The result of this was the establishment of a one-man power; soon none dared oppose him.

"Last winter my father's health was bad, so that his handwriting on rescripts was sometimes illegible. Ho Shen actually presumed on one occasion to say: 'Better tear off that rescript and use one that I have written instead.'

"Last month Ho Shen suppressed an official report from Kokonor concerning robbery under arms by bands of Mahomedans, who had murdered two Tibetan merchants, in the employ of the Dalai Lama. He returned the memorial to the sender and made no report to the Throne.

"After my late father's death I gave orders that any Mongol Princes and Dukes who had not had the smallpox should be excused from coming to Peking. Ho Shen disregarded these orders, and stopped all Mongol Princes from coming, whether they had had smallpox or not. In so doing, he violated the Throne's policy of showing courtesy to vassals. His motives defy conjecture.

"The Grand Secretary Su-ling-a was stone deaf, far gone in senile dotage. He was, however, the father-in-law of Ho Lin, Ho Shen's brother, and for this reason the Throne was never advised of his utter incapacity. Wu Sheng-lan, the Vice-president, and Li Kuang-yün, Director of the Imperial stud, were originally tutors at Ho Shen's private residence, which alone accounts for their extraordinary advancement. In fact, Ho Shen was a dictator, and did not hesitate to dismiss secretaries on the Grand Council at his own sweet will.

"Ho Shen's property has just been examined. It appears that he has built himself a mansion of Imperial cedar wood. the use of which constitutes *lèse majesté* on the part of a subject; the style of architecture is in exact imitation of the late Emperor's Palace of Imperial Longevity in the Forbidden City, whilst the pleasure gardens and pavilions are copied from the scheme of decoration used in the 'Terrace of the Fortunate Isles' at the Summer Palace. Into his motives in this matter let us not inquire too closely!

"Of jewels and precious stones he has collected two hundred pearl necklaces, a number greatly exceeding those in the Imperial Palace. He possesses one particular pearl far superior, both in size and lustre, to that worn by me in the Imperial hat of State.[1] In his collection there are jewels which were meant exclusively for the Emperor's use and to which he had no right; the number of his uncut stones is legion, far surpassing those of the Imperial household. The inventory of his hoard of bullion is incomplete, but the amount is certainly several million ounces.

"Such a career of venality and corruption may be called unique. Ho Shen has acknowledged the truth of each separate count of the above indictment, after undergoing a severe examination [2] at the hands of the Princes and Ministers.

"The fact now stands clearly revealed that Ho Shen is a deep-dyed traitor, lost to all moral sense, who has betrayed his Sovereign and jeopardised the State. As self-constituted dictator he has usurped supreme authority.

---

[1] The famous pearl worn in the Imperial hat was known as the K'ang Lung Chiao Tzŭ ("The azure dragon instructing posterity"). The pearl in Ho Shen's collection here referred to was even more famous. It was called the Cheng Ta Kuang ming ("Of glorious good omen"), and had been brought to the Ming Emperor Yung-Lo from Ceylon by one of his eunuch envoys in the 15th century. It disappeared from the Palace, stolen by the eunuch Wei Chung-hsien, in 1625, and remained in the South till 1781, when it was sent as tribute to Ch'ien Lung from Chêkiang and appropriated by Ho Shen. There was an ancient prophesy concerning it, that its loss would always mean ruin to the dynasty. After Chia Ch'ing had confiscated it from Ho Shen's estate, he referred to this prophesy. The last occasion on which it was seen at Court was at the Empress Lung Yü's reception to the ladies of the Diplomatic Body in 1911, when the child Emperor Hsüan T'ung wore it in his cap. Rumour declares that it was stolen in August 1911 by a eunuch named Shen Lo-t'ing.

[2] Under torture.

He has lent himself to the most flagrant abuses, but his venal greed and insatiate lust for lucre are comparatively light crimes as compared with the depths of his treason.

"To my father, who lavished favours upon him, he was guilty of most wanton ingratitude. Had any of his colleagues impeached him years ago, my father, in his divine wisdom, would surely have decreed his immediate decapitation, but not a word was ever breathed against him. My officials may now pretend that their silence was due to a loyal desire to avoid causing distress to my aged father, but I know all too well that the real reason lay in their fear of Ho Shen's power. That alone kept their lips sealed.

"Ho Shen's offences against my father are innumerable, exceeding in number the hairs of the head. If I condone them, how can I comfort the soul of my father in Heaven? The necessity for painful measures is forced upon me; I shall be glad to know the opinion of my Viceroys and Governors in the matter. My metropolitan officials have already been ordered to advise as to the sentence to be inflicted; Viceroys and Governors are hereby ordered to submit their views, together with any further details of Ho Shen's crimes that may be within their knowledge."

When the Great Man falls in China he brings down many in his ruin. Chia Ch'ing's blood was up; he commenced a general proscription against the *protégés* of Ho Shen in high places, making careful selection of those with squeezable estates. The first victim was the Manchu Governor of Shantung. The decree concerning him said:
"Amongst the memorials received by Imperial courier to-day from I-chiang-a, Governor of Shantung, I find a private letter addressed to Ho Shen, which states that the Governor had learned that the late Emperor had 'become a guest on high,' and goes on to exhort Ho Shen to subdue his grief and devote himself to his duties. He ignores me entirely, saying nothing about the awful loss

which I have sustained, though even the ordinary social relations of private life and common politeness require that a line of sympathy and condolence be addressed to a son who had just lost a father. I-chiang-a, in fact, sets himself to console Ho Shen, bidding him moderate his grief, but to me he sends only a routine memorial asking after my health, after which he proceeds to report on the affairs of his province, as if nothing unusual had occurred. The Provincial Treasurer, Wu Hsuang-kuang, is a Chinese, and not a Manchu like I-chiang-a, but he has had the grace and good feeling to send me a memorial expressive of the deepest sympathy and couched in most touching terms. Immediately on hearing of the late Emperor's death he wrote beseeching me to take comfort, writing, in fact, as a Minister should write to his Sovereign. I-chiang-a, a Manchu and the son of a Grand Secretary, cannot plead ignorance of etiquette, especially as he served for many years as Secretary of the Grand Council. He treats my father's death with callous hardness, and by thus tactfully condoling with Ho Shen, shows all too plainly that my father was nothing to him in the past and that I am nothing to him in the present. It is Ho Shen whom he worships and flatters. He is a monster of black ingratitude, and I transmit to him hereby my stern rebuke, besides demanding an explanation and referring his case to the proper Ministry for the determination of a penalty."

In due course I-chiang-a forwarded an explanatory memorial, but it failed to appease the Emperor. "He now puts forward the cunning quibble that the official intimation of my father's death had not reached him. He adds that he has never had any personal relations with Ho Shen, and wrote merely to express the hope that this national loss would inspire Ho Shen to display zeal and devotion for the State. All this is simply ridiculous; what devotion to the State could be expected from a man like Ho Shen, whose crimes have now been made manifest to the world, and whose whole career is one long record of self-seeking corruption? If I-chiang-a were really unacquainted with Ho Shen, will he kindly inform me into whose pocket went the extra receipts under the heading of tribute rice, in regard to which matter he has already been denounced? I-chiang-a has been guilty of grave offences. He is hereby cashiered and ordered to Peking to await my further pleasure."

Referring to the tribute from the provinces, Chia Ch'ing declared that Ho Shen had retained nine-tenths of it, and that Ch'ien Lung had been disgracefully cheated. He issued a decree forbidding any further remittances of tribute in kind from the provinces, excepting only medicines, sables and pearls from Manchuria, ginseng and porcelain. He particularly objected to the annual presentation of Ju-i ("As you like it") sceptres from each province to the Throne, and remarked that to him these articles were anything but pleasing, inasmuch as the people were taxed to provide them.

At the Emperor's word, Ho Shen's friends and followers now began to fall away from him. The Viceroy of Chihli, Hu Chi-t'ang, who owed all he had to Ho Shen, turned, after the manner of the mandarin, on his patron in disgrace, and thus memorialised the Throne: "Ho Shen is bereft of moral sense; he cannot be regarded as a human being. His dastardly treason to the Throne and cruel oppression of the people have put him on a level with the rebels in the west. Infatuate in his madness, he knows no law, human or divine; basely ungrateful, he wallows in crime. I beg to recommend that he be sentenced to the lingering death. I have also ascertained that in his usurping arrogance he has built himself a lordly sepulchre at Chi-chou, as magnificent as the Imperial tombs."

After receiving these thoroughly impartial views from the Viceroys and Governors, Chia Ch'ing (whose talent for long-winded reiteration exceeded even that of Yung Cheng) proceeded once more to recapitulate the list of Ho Shen's crimes. He recited twenty of them with much wealth of detail, and observed that there were more behind, though the whole Court was well aware that the fallen Minister's one vital crime was his enormous wealth. Once more, playing to the gallery and posterity, the indignant Monarch asks the Court to deliberate upon an adequate sentence.

Of Ho Shen's fellow-victim and offender, Fu Ch'ang-an, he observes: " Fu Ch'ang-an's grandsire, sire, uncle, and brothers all received hereditary honours from the Throne. Fu Ch'ang-an himself served for years on the Grand Council; his daily relations with Ho Shen were of the very closest kind. He knew full well the nature of Ho Shen's disgraceful greed; moreover, as he was constantly in intimate attendance on my late father, privileged to have access to his presence when alone, he could, had he so wished, have informed His late Majesty of Ho Shen's treasonable and ambitious designs, and my father would have realised that such a warning, based on intimate knowledge, was worthy of confidence and serious attention. In that case, there can be no doubt that Ho Shen would long ago have suffered the penalty of death, and the State would not then have had to deplore the present disastrous condition of affairs.

" If he really thought that the shock of such a revelation would have been dangerous to my aged father, why did not Fu Ch'ang-an report the matter to myself? But during the three years that have elapsed since my accession, not a syllable has he ever uttered about Ho Shen's guilt; his silence proves him to have been an accomplice and abettor. Had he even hinted to me of Ho Shen's crimes, I should have spared him to-day. As it is, the schedule of his confiscated property, though vastly less than that of Ho Shen, discloses total assets considerably exceeding ten million taels, which must surely be regarded as excessive for a man in his position. His remorseless greed is second only to that of the chief culprit. I command, therefore, that the two cases be treated identically, and a report submitted accordingly."

On the 17th, a fortnight after the death of the old Emperor, the Grand Secretaries and Ministers submitted their report. Many of them owed their advancement in life to Ho Shen, but the ship was sinking and the rats made haste to leave it. The fallen Minister's friends fell from him—none so poor to do him reverence. They advised the Throne to inflict the lingering death on Ho Shen and decapitation on Fu Ch'ang-an, the former being found guilty of high treason and the latter of having been an accomplice before the fact. Ho Shen's usurpation of supreme power constituted, they declared, a capital offence, excluding him from all hope of mercy at the hands of the law.

Chia Ch'ing had now observed the usual hypocritical decencies, and saved his face in the orthodox manner by placing on his Court the nominal responsibility for the official murdering of Ho Shen and the plundering of his vast estate. His object being to possess himself of the wretched Minister's ill-gotten wealth, he could afford to dispense with the lingering death, so long as death in some form were inflicted. His next decree, therefore, took into gracious consideration " the undesirability of executing the chief Minister of State like a common felon in the public square, and, because the Court was in mourning, allowed him the privilege of committing suicide, as a mark of high favour, and out of regard to the dignity of the nation." As to Fu Ch'ang-an, " as his property does not amount to a tenth of that illegally amassed by Ho Shen, his punishment is commuted to confinement pending decapitation."[1] As a refinement of clemency, the

[1] A sentence equivalent to imprisonment for life.

THE COURT OF PEKING

Emperor ordered that Fu Ch'ang-an was to be taken under guard to Ho Shen's place of confinement and there compelled, on his knees, to witness his late chief's suicide, after which he was to be escorted back to prison.

Ho Shen's brother, Ho Lin, had received an hereditary dukedom from His Majesty Ch'ien Lung in recognition of his meritorious services in Tibet, and his name had been inscribed amongst those of the heroes of the dynasty in a side-shrine of the Temple of Ancestors. Chia Ch'ing, after contemptuous references to Ho Lin's capacity and career, ordered that his dukedom be taken from him and that his shrine in the august company of the nation's heroes be dismantled and overthrown.[1]

One of Ho Shen's sons had married an Imperial Princess, Chia Ch'ing's sister, and as it would have been inconsistent with the dignity of the Imperial family to reduce him to the rank of a plebeian, he was permitted to retain an hereditary earldom, on the understanding that he was to be confined to his own premises and behave himself circumspectly. Other members of the family were degraded, and the whole clan was removed from the highest Manchu banner—to which Ch'ien Lung had promoted it—and ordered to revert to the Plain Red division.

Ho Shen met his end with the calm dignity of a brave man and a philosopher. He was commanded to kneel and listen to Chia Ch'ing's long-winded decree ordering him to commit suicide. On its conclusion, he said: " His Majesty is most gracious; I thank him for his clemency." Then, after kotowing in the direction of the Palace, he addressed his son and Fu Ch'ang-an. To the latter he said: " We two have served our old master together; it is in accordance with ancient practice that the Minister

[1] In the eyes of the orthodox, Chia Ch'ing by this act reached the lowest depths of filial impiety, and became a criminal in the sight of God and men. This sin was sufficient in itself to account for the subsequent visitation of Heaven's wrath upon him.

should follow his lord to the Nine Springs. I shall now attend His sainted Majesty, as of old, and receive his wise counsel. The present Emperor has loyal servants about him and is well rid of men such as you and I."

Then he mounted the daïs and hanged himself, tying the noose without assistance. His last words were: "His late Majesty will feel indignant wrath in the Halls of Hades." This was at 1 p.m. In a minute or two life was extinct. When the news of his death was brought in haste to the mean-spirited Chia Ch'ing, they found him kneeling before his father's coffin offering propitiatory libations of wine.

Peking was greatly excited, and the official world went in terror of a wholesale proscription, such as took place when the eunuch Wei Chung-hsien held sway at the end of the Ming dynasty. Chia Ch'ing was urged by his two elder brothers to issue a reassuring decree. Knowing himself to be extremely unpopular, and fearful of assassination, he followed this advice. He said, in his best manner: " Ho Shen is dead. Unless the Empire's chief cause of evil were pulled up by the roots, how could my Government be purified and officialdom purged of its corroding influence? His case is concluded, but he held at his disposal many of the highest posts, and his partisans in Peking are legion. The provinces swarm with the sycophants who fawned at his gate and bribed their unlawful way into his favour. Should I proceed to investigate every case I would have to indite at least seventy per cent. of the higher officials, which is clearly impracticable, for there would be no means of making the punishment fit the crime. The times are out of joint. So many and great abuses exist in our Government that time fails me to recapitulate them, I have mentioned the worst in my decrees regarding Ho Shen. But if my officials misconstrue my motives and begin denouncing their private enemies to me on trivial grounds, inventing plausible evidence for the wreaking of old grudges, there will be no end to the reign of terror and no one will be safe. I have no desire to be at the head of a party, nor to allow my Government to be divided into opposing groups, each animated by vindictive feelings towards the other.

"I dealt severely with Ho Shen because his usurping ambition jeopardised the safety of the State; his venal corruption and subterraneous trafficking were comparatively trivial offences. After I decided to strike I struck promptly and without mercy. But if only warning be taken for the future, I am ready to let bygones be bygones. I trust, therefore, that none of you will harbour nervous fears. Most of you are men of second-rate abilities, but if you will exert yourselves conscientiously in the service of the State, there is no reason why you should not improve in course of time. Some of you in your haste have gone astray; you must now cleanse your hearts and purge yourselves of error in the hope of becoming respectable members of society and not mere wastrels and encumbrances. Trembling obey this my mandate; let the whetstone of conscience make you keen to conform to my desire for the dawn of a better day!" (With many more platitudes to the same effect).

Chia Ch'ing's decrees are sufficient in themselves to show that his first idea, upon the death of his father, was to deprive Ho Shen of his power and his fortune, and this from purely vindictive and avaricious motives. But because "face-saving" traditions and the elaborate parade of elementary justice retained with him and with his Court an atavistic force of instinct, the judicial murder of his Chief Minister and the plundering of his worldly goods had to be carried out with due observance of time-honoured formalities and retributive justice. There could be no doubt that he and his immediate adherents, jealous of Ho Shen's wealth and power, had long since planned the impeachment and destruction of Ch'ien Lung's favourite, but when the time came, they were careful to cover the infamy of their proceedings with a fine texture of plausible justification. The Emperor's sole motives were jealousy and greed, but he compelled his victim, under torture, to invest them with the virtue of righteous indignation.

In the ransacked and chaotic jumble of the Grand Council's archives, a portion of the original report, submitted by the Council on the indictment of Ho Shen, has recently been found. Unfortunately, most of this document is missing, but what remains is extremely interesting. The first portion is a memorandum of His Majesty's orders, verbally communicated, concerning the several matters on which the Imperial Commissioners were directed to cross-examine the prisoner, under torture if necessary. It is unnecessary to reproduce the whole of this *dossier*, but the Emperor's first two questions may be quoted as proof of his grasping and thoroughly sordid intentions.

The first question was: "Amongst the mass of property seized in your various residences I find a quantity of ceilings and panellings of Imperial cedar wood, the use of which by a subject is tantamount to gross *lèse majesté*. All the furniture and fittings of this woodwork are an exact reproduction of those in the Palace of Tranquil Longevity. What was your motive in committing these acts of treason? Did you aspire to the Throne?

Ho Shen's reply (real or alleged) amounted, as did all the rest of his statements under "cross-examination," to an unqualified and humble confession of guilt. There can be no doubt that if he made the statements recorded against him, he did so because he knew that his doom was sealed, and wished to save himself and his persecutors further trouble. His answer to the above question is set down as follows:

"Your slave had no right to have in his private residence ceilings and panellings of Imperial cedar, with screens and woodwork in imitation of those in the Palace. The fact is, I sent a eunuch named Hu to the Palace to have the fittings copied. The cedar wood I purchased myself, but it is true that I took from the Palace several pillars of crystal and glass. For this your slave deserves to die the death."

The second question was: "Amongst the great assortment of pearls and jewels which were seized yesterday at your residences and handed over to me for inspection, I find over two hundred exquisite Court necklaces of pearls. I, the Emperor, only possess about eighty Court necklaces, including those formerly worn by my grandfather and great-grandfather. Your necklaces outnumber mine three to one. Amongst your large single pearls there is one much larger than the one I wear in my official hat. You have no right to wear such a pearl. How did you acquire this immense collection? Besides, you have innumerable quantities of other gems, more lustrous and larger than any I possess. Is not this of itself convincing proof of your covetous wickedness?"

To this Ho Shen replied giving the names of the various officials from whom he had received presents of pearls and other jewels, chiefly military commanders.

For the rest, the wretched man either confessed, or was reported to have confessed, that all the other charges against him, as set forth in the Emperor's indictment, were true. He had " appropriated Imperial handmaidens of exceptional comeliness for his own purposes"; he had ridden on horseback in the Forbidden City; he had revealed State secrets and suppressed despatches from the seat of rebellion; he had prevented the Mongol mission from coming to Peking, and done many other evil things, for all of which, " he deserved to die a thousand deaths."

But all these interesting formalities, in the case of a man irretrievably condemned before this farce of an "inquiry" began, were nothing more than by-play, as the Court was well aware; an empty parade of legality intended to serve the purposes of " historical accuracy " in the dynastic records. The real object of the inquiry was to elicit from Ho Shen the total amount of his property and the places in which it was to be found. In this matter he was less frankly communicative; after three " examinations," the list of his possessions included 60 million ounces of silver; 27,000 ounces of gold; 56 necklaces and bracelets of pearls; 456 rubies and 113 sapphires. The large Court necklaces were not included in the official schedule, because the Emperor had confiscated them for his own use on the day that they were handed to him for inspection. (The famous pearl-embroidered jacket, frequently worn by the Empress Dowager Tzŭ Hsi, was similarly confiscated from Ho Shen's collection.)

Ho Shen had to be repeatedly and severely beaten before he declared the total amount and the hiding-places of his wealth. Eventually, after the Eighth Prince and two Grand Secretaries had personally superintended the " inquiry " and the application of severe torture, Ho Shen disclosed the fact that most of his treasure was buried in his garden outside the city. Prince Ting, a grandson of Ch'ien Lung, was sent to dig it up, whilst the Eleventh Prince, with two other Grand Secretaries, made a thorough search of all the victim's city residences. The Court was hot on the scent for loot.

Eight days later the treasure-hunters sent in their report. Ho Shen's property was classified under 109 schedules, 26 of which showed a total value of 223 millions of taels (roughly at that time, 70 millions sterling). These figures, the result of an official valuation, were quoted in an Imperial decree, and may be regarded as approximately correct. His entire estate, roughly calculated on the same basis, must have been worth about 900 millions of taels. The bullion confiscated was handed over to the

THE COURT OF PEKING

Board of Revenue, ostensibly for the campaign against the rebels in Ssŭ Ch'uan and Hupei.

The official inventory, under the first 26 schedules of Ho Shen's estate, deals principally with his main residence, which Chia Ch'ing, in his disinterested zeal for the purity of the State, presented to his younger brother, Prince Ch'ing.[1] The gardens to the east of it, adjoining the Lake of the Ten Pagodas (Shih ch'a hai), were given to another of his brothers, Prince Ch'eng, and until quite recently belonged to his descendant, the "Beileh" Hsiao.

The flower garden, presented to Ho Shen by Ch'ien Lung himself, was one of the wonders of the capital. It contained sixty-four pavilions, some of them decorated with Imperial yellow tiles, and had high towers at its four corners, after the design of the Palace precincts, which was undoubtedly inviting disaster. In these towers Ho Shen kept a considerable force of night watchmen under arms to protect his vast wealth; there were 420 altogether in the pleasure garden.

Ho Shen's wealth was indeed sufficient to excite the jealous cupidity of a small-minded man like Chia Ch'ing. To be very rich is always dangerous under an Oriental Court, but the hoarding instinct is usually stronger than the fear of death itself in a race with which the horror of poverty seems, through ages of the fiercest life-struggle, to have accumulated the blind force of unreasoning instinct. The manner in which the Great Man invested and concealed his riches was typical of his class, and not without interest as illustrating the economic conditions then obtaining. To-day, the much-looted modern mandarin has discovered new and safer means of investing his money—in the fixed deposits of European banks and

---

[1] The western half of Ho Shen's residence is now the property of his grandson by adoption, the venal Prince Ch'ing, whose corrupt practices were notorious throughout the latter part of the reign of Tzŭ Hsi. The eastern half, divided from it by a street, is the Palace of Prince Hsiao.

real estate at the Treaty Ports; but until 1900, the methods adopted by Ho Shen were those common to the wealthy official class.

According to the 26 schedules above mentioned, Ho Shen was the owner of 75 pawnshops, 13 curio-shops, two storehouses of white jade and two of silk. In his fur treasury there were 1907 rare fox skins and 67,000 other pelts. He had a separate storehouse for sables and fur coats, in which were found 1417 fine sable robes and over 4000 other fur garments, together with large quantities of sable-lined boots and hats. His wood treasury was a building of 22 rooms, containing 8640 pieces of the choicest woods. The contents of the pawnshops and curio-shops alone were valued at 60 millions of taels.

His private residences were furnished with a magnificence which the China of to-day knows only by tradition, the magnificence of art treasures accumulated through long centuries, but which, looted in successive rebellions, or sold by their impoverished owners, have gradually found their way into the hands of foreigners and left the country for ever. The list of curios found in Ho Shen's principal residence included amongst others the following objects:

- 11 bronze tripods of the Han dynasty.
- 18 jade tripods.
- 711 antique ink slabs (some of the Sung dynasty).
- 28 Imperial gongs, of jade.
- 10 ancient Japanese swords.
- 38 European clocks, inlaid with gems.
- 140 gold and enamel watches.
- 226 pearl bracelets.
- 288 large rubies, 4070 sapphires.
- 10 trees of coral, 3 feet 8 inches high.
- 22 statues, in white jade, representing the Goddess of Mercy, the Lohans, etc.

THE COURT OF PEKING

    18 solid gold Lohans, 2 feet 4 inches high.
9000 sceptres "Ju-i" of solid gold, each weighing forty-eight ounces.
 507 jade sceptres, several of them engraved upon the handle with original verses by the Emperor Ch'ien Lung.
3411 small jade sceptres.
 500 pairs of chopsticks, ivory and gold.
     A gold table service of 4288 pieces; another similar service of silver.
  99 large soup-bowls of topaz; 154 of jade.
 124 wine beakers of white jade.
  18 plates of jade and eighteen of topaz, forty inches in diameter.
2390 snuff-bottles of jade, cornelian and topaz.
   1 solid rock of jade, carved and engraved with poems of the Ming Emperor Yung Lo and His Majesty Ch'ien Lung, about 8 feet long.[1]

Even the wash-basins, spittoons, and chamber utensils of the great man's house were of solid gold, or jade—only a few were of silver. Of small screens he had 23 of solid gold, and 40 of gold and lacquer; 24 large lacquer screens; 144 couches decorated with gold work and lacquer, inlaid with gems. Finally, in the treasury of this house alone and in the garden *caches* they found gold bars to the value of 35 million taels, besides 28,000 articles of jewellery, large and small.[2]

[1] This *objet de vertu* is now in the Metropolitan Museum at New York; it was taken from Tzŭ Hsi's apartments at the Summer Palace by an officer of the allied forces in 1900, and sold by him to an American connoisseur and diplomat. The Old Buddha was very fond of this curio, and was much distressed, on her return from exile to Peking in January 1902, to find that it had been looted.

[2] It is interesting to observe that the valuation placed on Ho Shen's property under these 26 schedules—roughly a quarter of his estate—taken at the rate of exchange at that period, would suffice to pay off the whole Boxer indemnity.

Small wonder if the Court officials were zealous in the work of compiling these interesting schedules, and small wonder if His Majesty Chia Ch'ing placed his own brothers (under the watchful eyes of Grand Secretaries) to make a full record of such splendid plunder. Once the work of the Imperial looters had been done, His Majesty deprecated any further references to the matter, or to the ultimate disposal of Ho Shen's property. Nevertheless, some four months after his death, a certain Lieutenant-General of a Banner Corps, named Sa, ventured to memorialise, saying that a good deal of leakage had occurred in compiling the official returns of the various properties, that there was still much treasure hidden, and that a good deal more had found its way, as hush money, into the pockets of the Imperial Commissioners who "tried the case." To this the Emperor replied in an edict, assuring the memorialist that he must be mistaken (Chia Ch'ing had no intention of muzzling the ox that trod out such good corn). Once more the tactless bannerman returned to the charge, evidently hoping to be well rewarded for his zeal. He declared that Ho Shen's treasury accounts had been in the hands of four female secretaries, and that a cross-examination of these women would bring many things to light. But Chia Ch'ing needed no further light on this subject. His decree rebuking the unfortunate Sa is interesting reading. The following is taken from its concluding paragraphs:

"Yesterday We appointed Prince Ch'eng, in company with the memorialist, to summon the four female secretaries to an investigation, so as to clear up the matter at once. The result is, as We expected, that they all deny the existence of any more treasure. Our original surmise as to the completely fictitious nature of Sa Pin-tu's information has thus been amply justified.

"None of the Princes or Ministers have ever suggested in Our presence that portions of Ho Shen's hoard had

THE COURT OF PEKING

been secreted or removed. It was left for Sa Pin-tu to deliver himself of these wild surmises, which clearly indicate his belief that We are animated by avaricious motives, and that We desire to accumulate vast wealth during Our reign. In his folly he has imagined that he would greatly interest and please Us with his stories about further hoards of treasure to be found.

"Now be it known that the only object in confiscating a Minister's property is to provide a solemn warning for the guidance of grasping officials. There is not the faintest idea of Our starting a wholesale proscription, so as to divert other ill-gotten gains into the Imperial coffers. The actual amount of Ho Shen's treasure is a matter of supreme indifference to Us; We are concerned only to vindicate the principle of official honesty. Even supposing for a moment that much of Ho Shen's property still remains unaccounted for, and has been wrongfully diverted to the possession of other private persons, We would make the obvious retort that its hiding-place cannot be very distant and that, no matter who has acquired it, it remains accessible if need be. Its present owners cannot conceal it indefinitely nor spirit it away.[1]

"Why, then, should We trouble ourselves about making too meticulous an inventory, or permit further ramification of this inquiry, which would convey an impression of covetous extortion?"

So Ho Shen died, because of his great wealth, and all his treasure was scattered. Chia Ch'ing did his work thoroughly. A month after the proscription and punishment of the deceased Minister's family, when he was busy with the counting of the spoils, one of his brothers, Prince Ting,[2] discovered another magnificent Court necklace of

---

[1] The meaning of this was plain; it conveyed an indirect intimation to those concerned, that His Majesty had his suspicions concerning the division of the spoils and that he wanted a larger share of the bullion, which was forthcoming.

[2] Eldest grandson of Ch'ien Lung.

pearls of which no mention had been made in the cross-examination of Ho Shen. It was his favourite and particular treasure, the apple of his eye. Whilst unable to conceal his delight at the find, Chia Ch'ing deals a spiteful final blow at Ho Shen's son, his brother-in-law, for not having declared the existence of this necklace. His edict reveals almost incredible depths of meanness, and may fittingly be cited as the last word in the history of Ho Shen :

" After the exposure of Ho Shen's abominable crimes and corrupt practices, We ordered Prince Ting to make a further inventory of his property. Mien En now informs Us that he and his fellow Commissioners have discovered an Imperial Court necklace of pearls, which he has submitted for Our inspection. When contemplating this article We are simply astounded, inasmuch as a Court necklace of pearls may only be worn by an Emperor, and no subject of the Throne is even entitled to own one. If it be now suggested that Ho Shen might have intended to present this necklace as tribute, Our reply is that in that case the pearls would not have been strung on dark yellow braid. We are thoroughly convinced that he had retained it for his own use.

" We therefore bade Prince Ting institute inquiries in the Ho Shen household, several members of which have now stated that although Ho Shen never wore this necklace by daylight, he would often put it on at night, when no strangers were present, and would then stand before the mirror contemplating himself with evident satisfaction. He would assume various attitudes, smile and mutter to himself, and walk up and down the apartment, assuming the gait of His late Majesty and even imitating his sacred voice. His words were generally indistinct, but the witnesses declare that they could hear the word 'Chen' (the Imperial 'We'), as if, indeed, he believed himself to be the Emperor.

THE COURT OF PEKING

"It is, in Our opinion, perfectly plain that he entertained designs of usurping the Throne. Had these facts come to Our knowledge before the 18th day of the 1st Moon We should assuredly have decreed Ho Shen's decapitation, even if We had spared him the lingering death and dismemberment.

"However, he has already been permitted to commit suicide, and thus luckily escaped the extreme penalty of public execution. We do not, therefore, insist on his corpse being hacked to pieces.

"As to his son, Fengshenyinte, the husband of an Imperial Princess, had he known of the existence of this necklace and had refrained from informing Us We should have ordered his dismemberment as an accessory before the fact. But a most vigorous cross-examination has elicited from him naught but repeated denials of all knowledge of its existence, and of Our grace We are pleased to order that no further investigation of the matter is required. Nevertheless, We cannot allow him to retain his hereditary rank, and We therefore deprive him of his ancestral earldom, merely allowing him to hold brevet rank as a Supernumerary Minister of the Presence. Prince Ting has shown much energy in the investigation of Ho Shen's property, and is to be referred to the Ministry concerned to determine a suitable reward."

CHAPTER XV

CHIA CH'ING: THE BEGINNING OF THE END

The example and results of Ho Shen's venal practices, and the presence at the provincial capitals of many of those who had studied the art of Government under his patronage and direction, speedily produced unmistakable symptoms of demoralisation throughout the public service, which, in its turn, resulted in wide-spread disaffection and unrest amongst the people. The mandarins who administered the Government under Chia Ch'ing were conspicuously inferior, in efficiency and moral character, to those who had held high offices under Ch'ien Lung. In China, more than in any other country in the world, because of the solidity of the patriarchal traditions of Government, the thoughts and deeds of the masses reflect in a high degree the moral qualities of the official class. The Chinese people are like the rest of humanity in that they cannot be made moral by Acts of Parliament, or wise by the inauguration of a Republic; but as regards the maintenance of public order and the pursuit of industry in preference to predatory activities, they are very greatly influenced by the moral qualities or defects of those placed in authority over them. If Chia Ch'ing had been a man of the same stamp as his father; had he pursued and despoiled Ho Shen and other offenders from a sense of duty and for the purification of the State, the public service would, no doubt, have recovered from the poison of corruption and gross living with which Ch'ien Lung, in his old age, had allowed Ho Shen to infect it. But, except in matters of personal revenge and covetous greed, Chia Ch'ing displayed neither initiative nor intelligence. Grasping, suspicious and thoroughly insincere, he lacked the quality of firmness and the sense of justice requisite to make a successful ruler of China; and his officials faithfully reflected their Sovereign's methods in their administration of the provinces. As a result, the spirit of rebellion, ever latent in the struggling mass of China's congested population, which manifested itself at the beginning of his reign, continued to grow and spread, until it became a chronic ailment of the body politic and an unmistakable indication of the approaching end of the Manchu power. Officials, civil and military, whom Ch'ien Lung would have recalled and executed for their failure to suppress local risings, were allowed by Chia Ch'ing to sow fresh seeds of disaffection, by wholesale and indiscriminating proscriptions of the wealthy, wherever an insurrection afforded them some pretext for filling their own pockets. And Chia Ch'ing shared this plunder, whilst bemoaning the evil destinies of his country in platitudinous decrees.

The insurrection of the White Lily society resulted in the devastation of four provinces before the new Emperor, after eight years of anxious struggle, felt himself secure upon the Throne. It eventually subsided in 1807, after wholesale extermination in suspected districts; but in 1812 an attempt was made upon the life of the Emperor at Peking, which revealed the existence of another widespread anti-Manchu organisation, and prepared the Government for the serious outbreak which the "Heavenly Reason" secret society was already planning in Honan.

The would-be assassin was a Manchu, named Ch'eng Te, employed as cook to the Imperial Household. Waiting for the Emperor on his way to the Summer Palace, he suddenly rushed towards the palanquin, sword in hand.

The bearers, seeing him, dropped the sedan and fled, the bodyguard seemed paralysed with fear, and the terrified Monarch collapsed in a fainting condition. He would undoubtedly have been slain had it not been for an officer of the guard, who galloped to his side just in time to overpower his assailant.

Chia Ch'ing, suspecting that the assassin had been hired by kinsmen of the late Grand Secretary, Ho Shen, had him examined with every refinement of lingering torture, but could extract nothing from him to prove the existence of an organised plot. All the man would say was: " If my plans had succeeded none of you would be where you are now." He was finally put to death by the slow slicing process, after his two sons had been beheaded before his eyes.

The annals of the dynasty contain no explanation of this attempt on the life of the Emperor; nevertheless, there is evidence to show that Ch'eng Te was one of a band of conspirators who, in the following year, made a determined attempt to seize the Palace and to overthrow the dynasty. The facts were made known to the Governor of Shantung, through a report forwarded to him by the District Magistrate of that province, who had arrested one of the leaders of the conspiracy, and elicited from him the information that the man Ch'eng Te had been a member of his band. The Governor thought it best to preserve a discreet silence on this matter, lest Chia Ch'ing should punish him for not having discovered and nipped the conspiracy in the bud. It was undoubtedly organised by some of Ho Shen's faction, acting in concert with the anti-dynastic societies in the provinces.

It was on the 15th day of the 9th Moon in the year 1813 that a considerable force of armed men suddenly forced their way into the Palace, and for a time actually held its gates. Their plans for gaining access to the Forbidden City were well laid, but as usually happens with Chinese risings, they had no capable leader, and once inside the Imperial precincts there was no definite plan of concerted attack. Chia Ch'ing was absent at the time, on his way to perform sacrifice at his father's tomb. His subsequent decree on the subject states the main facts accurately enough, as follows :

"Without warning, at noon of the 15th day of the 9th Moon, a band of rebels dared to enter the Palace by the Gate of Azure Thunder, where they were successfully stopped by eunuchs. An hour later another party climbed over the inner wall of the Forbidden City and entered the Palace, where my son, Mien Ning,[1] was at his studies.[2] Seeing that the situation was dangerous the Prince picked up a fowling-piece and drew his sword. He picked off the rebel leader, who, with a white flag in his hand, was directing operations. My son pleads guilty to rash presumption in having fired, but adds that the situation was desperate. He acted with true courage and commonsense, most remarkable in a young Prince still engaged in his studies. No sooner had the alarm been given than he rushed out and killed two more rebels, and by his prompt action caused the band to scatter in alarm. In spite of this my son apologises for his presumption in words which display admirable good taste and modesty. I can hardly guide my pencil as I write, for my eyes are blurred with tears, so deep is the gratification which I feel at his conduct. The sacred enclosure of the Forbidden City contains the spirit tablets of my ancestors and of my late father, and the Empress Consort is living there now. My son has bravely defended its sanctity and has acquitted himself with rare loyalty and filial duty. I confer upon him the title of Prince of the

---

[1] Who subsequently reigned as the Emperor Tao Kuang.

[2] The Prince was then thirty-one years of age. Chia Ch'ing kept him and his brothers in tutelage much longer than was usual, warned by the example of K'ang Hsi's rebellious family. Though married at the age of fourteen, he did not set up an independent establishment till 1816.

First Order, with the title of 'Wise,' and double his emoluments, raising them to T. 12,000 per annum. My third son, Mien K'ai, deserves praise also for the help he rendered. If my Ministers display merit I reward them as a matter of course. Naturally, therefore, if my own sons display courage and loyalty, I can hardly refrain from suitably recognising their deserts. This is only common fairness, and I trust that my Ministers will realise this and be inspired to equal bravery.

"A further memorial from my brother, Prince Yi, and others reports that the attack was suppressed by 3 p.m., the number of rebels taken alive being altogether two hundred. I would observe, however, that the list of their names only mentions thirty-one persons, and I should be glad to know what has become of the other hundred and sixty-nine. This memorial is sadly lacking in lucidity.

"My brother, Prince Ch'eng, after cross-examining several rebels, learns that there is still a band of some five hundred of them outside the Imperial City, but he does not state whether these took any part in the disturbances or how their presence came to be revealed. I desire information on this matter. On the occasion of so sudden an irruption of desperadoes, who have dared to enter the sacred precincts and lurk in the Imperial kitchen, the Princes and Ministers have shown remarkable courage. Those who made arrests in the inner enclosure of the Palace deserve the highest praise; next in merit are the defenders of the outer precincts. In the bestowal of rewards and honours those who were slain in repelling the attack are to be included under the first class; the severely wounded under the second class, and those slightly wounded under the third class. All names must be given irrespective of rank, and no favouritism shown. Upon my arrival, my second son is to meet me inside the gate of the Palace, and to prostrate himself in obeisance

THE COURT OF PEKING

for the honour I have bestowed upon him. He is excused from awaiting the cortège outside the city."

Chia Ch'ing countermanded his visit to the tombs and hurried back to Peking. In the course of a characteristic penitential decree he made the following remarks on the causes of national demoralisation:

"My dynasty has now ruled over this Empire for one hundred and seventy years; my glorious predecessors have, each in his turn, displayed a bountiful affection for their subjects, treating them ever as beloved children. No pen can describe their sage virtue and justice. Although I may have failed in reaching their standard of perfection I have not been a cruel or grasping ruler. This sudden disaster is quite inexplicable to me; it is, I suppose, a proof of my own scanty merit and a punishment for my many offences. The revolution broke out suddenly, but it must have been long in preparation. The besetting sin amongst my officials may be summed up in two words: 'Incurable procrastination.' I keep warning you all till my lips are sore and my tongue is dry, but you take no notice, and continue to govern in the old casual way. Because of this a calamity has befallen us, unparalleled under this or any other dynasty, infinitely worse than the episode which occurred under the Mings, when a man armed with a cudgel made an attempt on the life of the Heir Apparent of Wan Li.[1] I cannot bear to speak of this thing any more. All I can do is to repent me of my errors and to purify my heart, in order, on the one hand, to show my gratitude to high Heaven and, on the other, to lessen my subjects' disaffection towards their ruler.

"If you, my officials, desire truly and loyally to serve my great Manchu dynasty, then must you become as little children and toil zealously for the State, in order to redeem my errors and to reform the habits of the people. If, however, it please you better to remain sunken in

[1] *Vide supra*, p.

degeneracy, then you had better hang up your officials' hats and seek refuge in retirement for the remainder of this existence. Cease from placidly accepting the emoluments and sweets of office, like the mourner who takes the place of the corpse and presides at the funeral feast, in dignified nonchalance, for thus you will only enhance your Emperor's guilt. I have written so far, but tears gush forth and blot the paper. Let this be made known everywhere."

The name of the leading conspirator was Lin Ch'ing, whose influence over his numerous adherents of the Heavenly Principles Society seems to have been (like that of the Boxer leaders in 1900) largely mystical and religious. His avowed aim was the foundation of a new dynasty, with himself as the Heaven-sent ruler of China. Preparations were being made for a general rising on the 15th day of the intercalary 8th Moon,[1] but the plot was discovered, in April 1812, by the Manchu Prefect at Tamsui in Formosa, who happened to arrest one of its moving spirits, engaged there in spreading anti-dynastic sedition. This man disclosed the aims of the secret society, and named Lin Ch'ing as its leader. The Prefect informed the Governor of the conspiracy, but the Governor took no steps to warn Peking, for fear of getting into trouble himself.

On the day before the attack on the Palace, a Police Inspector at Lu K'ou Ch'iao, six miles south-west of Peking, sent an urgent message to the Governor of the city informing him that Lin Ch'ing had given orders to his men to enter the capital next morning. Again, the Governor, fearing to be the bearer of alarmist news, took no action in the matter.

As the result of the investigation held and the evidence of the prisoners, it transpired that several of the Palace eunuchs had taken part in the conspiracy. Chia Ch'ing's

[1] Intercalary 8th Moons seem to be especially selected by the astrologers of secret societies for the outbreak of rebellions.

edict on the subject is interesting, inasmuch as it reveals the increasing demoralisation of the Imperial Household. It reads as follows:

"Before the attack on the Palace certain seditious characters had been arrested in Shantung and Honan on charges of murdering officials. They confessed under examination that they belonged to the Heavenly Principles Society, and that their leader, Lin, was hiding in Peking. I was about to give orders for his arrest, when the Forbidden City was invaded by armed rebels, all of whom have been captured. It was learned that their leader, the aforesaid Lin Ch'ing, was in hiding at a village near Peking, and his capture was effected. He admits that he was the originator and organiser of the conspiracy. He propagated treasonable doctrines and planned to have me assassinated; his guilt is heinous in the extreme. I am deeply grateful to the protection of Heaven and of my ancestors for frustrating his designs, and command that he be punished with the utmost rigour of the law. I am greatly astounded to learn that several eunuchs, Lin Te-ts'ai and others, belonged to this heretic sect. That minions in the service of the Palace should dare to join a society so pernicious and abet its treasonable designs by opening the Palace gates to the rebels, reveals an unprecedented degree of guilt. The eunuchs under arrest must be examined separately under torture, and the whole truth extracted, without evasions or false witness. These guilty eunuchs must all be sentenced to dismemberment, of course, and their families will share their fate. The eunuch ringleader, Lin Te-ts'ai, is to be held until my return to the Palace, when I shall examine him myself, together with his chief accomplice. When I have rigorously cross-examined them, they will be duly punished by the lingering death."

On the following morning Chia Ch'ing re-entered Peking, taking the opportunity of exhibiting himself to the people by riding on horseback instead of being borne in the Imperial palanquin. He immediately set himself to the congenial task of examining the culprits under torture. The names of other ringleaders were revealed and the objects of the society, which was frankly anti-Manchu, disclosed. It was originally called the Eight Diagrams Sect, and had a great number of adherents in the northern provinces. In some respects its methods of worship resembled those of the Boxers of 1900.

After ordering the dismemberment of the leading criminals, the Emperor recorded his further views on the eunuch question, as follows:

"I have personally examined the guilty eunuchs, who assure me that they had no accomplices in their crimes. There are seven of them in all. There are several grades of eunuchs; all those in attendance on my person are extremely well behaved. These who are now under sentence have only been employed about the Palace in the humblest duties and have never had access to my presence. Their names are unknown to me and they have never formed part of my suite at the Summer Palace. Nevertheless, the Chief Eunuchs are greatly to blame for not exercising a more vigilant control. When I asked the culprits why they had plotted treason, all hung their heads and were silent. Then I asked whether I had ever ill-treated them, to which they replied: 'Your divine bounty is limitless, how could we harbour any ill-feelings against you?' They kept on saying: 'Lord Buddha,' (meaning me), 'save us.' It is, indeed, sad that they should have allowed themselves to be corrupted by evil influences outside the Palace. In future no eunuchs are to be allowed outside except for a limited number of hours, and in no case except in groups of three or four. By this means I hope to prevent subterranean intrigue and visits to the residences of officials. I am glad to think that the guilt of these owl-like monsters is confined to a very few. The other eunuchs ought to be grateful for their master's bounty and refrain from harbouring unworthy fears and suspicions. I shall never punish the innocent. Let this decree be inserted in my Palace annals.

"The 6th day of next Moon is the anniversary of my birth, but I have lost face by recent events and have now no heart to receive congratulations. Rebellions are raging and seditious sects flourish; what heart could I have for revelry? It would be the shadow without the substance. It has been your custom to present me with jade sceptres of good luck, which I have invariably returned to the donors. The recent conspiracy certainly does not denote 'good luck,' and I beg that my officials will offer me no more such 'luck' tokens. I grieve to think that you still desire to celebrate my birthday, but feel that I must sanction your request. In the meanwhile, I hope that each of you will commune with his heart in the night watches, asking himself what manner of man he desires to become, and what ambitions he cherishes. Do not jeopardise your careers! I have lost face by these events and am aweary of these perpetual admonitions."

[There is evidence in contemporary writings that the Court was equally weary, and that Chia Ch'ing had by this time written himself down as a complete failure.]

The demoralisation of the Court and the Emperor's lack of statesmanship were signally demonstrated in connection with the special embassy, under Lord Amherst, sent by Great Britain in the summer of 1816, for the purpose of arranging at Peking for improved trade relations and facilities at Canton, where serious differences had arisen between the East India Company's agents and the Chinese authorities. The history of that mission, and the reasons which led to its failure, have been fully described in Ellis's *Journal* (London, 1817) and other works. Suffice it to say that the breadth of vision which led Ch'ien Lung to dispense with the ceremony of the kotow in the case of Lord Macartney's Embassy was lacking in his ignorant and arrogant successor. China's military strength had greatly deteriorated in the twenty years that had elapsed since Lord Macartney's day, but the self-sufficient conceit of her ruling class had increased with their corruption and inefficiency. The truth of this statement is sufficiently revealed by Chia Ch'ing's edicts in regard to Lord Amherst's mission.

In the 7th Moon (end of August) 1816, the official Chinese point of view was thus recorded in an Imperial decree:

" Imperial mandate to the King of England: Whereas your country, though lying far beyond the wide seas, was sincerely desirous of attaining the blessings of civilisation, in the fifty-eighth year of Ch'ien Lung, when my sainted father was on the Throne, you sent a special mission to pay homage. At that time your Ambassador performed the ceremony required of him with the greatest respect and committed no breach of decorum or etiquette.[1] It was his high privilege, therefore, reverently to receive the gracious kindness of His late Majesty. He was admitted into his presence and was given a banquet and many presents.

" You have now sent another mission bearing a memorial and offerings of your produce. Your respectful homage has met with my appreciation, and I was glad of the coming of your mission. I examined into the details of the ceremonial adopted on the previous occasion, and bade my Court arrange for your Envoy's reception by myself,

---

[1] This is a deliberate perversion of the facts. The ceremony of the kotow was definitely waived by Ch'ien Lung after repeated, but futile, attempts on the part of his Ministers to induce Lord Macartney to perform it.

and to provide a banquet and presents, in exact accordance with the ceremonial prescribed by His late Majesty. On the mission's arrival at Tientsin, I ordered that a banquet should be given there in my name. To my great surprise your Ambassador, on returning thanks, failed to conform with the prescribed etiquette. Nevertheless, I bore in mind that a lowly official of a distant nation could hardly be expected to show familiarity with our ceremonial usage, and I was pleased to pardon his remissness.

" I commanded my officials to inform your Envoy, on his approaching the metropolis, that his predecessor, your former Ambassador, in the fifty-eighth year of Ch'ien Lung, did duly perform the whole prescribed ceremony, including the genuflexion and kotow. How, then, could any deviation from this course be permitted on the present occasion? Your Envoy replied to my Minister that he would certainly perform both genuflexion and kotow at the time of his audience, and promised that there should be no violation of etiquette.[1] My Ministers duly informed me, whereupon I issued a decree commanding your Ambassador to attend for audience on the 7th day of the 7th Moon. On the 8th day I arranged for a banquet in the Hall of Perfect Rectitude and Enlightenment, when the bestowal of presents was to take place, after which he was to be regaled with a further entertainment in the Garden of Universal Joy. On the day following, the 9th, he was to be received in farewell audience and to be taken over the grounds of the Summer Palace. On the 11th he was to proceed to the gate of the Main Hall of the Forbidden City, there to receive my mandate and gifts for presentation to yourself, after which he was to be entertained at a banquet by my Board of Ceremonies.

---

[1] Vide *Ellis's Journal*, p. 172. On the 27th of August a note was addressed to Chia Ch'ing's Ministers, stating Lord Amherst's final and irrevocable determination not to perform the kotow, a determination in accordance with all his previous declarations.

On the 13th he was to be ordered to take his departure.

"My Minister informed your Ambassador of the dates and details of the above programme. On the 7th, the date fixed for audience, the mission had reached my Palace gate, and I was about to take my seat on the Imperial Throne, when your Chief Ambassador suddenly announced that he had been attacked by a sudden illness and was unable to move. Admitting that this might possibly be the case, I merely commanded the presence of the two subordinate Envoys, but they also simultaneously excused themselves on the plea of sickness. Such gross discourtesy is utterly unprecedented; nevertheless, I administered no severe reproof, but confined myself to ordering their immediate departure from Peking. As the mission was not received in audience, your memorial, strictly speaking, should not have been presented, but I remembered that your country is afar off, and that the feelings were praiseworthy which led you to memorialise Us and send tribute. Your Envoys are alone to blame for their gross breach of respect; I fully recognise the spirit of reverent submission which animated you. I have consequently accepted the whole of your tribute, including maps, pictures, and portraits, and I duly acknowledge your devotion. Moreover, in my turn, I confer upon you a white jade and a green jade sceptre, a Court necklace, two pairs of large pouches to be worn at the girdle and eight small ones, that my bounty may be made manifest.

"You live at such a great distance from the Middle Kingdom that these Embassies must cause you considerable inconvenience. Your Envoys, moreover, are wholly ignorant of Chinese ceremonial procedure, and the bickering which follows their arrival is highly displeasing to my ear. My dynasty attaches no value to products from abroad; your nation's cunningly wrought and strange wares do not appeal to me in the least, nor do they interest me. For the future, O King, if you will keep your subjects in order and strengthen your national defences, I shall hold you in high esteem, notwithstanding your remoteness. Henceforward, pray do not trouble to dispatch missions all this distance; they are merely a waste of time and have their journey for nothing. If you loyally accept our sovereignty and show dutiful submission, there is really no need for these yearly appearances at our Court to prove that you are indeed our vassal. We issue this mandate to the end that you may perpetually comply therewith."

England in 1816 was busy with matters weightier even than the indignities offered to Lord Amherst's Embassy and the grievances of the East India Company at Canton, but China lost nothing by waiting for the day of reckoning which the arrogance and bad faith of the mandarins had now rendered inevitable. It was clear that the dignity of Great Britain could not tolerate indefinitely the ignorant presumption of the Chinese, nor the ill-treatment of British subjects at their hands. With the abolition of the East India Company's charter, seventeen years after Lord Amherst's ignominious dismissal from Peking, Lord Napier appeared at the gates of Canton; on that day began the long and painful process of disillusion, which, through bloodshed and humiliation, was to convince the rulers of China that their attitude of complacent superiority and over-lordship of the world was untenable.

If the Emperor Chia Ch'ing's decrees on the subject of the Amherst Mission are compared with the British records of what actually occurred at Peking, the fact stands out clearly that both the Emperor and the British Envoy were deliberately hoodwinked and misled by the Chinese and Manchu officials deputed to arrange with Lord Amherst the details of the presentation ceremony. The purblind mandarins, who had advised the Throne to insist on the performance of the kotow, were afraid to " lose face " by having to confess that they were unable to persuade the British Envoy to accept it;[1] they therefore lied to the Emperor about the Mission's attitude, and to the Mission about the Emperor's, until at the last, in order to extricate themselves, they were compelled to get rid of the foreigners at all costs. This they did by making it appear that the Envoy had been disrespectful to His Majesty, and by taking steps that the Mission should be illtreated and insulted.

Notwithstanding the wording of his mandate to the King of England, Chia Ch'ing felt that he had been grievously ill-used, and that by the departure of the Mission he had lost much face. He proceeded, therefore, as usual, to scold his Ministers, in the following querulous decree:

" On the occasion of the tribute Mission from England landing at the port of Tientsin, I commanded Su-leng-e and Kuang Hui to give a banquet in my name and to compel the members of the Mission to return thanks for the same by the three genuflexions and the nine prostrations. If these obeisances were duly performed the Mission was to be conducted to Peking, but in the event of any failure to observe the proper ceremonial, or if it were clumsily rehearsed, the officials above named were to memorialise and await my further commands. The Embassy's ships were not to be permitted to leave, so that they might be available to take the Mission back by the way it had come.

" My orders have been wilfully disregarded. The Mission has been allowed to come up to Peking, and the ships have taken their departure without leave from me.

---

[1] Vide *Ellis's Journal.* p. 173. It is interesting at this date to recall the fact that had it not been for the presence and firmness of Sir George Staunton, who had been a member of Lord Macartney's suite at Jehol, Lord Amherst would have yielded to the Chinese and kotowed.

THE COURT OF PEKING

Herein lies a gross dereliction of duty on the part of these two officials.

"Furthermore, I commanded Ho Shih-t'ai and Mukdenga to proceed to T'ungchou, where they were to direct the Mission to rehearse the ceremony. For this I gave them till the 6th day of the 7th Moon, by which time, if the Mission had acquired proficiency in the requisite etiquette, they were to be brought on to the capital; if not, the tribute Mission was to be denounced and my decision requested forthwith. On the 5th instant I received a vaguely worded memorial from Ho Shih-t'ai and his colleagues, and on the 6th the Mission was escorted into Peking. At 1.30 p.m. on that day I took my seat on the Throne in the Hall of Diligent Government and summoned Ho Shih-t'ai and Mukdenga to an audience. First I inquired as to the rehearsal of the ceremony at T'ungchou. Hereupon the two officials removed their hats and with repeated kotows confessed that no rehearsal had taken place at all! I asked them why, this being the case, they had not carried out my instructions and denounced the Mission to the Throne. Ho Shih-t'ai answered:[1] 'When the audience takes place to-morrow I will guarantee that the ceremonial will be performed in full.' For this blundering they are responsible, and just as much to blame as the first two officials. On the morning of the 7th I partook of breakfast, and at 6.30 a.m. issued a decree saying I was about to proceed to the Throne Hall, where I would receive the Mission in audience. To this Ho Shih-t'ai at first replied: 'The Mission is delayed on the road; so soon as it reaches the Palace gates I will inform Your Majesty.' In a little while he reported further, saying: 'The Chief Ambassador has had a severe gastric attack; it will be necessary to postpone the

---

[1] On the same day, Kuang Hui reassured Lord Amherst saying that "the affair was settled, and he might be perfectly easy. The ceremony would not be mentioned again."

audience, giving him time to recover.' At last he reported: 'The Ambassador is too sick to appear at audience at all.'

"I directed that the Ambassador be taken back to his lodging, and supplied at once with medical aid, after which I desired the immediate attendance of the Deputy Ambassador. To this Ho Shih-t'ai replied that the Deputy Ambassador had also been attacked by sickness, and that both would attend together on the Chief Ambassador's recovery.

"China is lord and sovereign of the world; was it possible for Us to submit calmly to such a wanton display of irreverent arrogance? Therefore I issued a decree, commanding the expulsion of the Mission from China. Nevertheless, I inflicted no punishment upon the Ambassadors; I bade Kuang Hui escort them back to Canton and see to it that they set sail from there. It has only now been reported to me by the Grand Council that the Mission had had an all night's journey from T'ungchou to the ante-chamber of the Imperial Palace at Yüan Ming yüan, and that the Ambassador, whose Court dress had not arrived, had strongly protested at the idea of appearing before His Imperial Majesty the Emperor in travelling clothes. Why did Ho Shih-t'ai not inform me of these facts? If it was because he overlooked them at the moment, he could easily have asked for another audience that evening or the next day. He did nothing of the sort, and allowed me to remain in ignorance until I was proceeding to take my seat on the Imperial Throne. The guilt of Ho Shih-t'ai and his colleague greatly exceeds the errors of the other two. Had they informed me of the true state of the case I should have postponed the ceremony to a later date. I am astounded at the way in which my stupid officials have mismanaged this business, and I feel that I have completely lost 'face' in the eyes of my Court. All I can do is frankly to acknowledge my mistakes.

THE COURT OF PEKING

" I shall deal with the four officials' punishment [1] after the Board of Civil Office has recommended an appropriate penalty. In the meantime, I record the facts for the information of my officials throughout the Empire and the Mongol Princes."

It was months before Chia Ch'ing recovered from this loss of face.

[1] One was deprived of his post of Board President; another was reduced from the rank of Comptroller-General of the Household to that of an official writer of the eighth rank. The other two, highly placed Manchus both, were cashiered.

CHAPTER XVI

TAO KUANG. THE IMPACT OF THE WEST

WHEN Chia Ch'ing died, struck by lightning, in 1821, he left to his son, Tao Kuang, an Empire from which the glory of his father's reign had departed. No more victorious armies would march, under Manchu leaders, to wars of conquest in Central Asia. For the future, China was to be harassed by rebellions within and by attacks from without, but the Manchu's power of ruling the country was steadily waning. The canker worm of effeminacy had already eaten deep into the heart of the Manchu military organisation; its garrisons in the provinces were fast losing the virility of Nurhachi's days and with it the respect of the Chinese. In the public service, as we have shown, corruption and cowardice were rapidly doing their work of demoralisation: and all the while, new forces and new foes were preparing to destroy the splendid self-sufficiency of the Middle Kingdom. Until now, China had settled her affairs and paid the price of her rulers' sins within her own borders: if she had had invaders and suffered the domination of aliens, at least they had been Asiatics, and the sons of Han had eventually conquered the conqueror by the moral force of their superior civilisation. But now, new conquerors were advancing who, in addition to material strength of a kind undreamt of in China's star-gazing philosophy, were to dispute even the moral supremacy of the Canons

THE COURT OF PEKING

of the Sages, and finally to take from China her great inheritance, her contempt for the outer barbarians, her false pride and pinchbeck supremacy, fast set in its massive frame of complacent ignorance.

When Tao Kuang came to the Throne, in his thirty-ninth year, it seemed at first as if he might fulfil the promise of courage and decision which he had given at the time of the rebel attack on the Palace in 1813. As a youth, he had shown energy and much fondness for sports; it was recorded in the Palace annals that in the year 1790, being then a boy of nine,[1] he accompanied his grandfather Ch'ien Lung on a hunting trip to Jehol and so delighted the Emperor with his skill at an archery competition that the aged monarch presented him with a Yellow Jacket and allowed him to wear it. But the process of degeneration, at Peking and in the provinces, had gone too far to be checked by the single-handed efforts of any Sovereign, and the men about Tao Kuang's Throne were remarkable neither for virtue nor for statesmanship. He reigned, *tant bien que mal*, for thirty years, but after the first ten, he displayed little energy in State affairs, gradually relegating them to his two principal advisers, the Manchu Grand Secretary Mu Ch'ang-a and the Imperial Tutor, Tu Shou-t'ien. At the close of his reign, when the pride of the Dragon Throne had been humbled by the British barbarians at Canton and Nanking; when the wide-spread elements of unrest and discontent, were about to blaze out into the great Taiping rebellion (from which the Manchu power would never have emerged had not the "barbarians" upheld it); when the Empire was visibly tottering to its ruin—Tao Kuang's mind was chiefly concerned with two matters, first; how to keep down the "squeezes" of the eunuchs in his Imperial Household accounts; secondly, how to prevent the Censorate from

[1] By the Chinese reckoning of age, which makes a child a year old at birth. Tao Kuang was born in 1782.

wearying him with their long-winded and futile denunciations of abuses which he was powerless to check.

It was Tu, the Imperial Tutor, who devised the method for muzzling the Censorate which Tao Kuang adopted, with results satisfactory to his own comfort but injurious to the State. The Emperor had asked him to suggest a way of punishing a certain Censor who persisted in propounding questions displeasing to His Majesty. Tu replied: "That is not a difficult matter. Whatever the subject of the memorial may be, let Your Majesty issue a decree finding fault with some particular mode of expression or error in its wording, and order that the writer be handed over to the Civil Office for the determination of a penalty. The Censorate will realise that if Your Majesty is not prepared to overlook trifling errors in composition and caligraphy, your displeasure is likely to be seriously visited on those memorialists who venture to deal with high questions of State! Nobody will be able to suggest that Your Majesty is opposed to criticism, but in future criticism will automatically cease."

Tao Kuang was pleased to follow this advice, and in a little while the Censorate ceased to urge its views upon the Emperor. This suited his chief advisers, who were able to handle affairs in their own way and without daily denunciations. The Emperor never suspected that the advice was given with this motive, being himself of a trusting and straightforward disposition. When Tu died, Tao Kuang lavished posthumous honours upon him, frankly confessing that his advice had become more or less indispensable. It was Tu who also set the fashion of "ploughing" literary degree candidates for blemishes in caligraphy, irrespective of the merits of their compositions. In this way he degraded the standard of learning and scholarship and with it the general standard of intelligence and efficiency in the public service.

As illustrating the tone of the public service towards

the end of this well-meaning but unfortunate monarch's reign, the following verses, sent by an anonymous wit to the Grand Secretary Ts'ao Chen-yung are interesting:

" If you wish to intrigue successfully and to rise in the world, make you friends at Court, by occasional gifts of money;

" If you would be reckoned a hero, avoid all reference to vexed questions, be noncommittal and invariably humble;

" The key to success in a high official is to take things easily, neither asserting merit nor protesting loyalty;

" In all your duties be plausibly evasive; never criticise adversely and never condemn;

" Just as in the country a peaceful district enjoys good harvests, even so, an absence of friction conduces to official advancement;

" In dealing with your colleagues, be yielding and soft-spoken; cover up their defects, but avoid praising their virtues;

" By so doing you may comfortably rise to be a Grand Secretary: your wife will receive a patent of honour and your son a sinecure;

" You will leave behind you a fragrant memory imperishable; and if you are not canonised as ' Learned and Loyal,' you will at least go down to history as ' Learned and Polite.' "

It was the same Grand Secretary Ts'ao who, when asked to advise an aspirant to office on the best means of securing preferment, cynically replied: " It is really quite simple; just go on kotowing, and never commit yourself to any final opinion on any subject." Ts'ao indulged in cynicism because, though he could no nothing to stem the tide of decadence, he himself was honest and patriotic, as the times went. His family made a large fortune from the salt trade of Anhui; much of which escaped payment of the Government's dues; but when the Viceroy of Nanking, hard put to it for funds adequate to fight the rebellion, drew his attention to these leakages he replied: "Institute your reforms, by all means, and pay no heed to my family's means of livelihood. I have never heard of a Grand Secretary dying of starvation."

If the annals speak truly, Tao Kuang's most marked characteristic was his housewifely thrift, which in his old age verged on parsimony. Although, like most of his house, he was fond of the pleasures of the table, the best dinner was unpalatable to him if he thought that he was paying too much for it. He had all the frugality and fussiness which subsequently distinguished the Empress Dowager, Tzu Hsi, but lacked her saving grace of humour. He gradually cut down his domestic expenditure in the Palace to about 200,000 taels (say £60,000) a year, so that the Secretaries, Chamberlains and eunuchs of the household were hard put to it to make a bare living. Some of their manœuvres were as determined as the Sovereign's stinginess. It is recorded that on one occasion, His Majesty desired to have some macaroni soup, made in a special way, and gave orders accordingly. Next day the household humbly reported that it would be necessary to build a special kitchen for the preparation of this dish and to place an official in charge of it. For this they submitted estimates amounting to over 600,000 taels, as well as a yearly expenditure of 15,000 taels. The Emperor frowned: "Never mind about it: I know a good eating-house, outside the Ch'ien Men, where they make this soup excellently, you can buy it for forty cash a bowl. I shall send a eunuch every day to buy some there."

A few days later the Minister of the household came again and reported that this particular eating-house had closed its doors. The Emperor sighed: "I have always refused to waste a cash on my food," he said, "but it does seem hard that I, the Son of Heaven, cannot be allowed to procure any little delicacy I want."

THE COURT OF PEKING

Tao Kuang was not destined, as was his son, to see his capital invaded and his Palace burned by the outer barbarians; but his father's fatuous arrogance, and his own incapacity to realise the seriousness of the new dangers that threatened his Empire, cost him and his advisers a first heavy instalment of humiliation by loss of territory and of " face." The events which led up to the Treaty of Nanking and the cession of Hongkong to Great Britain do not come within the scope of the present work. It may be observed, however, now that the opium question in China has become a question of religious and sentimental polemics in England, that the action taken by the Viceroy Lin at Canton in destroying the British merchants' opium was due, not to moral considerations, but to his uncompromising contempt for the foreigner and all his works. Our first war with China as been persistently described as an " opium war," by persons vocationally identified with opium abolition as a prominent plank in the missionary platform; nevertheless, the fact remains, clearly demonstrable to all who are not carried away by their prejudices, that neither the Peking Government nor the Viceroy at Canton regarded the opium question from any point of view other than the political, fiscal and economic. One party at Peking, under Mu Ch'ang-a, was in favour of legalising the drug (as Sir H. Pottinger advised) just as it was in favour of granting many other reasonable trade facilities to the foreigner. The other party, the irreconcilable conservatives and chauvinists, were all for excluding it, on precisely the same grounds as they opposed the opening of new ports to trade. Lin Tse-hsü, the Viceroy of Canton, was the real cause of the war, because his attitude of contemptuous insolence and his methods of barbarism were not such as any self-respecting nation could tolerate. The following extract from a letter addressed directly to Queen Victoria by this stiff-necked patriot of the old school, contains, in a few lines, the whole pitiful tragedy of China's collapse before the impact of the West.

" You savages of the further seas have waxed so bold, it seems, as to defy and insult our mighty Empire. Of a truth it is high time for you to ' flay the face and cleanse the heart,' and to amend your ways. If you submit humbly to the Celestial dynasty and tender your allegiance, it may give you a chance to purge yourselves of your past sins. But if you persist and continue in your path of obstinate delusion, your three islands (sic) will be laid waste and your people pounded into mincemeat, so soon as the armies of his Divine Majesty set foot upon your shores."

Lin addressed this dispatch to the Queen of England in the style which Chinese officials habitually use in addressing their equals, and not in the form of a memorial to a crowned head. It was not a wise policy for one to adopt who proposed to destroy the British fleets with stinkpots.

At Peking, counsels were sharply divided between making peace on the terms demanded by the British and war *à outrance*. The rabid conservatives were then, as they are to-day even in Young China, all bombast and bravado, and they fiercely denounced Mu Ch'ang-a and his policy of truckling to the barbarians. There were amongst them, as there are to-day, sincere patriots who sinned in ignorance, and there were brave men, like the Manchu commander of the Tartar garrison at Chinkiang, who fought valiantly and died for their blind faith in the invincible supremacy of the Middle Kingdom. In the beginning of 1841, the Emperor's opinions, after several vacillations, were identical with, and probably inspired, those of the Canton authorities. In January he issued a decree (similar to those of Tzŭ Hsi in 1900), ordering his faithful people to drive the hated foreigner into the sea. But within a few months, after Chusan and Ningpo had fallen into the hands of the British, wiser counsels began to prevail.

A typical example of the Chinese patriot of those days was Wang Ting-lin, Grand Secretary and Grand Councillor. With all the strength of a masterful and sincere nature, he opposed Mu Ch'ang-a's peace policy and advocated war at all costs. He impeached Mu at audience, comparing him to the historic traitor Ch'in Kuei of the Sung dynasty;[1] and protesting against the signing of any treaty of peace with the barbarians. He criticised severely the Emperor's action in cashiering the Viceroy Lin Tse-hsü, and frankly expressed his opinion that Mu Ch'ang-a was working for his private ends, actuated by personal grudges. The Emperor refused to listen to him, and, shaking his sleeve in token of dismissal, rose from the Throne. Wang, moved to the point where etiquette is forgotten, clung to the Emperor's robe and continued to pour out impassioned words. Tao Kuang looked away and left him, without reply. Wang Tin-lin thereupon went straightway to his own house, indited a valedictory memorial impeaching Mu, begged the Emperor to behead him in order to satisfy the national conscience, and hanged himself.

So died a sincere but misguided patriot. But the sequel was equally significant, illustrating the cross-currents and inscrutable depths of life in the Forbidden City. On the morning after Wang's suicide an official named Ch'en, one of Mu's partisans and a Secretary of the Grand Council, noticed that Wang did not appear as usual for audience. As soon as his routine duties were ended, he hurried to Wang's house to ascertain the cause of his absence. There, in the main hall, he found the body still hanging, it being the unwritten law that

[1] Who weakly advocated making peace with the Ch'in Tartars. His statue is still spat upon by the vulgar in the temple where it stands.

when a member of the Council commits suicide (no infrequent penalty of greatness in China) the body must not be cut down until the Emperor has been informed and issued his further orders in the matter.

Wang's son showed the valedictory memorial to Ch'en, who read it and said: "The Emperor was very angry with His Excellency your father yesterday. If you present this memorial, your father will obtain no posthumous honours and your own career will be ruined. You had better suppress it." A fellow-provincial of Wang's, also of Mu's party, came in at this moment and concurred in the advice which Ch'en had given. Wang's family thereupon begged Ch'en to indite and substitute another memorial; Ch'en did so, adding that Wang had died suddenly of heart failure. Tao Kuang was greatly grieved and full of remorse for what had happened, conferred high posthumous honours on his faithful servant. Afterwards, when Ch'en showed the valedictory memorial to Mu, he was much startled and expressed deep gratitude for what Ch'en had done. His gratitude was genuine and resulted in Ch'en's rapid promotion. In ten years he rose to be President of a Board.

The Chinese, firm believers in the Asiatic doctrine which visits the sins of the father upon the children, even unto the third and fourth generation, point to the fact that Mu Ch'ang-a's descendants have fallen upon evil days. Mu's son was a superintendent of the Imperial Granaries —the Bannermen's Tribute Rice Intendency—but his grandson is a well-known actor of more than doubtful reputation, who plays female parts and is known in the tea-houses by the nickname of the "Virtuous Young Gentleman"—a Chinese Charmides. The moral sense of the *literati* considers this a fitting sequel to the career of Mu Ch'ang-a, whose only proved offence was that he advised making peace with enemies whom he knew to be stronger than anything that China could bring to bear

THE COURT OF PEKING

against them. Wang's sons were greatly blamed for suppressing their father's patriotic memorial.

The Treaty of Nanking was Mu Ch'ang-a's work, and it served beyond all doubt to postpone for a time the appearance of a British force at the gates of Peking. After the suicide of Wang Ting-lin, there was only one of the Grand Council who opposed Mu's policy, and this in a half-hearted manner.

When the draft of the proposed Treaty of Peace was handed in by Mu, the Emperor took it away with him from the Council. He spent the rest of that day and most of the night in pacing up and down the corridor of his Palace, deep in anxious thought. Several times he was heard to mutter " impossible " and to sigh deeply. At last, at 3 a.m., he stamped his foot and proceeded to the audience chamber, where he affixed the " vermilion pencil " to the draft. This done, he sealed it securely in an envelope and sent it by the hand of a eunuch to the office of the Grand Council. " The Councillors have not arrived," said the eunuch, " the Palace gates are still closed." " Wait there," replied Tao Kuang, " until Mu Ch'ang-a arrives. Give him this envelope but don't let any one else see it." The document sanctioned the signature of the Peace Treaty, but it was only with great reluctance and bitterness of soul that Tao Kuang accepted it. Such was the effect of the first serious impact of the west on the Dragon Throne.

It was in the summer of 1840 that the British fleet first blockaded Canton and, sailing northwards, seized the island of Chusan, which led to the degradation of Lin Tse-hsü and to the appointment of the Manchu Ch'i Shan[1] to be Imperial Commissioner at Canton. It was Ch'i Shan who agreed to the cession of Hongkong (occupied

---

[1] Commonly known in contemporary writings (*vide* Huc's *Tibet*) as Ki shan or Ki shen (Boulger). He was the grandfather of Jui Ch'eng, who surrendered Wu Ch'ang to the rebels in October 1911.

by the British on 26th January, 1841) in exchange for the rendition of Chusan. This-surrender so enraged Tao Kuang, at that time under the influence of the war party, that he deprived Ch'i Shan of his Grand Secretaryship and refused to recognise his negotiations. The Throne (as above stated) insisted on war to the knife and the extermination of the barbarians. Ch'i Shan, according to the Chinese chroniclers, did his best to retrieve the situation by a characteristically Chinese *acte de guerre;* He sent privily to the British Commissioner (Elliott) offering him a beautiful concubine and curios in the hope of cancelling his territorial negotiations; but the barbarians were not amenable to reason in this form, for they proceeded to bombard Bocca Tigris. It was at this stage that Ch'i Shan memorialised the Throne, frankly stating his opinion that further fighting would only make matters worse, " We possess no impregnable defences," said he, " and our military equipment is utterly useless. Our troops are feeble and our subjects disloyal. If we engage in hostilities, disaster will overtake us. For the present, wisdom dictates the adoption of measures of expediency."

Subsequent events and their results, as embodied in the Treaty of Nanking (August 1842) justified Ch'i Shan.

Towards the end of Tao Kuang's reign, a great soldier and statesman made his appearance on the scene, who was to achieve fame in years to come and to assist the great Empress Dowager Tzu Hsi in restoring, for a time, the prestige of the Manchu dynasty. This was Tseng Kuo-fan.[1] Concerning him an interesting story is told by the Chinese annalists, illustrating the inveterate faith in omens, which Tao Kuang shared with all the Sovereigns of the Manchu dynasty.

One night, greatly troubled by tidings of internal rebellion and the persistent truculence of the British,

[1] Vide *China under the Empress Dowager*, p. 64 *et seq.*

he dreamed that the Forbidden City was invaded by a band of ruffians: armed with staves and swords, they pressed upon the Imperial Throne and overturned it. It seemed to him, in his dream, that he stood there, alone, confronting the rebels and helpless to resist them. He called for help, but all his attendants had fled. He was just about to fly from the Palace in hopeless shame and confusion, when a man rushed forward, dispersed the rebels, and replaced the Throne in its former position. The Emperor, overjoyed, was on the point of thanking his rescuer, when he awoke. He never spoke of this dream, but often thought of it, and his deliverer's features were clearly impressed on his memory. Two years afterwards, when a batch of newly elected Hanlin doctors was presented at Court, he recognised in one of them the hero of the dream. This was Tseng Kuo-fan, whose rapid promotion was from that moment assured.

Another story, told by the Chinese to account for Tseng Kuo-fan's meteoric advancement, may, or may not be true, but in any case it throws some light on the relations existing between the Sovereign and his chief advisers and on the secret of Mu Ch'ang-a's great influence at Court.

Mu, knowing Tseng Kuo-fan as a member of the Hanlin Academy, had a high opinion of his talents. One day when the Emperor was discussing with him the literary ability of the Academicians, Mu replied: "There is literary talent in abundance, but Tseng Kuo-fan is almost the only one worthy of high office. He has remarkable knowledge of State affairs and never fails to notice everything." Mu subsequently told Tseng what he had said, and a few days later there came an order from the Emperor for Tseng to attend for audience. He went out to the Summer Palace and was given the menu for the day, which by prescribed custom, officials received at special audience must take with them to the audience chamber and formally present to the Emperor. He was escorted by a eunuch to a small chamber and directed to await the Imperial summons.

The day wore on to sunset, but no summons came. At last a message was brought, ordering him to present himself again on the following morning. Tseng, quite at a loss, hurried to Mu's residence, to ask him the meaning of the procedure. For a while Mu was perplexed, but suddenly a light seemed to flash upon him. "Were there any scrolls or books in the room in which you waited?" he asked. "Yes, the walls were covered with scrolls, but I was so nervous about my audience that I never noticed them."

Mu stamped his foot : "That's bad," said he. He then summoned his confidential servant and handed him a bank note for 400 taels. "Take that to the Palace and find out into which room Tseng *tajen* was shown to-day. Then bribe the eunuch in charge to allow you to copy every one of the scrolls on the wall. Come back as soon as possible."

Turning to Tseng, he said : "You had better stay here to-night; we will go to the Palace together in the morning." About midnight the messenger returned and handed a copy of the scrolls on the wall to Mu. They were all autograph homilies by the last three Emperors, advice on the art of government and admonitions to officials. They contained allusions to various events and to many officials of the three reigns. Only a man possessed of exceptional knowledge of Chinese political history could explain these allusions. His Majesty had wished to test Tseng's abilities and to ascertain if Mu's commendation of him was fully warranted. Mu handed the document to Tseng : "Study this carefully," he said, "You will find it a ladder to promotion."

Next day, when the hour of audience arrived, the Emperor questioned Tseng for nearly an hour concerning

THE COURT OF PEKING

the various matters recorded on the scrolls, and was greatly pleased by Tseng's apt answers.

Tao Kuang's successor, his fourth son, who misgoverned the Empire under the reign-title of Hsien Feng, was the worst example of debauched degeneracy in the history of the dynasty. Here again the Chinese chroniclers tell a tale which, if true, shows how the wit of one man, intelligently applied to things apparently trivial, may upset the counsels of kings and affect the destinies of millions.

Towards the end of his reign, Tao Kuang, concerned as to the succession, had practically decided to confer it upon his sixth, and favourite, son Prince Kung, a young man infinitely superior in character and intelligence to him who eventually became Heir to the Throne. It happened, however, that the latter's tutor, Ts'ao Chen-yung, knew of the Emperor's predilection, and, naturally, desiring to enhance his own position, cast about for some means of inducing the Sovereign to change his mind and to confer the succession upon his pupil. In this he was successful.

The Emperor, following the dynastic tradition, had given orders one day that his sons should go hunting in the Southern Park. Etiquette required that a Prince who had not completed his studies should ask his tutor for permission to absent himself for the day. The fourth Prince therefore attended at the lecture room in the Palace, and found his tutor there alone. The Prince went up, and making the bow which ceremony requires, asked for leave. Ts'ao asked for what purpose, and he answered: "The Emperor wishes me to take a day's shooting." Ts'ao whispered to him: " A-ko,[1] take my advice: when you reach the park, sit you and watch the others shooting. Do not fire a shot, and give orders to

[1] The Manchu word used in addressing or speaking of Princes, meaning literally " Elder Brother."

your huntsmen not to set any traps. If the Emperor asks you for your reason for this, at the end of the day, tell him that at this spring season it is not right to take life, because both beasts and birds have their young to take care of, and such slaughter is a violation of natural harmony. Take care not to quarrel with your brothers but do not endeavour to emulate them. If you, A-ko, will only remember this, you are certain to win His Majesty's approval, for I know his disposition. On this hinges your whole future, either one of glory or comparative obscurity. Be careful; do not forget."

The Prince carried out these instructions, and Prince Kung secured the largest bag. He was elated, and seeing his brother's beaters standing empty-handed around him, chaffed him on having taken no part in the chase. He then asked him his reasons for not shooting. "Oh, for no particular reason. I am not very well and did not feel like violent exercise."

When the Princes returned in the evening, and reported to their father, only Hsien Feng had an empty bag. To Tao Kuang's questions he replied exactly as his tutor had told him to do. The Emperor was greatly delighted, and said: "This is the conduct of a superior man," and from that day decided to make him his heir.

In later years, when Tao Kuang had passed away, Hsien Feng raised his tutor to the rank of Assistant Grand Secretary, but he died before attaining to still higher honours. The Emperor wept bitterly and proceeded in person to offer a sacrifice to his remains, besides conferring upon him the highest posthumous honours given to a Chinese during the last century.

So Hsien Feng, winning his father's favour after the manner of Jacob, reigned in his stead and hastened the swift decline of the Manchu dynasty.

CHAPTER XVII

HSIEN FENG AND T'UNG CHIH: THE FACILE DESCENT

THE inner history of the Court and Government of China, from the accession of Hsien Feng in 1851 down to the death of the Empress Tzŭ Hsi in 1908, has already been told in *China Under the Empress Dowager*. The following chapters are supplementary to that work, and intended only to throw some additional light on the men and chief events of that period, and particularly on the life of the Court.

In the persons of the two Emperors, Hsien Feng and T'ung Chih, father and son, the tree of demoralisation brought forth its predestined fruits, whose evil savour was to infect the Forbidden City henceforth until the passing of the dynasty. Hsien Feng came to the Throne, at the age of nineteen, a thoroughly dissolute and depraved specimen of humanity, physically and morally contemptible. He lived to see his Empire ravaged by the Taiping rebellion and preserved only by the timely help of the despised European. He died, a fugitive from Peking, his capital desecrated for the first time in the history of the Manchus by the presence of invaders, his Palace burned and his treasures looted. Peking, that for over two hundred years had known security under the Manchu rule, learned under Hsien Feng the first of many bitter lessons, receiving in the mild visitation of the

Anglo-French armies a warning and a foretaste of the grievous calamities that have now left it a city of the destitute.

Before two years had passed of the ten years of his ill starred reign, Hsien Feng's Throne was tottering under the repeated blows struck at it by the triumphant forces of the Taipings; the rebel chief had proclaimed himself Emperor and established his capital at Nanking. Whatever was left of virility and patriotism at Peking gnashed its teeth in impotent rage, not so much because of the imminence of the danger, as because of the hopeless depravity of the Sovereign and the men whom he delighted to honour. Rome was burning whilst China's Nero not only fiddled, but danced obscenely to his own music. Whilst province after province passed through fire and sword to acknowledge the sway of the Rebel Emperor, the Lord of Heaven busied himself with the provision of new lights for his harem or joined his evil genius, the notorious Minister Su Shun, in orgies of unspeakable debauch in the low haunts of the Chinese quarter.

The following well-authenticated story illustrates the frame of mind in which the Emperor and the Court of the Great Pure Dynasty prepared to meet the most serious crisis of the Taiping Rebellion, at the moment of the fall of Nanking (March 1853). It recalls vividly to mind the attitude of the eunuch-ridden Mings, eating, drinking and making merry when Li Tzŭ-ch'eng and his army were at the very gates of the capital. The parallel is completed by the fact that, thanks to the evil influence of men like Ho Shen and Su Shun, the eunuchs' power in the Palace had been slowly but surely increasing since the death of Ch'ien Lung, and was now a conspicuous factor in the corruption of a Court sunken in luxury and gross living.

The spring of 1853 had been appointed for the selection of handmaidens of Manchu stock to enter the Palace.

THE COURT OF PEKING

The Court Chamberlains and eunuchs had listed and collected a large number of nominees for the harem, and on the day after that which brought the news of the fall of Nanking, a long line of these young women stood waiting, at dawn, outside the gate of the Palace of Feminine Repose. Amongst these girls was one, the daughter of a retired Manchu lieutenant, named Tuan, who wept bitterly at being compelled to leave her father, now a widower, sixty years of age and very poor. She had been able to supply him with the necessaries of life by giving lessons and by needlework, and now she feared he would die of sheer want, for he had no sons or brothers to help him. But there was no way of escaping from her present position: her name had been included in the list of handmaidens eligible, and the captain of her Banner was responsible for her appearance.

The news of the fall of Nanking naturally and forcibly disturbed the even tenour of Hsien Feng's day, and compelled him to discuss with the Grand Council a situation so fraught with danger to his Government and House. Even Su Shun himself was greatly disturbed, the Censorate buzzing like a wasps' nest and memorials pouring in. The moment was unpropitious for dalliance; audiences must be held and orders given. It was nearly sunset before the business of the day was done and Hsien Feng could give a thought to the bevy of women expectant at his gates. They had stood about waiting patiently all day, many without food and all very nervous; by evening most of them were completely exhausted and many were in tears.

One of the eunuchs in charge rebuked them for weeping, and said: " His Majesty will soon be coming to inspect you. How dare you behave in this unseemly way? Has the whip no terrors for you?" On hearing this they all trembled and wept the more, and none dared reply to the eunuch except the motherless maiden, who answered him in a clear, firm voice, saying: "I have been forced to leave my home and to enter the Palace. If I am selected for service here, it means that I shall be imprisoned for the rest of my days and never see my father again. In life we shall be separated; in death divided. Can you wonder if I weep? Any one with a heart must do so. I am not afraid to die, and care nought for your threatened punishment! Have not the Taipings seized the Yangtsze Valley, and now that Nanking has fallen, is not half of the Empire as good as lost? Yet the Son of Heaven is not concerned to find competent generals to take the field and repel the invader, so that his Empire may be saved; his time is given to the selection of women who may minister to his pleasures. He drags the daughters of the people from their homes and imprisons them in his Palace, where they will never breathe again the air of freedom, so that he may enjoy himself for a brief space! Little he recks of the impending fate of his ancestral altars and the tutelary gods! The Taiping host will soon be knocking at his Palace gates, and then the nine spirits of his ancestors will lack their burnt offerings and worship of appointed days. I do not fear death: and for your threats of the whip I care nought at all."

At this outburst, spoken in a loud voice, the eunuch endeavoured to quiet her by putting his hand over her mouth, but at that moment the Emperor, in his chair, appeared upon the scene. The eunuch bound her hands and led her to the presence, bidding her kneel. But she refused to do obeisance and looked defiantly at the Emperor. Now His Majesty had heard the last few words of her speech, and good-naturedly asked what all the trouble was about, whereupon she deliberately repeated what she had said. Hsien Feng was delighted with her spirit: "You are a true heroine," said he; "untie her hands and lead her to see the Empress." The Chinese chroniclers, who like to make such stories end happily

THE COURT OF PEKING

and with a good moral, aver that Hsien Feng gave this outspoken maiden in marriage to one of the Imperial Princes who had just lost his wife (it being the custom for the Emperor to decide the matrimonial affairs of the Imperial Clan), and in this position she was able to support her father in his old age.

At the beginning of Hsien Feng's reign there were, as usual, two parties about the Throne, the one honest and patriotic according to its lights, the other utterly corrupt. The acknowledged leader of the powers of evil in high places was the Imperial Clansman Su Shun, who set himself to debauch the body and soul of the young Emperor by every kind of wickedness. Not that Hsien Feng required much enticing in that direction, for his tendencies were those of a vicious sensualist from his youth up. Su Shun merely supplied the match of experience and suggestion to a brand all ready for the burning. Before long he became the *âme damnée* of the depraved monarch, whose physical condition bore testimony to his way of living; often, after a night of prolonged orgies, his legs tottered under him at the hour of audience and on one occasion he was unable properly to perform the sacrificial rites at the Temple of Heaven.

The only official who bravely tried to counteract the evil influence of Su Shun at Court was the Grand Secretary, Po Sui;[1] an honest, straightforward man, whose blunt speech and fearless criticisms gradually came to offend the Emperor. Su Shun conspired with the Princes Yi and Cheng (who later, upon Hsien Feng's death, joined him in usurping the Regency) to get rid of their uncompromising and plain-spoken opponent, and, judging by documentary and circumstantial evidence, there appears to be good reason for believing that Hsien Feng was a party to the plot. It ended in Po Sui's decapitation

[1] Vide *China under the Empress Dowager*, p. 31, where, by a clerical error, his name is wrongly given as Po Chun.

on the public execution ground, and the complete supremacy of Su Shun and his party from 1859 until the death of Hsien Feng, and Tzŭ Hsi's successful *coup d'état* against the usurping Regents.

The scheme which Su Shun initiated for the undoing and judicial murdering of Po Sui is worth describing, because it reveals something of the depths of subterranean intrigue that lay behind the gilded splendour of the Dragon Throne; at the same time it illustrates and explains the complicated machinery by which the instinct of Chinese rulers has always fairly safeguarded the road to public office—that is, the road to wealth—from the worst abuses of venality and nepotism. The system of public service examinations, with all its elaborate (and, on the whole, effective) precautions against chicanery and fraud, has probably contributed more than any other factor to the permanent stability of China's civilisation. It is surely a striking testimony to the intuitive wisdom of that civilisation and to its binding force, that, even in times of chaos and corruption, China's worst rulers have usually realised the all-importance of honesty and fair play in the examinations for the literary degrees, whereby the humblest subject could rise to the highest offices in the land. Even the Taipings established a similar competitive system, at their Court of a day, in Nanking.

At the examinations held for the Metropolitan degree, in the autumn of 1858, Po Sui was Chief Examiner. Thoroughly honest and incapable of favouritism himself, he seems to have suffered from the failing, common enough amongst high officials, of taking too much for granted in his subordinates. The position of Chief Examiner, at all times one of great dignity, was then one of peculiar and dangerous responsibility, because for some time past there had been ugly rumours of bribery and impersonation in connection with other examinations.

THE COURT OF PEKING

It is doubtful whether these had come to the ears of Po Sui, whose character was easy-going and trustful; in any case, contemporary opinions and posterity alike have acquitted him of all suspicion in reference to the cases which, thanks to the malevolence of Su Shun, cost him his life.

Po Sui had a confidential servant (of the type of Gehazi) named Chin Hsiang, who saw and seized opportunities for himself in his master's high office. To him there came secretly a Manchu named P'ing Ling, a man of good family but disreputable habits, who made a living by singing at banquets in woman's attire with his face powdered. Being young and good-looking, this ne'er-do-weel cherished ambitions to enter the public service. He therefore bribed Chin Hsiang with a thousand taels to secure for him a high place at the examination. Chin Hsiang arranged for a substitute to enter in Ping's name, whose essay was awarded the seventh place on the list.

Another rich but illiterate candidate, a native of Canton, named Lo, also bribed Chin Hsiang, who in this case went so far, with the help of the assistant examiner, as to tamper with the order of the successful papers, including Lo's amongst them, after it had been relegated to the supplementary list by the examiners. When the revising examiner came to inspect Lo's essay, he saw at once that an irregularity had been committed, but, thinking that it must have occurred with Po Sui's knowledge, made no comment at the time. It is possible that he foresaw an opportunity of making friends of the mammon of unrighteousness and gaining the favour of the powerful Su Shun. In any case, he informed one of the Censors, named Meng, of Lo's case, and Meng prepared a memorial impeaching the whole staff of examiners, with Po Sui as their responsible chief.

Before handing in the memorial, Meng happened to be dining one evening at the Restaurant of Abundant

Blessings in the Coal Market Street, when he overheard a conversation between P'ing Ling and a couple of actors who were dining with him. P'ing Ling was in his cups and was talking in a loud voice. The Censor did not know him by sight, but pricked up his ears at the following remark: "Not long ago I was no better off than either of you; people looked down upon me as the scum of society. But now I have taken a high place at the examination and that is all over. If you like I can help you fellows to attain success by the same means, when the next examination takes place. It is only a matter of paying big squeezes, and there's no reason at all why you shouldn't come out near the top of the list."

Upon this the Censor made inquiries, and ascertained P'ing Ling's name. Waiting until the actors had become thoroughly fuddled with wine, he proceeded to introduce himself as an old family acquaintance to P'ing. Telling him that he was one of the unsuccessful candidates from Nanking, he asked how he could arrange to be successful at the next attempt. P'ing, too drunk to be suspicious, told him the whole story. Next day the Censor, adding this new material to his memorial, laid the whole plot before the Throne. Hsien Feng was greatly incensed and bade the Board of Rites bring for his inspection the successful essays of P'ing Ling and Lo, which, in accordance with custom, had been filed in the archives. After perusing the essays, the Emperor ordered that these two candidates should forthwith undergo a special examination in the Imperial library. The Emperor himself selected the themes, the prose essay being "In what does happiness consist?" and the verse theme, "A wise man hesitates to talk in front of a parrot." Prince Cheng and Su Shun were appointed supervisors of this examination. As both the candidates were illiterate, the result, as may be imagined, was laughable enough, except for those concerned. Their names were erased from the list of successful candidates; Lo committed suicide, and P'ing Ling died in prison. The examiners were then handed over to the Board of Punishments.

At this stage Su Shun appeared upon the scene. Fate had delivered his adversary into his hand, for he, Su Shun, was President of the Board of Punishments. When first the Board reported on Po Sui's case, Hsien Feng was reluctant to impose the death penalty, upon which Su Shun and his confederates (the Princes Yi and Cheng) insisted, but Su was able to persuade the weak and dissolute young monarch to adopt stern measures. Hsien Feng knew that Po Suï was a just man and rightly popular, even as he knew that Su Shun was detested for his avarice and cruelty; he knew that Po Sui had deserved well of the State and that his offence in the present instance was one of carelessness at most; he therefore hesitated and summoned the Grand Council to discuss the matter. Finally he was persuaded to issue the decree which condemned Po Sui to death, and appointed Su Shun and Chao Kuang to superintend the execution. This decree reads: " Prince Yi and his colleagues have memorialised me in regard to the examination abuses case of last autumn, and submitted their proposals as to the penalties to be imposed. I have carefully perused and considered their report. There are certain points in it to which I desire to call the attention of my Ministers. The examination system is intended for the selection of candidates for government service, and severe penalties are imposed for malpractices and favouritism on the part of the examiners. So far, during our dynasty, there has been no case of a member of the Commission endangering his life by conniving at malpractices. But now, to our sorrow and surprise, the Grand Secretary, Po Sui, has gone so far as to defy the law and to forget the benefits bestowed upon him. As a Grand Secretary and Minister of the Presence for many years, besides having held office as Grand Councillor and

Comptroller of the Household, how could Po Sui have been ignorant of the law, especially as his own career began at a public examination? He acceded to the proposal of his servant, Chin Hsiang, to be allowed to substitute a revised essay for that of one of the candidates. If Chin Hsiang were still alive, there would be no difficulty in establishing the facts before the Tribunal of Justice. I have precedents to guide my decision in the dynastic laws, and am by no means straining a point to serve the ends of justice. All I am now considering is the evidence of Po Sui himself, to which I have given careful consideration, as I find that although there are certain extenuating circumstances, the law must be allowed to take its course.

"At this point I pause and the tears flow down my cheeks.[1] In accordance with the advice of my Princes and Ministers, I command that Po Sui be summarily decapitated and that Su Shun and Chao Kuang shall duly superintend his execution in the public square. The examination secretaries, P'u An, Lo Hung-yi and Li Hung-ling, are also to be decapitated, that the law may be vindicated. The assistant examiner, Chu Feng-piao, is to be cashiered, for I cannot believe that he actually connived at his colleagues' misconduct; otherwise, he, too, would have been severely punished. The Hanlin Compiler, Tsou Shih-lin, who, in his capacity as junior examiner, amended the composition of the successful candidate (P'ing Ling), since cashiered, is henceforth and for ever debarred from official employment. Twelve of the successful candidates are to be brought up for further inquiries, and the Ministry of Rites is to report on the penalties to be imposed on the remainder of the examiners. The proctors who were on duty during the examination are to report, explaining how two characters in one of the essays came to be altered during the process of collecting

[1] In reading Imperial decrees of this type one is frequently reminded of Mr. Pecksniff and " the duty he owed to society."

the papers. Three of the candidates, Hsieh Sen-chih, Hsiang Yüan-p'ei and Li Tan-hua are to be sent under escort from their native places for trial at Peking.

"Henceforward, the examiners at all all-important public examinations, must cleanse their hearts and rid themselves of every sort of prejudice, so that no candidate shall enter the Government service by unfair means. The candidates are each and all to pay more heed to their moral character and to inculcate self-respect; let them refrain from intrigue and from base attempts to win favour, taking warning from the present example. Thus will my object be attained, which is to raise the standard of morals among the scholars of the Empire: with this ideal before me, I have not shrunk from administering exemplary punishment as the law demands. Surely you, my Ministers, will sympathise with my ideas, and appreciate the motive which animates me."

So Su Shun and the powers of evil triumphed. On the day fixed for Po Sui's decapitation, he and the other condemned officials were conveyed in carts to the place of execution, known as the Western Market, where they were to await the arrival of the Palace decree finally confirming the order. Po Sui wore the costume which custom requires in the case of high officials condemned to be beheaded; he was dressed in plain black silk and his official hat was shorn of its red tassel—a sign of mourning. On arrival at the place of execution he prostrated himself in the direction of the Palace and gave thanks for favours received in the past. After this he turned to his son, Chung Lien, saying: "The Emperor will surely spare my life; he is sending me to the execution ground as a warning, but at the last moment I feel sure that he will grant a reprieve. When it arrives, I shall go to the Temple of the 'Evening Ray' and wait there until arrangements are made for me to set off to my place of banishment. Do you return home and prepare the various things which I shall need on the journey." (When high officials are sentenced to death, the Throne frequently commutes the capital penalty at the last moment to one of perpetual banishment. Po fully expected to be sent to Turkestan or to the post roads).

He had scarcely finished speaking, when Chao Kuang, the second official supervising the execution and one of Po Sui's oldest friends, arrived in his chair. His eyes were red with weeping. He had been waiting at the Palace for the final confirmation or modification of the sentence. As soon as Po Sui saw him, he said : " It's all over. Left to himself, the Emperor would never have been so pitiless : Su Shun has been my evil genius from first to last. It is he who has hardened His Majesty's heart. After all, what does my death matter ? The day is close at hand when Su Shun will share my fate. You must look forward to that day."

With that, he beckoned to the headsman, who came forward and fell on one knee, saying : " If Your Excellency the Grand Secretary will be pleased to kneel down, I will give you a reverent send-off to the next world." Po Sui did so, and the executioner, with knee bent in respect, deftly cut off his head at the first stroke.

Before signing the fatal order, Hsien Feng had summoned Chao Kuang to the presence. The Emperor was seated on the Throne with the vermilion pencil in his hand but seemed reluctant to sign the death warrant. For a long time he hesitated, repeatedly exclaiming : " Although legally his crime deserves death, there are extenuating circumstances." Su Shun replied : " Whatever the circumstances, this is no case for your clemency. Your Majesty has admitted as much."

The weak monarch still hesitated to sign. Finally, in desperation, he handed the pencil to Su Shun, who promptly marked against Po Sui's name the fatal hook. Chao Kuang burst into tears and departed for the place of execution.

THE COURT OF PEKING

After Po Sui's death, one of his *protégés* presented the following pair of memorial scrolls, which were much admired as an example of skill in dealing with a delicate subject:

" In life he attained to high honours, in death he was unfortunate. Come bounteous dew and rain, or come the thunder bolt of wrath, all proceed alike from the Imperial will."

" The Minister's gate may have been like a market,[1] but the Minister's heart was pure as water. Do you, majestic Heaven and divine earth, look down on him with pity, loyal and forsaken."

Two years afterwards, when the masterful statecraft of Tzǔ Hsi had defeated all the plots of the usurping Regents, Su Shun met his death on the same spot which had witnessed the execution of his victim, Po Sui.[2] But whereas Po Sui's death was universally deplored, that of Su Shun was welcomed by the populace of Peking with general rejoicings. He went to his doom, clad in a long white robe of sackcloth. As he emerged from the Shunchih gate of the inner city on his way to the execution ground, it was noticed that his face was covered with dust, for a high wind was blowing. Arriving at the Western Market, he alighted somewhat feebly from the open cart in which the condemned are conveyed, and began to say a few words of farewell to Prince Jui, who had been commanded by Tzǔ Hsi to superintend the execution. He was not given time to finish, but was dragged forward, made to kneel and in a moment his head fell, his death being greeted by loud applause from the crowd. The same headsman officiated who had dispatched Po Sui two years before. Not one of Su Shun's family was present to see the last of him: his sons had gone to the gate of the prison, but

[1] This in allusion to the train of clients attending on an influential personage.
[2] Vide *China under the Empress Dowager*, pp. 47, 48.

had been driven away by the gatekeepers with whips. Rarely had any high official achieved Su Shun's measure of unpopularity with the people of Peking.

When officials of high rank are unfortunate enough to suffer the fate of public decapitation, it is the custom that the executioner, in exchange for a heavy fee, stabs his victim to the heart before severing his head, the idea being that by this means little or no blood would be shed. On coming forward, the executioner is presented with a basin and towel wherewith to perform ablutions. In Su Shun's case, however, all these delicate attentions were omitted. It is also the custom that after the execution the headsman shall immediately sew the head on again, almost as it as soon falls to the ground : for this a fee of 1000 taels is usually claimed.[1] But Su Shun's body was left where it fell, and the dogs came and licked up his blood. His head was hung for many days in the public square.

Su Shun's confederates, the usurping Regents, the Princes Yi and Cheng, shared his fate in 1861, by order of Tzŭ Hsi. Both met death with philosophic calm. Prince Yi's family were permitted to be present in the Court of the Imperial Clan, and he gave them elaborate instructions as to his funeral and the division of his property. He desired to be clad in white silk robes and particularly asked that his portrait (which is always painted after death and has a semi-sacred significance in connection with the rites of ancestral worship) should also be mounted on plain silk. Prince Cheng showed signs of agitation, and his last utterances were indistinct, but in his case, too, the family was present.

The nooses used for both were covered with delicate silken material. Two low tea tables were placed in the "empty chamber" of the Clan Court,[2] and the two

[1] This was done in the case of Chi Hsiu, who was decapitated in 1901 in the presence of the allied troops.

[2] The name is euphemistic, in the sense that the room was never to be tenanted except by Princes or Clansmen under sentence.

THE COURT OF PEKING

Princes were then invited to mount the tables and adjust the nooses on their necks amidst the lamentations of their respective families. Prince Yi had no sooner complied, and the table been drawn away, than he expired. Prince Cheng was less fortunate. He was a man of enormous weight, and no sooner had he placed the noose around his neck than the rope broke and he fell heavily to the ground. At the second attempt he was successful. The underlings at the Clan Court naturally availed themselves of the opportunity to squeeze the unfortunate families of the once all-powerful Princes. Their relatives had to pay out over one hundred thousand taels before being allowed to remove the bodies and arrange for their honourable burial.

In August 1861, Hsien Feng died, a fugitive and a physical wreck, at Jehol, in his thirtieth year, leaving the Throne to his only son, the Emperor T'ung Chih, then a child of six. During his minority, under the Regency of Tzŭ Hsi and her colleague the Empress Tzŭ An, the tide of disintegration was temporarily checked, the Government being largely in the hands of wise and liberal statesmen of the type of Prince Kung and Wen Hsiang, and the Imperial armies led by capable generals, like Tseng Kuo-fan and Tso Tsung-t'ang.

Of T'ung Chih's reign and his personal influence on the destinies of the Empire, it is unnecessary to say much, for he attained his majority and assumed nominal control of the Government in February 1873, and died in January 1875. That he was never intended to live and to deprive Tzŭ Hsi of her undisputed authority, is certain. Equally certain that she encouraged, or took no steps to restrain, the vicious tendencies which were matters of notoriety in Peking, and which eventually led to his death from a disease contracted in the low haunts of the Chinese city.[1] But the following notes, taken from the reminiscences of

[1] Vide *China under the Empress Dowager*, pp. 119, 120.

an aged eunuch, retired from the Palace after the death of Tzŭ Hsi in 1908, afford instructive information regarding certain details of the inner history of the Court at that period, and notably on T'ung Chih's marriage to the virtuous and pathetically unfortunate A-lu-te.

Before his marriage, says this eunuch's diary, the young Emperor was in the habit of visiting the theatres and brothels of the Ch'ien Men quarter in the company of a eunuch named Chou, for which purpose (as the Palace gates were closed) he had an opening made in the wall just outside the Western Gate of Perpetual Peace. At this point Chou's cart, drawn by a fast pacing mule, would await him, and it became matter of common gossip in the capital that the Son of Heaven was frequently mixed up in drunken and disreputable brawls, and would often return to the Palace, even after he had attained his majority, long after the hour fixed for audiences. In the day time he would frequent, incognito, the book and picture shops of the Liu Li-ch'ang to purchase lewd carvings and paintings of the kind to which the dissolute patricians of Peking have always been partial.

T'ung Chih hated and feared his mother's favourite Chief Eunuch, the notorious An Te-hai—who, if the common report of the Palace spoke truly, was no eunuch. He also disliked Su Shun, who used to bully and tease the boy.

When the time arrived, in the autumn of 1872, for arranging the young Emperor's marriage, which took place early in the following year, the two maidens selected from the large number of eligible candidates were A-Lu-te, (the daughter of Ch'ung Ch'i), and a daughter of Feng Hsia, the friend of Jung Lu. Tzŭ Hsi preferred the latter, whilst her colleague, the Empress of the Eastern Palace, preferred A-Lu-te. As the Co-Regent Empresses could not agree, Tzŭ Hsi finally proposed that T'ung Chih should be left to make his own choice: "Let him see both girls [1] and he can select the one he prefers." Tzŭ Hsi felt no doubt that T'ung Chih would be guided by her wishes, and she was therefore much displeased when the Emperor, on being ushered in, and having the position explained to him, replied without hesitation: " I choose A-Lu-te as my Empress." Tzŭ Hsi could not very well say more at the moment, so A-Lu-te became Senior Consort, and the Discerning Concubine, as Lady Feng was now called,[2] became Senior Secondary Consort.

After the marriage, Tzŭ Hsi used often to scold and revile her son for his foolish choice. " You ought to have done as I bade you and chosen the Discerning Concubine. I find her intelligent and dutiful, whilst A-Lu-te is a feather-head, who knows nothing about Court etiquette. Unless she amends I shall have to consider her deposition. In any case, I must ask you to cease dallying about her Palace, instead of attending to Government business." She would also frequently instruct the eunuch Li Lien-ying to convey the " Discerning Concubine " at night to the monarch's bedchamber, in the hope that she might present him with an heir to the Throne, and thus secure for herself (Tzŭ Hsi) a long and undisputed tenure of the Regency As etiquette prescribes, Li would carry the Discerning Concubine on his back, with only a cloak thrown over her person, and leave her at the lower end of the Dragon couch, from which position it was her duty to raise herself gradually till she reached the level of the Imperial pillow.

But T'ung Chih cared nought for the lady and avoided her as much as possible. Worried by his mother's inter-

[1] An unusual proceeding, which custom prohibits before the marriage ceremony, as the bridegroom has nothing to do with the selection of his wife.
[2] This lady caused trouble in 1909, by insisting on remaining, in resentment which simulated mourning, at the Eastern Mausolea after the Old Buddha's interment, but the Empress Lung Yü tempted her back to Peking by means of certain concessions as to her precedence and emoluments.

ference in his domestic affairs, he sought distraction in the haunts of the Chinese city, and when he did happen to pass a night in the Forbidden City, he would frequently leave the Discerning One to undisputed possession of the Dragon couch, and take up his quarters in the Palace of Heavenly Purity.

When he fell sick, Tzŭ Hsi pretended to put the blame on A-Lu-te. and soundly rated her for having seduced the Emperor from his mother's influence. His death was a sore blow to his unhappy widow, whose eyes were swollen with weeping. One day her father, a time-serving wretch, came in to see her, and subsequently reported to Tzŭ Hsi as follows : " If the Empress is so melancholy the best thing she can do, for every one's sake, is to follow His Sainted Majesty to the tomb as speedily as possible."

Two hours later she died, and the uncharitable say that Ch'ung Ch'i, anticipating Tzŭ Hsi's wishes, gave her the opium which enabled her to commit suicide, because he foresaw trouble ahead if she gave birth to an heir, and realised that his own position would then be compromised with Tzŭ Hsi. A large and influential party at Court would demand the heir's elevation to the Throne, and unless they succeeded in depriving her of power (which was not likely) Tzŭ Hsi would surely wreak vengeance on A-Lu-te's family. So, like a wise man, he took precautionary measures.

After the death of Hsien Feng in 1861, the vigorous and intelligent policy of his young widow (Tzŭ Hsi), loyally backed by Generals of the stamp of Tseng Kuo-fan and Tso Tsung-t'ang, succeeded in stamping out the Taiping rebellion—greatly assisted, it is true, by Chinese Gordon's "ever-victorious army." It had lasted for thirteen years— devasting nine provinces and bringing death and desolation to untold millions. Since 1855, the first high incentive and semi-religious character of the movement had completely disappeared; it had become a vast and ruthless horde of undisciplined bandits which lived, *au jour le jour*, upon the country. As it is to-day, so it was then; China's rebels could fight and could take cities, but they had no system and no cohesion to offer in place of that which they had contrived to overthrow. As it is to-day, so it was then; the plunder lust, the insatiable frenzy of loot, demoralised both rebels and Imperialists; so that, until the arrival on the scene of General Gordon and new military ideals, hostilities dragged on almost aimlessly, to the ever-increasing distress of non-combatants.

Nevertheless, it is well to remember that the Taiping rebellion, like all other great risings in China against an unpopular dynasty, represented originally a genuine intention on the part of its leaders to put an end to very real grievances and to replace the Manchu dynasty by something more efficient and more righteous. The annals of the time prove that, even at the last, the movement retained a remnant of leaders who kept their first high ideals and endeavoured to restrain their lawless forces. The following brief extracts from contemporary chronicles relate to the last days of Li Hsiu-ch'eng, with whose death, after the fall of Nanking (July 1864), the rebellion was practically ended.[1]

To this man, known far and wide throughout Kiangsu as the "Patriotic Prince," the Taiping rebellion owed much of its original success, and whatever semblance of orderly government it had been able to evolve at the Court of the "Heavenly King." His military genius was undeniable, and his personal character entirely admirable; so much so, that not only was he idolised by his soldiers, but by the people, whom he protected, so far as in him lay, against oppression. He was a strict disciplinarian, insisted on the regular payment of the troops under his

[1] For an account of his death at the hands of Tseng Kuo-fan, *vide* the latter's memorial, *China under the Empress Dowager*, p. 73.

command, and punished rape with decapitation. He combined the qualities of a good fighting man with a gentle and pious nature; a conscientious observer of the rites of his Buddhistic faith, he gave liberal allowances to the families of those who had fallen in battle, and instituted an annual service of commemorative masses on the Buddhist All Souls' Day, at which he was wont to appear in person, burning incense and joining in the litany for the dead. A brave fighter and a gentleman.[1]

It was Li Hsiu-ch'eng who held Soochow against Gordon's army in the winter of 1863. Just before the fall of the city, in December, the rebel garrison and the populace were in desperate straits. The troops had had no regular meals for days; nevertheless, the example of Li's indomitable courage kept up their spirits. He dispatched one of his officers with a letter, asking for help, addressed to Hung, the "Heavenly King," at Nanking. His messenger was captured and killed by the Imperialists, and his letter was preserved by the officer into whose hands it fell, who subsequently—admiring Li's splendid courage—sent copies of it to his friends. The letter was written in a fine running hand, and shows not only a brave spirit but every evidence of deep scholarship:

" From this beleaguered city," it reads, " I indite these lines. Our provisions are exhausted; in the camp, the cooking pots are empty. The stove is cold and there is no drug that can allay the pangs of hunger. Corpses are

[1] It is interesting to note that President Yuan Shih-k'ai gave orders last year, to the office for conferring Patents of distinction, to make inquiry concerning the descendants, now surviving, of the Taiping leaders. The Office reported that the eldest son of Li Hsiu-ch'eng, named Li Cheng-hsiang, is now in his fifty-sixth year. He has forwarded to the Patent Office a record of the Taiping rebellion, written by his father, which is to be incorporated in the official history of China. Posthumous honours will probably be conferred upon Li Hsiu-ch'eng. From this it will be seen that no man's words or deeds are ever finally condemned in Chinese history. The filial piety of his descendants, and other things, will serve in time to rehabilitate his character for posterity.

carved in pieces and mothers sell their sons for food. For many days past we have been shouting 'Dinner is ready' at meal times, so as to deceive the enemy concerning our lack of provisions. Our plight is grievous, resembling that of the turtle in the tureen : our danger is as that of the tiger at bay upon the mountain precipice. Your Majesty has founded a new Empire, but if its roots be shaken, the branches are agitated. Soochow is your Majesty's lower jaw : if the lips perish, the teeth must speedily decay. As soon as you have been able to force a way through the beleaguering armies which invest Nanking, it behoves you to dispatch troops to our assistance. I send these few lines beseeching you to take care of your health. Interrupting the whetting of my spear, I write this message, earnestly praying for your welfare."

Li escaped from Soochow, that city of dire carnage, and lived to take part in the final act of the great drama when, at the fall of Nanking in the following July, the "Heavenly King" met his fate. Li escaped from Nanking, accompanied only by two lads. One of them was the second son of the "Heavenly King," Hung Fu-tien, and the other was Li's own page. Hung could not ride, and soon got separated from his companions (he was subsequently captured by the Imperialists). Li and his page hurried on in the darkness and finally lost their way. They were resting at daybreak on a wooded hill when eight woodcutters came up. One of them recognised Li and addressed him as the Patriotic Prince. Li begged them not to betray him. "If you can find a way of taking me safely to Huchou in Chekiang, I will give you 30,000 taels." The men, moved to tears at his plight, agreed to do so.

At evening they descended the hill and came to their hamlet of Chien Hsi—"West of the Ravine." Their movements were hampered because Li and his page were burdened with a quantity of jewels, besides having a pack mule loaded with gold bars and pearls. The woodcutters hid them in an inner room, and advised Li to disguise himself by shaving his head.[1] He refused, saying: " I am the subject of the Taiping dynasty; our Empire is overthrown and our Sovereign dead. If I am captured and brought before the Manchu Commander, my fate is sealed, I know. But were I to escape capture by shaving my head, I should be false to the principles which made me a rebel."

One of the woodcutters, a man named T'ao, cunning and greedy by nature, longed to secure the large reward offered for Li by betraying him, but he feared his companions, who were loyal to Li. So he found a pretext to go out, and sought acquaintance in the Manchu camp of General Hsiao, whose advice he asked. This man naturally informed one of the General's bodyguard of Li's presence in the neighbouring village, and the General, on hearing the story, detained T'ao, entertaining him with food and wine, and hurriedly dispatched a troop of horsemen to arrest Li. They brought him back, and with him his treasure, which the General seized. Hoping to keep the matter quiet, he then gave orders to have T'ao beheaded, but the man had fled; he subsequently fell a victim to the wrath of his companions, who killed him for his treachery. The General received high hereditary rank for his capture of Li and his treasure, but several of his men were slain by the woodcutters, who, after slaughtering them, made sacrifice to Li's spirit. Tseng Kuo-fan heard of their doing so and had them brought to his headquarters. Boldly and frankly they confessed the truth. Tseng, who greatly admired the rebel leader, praised their loyalty and made them presents, which they reluctantly accepted. Chinese chroniclers deplore the fact that the names of these worthy woodcutters have not been recorded.

The following story describing the manner in which the

[1] The Taipings discarded the tonsure in token of rebellion against the Manchu dynasty.

THE COURT OF PEKING

Imperialists finally took Nanking, goes to show that there was love as well as war in the rebel capital. When the city was finally invested by Tseng Kuo-fan's forces, the key to the position lay at the " Islet of Nine Eddies," and there Hung Hsiu-ch'üan, the rebel king, had stationed a large force. As soon as the Imperialist forces had captured this islet, Nanking was practically at their mercy. Tseng Kuo-fan is usually credited with this exploit, but the fact is that one of the rebels betrayed the secret of the distribution of their forces and this enabled the Imperialist attack to concentrate on the weakest spot.

During the reign of the " Heavenly King " at Nanking, two civil service examinations were held, at the second of which a Kiangsi scholar named Pu Ying-ch'i was third on the list. He was an unusually handsome man and used to call himself a second Ch'en Ping, after a certain beau who played a prominent part in the foundation of the Han dynasty in the second century B.C.

While the Palace examination was proceeding, the " Heavenly King's " younger sister, Hsuan Chiao, watched the candidates from behind a curtain, and was much taken with Pu's good looks. It was she who induced her brother to place him third on the list. When, in due course, he appeared at Court to return thanks, Hung said to him : " You ought really to thank the Divine Sister," and bade a eunuch take him to her presence. Pu knelt before her, and the Divine Sister held out her hand to him, saying : " We shall often meet, for I intend to secure you a good post at Court."

A few days later he was made Chamberlain, and before long his relations with the Divine Sister became something more than brotherly. The Divine Sister had a husband, Li Shao-shen, who was greatly distressed, but feared to interfere in her intrigue.

Now it happened that the " Prince of the East," Yang Hsin-ch'eng, like all the other rebel princes, maintained a staff of ladies who served him as majors domo, ushers, and in other capacities. One of these women, the daughter of a literary man, possessed great skill with her pen, and besides this was superior to the Divine Sister in the matter of good looks. She, too, became infatuated with the handsome Pu, and was for ever inviting him to her boudoir. As this liaison developed, the Divine Sister became exceedingly jealous, but had to endure it, as the "Heavenly King" could not afford to quarrel with the "Prince of the East." For a time Pu played the Don Juan with both fair ladies, but gradually became tired of their charms, and, realising that the Taipings were nearing the end of their tether, he decided to quit Nanking by stealth, and to try to return to his home in Kiangsi.

In this attempt he was captured by General Fu Ssu's men and, hoping to save his life, said: "I have a secret to communicate." Ushered into the General's presence, he said: "The rebels depend on the Islet of Nine Eddies for their supplies; for all their reinforcements come in by that route. This alone has enabled them to hold out so long. You will never take Nanking until you capture the islet. I have with me a plan, upon which you will see marked the disposition of their forces and the emplacements of their guns. One side is practically impregnable, but there is one spot which is open to attack. Take them unawares from that side and you will capture the position as easily as spitting on your fingers. Once the islet is in your possession, their communications are cut and they will be like rats in a trap."

The Imperialists acted on this information and Nanking fell. Pu Ying-ch'i was rewarded with a lieutenant colonelcy, but Chinese chroniclers, who seem, as a class, disposed to sympathise with rebels of all kinds, condemn his action, unkindly observing of him that he served two dynasties, one in a civil, and the other in a military, capacity.

CHAPTER XVIII

THE SORROWS OF HIS MAJESTY KUANG HSÜ

The personality of His Majesty Kuang Hsü was always so overshadowed and dominated by that of the masterful Tzŭ Hsi, even during the years (1889–1898) when he was theoretically in control of the Government, that his individual abilities and aspirations had little scope to shape themselves to any good purpose; and the dynastic annals, compiled under the direction of the "Old Buddha," treat him, generally speaking, as a negligible quantity. For although during her years of nominal retirement, Tzŭ Hsi divested herself of the outward symbols of supreme power, the Emperor himself and all his Court were well aware that the final arbiter of all important questions was still the autocrat who watched events from her retreat at the Summer Palace, whose confidential agents and partisans constituted the dominant party in the metropolitan and provincial Yamêns. At no time did she surrender to the Emperor the fundamental authority to which the official world looked for rewards and punishments; in her hands remained the appointment to all high offices, by which means she created and strengthened ties of personal loyalty to herself. The Emperor on his Throne was a cipher in the inner councils of the State, which drew their inspiration from the fountain head of all favours; of far less account, in the estimation of the mandarinate, than the Chief Eunuch, Li Lien-ying. Except during the hundred days of Reform, which precipitated Tzŭ Hsi's *coup d'état* in 1908 and her return to full and undisguised supremacy, the unfortunate monarch was never able to muster courage or supporters sufficient to enable him to assert himself.

There were, it is true, occasions when he endeavoured to throw off the yoke and to claim rights of independent initiative, especially during the short time when he relied upon the influential support of Chang Yin-huan and the reform leaders at Peking; but his attempts were ever doomed to spend themselves in futility against the solid wall of vested interests and privileges with which the genius of Tzŭ Hsi had surrounded him.

In January 1894, before the outbreak of war with Japan, His Majesty's mind was much exercised at the increasing demoralisation of the public service, brought about by the Chief Eunuch's shameless trafficking in Government appointments of all sorts. In this matter he felt sure of the sympathies of the best men in the public service, whose sense of decency was undoubtedly violated by the outrageous proceedings of Tzŭ Hsi's favourite, and whose interests were thereby imperilled. The *literati* generally and the bulk of conservative officialdom were becoming scandalised by the flagrant venality which sold offices without regard to the qualifications of the buyer, so that Kuang Hsü was emboldened to assert himself. The following instance of a case in which he did so, without evoking a display of the "Benevolent Mother's divine wrath," is instructive.

When the Shanghai Taot'ai-ship fell vacant, on Nieh Ch'i-kuei's promotion to a judgeship, in January 1894, the Grand Councillors handed Kuang Hsü a list of the Taot'ais eligible for preferment and asked His Majesty to make a selection. The Emperor said nothing, but produced a slip of paper from his sleeve, on which was written the name "Lu Po-yang." With a frown he handed it to the Council, and told them to report as to the man's previous career and record. The Councillors retired and investigated their files, but found no such name on any of their lists. They reported accordingly, whereupon Kuang Hsü ordered that the Presidents of the Boards of Civil Office and Revenue be summoned, and instructed to examine into the matter. The Councillors saw that the Emperor had received a hint from Tzŭ Hsi to appoint Lu Po-yang, whatever his record, so they tactfully replied: " If Your Majesty knows the man, it would be best to appoint him without further investigation. It is possible that his name is neither on the Board of Revenue's list nor on that of the Civil Office. And it would not look well to give him the post, after we had inquired and ascertained that he had no claims." Kuang Hsü sighed, and made the appointment.

Not very long afterwards occurred the more flagrant case of Yü Ming. This man was a Manchu attached to the Imperial Household: he had never held any official post, was the head manager of a large firm of building contractors at Peking, and had purchased the brevet rank of Sub-prefect. The lucrative post of Taot-ai in charge of the Tea and Salt industries in Ssŭ-ch'uan fell vacant, and Yü Ming, under pressure from Tzŭ Hsi, was given the position.

In due course he appeared before the Emperor in audience to return thanks. Kuang Hsü said to him: " In which of the Government Boards have you served?" He replied: " Your slave has always been attached to Kuang shun." (Kuang shun is the name of the very wealthy firm of contractors above referred to.) The Emperor did not understand him and repeated the question. Yü Ming replied: " Has Your Majesty never heard of the Kuang shun firm? They are the biggest contractors in the West city. Your slave has been manager there for a long time." The Emperor smiled:

"Oh! I see: you mean that you have always been in trade. Well! To be manager of a big firm of contractors is a highly lucrative post. Why do you want to exchange it for an official career?" The answer came glibly: "Because I have heard that the perquisites to be made out of this Tea and Salt Taot'ai-ship are worth at least ten times as much as I can make out of business."

By this time Kuang Hsü was greatly incensed at the man's effrontery, but suppressed his wrath for the moment. "Can you write or speak Manchu?" said he. "No, Your Majesty." "Can you write Chinese?" Yü Ming hesitated for a long time and then stammered out: "Yes." The Emperor then threw some paper and a pencil on the ground and directed the eunuch in attendance to take Yü Ming outside. "Go and write out a statement of your official career on the steps outside the hall, where I can see you."

After a very long interval Yü Ming re-entered the hall of audience and handed the paper to the Emperor. All he had written was: "Your slave, Yü Ming, Manchu of the striped Yellow Banner." The characters were the size of tea cups (etiquette requires that for presentation to the Throne they should be small and exquisitely formed in round hand). Yü Ming's writing sprawled all over the page, was hardly legible, and one of the two simple characters comprising his name was wrong.

At this the Emperor flew into a passion: "You may keep your former brevet as Sub-prefect," he said, "and await your turn for promotion." (This meant that he was relegated from the high position of Taot'ai-elect to that of an expectant of low rank, who would most likely never get a position at all.) "I hereby appoint Chang Yuan-p'u to the post: let the Council report immediately." Thus did Kuang Hsü for once defy Tzŭ Hsi.

The chronicler relates that Yü Ming returned to his business as a contractor and, with the help of Li Lien-ying, made a great deal of money out of a contract for the building of a shrine in memory of Prince Ch'un, Kuang Hsü's father. Having " squeezed " large profits out of this lucrative work, he proceeded to bribe the eunuchs in the employ of the young Prince Ch'un (subsequently the Regent) to steal and sell to him jewels and curios from the Prince's residence. He was found out, and the Emperor ordered his arrest, but he contrived to escape by shaving his head and becoming a priest. He found shelter at a temple of the Western hills, and was well known to several foreigners there some years ago. Eventually he was ejected from the priesthood on account of a scandal in connection with a lady of high degree at Peking. As for Lu Po-yang, the Taot'ai-elect of Shanghai, the incorruptible Nanking Viceroy, Liu K'un-yi, who knew of his disreputable antecedents, refused to allow him to take up the post, and impeached him on a charge of bribery. He was dismissed from office, and the 700,000 taels which he had paid to Li Lien-ying (to be divided between the eunuch and his Imperial mistress) were money wasted, for he never occupied the post. In disgust with public life, he too became a Taoist priest. So that Kuang Hsü's firm stand was justified by results, and Tzŭ Hsi gave no sign of disapproval.

It is not to be supposed that his unfortunate Majesty was entirely without friends and counsellors : there were many at Court who hated, while they feared, the *régime* of the grasping Chief Eunuch and his imperious mistress. But her hand lay heavy upon them, and though the atmosphere of the metropolis does occasionally breed heroism in the orthodox mandarin, it is usually of the valedictory death-scene order rather than the kind which displays itself steadily in every-day routine. Those whose sympathies were with the Emperor, and those who regarded the Empress Dowager's continued usurpation of the supreme power as dangerous to the Empire, endeavoured (timorously enough) to persuade the Old Buddha by constitutional procedure to relax something of her firm grip upon State affairs.

To give one instance. Early in 1896, when the Empress Dowager was *en retraite* at the Summer Palace, the Censor Wang P'eng-yün put in a memorial of remonstrance against the Emperor's repeated visits to the Summer Palace to pay his respects to Tzŭ Hsi. He said: " These journeys to and fro waste most of the day and distract His Majesty's attention from State affairs. Every few days he leaves the Palace before dawn and does not return to Peking till dusk. Should the Emperor contract an illness from chill or fatigue, no one would be more sorry than the kindly Mother. I therefore venture to recommend that the Emperor should attend to his duties and not waste time in these ceremonial excursions."

The real meaning of this memorial was that the Emperor was far too much under Tzŭ Hsi's control and afraid to take any important step without her approval; in other words, Wang desired to see Kuang Hsü emancipated from petticoat government. As it happened, the Old Buddha was at the time in one of her good-humoured and lenient moods; had she not been so, this memorial might well have cost the Censor dear. Only a month before, a eunuch named K'ou had been summarily beheaded for venturing to advise the Emperor to select his own staff of personal attendants, so as to avoid the constant espionage of the Empress Dowager. Since then the Grand Council had gone in daily terror for fear that some Censor should denounce this execution or impeach the Old Buddha; when therefore, Wang P'eng-yün's memorial reached them, they were much perturbed. Prince Kung and Li Hung-tsao discussed it anxiously. Li remarked : " Truly, we should be thoroughly ashamed of ourselves, when a small official ventures to speak out thus openly against the Old Buddha, while none of us have dared to criticise her in any way. Let us try, at least, to shield him from any serious consequences. When Your Highness is received in audience by His Majesty, you must think of some way whereby the Emperor may pacify Her Majesty or else suppress the memorial." Prince Kung agreed, but observed that the suppression of the memorial would be difficult. When summoned to audience he handed up the memorial to Kuang Hsü, who after perusing it said: " Her Majesty will certainly demand his execution. What do you advise? " Kung repeated what Li had said. " That's all very well," replied the Emperor, " but do you forget that K'ou was decapitated the other day for criticism far less outspoken? " Prince Kung answered: " A eunuch has no right to memorialise at all nor to interfere in affairs of State. In putting him to death Her Majesty was only acting in accordance with dynastic house-law. But a Censor is entitled to criticise without restriction and his person is—or should be—inviolable."

Kuang Hsü sighed: " Do not think that I wish to restrict their criticisms, but you know how I stand. I fear that Her Sacred Majesty will be greatly incensed when she sees this document. Present it I must, for if I did not she would surely hear about it. I think that you had best discuss the situation again with Li Hung-tsao. At least you can stop the presentation of any further memorials of this kind."

Prince Kung retired and, with Li's help, drafted a memorial in which the following passage occurred: " The Censor is greatly daring when he raises such questions, but his action is actuated by a misguided sense of loyalty and not by any radically evil propensities. We have carefully perused his memorial and find therein no treasonable matter nor anything derogatory to Her Majesty's beneficent virtue. We therefore implore Your Majesty to forgive him." Kuang Hsü then left for audience at the Summer Palace, taking the two memorials, which he submitted, meekly kneeling, to Tzŭ Hsi. The Old Buddha, who was in a particularly good temper that morning, read the documents and then said with a smile: " You seem dreadfully nervous about this effusion, but there is really not the slightest reason for you to fear that I should be displeased. I welcome criticism from the Censors: that is what they exist for."

On returning to the Forbidden City Kuang Hsü said to Prince Kung: "On this occasion Her Majesty has taken a lenient view, but I am sure that if the subject ever comes up again in a memorial, not only will its author be beheaded, but Wang, who now escapes, thanks to the Old Buddha's good humour, will also suffer death."

Nevertheless Tzŭ Hsi took the hint which, after all, was reasonable enough, and thereafter required fewer visits from the Emperor, besides which she arranged matters so that he could get back to Peking at an earlier hour.

At the time of the *coup d'état*, many of the friends of the Reformers wondered how the Old Buddha had so swiftly possessed herself of all the details of K'ang Yu-wei's plot and the names of his confederates. The explanation is as follows: For some days before Tzŭ Hsi's *coup d'état* the Emperor, realising the hostility of the reactionaries to K'ang Yu-wei, had ceased from calling him to audience. Instead he made use of the reformer Lin Hsü, who transmitted messages to and from K'ang. He spoke with such a strong Fukhien accent that the Emperor had difficulty in following him, and therefore directed him to write down everything of importance and leave the memoranda with him for subsequent perusal.

A week before the fatal 5th day of the 8th Moon, the Old Buddha suddenly came in, unannounced, from the Winter Palace to pay the Emperor a surprise visit, and see what he was about. It was only when she had actually reached the West Gate of the city that an outrider was sent on ahead to inform the Emperor, so that

THE COURT OF PEKING

he might hasten to the entrance of the Western Palace and welcome Her Majesty, as usual, on his knees.

Kuang Hsü and Lin Hsü were discussing matters in the Palace of Heavenly Purity, when a eunuch rushed in and said: "The Old Buddha will be here in twenty minutes. I have ordered your chair for you to go and meet her." The Emperor hurriedly bade Lin Hsü gather up his papers and leave the Palace, while he himself proceeded to meet the Empress. Unfortunately Lin Hsü, in a great state of nervousness and fear, was so anxious to get away before the Empress's eunuchs should see him, that in his haste he accidentally dropped the most important of all his documents, one in which he had outlined the plan for surrounding the Summer Palace and seizing the person of Tzŭ Hsi. This paper was picked up by one of Li Lien-ying's henchmen and handed by the Chief Eunuch to Her Majesty. It was the death warrant of the Reformers.

For the next two years, Kuang Hsü was virtually a prisoner and treated by the Old Buddha and Li Lien-ying with studied rudeness and neglect. He became afflicted with a deep, chronic melancholy, fully aware, during the period of his solitary confinement, that his life hung upon a thread, at the mercy of the Old Buddha's cold-blooded policies and vengeful moods. After the *coup d'état*, Tzŭ Hsi used frequently to visit her wretched nephew in his lonely pavilion prison on the "Ocean Terrace," and would calmly announce to him the arrangements she proposed to make after his decease, which, as he well knew, was being planned with all due regard to precedent and decorum.[1] Knowing his proudly sensitive nature, she would taunt him with the illegality of his succession to the Throne (her own doing) and declare that his reign would be recorded in the dynastic annals as an interregnum, as was done in the case of a similarly unfortunate

[1] Vide *China under the Empress Dowager*, p. 212.

monarch, named Ching Tai, of the Ming dynasty (1450–1457).

Kuang Hsü took a melancholy interest in the history of his prototype, on which he used to meditate for hours. There were indeed many curious features of resemblance between the Ming Emperor's destiny and his own. Ching Tai had been placed upon the Throne by command of the Empress Dowager of that day, in the place of his elder brother who had been carried into captivity by the Mongols. He was treacherously murdered by eunuchs, whilst performing sacrifice. His reign was expunged from the dynastic annals (though eventually restored), and his body was buried, not in the Imperial mausolea to the north of Peking, but in a comparatively humble grave at a site adjoining the Summer Palace.

After his release from solitary confinement, and when the Old Buddha's heart had been somewhat softened towards him by their common misfortunes after the flight from Peking in 1900, Kuang Hsü maintained his melancholy devotion to the memory of Ching Tai. From a window of the Summer Palace he could see the grave of his luckless predecessor, and lamenting its neglected state, he persuaded one of his eunuchs to plant new pine trees about it and to repair the pillars of the main hall of sacrifice. But he bade the eunuch take care that the Old Buddha should not know by whose orders these things were done. If she knew it was the Emperor's doing, she would no doubt be angry : if discovered, the eunuch was to say he was " acquiring merit " at his own expense, and Tzŭ Hsi would probably praise his virtuous conduct. But every one at Court knew of Kuang Hsü's pathetic interest in the fate of Ching Tai, so much so, that after his death in 1908, Chang Chih-tung cynically proposed to the Regent to give him the posthumous title of Ching (Illustrious) in commemoration of this interesting affinity.

Towards the end of Kuang Hsü's mysterious and fatal

THE COURT OF PEKING

illness, in November 1908, he suddenly displayed an unusual initiative and independence of mind. On the 11th of November, two days before his death, he arose from his couch and expressed his intention of presenting himself at Tzŭ Hsi's bedside, to inquire after her health. The dynastic annals recorded his pious solicitude for Her Sacred Majesty, but the real incentive was probably his desire to verify for himself the fact that his relentless oppressor was mortally stricken. The effort, whatever its motive, was too much for him, and he collapsed after walking a few steps. His eunuchs carried him to a couch on the south side of his bedroom, from which he never rose again.

On the 10th of November, when Dr. Chou was summoned to advise on the state of His Majesty's health, he was amazed at the evidences of neglect which he found in the mean equipment and general squalor of His Majesty's apartment. It was heated by means of one of the common white-clay stoves which are to be found in the poorest houses in North China, things that cost a few pence and emit noxious fumes of charcoal gas. His bedding was meagre and coarse, of the kind a shop apprentice might use. There were a few historical books by his bedside, but no ornaments or comforts of any kind; the yellow tablecloth was dirty and had evidently not been changed for months. When, after his death, his coffin was borne to the Western tombs, to be deposited in a temporary shelter pending the building of his mausoleum, the articles which he had had in daily use were carried, as custom requires, in the funeral procession, and it was observed by the populace that they were no better than those of the ordinary shopkeeper's household. There was no money wasted on the Son of Heaven under the administration of the insolent Chief Eunuch, Li Lien-ying.

From his death-bed, the Emperor addressed a last request to the Old Buddha, which showed how vividly the tragic events of 1900 had impressed themselves upon his mind, and how steadfastly he cherished the memory of the one woman who had cheered his unhappy life with affection and loyalty. This was the "Pearl Concubine," murdered by order of the Empress Dowager on the morning of the flight from the Palace, after the entry of the allied armies into Peking. The hand that sent this loyal soul to her doom was the hand of Li Lien-ying, who threw her into the well, but the man who had poisoned the Empress's mind against her, and who was therefore chiefly responsible for her death, was a eunuch named Tsui. This wretch had hurled stones down the well upon the victim of his malignant intrigues and had mocked the Emperor in his grief. Kuang Hsü had not forgotten or forgiven, and at the last he sought to be revenged on one who had added insults to the deadliest injuries. He asked the Old Buddha that the eunuch Tsui might be dismissed from the Palace and all his vast fortune confiscated. Even then, remembering Her Majesty's ultra-sensitiveness in matters where her supreme authority was concerned, he avoided all direct reference to tragic events of which, he believed, she had repented, and requested the eunuch's punishment on the ground that " he was planning treason against Her Majesty's person." His wish was granted (Tsui's fortune was probably an important factor in the decision) and on the day of Kuang Hsü's death, the eunuch was ignominiously driven from the Palace.

Many were the slights and indignities placed upon the miserable monarch by these " rats and foxes " of the Palace, who seemed to delight in wounding his sensitive nature. Li Lien-ying invariably checked the Empress Dowager in any kind impulse of compassion towards him by representing the Emperor as persistently disrespectful to herself.

When the Emperor was confined by the Old Buddha's orders at the Ocean Terrace, which was connected with the rest of the Palace by a single drawbridge that spanned the surrounding narrow lake, he practically saw no one excepting the two or three eunuchs appointed to watch over him. Even his wife and other ladies of the Palace were seldom allowed to come near him, and the Old Buddha's occasional visits were hardly calculated to cheer him. His apartments were untidily kept and scantily furnished; even the bamboo screens were usually in tatters and the paper windows in holes. When the electric light was installed in the Palace only the Emperor's rooms were not connected. The Imperial Household officials took their cue from the Old Buddha, and knew better than to show concern for the Emperor's comfort. On one occasion, Kuang Hsü asked Chi Lu, a Chamberlain of the Household, to get him some new bamboo screens to replace his old ones which were dropping to pieces. Chi Lu did so. Next morning the eunuchs in attendance on Her Majesty took pleasure in informing him that the Old Buddha had been graciously pleased to present fine sable robes to all her other Chamberlains, whilst on him she had bestowed a foreign dog. This gentle hint, typical of Tzŭ Hsi's way of doing things, effectually checked any further attempts on the part of Chi Lu to make things easier or pleasanter for poor Kuang Hsü. It is only fair to say, however, that after the return from Hsian he was better served, and was eventually allowed to have his own attendants about him, and certain benefits from the Privy Purse.

CHAPTER XIX

MEMOIRS OF THE BOXER YEAR (1900)

THE inner history of the Court of Peking during the height of the Boxer crisis and the siege of the Legations was fully narrated in the diary of His Excellency Ching Shan, published for the first time in *China under the Empress Dowager* in 1910. Since then, the observations of Europeans who went through that siege, and the criticisms of Chinese apologists on the subject, have confirmed the opinion that Ching Shan was not only well-informed but remarkably accurate in his record of those stirring days. Until the abdication of the Manchus, it was almost impossible to obtain authoritative evidence confirmatory of Ching Shan's sensational revelations. Tzŭ Hsi's successor as Empress Dowager, Her Majesty Lung Yü, by whose orders a special Chinese translation was made of *China under the Empress Dowager*, forbade the vernacular press from publishing any reference to a work which, naturally enough, she regarded as *lèse majesté* of the worst description. Since the inauguration of the Republic, however, the writings, public and private, of many Chinese and Manchus have thrown no little light on the principal events of the reign of Tzŭ Hsi, and indeed on the history of the dynasty. Making all due allowance for the Oriental failing, common to most Chinese annalists, of believing and recording evil of those in high places, there is much in these posthumous papers which serves to amplify and to check our knowledge of important details.

THE COURT OF PEKING

The most significant feature common to all these documents lies in their tacit acceptance of the fact that a time of political chaos implies the wreaking of vengeance for private grudges by whichever party happens to be possessed of the balance of power at any given moment. The Old Buddha's acceptance of the Boxers' programme of " driving the hated foreigner into the sea " was used by the leading Boxer politicians—Prince Tuan, Hsü T'ung and Kang yi—not so much for the furtherance of that policy and the good of the State, as for the castigation of their personal enemies and rivals. Even when the allies were at the very gates of Peking, the thoughts of these men were directed less towards the defence of their city and their sovereign than towards revenge on their political opponents. The grim drama of human passions which was enacted around the Dragon Throne during those days of terror is made grimmer by the fact that those who describe it regard it as a matter of course, unconscious of all it implies in the history, past and future, of their country.

Before dealing with some of the most noteworthy incidents in this drama, we may take from the diary of a Manchu official the following account of the vicious profligacy which characterised the Princes and nobles of the Imperial Clan long before they became leaders of the Boxer movement. The author heads his reminiscences: " Signs of a Decaying dynasty."

" It has ever been the case in Chinese history," he says, " that whenever a dynasty has lost its virility and exhausted the mandate of Heaven, its Princes and nobles, becoming effete and addicted to luxurious and unnatural vices, must be for ever seeking some new and strange way of gratifying their jaded appetites. In the years before the Boxer outbreak, the young Manchu aristocrats of Peking used to amuse themselves by dressing themselves as beggars and parading the streets in this guise. I cannot say who started this fashion, but it became quite the rage. Every young Prince would endeavour to surpass his fellows in a thoroughly realistic imitation of a true beggar's disguise. At first the craze was confined to the highest Manchus, but, as might be expected, it soon found imitators among the sons of Chinese in high places. Prominent amongst them were the grandsons of the powerful Board President, Pi Tung-ho. To-day this family is fallen upon evil days, and its fate is well deserved.

"I remember particularly one occasion, during the dog-days of 1892. It was a very hot day, and some friends had invited me to join them in an excursion to the Kiosque and Garden known as 'Beautiful Autumn Hillock,' just outside the south-west gate of the Southern city. The place is also called the Brick Kiln Terrace; it consists of a hillock about forty feet high, on top of which there is a wide level space of about a quarter of an acre in extent. This spot is well shaded by tall willows and poplars, and in the middle there is a pond, where water-lilies and rushes grow. There are no houses about it, so the place is delightfully cool, and visitors can take their tea quietly at the open-air restaurant, while enjoying the pleasant and busy scene. Pedlars and wine-sellers come here to ply their trade, acrobats and conjurors perform to earn a few cash from the idle rich, and there are strolling musicians. There are also sheltered nooks for the comfort of visitors, so that one might fancy oneself in the heart of the country.

"At the table next us sat a young man of about eighteen: his face was as black as soot and he looked thin and ill-nourished. His queue was plaited round his head and he had inserted a bone hairpin in his hair, after the manner of the Peking hooligan class in summer time. He wore no socks and was stripped to the waist. His only garment was a very shabby pair of short trousers, which hardly reached to the knee, all covered with grease and mud, and badly torn: in fact, he was scarcely decent. He wore a pair of dilapidated grass slippers, through which his toes protruded.

"Strange to say, this miserable-looking beggar had on his right thumb a large ring of green jade worth at least 500 taels (say at that time £80); and he carried a beautiful and very costly carved fan with a jade handle. He sat, with legs crossed, on the ground, drinking wine. His conversation was full of vulgar oaths and the lowest Pekingese slang. I noticed, however, that the waiters showed him a very particular and eager attention and hardly ever left his side. To their other patrons their behaviour was very different, being somewhat offhand and brusque. I was lost in bewilderment at this spectacle, wondering what it meant, when the sun began to sink behind the western hills and the guests to leave. All of a sudden I observed the arrival of a smart official cart with red wheels set far back,[1] and a train of some twenty well-groomed attendants. I then realised the truth and awaited developments with some curiosity. Two officials came up the hillock, both wearing the button of the third rank and peacock's feather. They were evidently officers of the bodyguard; one of them carried a hatbox and a bundle of clothes, while the other held a basin and ewer. They approached the young beggar, and reverently addressed him: 'Your Highness's carriage is ready. You have an engagement to dine at Prince Kung's palace tonight, and we ought to be starting.' So the young blood got up, took a towel and washed his face. We were all astonished at the transformation, and could scarcely suppress an exclamation of surprise. The dirty black of his face and been replaced by a delicate white complexion, and though thin, he had the distinctive features of the Manchu Princes. We perceived that he had daubed his face with charcoal.

[1] A type of vehicle which could only be used by persons of very high rank.

"He then attired himself in his proper clothes, with the jewelled buttoned hat which Princes wear, decorated with the triple-eyed peacock's feather. The two officers humbly escorted him to his carriage; he drove off and was soon lost to view.

"The head waiter then whispered to me: 'That was the Beileh, Tsai Lien.' I replied in amazement: 'What does he mean by such behaviour?' 'Oh,' said he, 'don't you know the latest craze of our young Princes in Peking?' He went on to tell he how Prince Chuang, Prince K'o, Prince Tuan, the Beilehs Lien and Ying, Prince Ch'ing's son Tsai Chen, the son of the Lieutenant General Ch'i Hsiu, Prince Chuang's sons, Huai-t'a-pu's boys, and many others, made a practice of adopting this guise, and were constantly causing disturbances in houses of ill fame, taverns, etc., and street rows, as the police were afraid to interfere with them. The Prince we saw was comparatively well behaved.

"I was horrified to hear this, and said: 'This surely portends evil to our Empire. Such things occurred just before the Sungs were finally defeated by the Mongols and also at the close of the T'ang dynasty. History is full of such examples. Mark my words, China will be plunged in dire calamities before ten years have passed.'

"My friends were all Manchus of the Imperial Household, in a position to learn much of the inner life of the Court, so I had no doubt as to the accuracy of their statements. My own opinion was confirmed in due course, for eight years later the Boxer outbreak occurred. Of the several Princes who had amused themselves by playing the beggar, Prince K'o was taken into custody by the foreign troops and set to work at burying the bodies of the dead: in his mortification he committed suicide. Huai-t'a-pu was forced by the Russians to clean out latrines: he complained to the officers that he was of high rank, but they only reviled him and flogged him with a whip; he did not dare to tell them of his near kinship with the Old Buddha, lest his Boxer proclivities should become known and a worse fate befall him. Eventually he also took poison and died. Ch'en Pi was forced to pull a ricksha. Scions of the Imperial family, men who had never done a day's real work in their lives, fell to tramping the streets not as sham, but real, beggars. Prince Tuan and his brothers were either exiled or cashiered: Prince Chuang was permitted to commit suicide. Ch'i Hsiu perished by the sword of the executioner. The hero of our day's outing, the Beileh, Tsai Lien, lost his title and rank as the result of complicity in the Boxer rising, and is now living in greatly straightened circumstances. I wonder if those who still survive of that bright band of gay blades ever feel any impulse to play at wallowing in the dung-heaps of the city with outcasts and beggars? Perhaps by now their jaded appetites are sated, and in their sober moments they may even brood sorrowfully over the piteous decline of their once proud Manchu dynasty."

The following, also from a Manchu's diary, explains how it came to pass that, after much vacillation and casting about for advice, the Old Buddha finally decided on defying the forces of the Western world.

"At the critical moment when the Taku ports were taken (17th June, 1900) by the foreigners, the three high officials who led the war-party at Peking were Prince Tuan, Hsü T'ung and Kang yi. Prince Ch'ing might have voted against the Boxers had not Prince Tuan been watching him closely: whereat he was afraid. Chao Shu-ch'iao could never come to any definite opinion one way or the other. When the news reached Peking that the forts had been taken, the Old Buddha, sorely perturbed, sent for each member of the Grand Council separately. Prince Ch'ing, though not on the Council, was first asked for his opinion. True to his crafty principles, he replied: 'Peace or war, each course presents its advantages, but it must be for Your Majesty to decide.' 'That is no answer to my question,' retorted the Old Buddha, 'you may go down from the Presence.' Jung Lu, the next to be summoned, implored Her Majesty to pause before taking action which would irrevocably end the Manchu dynasty. After being angrily rebuked by the Old Buddha, he gave place to Kang Yi, who advised war to the death. Chao Shu-ch'iao was then called in. The Old Buddha first told him exactly what the others had said and then observed: 'You have held many provincial posts' (he had been a Prefect at Feng Yang in Anhui for many years), 'and have had direct experience of the conditions under which my people live. In this respect you should be able to gauge the situation better than either Kang Yi or Jung Lu, who have never held office as magistrates. I shall therefore decide in accordance with your judgment.' Chao had previously promised Jung Lu to vote against war, but realising that the Old Buddha was bent on hostilities, he hesitated and finally stammered out: 'I hear that the Foreign Powers are sending large armies to China; I am afraid that a campaign is by no means certain to end in victory for our arms; nevertheless, a pacific policy presents obvious difficulties.' The Empress angrily interrupted him. 'Are you for peace or war? Make up your mind one way or the other and tell me.' Chao replied: 'Your Majesty might declare war to begin with, and then if we are defeated, it will not be too late to order a cessation of hostilities. Troops are pouring into Peking from the provinces to support Your Majesty; but even if we are completely defeated, *the foreign armies will never venture to penetrate far into the interior.*' This last argument greatly impressed Tzŭ Hsi, who used it in her subsequent speech to the Ministers and Princes as a good reason for declaring war."

THE COURT OF PEKING

When, under the Peace Protocol, Chao expiated his comparatively innocent part in the Boxer movement, the Decree in which Tzŭ Hsi recorded his sentence referred to his vacillation at audience; but he was ever a favourite of hers and she did her utmost to protect him from the death penalty.[1]

Of the three men who chiefly influenced Tzŭ Hsi's mind and turned the wavering scales in favour of war, Prince Tuan, the swashbucklering fanatic, is less interesting as a type than Kang Yi and Hsü T'ung, whose hatred of foreigners followed naturally from their conception of the orthodox and patriotic official's duty to his country and himself. Hsü T'ung's hostility towards Europeans and all their ways was cold-blooded and uncompromising, but at least it had the merit of being unconcealed. He carried it, indeed, to an excess which made him notorious in Peking long before the Boxer outbreak; for several years he made it a rule to leave his house (which was on Legation Street) by the side door leading to the wall rather than set foot on the foreigners' macadamised road. His son Hsü Ch'eng-yü, however, though by no means friendly to Europeans, was in the habit of taking foreign meals at the local hotel, and was on good terms with a certain foreigner who lived next door to the Grand Secretary's premises. It was through this European's kindly intervention that Hsü was able to escape from the besieged Legation quarter, and the Old Buddha fully intended to reward the foreigner for his friendly act.

Hsü T'ung's quarters during the next two months were at the former residence of the Grand Secretary, Pao Yün; he went to the Palace nearly every day and did more than any one, except Tuan and Kang, to persuade Her Majesty to place her trust in the Boxers.

When the Court fled south, Hsü would have liked to follow Her Majesty, but a decree made him Peace Plenipo-

---

[1] Vide *China under the Empress Dowager*, p. 368.

tentiary. His son, Hsü Ch'eng-yu, then said to his father: "Your Excellency is now over eighty years of age. Your policy has been an utter failure. What are you waiting for, that you still cling to life?" The old man angrily rebuked him for this unfilial speech. The son retorted: "Father, you have been disloyal to the best interests of the State. A disloyal minister cannot complain if he has an unfilial son." (These words were used by Wu San-kuei to his father in 1644,[1] when the latter submitted to the rebel Li Tzŭ-ch'eng, who proclaimed himself Emperor after overcoming and expelling the Mings.) The old man meekly replied: "Do as you think best then." With that, his son led him to a tree in the garden, hung a rope thereon and assisted the Grand Secretary to commit suicide. His action would have been meritorious, had he seen fit to die at the same time, but he clung to life, only to be beheaded five months later.

When the Boxer madness was at its height, Hsü T'ung, who was nothing if he was not thorough, used to say to his friends: "Before we can hope to drive these foreigners into the sea, we must exterminate one Dragon, two tigers and thirteen sheep." The Dragon was the Emperor, the tigers were Jung Lu and Li Hung-chang, and the sheep were the Yangtsze Viceroys, Prince Ch'ing, Yüan Shih-k'ai, Wang Wen-shao and the other moderates at Peking and the provincial capitals.

Yü Hsien, the "butcher" Governor of Shansi, on the black list of the Allies, was first sentenced to banishment by Tzŭ Hsi, and had proceeded on his way as far as Lan Chou in Kansuh, when Her Majesty's decree—reluctantly issued under pressure—reached Sung Fan, the Viceroy, whereby Yü Hsien was sentenced to decapitation. Sung Fan was an old friend of Yü Hsien, and the day before the arrival of this decree had invited him to a banquet. While the feast was actually proceeding, the order from

---

[1] *Vide supra*, p.

the Old Buddha was brought to the Viceroy, requiring Yü's immediate decapitation. Sung Fan read it, changed countenance and hurriedly concealed the document. Yü asked permission to see it, and on being refused, angrily put down his chopsticks and announced his departure. Sung, seeing no help for it, let him see the decree. In response to his friend's expression of grief, Yü smilingly said: " It is the fortune of war. I am a soldier and know that you must obey orders. The Sovereign commands, what can a Minister do but comply? Our feast, however, is a private matter; my decapitation is your public duty. Let us first conclude the banquet and speak of other things." Yü then drank most immoderately, took leave of his friend and spent the rest of the day quietly. Next morning the Viceroy sent his guard to convey him to the place of execution, which had been hung with red silk, and sorrowfully witnessed the beheading of his firend.

Kang Yi, after Hsü Tung the most determined fire-eater of the war party, was an ignorant and illiterate bigot, a great believer in magic and spells. His belief in the Boxers was the natural outcome of his puerile superstition; his favourite literature was the well-known magical romance, *Feng Shen Chüan*, a collection of fantastic legends which his secretaries had to read aloud to him almost daily. When serving on the Grand Council he was wont to say that though possibly there really were in Europe as many nations as Russia, England, Germany and France, all the rest of the countries of which foreigners spoke—Sweden, Holland, Austria and Spain—were surely nothing but lying inventions, intended to intimidate China.

On one occasion, in 1894, on coming up to Peking from Canton, where he had been Governor, he recommended one of his aides-de-camp for a high post. Kuang Hsü asked what were the nominee's qualifications. Kang Yi replied: "He is my Huang T'ien-pa."[1] Huang T'ien-pa had been the right-hand man of a certain magistrate in K'ang Hsi's reign, and is a legendary hero renowned for his bravery. Kuang Hsü perceived the allusion, but he only smiled slightly, for he knew that Kang's knowledge of history was derived from plays and ghost stories.

Looking back on the Boxer movement, and dispassionately considering its genesis and leadership, the childishness of its impulses and ambitions assumes a pathetic aspect, and, viewed in this light, the penalties imposed on China by the European powers appear to have been lacking in sympathetic recognition of many fundamental facts. One of the chief Boxer leaders, for instance, one of those who misled thousands of comparatively innocent human beings to their doom, was a woman, originally a low-class courtesan of Tientsin, who was known as "The Yellow Lotus Holy Mother." In the eyes of her superstitious followers, this woman became an Oriental Jeanne D'Arc. When the Boxer movement was in full swing, any one suspected of being friendly to foreigners was taken before her, and sentenced to death, or set at liberty, according to her decision. Li Hung-chang's eldest son, Li Chang-shu, who was in Tientsin at the time, was arrested by the Boxers and brought before the "Yellow Lotus." The "Holy Mother" bade him kneel, and then smiled graciously upon him. One of his attendants, who was intimate with a Boxer chief, purchased his release—for the "Yellow Lotus" had an eye to business.

The Viceroy, Yü Lu, invited her to his yamên and begged her to predict the result of the movement. At her coming he knelt in Court robes to receive her outside the main tribunal and made obeisance to her. He said: "The foreigners are near at hand. Have mercy and

---

[1] A well-known theatrical personage: it is not etiquette to cite heroes of the stage at an Imperial audience, least of all to compare one of them with an official.

deliver us from them by your magic power." She replied: "I have already arranged for an angelic host to destroy them with fire from Heaven. You need not be alarmed." She was eventually arrested and decapitated by order of Li Hung-chang.

The point of view of the man in the street, the humble, plunderable private citizen, was of little account in those days, when the great ones staked the destinies of the Empire on a single desperate throw. What the man in the street felt is fairly described in the following reminiscence of the crisis, penned at the time, by a Kiangsu man resident in Peking, styled Heng Yi.

"In the 26th year of Kuang Hsü," he wrote, "my house was at the western end of San T'iao lane, not four hundred yards from the Legations. After the murder of the German Minister on the 24th of the 5th Moon, the ruffian soldiery of Tung Fu-hsiang entered and sacked nearly every house in my neighbourhood. All through the 24th and 25th I could hear the shrieks of the women and children, whom they were butchering, and their shouts, in the Kansu dialect, 'Bring out the Erh Mao Tzu!'[1] On the 26th (June 22nd) a Manchu Censor impeached them to the Throne, and the Old Buddha sent for their General, Tung Fu-hsiang, and bade him make an example of the culprits. Accordingly, on the evening of that day, twenty soldiers were beheaded just at the entrance to my lane.

"Even this exemplary punishment did not abate their fury, for next day another large contingent started looting again, and in due course approached my house. My cousin ordered the gate man to draw the bars across the main gate, but I begged him to do nothing of the sort. 'Our only hope to escape being massacred is to parley with them.' My cousin agreed, so we collected the whole

[1] "Secondary Devils"—the term used to describe Chinese Christians.

of the family in one of the main rooms, and told them not to get excited or scream. I had scarcely mustered them when nineteen of the Kansu braves came rushing in. Their swords and clothes were still dripping with blood; as if they had come from a shambles. I went forward to meet them, saying politely: 'I know what you have come for: you are looking for secondary devils. However, none of us have "eaten" the foreign religion. You will see that we have an altar to the kitchen god in our back premises. The whole of our family is now here; will you not take a look through the house to see if there are any Christians in hiding?' I meant by this to imply that we should offer no opposition to their looting whatsoeve they pleased. I also called a servant to prepare tea. Our guests received these overtures pleasantly enough, and after a few minutes of energetic looting they returned to my guest room, and some of them sat down to take tea. One of them remarked: 'You seem to be thoroughly respectable people: what a pity that you should reside near this nest of foreign converts and spies.' After a brief stay they thanked us politely, apologising for the intrusion, and retired with their booty. It was then about 2 p.m. We lost about $4,000 worth of valuables. Shortly afterwards, flames were bursting from our neighbour's premises, so I made up my mind to remove my family to a friend's house in the north of the city. In spite of these deeds of violence, even intelligent people still believed that the Kansu soldiery were a tower of defence for China, and would be more than able to repel any number of foreign troops. A friend of mine reckoned that 250,000 persons lost their lives in Peking that summer. I used to revile the Boxers in the family circle, so much that my own kinsmen, who sympathised with them, would call me an 'Erh Mao Tzu,' and my cousin, fearing that the Boxers would murder me, induced me one day to kotow before one of their altars in the Nai Tzu fu. To

THE COURT OF PEKING.

this day I have regretted my weakness in thus bowing the knee."

Five high officials fell victims to the malignant passions and private enmity of the war party during the height of the crisis, while the Allies were advancing upon Peking. Of these, two were executed by the orders of the Old Buddha—Yüan Ch'ang and Hsü Ching Ch'eng—for having tried to protect foreigners.[1] The other three, Li Shan, Hsü Yung-yi and Lien Shan, were hurriedly sent to their death by Prince Tuan.[2] The death of Hsü Ching-ch'eng, a very brave and courtly gentleman, has been well described by an anonymous writer, in a memoir entitled, *Reminiscences of a Time of Suspicion and Panic*,[3] as follows:

"A certain old scholar of Chekiang had been a close friend to Hsü Ching-ch'eng in the days before Hsü had attained to official rank. He accompanied him on his first mission to Europe, and from that time never left him till the day of his death. This gentleman relates that on the day of Hsü Ching-ch'eng's arrest, all was quiet in Hsü's house and there were no particularly alarming rumours. After the midday meal they were sitting talking in the library, Hsü having ordered his carriage to go to the Tsungli-yamên. He had just put on his official robes, when the gate-keeper came in with a card to announce a visitor. The name was not familiar to Hsü, who told the gate-keeper to make his excuses, explaining

---

[1] Vide *China under the Empress Dowager*, p. 294.
[2] The diarist, Ching Shan, declares that this was done without the knowledge of the Old Buddha, but on the face of it, this is difficult to believe. It is most probable that, without premeditation, she allowed it to be done in one of her violent fits of rage, and was sorry for it immediately afterwards.
[3] Literally: "monkey-like suspicions and panic at the cry of a bird."

that he had an appointment at the Yamên and no time to spare. The gate-keeper went out but came back at once, to say that the visitor was a military official employed at the Yamên, and that his orders from Prince Ch'ing were to invite Hsü's immediate attendance: Prince Ch'ing and Prince Tuan were both at the Yamên already, and there was most important business on hand. Hsü thereupon went out and saw the man. On returning, he said to his friend: 'When we left the Yamên yesterday I heard nothing of any important business. I wonder why both Princes are attending there to-day?' To this his friend replied: 'No doubt something has happened. I shall go now into the Southern city to get the latest news.' The friend then went out, but immediately returned to say: 'That officer who came to fetch you is still waiting outside, close by the gate. He seems greatly excited; it all looks very suspicious. Besides, I know all the Yamên official messengers by sight, and I never saw this man before. I advise you, as a precaution, to take a larger suite with you than usual, and be sure to send back a messenger with a report.'

"Hsü smilingly ignored his friend's remarks, entered his carriage and drove as far as the end of the lane, where he observed several runners from the Yamên of the Metropolitan Gendarmerie standing about. Upon a sign from the officer, they all formed a bodyguard round Hsü's carriage. Instead of proceeding towards the Tsungliyamên they turned northwards, and when Hsü asked the reason for this he was told that to-day's meeting would be held in the Yamên of Gendarmerie. On arriving there, the officer came forward and assisted Hsü to alight. He then ordered Hsü's attendants to go home: 'You are not wanted here,' said he; 'His Excellency will have other men to wait upon him inside.' Hsü was rapidly conducted to a small room, the door was bolted and he was left alone. He could hear sounds of lamentation proceeding from some one in the next room. This turned out to be Yüan Ch'ang, but the two were not allowed to meet.

"Meantime Hsü's suite returned home, and his friend was greatly alarmed at this report. He hurried off to Wang Wen-shao (his fellow provincial) to find out what was afoot, and to beg him to save Hsü's life. Wang professed amazement: 'I have only just come from the Council,' he said, 'and to my knowledge Her Majesty issued no decree. Your story seems incredible.'

"Hsü's friend took his leave and spent most of the night in trying to find some means of succouring him; it was not till 3 a.m. that he heard definitely that both he and Yüan had been sent to the Board of Punishments. Early that morning he received a private note from a secretary of the Board to tell him that the heads of the Ministry had just come out from the great hall of Council, and that orders had been given for a supply of red yarn to be got ready, from which he knew that the execution of the two prisoners had been decreed, because an ancient custom requires that when a high official is to be beheaded, his face must be enveloped in red cloth.

"On receipt of this note Hsü's friend set off to visit Wang Wen-shao to intercede once more for Hsü's life, but he had only just started when he received a message saying that the cart conveying the condemned had already left the Board of Punishments. He hurried off to the execution ground outside the city, but on reaching it he found that the two officials were already dead, and that Hsü Chehg-ju (son of Hsü Tung) was on his way to the Palace to inform Her Majesty of the due execution of her orders."

As regards the death of Li Shan, the same writer observes that it is not correct to suppose that it was due to the Boxers' coveting his vast wealth. The real reason lay in a long-standing feud between him and Duke Tsai Lan, who was really responsible for his execution. Some years before, a well-known singing girl named " Green Monkey " was all the rage among the fashionable élite of Peking. Both Tsai Lan and Li Shan had had relations with her, and each wished to secure her for himself, because her beauty made her worthy in their eyes " of having a golden house built for her abode." At that time, however, Duke Lan had no official position and was in poor circumstances financially, so Li Shan succeeding in carrying off the " Green Monkey." For this Tsai Lan cherished a bitter grudge against him, which the Boxer rising gave him an opportunity to pay off.

As for the Chancellor of the Grand Secretariat, Lien Yüan, executed at the same time by order of Prince Tuan, he had put in a memorial urging that the bombardment of the Legations should cease. He was just emerging from the Palace when he met Ch'ung Li, ex-commandant of the Gendarmerie, just outside the gate of Brilliant Fortune. With an exclamation of surprise Ch'ung Li said : " What brings you to the Palace at this early hour ? " (It was not yet dawn; Lien had had to attend early in order to present his memorial.) Lien told him the reason. Ch'ung angrily replied : " Indeed ! Have you forgotten your Manchu birth that you behave like one of these Chinese traitors ? "

Lien refused to admit that he was in the wrong, and angrily turned on his heel. Ch'ung Li was furious, and reported to Prince Tuan. A few days later Lien met his fate at the " Western Market." Just before his head fell, a Boxer leader in full uniform came riding up at a hand gallop, dragging behind him something which was so completely covered with dust and mud as to be quite unrecognisable. It was not until the rider had pulled up his horse at the execution ground, that the bystanders perceived it was a man bound hand and foot. The features were mutilated beyond recognition, but on inquiry of the runners they learned that it was Li Shan.

The fate of the third victim, Hsü Yung-yi, was the hardest of all. A native of Chekiang, he began his career as a small official in the Board of Revenue, obtained by examination a post as clerk on the Grand Council, and finally, after nearly fifty years of official life, rose to be Board President. He was circumspect and careful by nature, an advocate of compromise in State affairs, honest and incorruptible, resembling the late Duke of Devonshire in his slow and weighty mode of speech. His death was a surprise to every one, because few knew that he had an enemy. Tzŭ Hsi always liked him, and subsequently declared that his execution was none of her doing.

Be this as it may, the man really responsible for his undoing was Hsü T'ung, who had long cherished a secret grudge against him, because of an apparently trivial incident in connection with an Examination Commission on which both men were engaged. On that occasion a candidate, protégé of the Grand Secretary, had been " ploughed " as the result of Hsü Yung-yi having detected an error in caligraphy which had escaped the notice of the other examiners. Hsü T'ung's mind was of the type which cannot forget or forgive loss of " face."

After the death of Li Shan and Lien Yuan, Prince Tuan Duke Lan and Kang Yi were by no means sated of their blood lust, and proposed to make a wholesale proscription of their opponents, including, if possible, Jung Lu. Liao Shou-keng, ex-President of the Board of Ceremonies (a native of Kiangsu) had been removed from the Grand Council some months previously, and had resigned from the Tsungli-yamên in June, 1910, but Kang and Tuan both had long-standing grudges against him. They fixed on the 22nd of the 7th Moon (*i. e.* August 16th) for the execution of Liao and several others, Liao being the first on their list of victims. They made no secret of their intentions, which were known all over the metropolis. Liao Shou-keng had sent his family home to the South, and was living at that time in a small temple outside the Tung-hua Gate. On hearing the news he was much alarmed, and implored a kinsman of his, an ex-Viceroy, to persuade Jung Lu to save his life. Jung Lu promised to do what he could, but next day he reported that all his efforts had been in vain. At audience that morning he had kotowed time and again to the Old Buddha imploring her to save Liao's life, but Her Majesty had refused to change her decision, and no appeal could move her. He therefore advised that Liao should commit suicide.

The message was duly delivered to Liao, but he could not make up his mind to act upon it. Herein he was wise, for on the 21st, one day before the date fixed for his execution, Peking fell, and thus he escaped. He left immediately for his home in the South, where he died not long after. The priest at the temple where he lived said afterwards that when Liao heard the news of his sentence, he wandered round and round the courtyard like a man in a frenzy, and hardly stood still a moment for several hours on end. He took no nourishment and was as pale as a corpse.

It is not generally known that Wang Wen-shao himself had a very narrow escape at that time. After the five officials above-named had been put to death, Duke Lan put in a memorial concerning the bombardment of the Legations. To this there was a supplementary memorandum attached, containing these words : " Most of the pro-foreign traitors have been put to death, and Your Majesty's Court is purged of their odious miasma. One man, however, still remains to pollute your presence. That man is Wang Wen-shao. Unless the weed be plucked up by the roots, disaster will ensue. I beseech Your Majesty to have him beheaded, so that Your Court may be thoroughly purified of traitors."

THE COURT OF PEKING

The memorial duly reached the Grand Council for presentation. Jung Lu opened and perused it. He said nothing to his colleagues, but hid the supplementary memorandum in his sleeve. He handed the memorial itself to Wang Wen-shao, who read it through, and then said to his colleague: "I understood that Duke Lan was putting in a supplementary memorandum as well. Where is it?" Jung Lu quietly replied: "Oh! probably it has been retained by Her Majesty, and will not be issued."

A few minutes later, the Councillors were all summoned to audience. After transacting routine business, Jung Lu took out the supplementary memorandum from his cleeve, saying: "This memorandum of Tsai Lan is really an abominable insult to Your Majesty's intelligence. Will Your Majesty be pleased to issue a rescript of severe censure?"

The Old Buddha glanced over the document, and the "benevolent countenance" grew black as thunder. She muttered to herself and sat with knit brows, her face wearing an expression which, as Jung Lu knew well, boded evil to the victim of her impending wrath. At last, she said sternly: "Will you guarantee that this man is innocent of all treasonable designs?" Jung Lu kotowed. "Although every man in Your Majesty's Court were a traitor and were plotting against Your Majesty, yet I would stake my life on this man's unswerving fidelity. I, your slave, will pledge the Grand Secretary's loyalty, as long as breath remains in my body. If I had a hundred voices I would proclaim it with every one, even though my head should fall under the headsman's sword for my temerity." The Old Buddha still hesitated, with an inscrutable look on her face and a demeanour of enforced calm. At last she said in a voice of deep warning: "So be it, then. I place this man under your charge, and if I find that your words are false and that he has been conspiring against me, both of you shall suffer the same penalty." Jung Lu again prostrated himself and thanked Her Majesty for her gracious kindness. The victory was won. He and his colleagues then took their leave.

Now, Wang Wen-shao was very deaf, and all this time had been kneeling at some distance from the Throne. He had no idea what the Old Buddha was saying to Jung Lu. Afterwards Jung Lu told his friends the story, remarking: "While I was pleading for Wang's life and the Old Buddha looked wrathfully in his direction, speaking in such a tone that Prince Li and I both trembled and turned deadly pale, while Kang Yi sneered at us, there was old Wang, looking perfectly happy and self-possessed, without the least idea of what was going on." To the day of his death Wang never knew of his escape, and would often ask Jung Lu what the Old Buddha was saying to him on that fateful morning of August 1900.

Finally, from notes written a month after the relief of the Legations, by one who signs himself "An Imperial Clansman," we take the following pathetic description of the death of Lien Yuan's son-in-law, Shou Fu, who with all his household committed suicide upon the entry of the Allies, fearing insult and outrage at their hands. Shou Fu was of a type not uncommon amongst the Reformers (of whom he was one)—earnest, honest and impulsive, but not very wise or well-informed. A blind impulse, born of ignorance, wiped out all his family; such tragedies were common, however, during those days of battle, murder and sudden death. For that matter they are common enough in China at this time of writing.

"At the beginning of the Boxer crisis Shou Fu was greatly concerned as to the state of affairs at the Palace. He sought everywhere to obtain accurate information, and in the end came to the conclusion that the Old Buddha's belief in the Boxers would bring ruin upon the State, and end the Manchu rule. To his family he expressed the opinion that the only hope of saving the situation would be to get the Emperor out of the hands of Tzŭ Hsi and Li Lien-ying—'a position of dire peril'—and let him then arrange matters with the Allies.

"When Prince Tuan and his confederates had won the ear of the Old Buddha, one of Shou Fu's friends implored him to leave Peking, but he sadly refused. He was then urged to allow his younger brother, Chang Fu, to take his wife and children to his villa in the country, but again he refused, saying: 'When the skin has perished, where shall the hair grow? When everything is in such dire confusion, why worry about individual misfortunes?' His brother Chang Fu agreed, saying that he also had lost all desire to live.

"Shou Fu's father-in-law, Lien Yüan, Chancellor of the Grand Secretariat, was a well-known authority on the philosophy of Chu Hsi. In 1898, while holding office in Hupei province, he heard that Shou Fu was a supporter of the Reform movement, and wrote him a very angry letter. After the interchange of some heated correspondence, all relations ceased for a time between the two men. Subsequently, when Lien Yüan came to hold office in Peking, he realised that his son-in-law's endorsement of the Reform movement arose from sincere patriotism and not from any love of new and strange ideas. When, in June, the crisis became acute, Lien Yüan was received in audience with the rest of the chief officials. There in the audience hall he wept aloud, and addressed a most vigorous remonstrance to the Empress Dowager, telling her that by the laws of nations, the persons of envoys are sacrosanct. At this Prince Tuan stepped out from his place at the head of the Princes, and angrily exclaimed: 'Lien Yüan deserves to lose his head.' Luckily for Lien, the Old Buddha made no sign, but continued to listen, apparently unmoved, while he finished his discourse. When he had done, all she said was: 'I am perfectly well aware of all you tell me, and I find these long-winded harangues very wearisome.' But Shou Fu rightly foresaw that his father would not escape the vengeance of Prince Tuan for thus openly defying him.

"Shou Fu's family moved to Lien's house four days after the latter's execution, *i. e.* on August 14th. From that day communications were interrupted, between various parts of the city, by the coming of the allied armies. On the 17th of August detachments of foreign troops had been seen in the West city, but it was rumoured that all who hung out the white flag would have their lives spared. Nevertheless Shou Fu and his brother proceeded to poison themselves with opium. Their unmarried sister, aged thirty-two, then swallowed some of the drug, and made her little sister, aged eight, do the same. Her slave girl named Sa'Erh, stimulated to heroism by her mistress's shining example, vowed that she too would give up her life. By this time, the foreign soldiers had entered the adjoining courtyard. Shou Fu was afraid, as the drug worked slowly, that death would not come in time to save them from insult by the troops, so he led them all into a room on the west side of the court. There he mounted the brick platform and hanged himself to the rafters; but he being very stout, the rope gave way, and he fell with a crash to the ground. His brother Chang Fu raised him and hurriedly assisted him to climb up again and to adjust the rope securely, and this time he succeeded in hanging himself.

"Chang Fu then quietly made ready the ropes for his sisters and the little maid. When he had done so, there was no more rope left, so he hurried out and found a piece of thin cord in an outhouse. With this he returned to the western room, opened the door and hanged himself to the rafter just inside, thus blocking the entrance. It was then ten o'clock in the morning of the 23rd day of the 7th Moon. Shou Fu's age was thirty-six, and his brother's thirty-two. Their wives were forcibly prevented by Lien's family from committing suicide, as they too wished to do.

"Later, when the foreign soldiers had left the house, the servants had to cut down Chang Fu's body before they could get into the western room. The five bodies were reverently laid out in the main hall, but the family had no money wherewith to bury them decently. A kind neighbour, named Fu, made them a present of a hundred taels, and with this they bought five coffins. The remains were taken to the garden at the back and there temporarily interred.

"Ever since the Japanese war," concludes the chronicler, "Shou Fu had realised that only by reform could China be saved from ruin. No doubt he would have preferred to serve his country by living to work for it, rather than by dying for it; nevertheless his heroic resolution must have afforded no small satisfaction to the soul in Heaven of his ancestor, Nurhachi, as well as serving to show his enemies how a true patriot can die!"

CHAPTER XX

CONCERNING THE OLD BUDDHA

READERS of *China Under the Empress Dowager* may remember that, in summing up the character of that remarkable woman, we drew attention to the fact that up to the time of her death, despite the mass of material existing in the diaries and archives of metropolitan officials and the personal reminiscences of those who knew her well, nothing of any human interest or value had been published in China concerning her life and times. The work issued by "Wen Ching," from the safe asylum of a British Colony, was so obviously distorted by hatred of the Manchus and so recklessly inaccurate on matters of verifiable detail, as to be useless. The diary of Ching Shan afforded for the first time authoritative evidence of the opinion in which Tzŭ Hsi was held by those most competent to judge of her faults and virtues. Regarded in the light of that evidence, which has undoubtedly been confirmed by popular verdict, the Empress Dowager "despite her swift changing and uncontrolled moods, her childish lack of moral sense, her unscrupulous love of power, her fierce passions and revenges, was no more the fierce monster described by 'Wen Ching' than she was the benevolent, fashion-plate Lady Bountiful of the American Magazines."[1]

In discussing the early life of Tzŭ Hsi, and the crimes with which her contemporaries and posterity have charged

[1] *China under the Empress Dowager*, p. 478.

her, we laid stress on the fact that she lived her life according to her lights and in strict accordance with the traditions of her race and caste. Her own mistress, and virtual ruler of the Empire at the age of twenty-four, with none to teach her to control either her moods or her passions, how could she learn to cleanse the Forbidden City of its barbaric cruelties and corruption? Remembering the utterly unscrupulous falsehood of the charges with which Chinese political opponents habitually assail each other, and making due allowance for Tzŭ Hsi's environment in a city of " infantile gaiety and sudden tragedy, of flashing fortunes and swift dooms " we held, and hold, that she was entitled to the benefit of many doubts.

Nevertheless, and making all these allowances, the fact has ever been indisputable that the licentiousness and wicked extravagance with which Tzŭ Hsi's name was universally associated during the minority of her son T'ung Chih, created widespread feelings of resentment and disgust amongst the better class of Chinese officials. These feelings bore fruit at several important crises of her career, and undoubtedly contributed in the end to inspire the Western-educated Cantonese party with the evolutionary ideas, which led to the overthrow of the dynasty. In 1898, for instance, one of the memorials submitted by the Reformer, Yang Jui, to His Majesty Kuang Hsü, advocating the seizure and imprisonment of the Empress Dowager, denounced her gross immorality and accused her of illicit relations with several notable persons, one of whom was Jung Lu. It compared the crimes and orgies of her Summer Palace with those committed under the infamous concubine, Ta Chi, of the Shang dynasty, and referred to her vicious practices as matters of common and undisputed knowledge. This, indeed, has generally been the attitude of the anti-Manchu movement of Young China; but, in assessing the value of its denunciations and the evidence which it now produces with impunity in support of its assertions, it is well to bear in mind the frankly prejudiced character of the writers, and to realise that their statements are no more worthy of complete confidence than the evidence of Tzŭ Hsi's own decrees and official apologists.

The principal crimes with which Tzŭ Hsi stands charged are crimes affecting the Imperial succession. Incidents such as the murder of the " Pearl Concubine " or her complicity in the Boxer madness, are not seriously denounced by her critics; by tacit consent it appears to be assumed that a ruler in China may forcibly remove all obstacles from the path of his, or her, supreme authority, except where the direct and legitimate succession to the Throne is involved. The instinct of Young China seems, in this matter, to be unconsciously at one with that of the orthodox *literati* of the old *regime*, and to spring from recognition of the principle that the whole social system of China, based on ancestor worship, is bound up with maintenance of the Throne and the regular transmission of the Goodly Heritage to legitimate heirs.

In discussing the untimely death of T'ung Chih's young widow, the virtuous A-lu-te, and her unborn child in March, 1875, we recorded the fact that " opinions have always differed, and will continue to differ, as to the truth of her alleged suicide," but that the balance of all available evidence undoubtedly pointed in the direction of foul play. Of all the crimes with which Tzŭ Hsi has been accused, this was, and is, the most heinous, the most cold-blooded and at the same time the most vitally necessary to the maintenance of her own position as ruler of China. Given the circumstances under which it occurred, it was inevitable that the death of this unfortunate woman should be laid at Tzŭ Hsi's door by a verdict of public opinion practically unanimous; but

THE COURT OF PEKING

it has been left to the pamphleteers and annalists of the Republic to set forth that which purports to be definite evidence of the crime. How far this evidence is based on testimony of competent witnesses, and how far evolved from the inner consciousness of the writers, it were hard to say. All the narratives in our possession are the work of men who set out with the avowed purpose of vilifying the Manchus in general and the Old Buddha in particular. In describing many of her alleged crimes; the murder of her colleague, the Empress Tzǔ An; the debauching of her son, T'ung Chih; the killing of A-lu-te, and the death of Kuang Hsü, these writers of Young China agree generally in their conclusions, but they differ very materially on important details of evidence, and their work, as a whole, suggests constructive memory developed to a very high degree of elasticity.

The following extracts from the recent work of four such writers are reproduced in order that the reader may form an impression of the opinion in which the Great Empress Dowager was held during her lifetime, not only by the ever-turbulent spirits of Canton, but by many of her detractors and secret enemies in the North. Whatever the truth or untruth of their conclusions in regard to the personal blood-guiltiness of the Empress Dowager, they present, separately and collectively, a lamentable picture of the inner life of the Forbidden City, where corruption festered around the foundations of the Dragon Throne, and where, in the shadows of the stately halls, love and pleasure ran swiftly, the grim Fates pursuing.

The first is the work of the brilliant scholar P'an Tsu-yin, a leader of the Southern party at Peking, in the early 'nineties, who died in 1897. His memoirs were published by his grandson, one of the Shanghai revolutionaries, shortly after the abdication of the Manchus. P'an Tsu-yin calls his reminiscences *Random Notes from the*

Chamber of the Cloudy Sea, this being the poetical name which he gave to his studio. For several years he was employed in the Palace as a sort of poet laureate, his duty being to compose Imperial inscriptions in the Palace library. The following paper, dealing with Tzŭ Hsi's first emergence into the arena of State affairs, was written in April 1880:

"When Su Shun was beheaded, after the abortive conspiracy of the usurping Regents in 1861, official pronouncements and common report agreed in expressing the conviction that he had plotted high treason and cherished designs upon the Throne after the death of Hsien Feng, and that a *coup de main* by his faction was only averted by Tzŭ Hsi's resource and courage. Her prompt and decisive action in putting him and his fellow conspirators to death has been lauded to the skies by many writers. Yet the commonly received version of this incident is very wide of the truth, as I, who have been intimately associated with Palace affairs for many years, have good reason to know. The Western Empress's real reason for putting Su Shun to death was that he knew too much about her, and had therefore to be put out of the way. Dead men tell no tales.

"When Tzŭ Hsi was first admitted into the Palace, she was not an Imperial concubine, but only a handmaiden of very low rank. Duties were assigned to her at the Summer Palace in an outlying building called "The deep recesses of the plane trees." There she performed her allotted tasks, embroidery and other duties suitable to females, with diligence. One of her chief gifts was a charming voice; she knew many Southern songs, which she had learned from a nurse who had been with her since her birth in the South. One day when Hsien Feng was strolling in the grounds of Yuan-ming-yuan, he heard from a grove close by a delicate voice trilling a Southern air. Greatly charmed, the monarch proceeded to make the acquaintance of the fair singer. This was his first meeting with Yehonala, for on entering the Palace she had passed before Tao Kuang and his mother, and he never had seen her. He spent the following evening in her company; she proved herself an adept flatterer, and was clever enough not to appear servile. She anticipated all the Emperor's wants and so delighted him by her *espièglerie* and power of mimicry, that on the following morning he took her back with him to Peking. In due course she bore him an heir, and from that day her high destinies were assured.

"On the occurrence of this auspicious event she was raised to the rank of Imperial concubine, in accordance with Manchu custom. Her elevation to this high rank completely changed her disposition; she grew most haughty and unruly. To the Emperor she was contumacious and wilful; to her colleagues, overbearing and sarcastic. She acted as if the future were absolutely in her hands, and Hsien Feng was quite unable to exercise any authority over her. He could not even restrain her indulging in unseemly dalliance with a young officer of the Guard, a kinsman of her own, Jung Lu. The Taiping rebellion gave her splendid opportunites for intriguing and forming cabals; the Throne was at its wits' end and the dynasty seemed to be doomed. Yehonala took command of the situation, and by recommending this or that officer for preferment at Court steadily increased the number of her faithful henchmen.

"Her power grew apace and soon overshadowed that of the Emperor himself; State papers were submitted for her inspection: all the while, the weak monarch regarded her with increasing jealousy and hatred. At that time Su Shun was by far the most prominent member of the Imperial Clan. Hsien Feng delighted to honour him and always sought his society in preference to that of his own sulky brother, Prince Kung. No one else at Court rivalled him in the Imperial favour. Yehonala knew that she had forfeited the Emperor's regard, and was therefore anxious to win Su Shun to her side; she did so in the only way open to a woman, by tempting him to woo her. Su Shun told her plainly that too many men had known her charms for him to wish to make one of that great company, and from that day Yehonala's resentment against him burned fiercely.

"On the occasion of the Dragon Festival, she persuaded the Emperor to take her on a boating excursion. Yehonala, an adept with the oar, entered the boat first and stood waiting for Hsien Feng and Su Shun to embark. Just as the Son of Heaven was getting in, she suddenly dipped her oar, causing the boat to tilt, whereupon Hsien Feng took an undignified header into the water, besides hurting his foot. This act of mischievous effrontery infuriated the Emperor. It was about this time that his sister, the Princess Imperial, reminded him of the ancient prophecy: 'The Manchu house will be overthrown because of a warrior woman of the Yehonala Clan.' He remarked to Su Shun, in the hearing of a eunuch, who told me these facts: 'I propose before long to follow the example of the founder of the later Han dynasty (A.D. 30) who decreed the execution of his concubine Kouyi. What do you say? Shall I kill the Imperial concubine, or not?' Su Shun declined to utter an opinion, but his silence was construed by the Emperor as assent. The same eunuch who informed me of these things, told Yehonala of her husband's proposal. Her proud spirit was curbed for a while, but she lost no opportunity for consolidating her position, and the Emperor's increasing debility made it difficult for him to take any decided action. At this juncture, the war with the barbarians broke out. Hsien Feng became paralysed with fear and fled from Peking in spite of

THE COURT OF PEKING

Yehonala's remonstrances. At Jehol his health grew rapidly worse: he fell into a state of chronic melancholy, shut up Yehonala in one of the side Palaces and forbade all intercourse with her. But for the loyalty of some of her admirers she would probably have starved to death.

"As he lay dying, the Emperor determined that his guilty consort should not live to enjoy the fruits of her scheming. With his own hand he penned a valedictory decree, brief and explicit: 'After Our death you are commanded to slay the Western Empress, so that she may attend Our spirit in the next world. She must not be allowed to live and by her misdeeds overturn Our dynasty.' Hsien Feng sent for Su Shun and handed him this mandate, with orders to see to its due execution. Su Shun placed it inside the Imperial pillow; it had to remain in the death chamber, lest men should say it was forged.

"Now it happened that a young eunuch named Li Lien-ying, in attendance on the Emperor, was an expert masseur and his ministrations gave some relief to the dying monarch, whose limbs were racked by rheumatic pains. He was waiting in the antechamber whilst the Emperor was conversing with Su Shun, and having overheard the decree, hurried off to inform Yehonala. Prince Ch'un and his wife (sister of Tzŭ Hsi) were in Jehol at the time, and were waiting in the Palace, expecting at any moment to hear of the Emperor's death. Li Lien-ying managed to get word to Princess Ch'un of the fatal decree, and implored her to succour her beloved sister. On the announcement being made that the Emperor was being arrayed in his robes of longevity (*i.e.* that he was *in extremis*) the Princess was admitted into the chamber to assist in performing the last rites. Tzŭ Hsi was also released from her confinement, and entered the death chamber with her son, the Heir to the Throne. The Senior Empress, Tzŭ An, had the decree in her hand, but

Yehonala and her sister between them persuaded her to give it up, and promptly burned it. It was commonly believed that Tzŭ An voluntarily surrendered it, not wishing to make trouble at such a time, firstly, because she had no love for Su Shun, and secondly, because she had in her possession another similar document which authorised her to slay Yehonala if at any time her conduct should prove a danger to the State. At any rate the fatal decree was burnt; Su Shun re-entered the death chamber after the final offices had been performed, and inquired at what hour His Majesty had ascended on high, because custom prescribed that this should be inserted in the Imperial decree announcing the sovereign's demise. Tzŭ Hsi angrily took out the watch which she wore at her girdle, and turning its face towards Su Shun, exclaimed in a freezing tone: "See for yourself; he died only a moment ago." She did not wish it to appear that any interval had occurred which would justify suspicion as to the destroying of papers. From that day she made up her mind to put Su Shun to death. She knew that several people in the Palace were aware of the Emperor's intention to remove her, so that Su Shun's death was necessary to ensure her own safety. How true is the saying in the Odes: 'Truculent is the feminine nature!' Yehonala was a she-wolf at heart, though in saying this I know that I am guilty of presumption towards one who has shown me favour."

We turn next to a memoir or pamphlet, circulated over the signature of "An Anhui official." After referring to the fact that the Manchus first became a power by their subjugation of the Yeho tribe, and that they lost their Empire as the result of the ascendancy of the Yeho Clan (wherein he descries the inexorable whirligig of Time), this writer proceeds to explain Tzŭ Hsi's responsibility for the Manchu decadence, as follows:

THE COURT OF PEKING

"At the beginning of Hsien Feng's reign, the young Emperor created a very favourable impression. But the anxiety induced by the successes of the Taiping rebels, and the temptations placed in his way by the Court eunuchs, led him before long into evil courses of debauchery, in which he eventually became hopelessly involved. Wearying of the Manchu women of whom his harem was composed, he turned a willing ear to the beguilements of Su Shun, who played on his weaknesses chiefly in order to lessen the influence of Yehonala. With the help of the Chief eunuch, Su Shun procured thirty beautiful Chinese maidens from Kiangsu and Chekiang and brought them to Peking. Now there is a dynastic house-law of the Manchus which forbids the introduction of Chinese women into the Forbidden City.[1] Su Shun accordingly suggested to Hsien Feng that the disturbed state of the Empire justified special precautions for his personal safety at the Summer Palace, and he therefore advised him to employ these thirty Chinese women as a special bodyguard on night duty in the proximity of the Imperial bedchamber. They were to be divided into watches, of three women each, and beat the watch rattle in the courtyard adjoining Hsien Feng's apartments. Hsien Feng found the idea attractive, and the Palace Amazons became a feature of his Court.

"Although Yehonala had given him an Heir to the Throne, Hsien Feng greatly disliked her, and frequently discussed with Su Shun the advisability of deposing her. On his death-bed he wrote a valedictory Edict which he handed to his consort (Tzŭ An) in which he said: "The Western Concubine being mother of the new Emperor,

[1] This law was introduced by the mother of Shun Chih, the first Manchu Emperor, in order to guard her son against debauchery and to preserve the purity of the Manchu stock. She had an iron pillar erected at the entrance to the Palace, bearing the inscription, "If any females with small feet dare to pass this gate, let them be summarily beheaded."

it will be necessary to raise her to the rank of Empress Dowager. But she is utterly untrustworthy, and capable of any crime. Do not let her influence you in matters of government, but decide everything for yourself. If she behaves herself, well and good; treat her with all kindness. But if her misdeeds become flagrant, you must summon the chief Ministers to your presence and show them this decree, which authorises you to compel her to commit suicide." Hsien Feng never contemplated the joint Regency: the valedictory decree subsequently produced by Yehonala was forged for her by Li Hung-tsao.

"Upon Hsien Feng's demise, a clear distinction was at once drawn between the two Empresses: the senior, Tzŭ An, received the higher title of 'Empress Mother,' while to Yehonala was given the inferior appellation of 'Holy Mother.' [To a European the distinction is hardly apparent; suffice it to say, that in Chinese eyes there exists a real gulf between the two titles.] There was a precedent for thus lowering the rank of the Emperor's actual parent in the reign of Wan Li [sixteenth century], where a similar course had been adopted to thwart an ambitious woman. Yehonala was furious, and intrigued to such effect that she soon secured a title which gave her rank with, but after, the Senior Empress. She became the 'Motherly and Auspicious,' a title which, for experts in honorifics, is less elevated than the 'Motherly and Peace-giving' which designated Tzŭ An.

"At Jehol, Yehonala first threw out suggestions of her scheme for seizing the Regency to some of the Council. The idea met with no enthusiasm, as was evident from the demeanour of the Ministers, but none of them dared openly to oppose the masterful young woman, except Tu Han, who boldly rebuked her and pointed out that such a course would constitute a flagrant violation of dynastic house-law. Yehonala said no more at the time. The Empresses' Regency was thus unwelcome to the Court when first mooted; if it subsequently came to be well received, this was because Su Shun made himself so highly unpopular by his overbearing manners and by his openly expressed contempt for certain Princes of the Imperial Clan, who headed a strong party against him. Posterity has done scant justice to Su Shun because of his high stomach. The man was really far from bad, and infinitely less venal than most of his contemporaries. At least he was no bigoted Manchu, and it was chiefly through his influence that high military commands were given to Chinese like Hu Lin-yi and Tso Tsung-t'ang. At Court they called him the " Emperor's alarum.

" As to Tzŭ Hsi: 'The true story of the inner Chamber cannot be told in its entirety.'[1] The Empire soon learned to know only too well what were the morals of the Empress: her *liaison* with An Te-hai, who was no eunuch, was in all men's mouths. It was rumoured at one time that she was *enceinte* and people whispered that, if T'ung Chih died without an heir, the next Emperor would be illegitimate, like the ' First Emperor ' of the Chin dynasty. It was because of this scandal that the Empress Tzŭ An decided to kill An Te-hai. His remains were never exhibited to the public, lest the fact should come to light that he was not a eunuch.

" When the time came for the marriage of her son, T'ung Chih, Yehonala was very anxious that a daughter of Feng Hsia should become Empress Consort, but in this she was thwarted by Tzŭ An. A-Lu-te, who was chosen, was chaste and well-read. Chastity had no charms for Tzŭ Hsi, who alternately flouted and ignored her. She even went so far as to forbid the Emperor to visit his Consort, and compelled him to pass his time in the company of Lady Feng, who had been given the title of ' Discerning Concubine.' T'ung Chih soon

[1] A quotation from the Odes.

wearied of the Discerning one, and for a time spent his nights in solitude at the Palace of Celestial Purity. It was not to be wondered at, perhaps, under these circumstances, that the eunuchs soon persuaded him to accompany them on long nocturnal excursions to the gay quarter of the capital; on these occasions he passed as the 'licentiate Ch'en from Kiangsi.' On one of these outings he met in a tavern the Vice-president Mao Chang-hsi, and nodded to him affably. Mao was greatly alarmed and promptly informed the police that the Son of Heaven was leaving the Palace incognito, so that after this T'ung Chih's steps were dogged by a number of guards. T'ung Chih was far from gratified by these attentions and at the next audience expostulated strongly with Mao for not minding his own business.

"When the Emperor fell ill of the disease which proved fatal, Tzŭ An sent for the Empress A-Lu-te and comforted her by allowing her to minister to her husband. Now it is an old custom of the Palace that whenever the Emperor desires to visit any one of his concubines, an order in writing must first be sent by the Empress Consort bidding the favoured one to await the coming of the Son of Heaven. This order must be sealed with the Empress's seal, for without her authority the concubine is not permitted to give admission to the Emperor. [This has been the rule ever since the attempt to assassinate the Emperor Chia Ch'ing in 1542, when Yang Chin-ying attacked him in one of the concubines' apartments.] When T'ung Chih was ill and quite unfit to leave his bed he nevertheless persuaded his Consort to seal an order authorising a visit to one of his concubines. Shortly after this, his condition became desperate, and realising that the end was near, he sent for Li Hung-tsao, in whom he trusted, and on his coming, bade him raise the curtain and enter the bedchamber. A-Lu-te, who was standing by the bed, wished to withdraw, but T'ung Chih stopped her, saying: 'The Imperial Tutor is the old and trusted servant of the late Emperor: you may stay and hear what I have to say.' Li went down on his knees and made obeisance: T'ung Chih bade him arise, saying: 'This is no time for ceremony.' Then, taking Li's hand, he went on: 'I am dying.' Both Li and A-Lu-te began to weep, but he told them to desist and listen, as his time was very short. Turning to his wife, he asked: 'In the event of my death, who, think you, should succeed me?' She replied: 'The nation needs a ruler who has attained to manhood. I have no desire to be Empress Dowager and to have the charge of an infant Emperor. A minority would be a disaster to China.' The Emperor smiled: 'That is well. I am delighted that you realise this; I need not be uneasy any more.' He next told Li that he wished his first cousin the Beileh Tsai Ch'u, son of the ninth Prince, to succeed him as heir to Hsien Feng.[1] He then dictated his valedictory decree, which he bade Li copy out by his bedside. It contained about a thousand characters and introduced elaborate safeguards against his mother's usurpation of power. The dying man perused it with satisfaction, saying: 'Capital! Go now and rest; I may see you again before the end.'

"Li Hung-tsao left the Palace deadly pale and trembling violently; no wonder, for he hurried straight to Tzŭ Hsi's Palace and demanded immediate audience of her. Yehonala bade him enter, whereupon, without preliminaries, he produced the valedictory decree from his sleeve. Her Majesty read it with her usual unmoved calm: but at the end her rage burst forth. She rose from her seat, tore the paper into pieces and trampled them under her feet. 'Leave us at once,' she said to Li. She then

[1] This Prince was sent to prison by Tzŭ Hsi in 1898, after the *coup d'état*; his rank was restored to him by the Regent, Prince Ch'un, on the day of Yuan Shih-k'ai's downfall in 1909.

gave orders that no more medicine or food of any kind was to be taken to the Emperor; and no one was to go near him. She herself hurried to her son's apartment only to find him already dead. Tzŭ Hsi always remained grateful to Li for this act of treachery. True, she dismissed him from the Council in 1884, but ten years later he was again high in office, and after his death he received the highest possible title of canonisation, 'Learned and Orthodox.' Li Hung-chang used to say that this one act of his had done more than any other to bring the house of Gioro to ruin, owing to the harm Tzŭ Hsi's second Regency did to China. After the *coup d'état* in 1898, he narrated the whole incident to Ma Chien-chung, one of his secretaries, and added: 'Li Hung-tsao ruined the dynasty by that one act of his. We have him to thank for the war with Japan and all our subsequent misfortunes.' It was Ma who told me the facts.

"It was dusk when T'ung Chih died; the Grand Council were summoned at once to the side hall, but they found there Yehonala alone. She was standing beside the Throne, wearing her every-day costume. The Princes and Ministers inquired after His Majesty; the news of his decease being as yet unknown. Yehonala smiled: "Oh! His Majesty is in splendid health," she said. That was all, but the Court knew that the Emperor was dead.

"A moment later, suddenly forcing an angry tone, Tzŭ Hsi exclaimed: 'The Emperor is dead,' and then went on, 'This is no time for ceremony; we have important business before us.' During the discussion which followed, only Wen Hsiang opposed Tzŭ Hsi, and pressed for the appointment of an heir to T'ung Chih instead of to Hsien Feng. He was greatly indignant at the wrong done to T'ung Chih,[1] whom he only survived by a few months.

[1] Vide *China under the Empress Dowager*, p. 135.

THE COURT OF PEKING

"During the first years of Kuang Hsü's reign, Tzŭ Hsi took but little interest in the government, and frequently abstained from appearing at audiences. This was in itself significant, and when, in February 1881, she was taken ill, and remained confined to her rooms for two months, it was generally believed that she gave birth to a child, of whom Jung Lu was believed to be the father. As it would have been contrary to etiquette for the Court physician to give her prescriptions appropriate for an illness resulting from confinement (Yehonala being a widow), they treated her as if for dysentery, and her state, instead of improving, grew worse. It was not till Dr. Hsieh Fu-chen was summoned from Kiangsu that he diagnosed her complaint correctly, but in ordering the proper remedies he was careful to write at the top of the prescription 'For dysentery,' so that the august patient might not lose face. [All prescriptions for the Palace must be recorded in the archives of the Court of Physicians.]

"Tzŭ An had discovered her colleague in several equivocal situations, and was well aware of her lack of feminine virtue, but she was of a generous and tolerant nature. On Tzŭ Hsi's recovery from the illness above mentioned, the Eastern Empress invited her to a party to celebrate the event. After the wine cup had been passed three times, Tzŭ An dismissed all the attendants, desiring to appeal to Tzŭ Hsi's better nature by talking confidentially over old times. She referred to their childhood and to her father's kindness to the stricken family of Yehonala, and then she spoke of the flight to Jehol and the plot of Tsai-yuan, which so nearly brought ruin to them both. Yehonala affected to be deeply moved, and shed many tears during this recital. The Eastern Empress proceeded: 'We are both getting old, my sister; it may not be long before one of us rejoins our lord and master Hsien Feng in the Halls of the Lower

World. We have spent some twenty years together, and on the whole we have never had a real disagreement. Now, I have in my possession something which I received from His late Majesty and which has become of no value. I am afraid of its being discovered in the event of my death, in which case people might be led to suppose that our relations had only been friendly on the surface, and that we were really at enmity. This would be a pity indeed, and would be contrary to the late Emperor's wish.' With these words she produced a paper from her sleeve and handed it to Yehonala, who read it, turned ghastly pale, and could hardly master her feelings. For the document was the mandate given to Tzŭ An by Hsien Feng, as he lay dying, authorising her to kill Tzŭ Hsi if necessary. When Tzŭ Hsi had read it through, Tzŭ An asked for it again, saying: 'Do not be angry, sister. Be sure I should not have let you see this if I had harboured any feelings against you. I wished you to see it, that you might realise the very real affection that I have for you.' She then took the paper and burnt it before Tzŭ Hsi's eyes, saying, with a smile: ' It is worthless now, and had better be destroyed. I feel that I have done my duty by His Majesty and have fulfilled his wishes.' Yehonala was enraged beyond measure, but managed to hide her feelings. She pretended even to shed tears of penitent gratitude, and clasped Tzŭ An's hand, while her breast heaved with sobs. Tzŭ An consoled her and advised her to return to her Palace and rest. It was then that Tzŭ Hsi made up her mind to kill the Eastern Empress. So true is the adage that ' He who is not accustomed to train savage beasts should do nothing to goad them to fury.' Tzŭ An would have done well to remember this saying.

"A few days later Tzŭ An visited her colleague and found her quite unlike her haughty self; she was a model of submissive affection, so that the eunuch attendants could not understand what had come over their mistress. As for Tzŭ An, she congratulated herself on her wise diplomacy and fancied that she had curbed Yehonala's proud spirit for ever. Before leaving, Tzŭ An complained of feeling hungry; Tzŭ Hsi thereupon ordered Li Lien-ying to bring up a tray full of sweet cakes. Tzŭ An took several and found them far more palatable than those served to her from the Imperial kitchen. Yehonala was glad and said: 'Oh! these are made by my sister, the Duchess Chao. If you like them, I will send word to her to-morrow and she will make some more.' Tzŭ An thanked her, and Yehonala said smilingly: 'My family is as your family. How, then, should my sister be deemed worthy of your thanks?' Two days later the Duchess Chao duly furnished several boxes of cakes precisely similar in appearance to those which Tzŭ An had so greatly enjoyed. Tzŭ An ate one or two and found the flavour somewhat bitter. Before sundown she was dead—poisoned.

"Now it chanced that, on the previous evening, Tzŭ An had not been feeling quite well, and had sent for the same physician who had treated Yehonala so successfully, Dr. Hsieh Fu-chen. He advised her, in a memorial, that there was nothing much the matter, and that she did not need medicine. The eunuchs insisted, however, on his prescribing, so he gave her a cooling mixture and withdrew. Next day he went to call on his friend, Yen Ching-ming, the Grand Secretary, and while the two were chatting, one of Yen's secretaries came from the Board of Revenue with a document for his Chief to sign. He mentioned that, when he left the office, a rumour was in circulation that the Eastern Empress had expired. 'They were ordering the "auspicious boards"[1] to be prepared,' said he. Dr. Hsieh could not believe his ears, and dropped the cup he had in his hand,

---

[1] In the Palace an Imperial coffin is thus described.

exclaiming, 'I saw Her Majesty only a very short while ago and she had nothing but a slight chill. It is impossible that it could have proved fatal. It is far more likely that the Western Empress has had a relapse, and that some mistake has occurred by confusing the names.' Presently, however, one of the Household came to tell the fatal news. When Dr. Hsieh heard it, he was greatly distressed and said: 'There are stranger things in Heaven and earth than ever I dreamed of. What have I to live for now?' Because of his skill in medicine he had recently been promoted to be Lieutenant-General of a Banner.

"During Tzŭ Hsi's sickness, audiences had been held by Tzŭ An alone. That evening, when Tso Tsung-t'ang attended at the Palace, before the report of Tzŭ An's death had been published, he inquired how she was. They told him she was dead, whereat he was horrified and amazed: 'I saw her at audience to-day and she spoke with all her usual vigour; I cannot believe that such a death can have been natural.' Prince Kung hurriedly stopped him from saying anything more, but the eunuchs had heard him and duly informed their mistress. Tso left the capital not long afterwards.

"The collection of poisons in the Palace comprised drugs of such potency that with some death followed on mere contact with the lips, while others took many days to operate and were not to be detected by any Chinese methods. Many of these drugs had come down from the Ming dynasty. Some of them were said to have been brought from Italy in K'ang Hsi's day by foreigners at the Court. It was with one of these drugs that Tzŭ Hsi poisoned 'Mysterious' Liu, one of the chief eunuchs, whose influence for a time exceeded even that of Li Lien-ying. This eunuch was senior to Li in standing, and though Li gradually rose in Yehonala's favour, Liu continued to attend Her Majesty daily and would not be supplanted by his younger rival. Li hated him and slandered him in every possible way to the Empress, but Liu was very cunning, and managed to anticipate calumny with explanations which always pacified Tzŭ Hsi. One day, however, he offended Her Majesty, who reproved him severely; this time, Li's abuse of his rival fell on attentive ears and Tzŭ Hsi, giving way to a passion of rage, ordered Liu to attend her immediately. When he appeared, she recapitulated the list of his offences, some thirty in all, and ended by saying: 'Do you not think you merit decapitation?' Liu realised that there was no hope, so kotowed, saying: 'Your slave deserves to die a myriad deaths, but I implore the Old Buddha to remember that I have served her, as her dog or her horse, for thirty years; let her grant me at least the favour of dying with a whole skin.' She pondered over this for a minute, and replied: 'Very well; you may go now, and await my further commands.' She bade her handmaidens conduct him to a small antechamber and lock the door on him. Then she burst out laughing, and called all her eunuchs and women to her side: 'I have a new amusement for you to-day,' she said. One of the women was told to bring a small case from her bedroom; Yehonala opened it with a tiny key which she wore at her girdle. It contained about twenty phials, one of which she selected and poured out some of the contents, a pink powder, into a wine-cup. She mixed some water with this and bade the attendant take it to Liu and say that he was to drink the contents and then lie quietly down. The attendant soon returned and reported that Liu had thanked Her Majesty for her benevolence and had done as directed. Tzŭ Hsi waited about ten minutes and then said: 'You may now see the fun I promised you. Open Liu's door and see how he fares.' The eunuch was lying apparently asleep; though dead, he showed no trace of suffering. Yehonala had a heart of iron: indeed, 'What in this world is so truculent as the feminine nature?'"

Another memoir, by "A writer on Court subjects," deals with the same tragic incident. It will be seen that his statements, based on the real or alleged testimony of one of Tzŭ An's confidential eunuchs, coincide with those of the "Anhui official" in regard to several of the main charges against Tzŭ Hsi, but the motives alleged for the sending of the poisoned cakes have nothing in common in the two narratives. It seems fair to conclude that in one instance (or both) the writer has drawn on this imagination for his facts, and constructed theories which seemed to him to meet the case and to supply a plausible indictment.

This writer professes to give the "main facts concerning the sudden death of Tzŭ An."

"When the Empress Dowager of the Eastern Palace died suddenly in 1881," he says, "suspicion pointed to Tzŭ Hsi, who had everything to gain by putting her colleague out of the way, but her guilt remained not proven, owing to the care with which Palace secrets were guarded. In April 1908, I was in Peking, and happened to meet a eunuch in a shop outside the Ch'ien Men, with whom I became intimate. He had formerly been Tzŭ An's confidential table boy; his name was Liu Wen-pin. It is hard to say why Tzŭ Hsi did not take his life, but the Old Buddha was always unaccountably loth to kill more people than was necessary. This man told me the whole story and, on the face of it, I should think his record was true. He said:

'The elevation of Kuang Hsü to the Throne was quite contrary to the wish of Tzŭ An; after his accession she took even less part in State business than during T'ung Chih's reign. Above all things she hated a scene, and was distressed by her colleague's somewhat hasty temper. She took to religious observances, became a devout

THE COURT OF PEKING

Buddhist, and fasted on all the occasions which custom enjoined. Bonzes attended her Palace and recited prayers daily, and in time of drought or flood she would pray for hours together.

'At that time the most fashionable actor in Peking was one Yang Yueh-lou, remarkable for his personal beauty and charm. Tzŭ Hsi summoned him to her Palace to play before her, became attracted by his good manners and gift of ready repartee, and ended by becoming intimate with him. He would come to her apartments at all hours of the day and night; finally, she installed him as doorkeeper, and although this caused some scandal, none of the Princes or officials of the Court ventured to remonstrate with her except one courageous Censor, who, in a memorial, plainly hinted at her flagrant violation of ancestral house law. Yang frequently spent the whole night in Tzŭ Hsi's company. One evening, Tzŭ An had occasion to go across to Tzŭ Hsi's quarters, in connection with some official appointment that was to be decided next morning. She appeared unannounced. Tzŭ Hsi was out in the grounds, but Yang was calmly reclining on the Old Buddha's "phœnix bed." Tzŭ An saw him quite plainly and beat a hasty retreat, after giving to the maids in attendance the message which she desired to be conveyed to Tzŭ Hsi.

'Tzŭ Hsi, on returning, was horrified to find that she was found out. As was her wont, she acted promptly. She ordered Yang to arise, and handed him a cup of clotted cream flavoured with apricot, saying: "The Empress of the East will be back almost immediately, so you had best be off. Here is a beverage, from my own table, which you may drink in my presence." The flattered minion partook of the delicacy and just managed to reach his home before dying in awful agony. The cup had contained a large quantity of arsenic, the poison which Tzŭ Hsi found most effective.

'Tzŭ Hsi then took to her room and gave out that she was too sick to attend to State matters. Tzŭ An had been much shocked by what she had seen. Had she been a strong woman, she could easily have degraded Tzŭ Hsi by issuing a decree recounting her misdeeds; indeed, she might have secured her death for so gross a breach of a widow's duty and disrespect to Hsien Feng's soul in Heaven. But she feared Tzŭ Hsi too much to venture on such a step, and it never occurred to her that in her own self-defence she would be wise to take action, inasmuch as Tzŭ Hsi was not likely to forget or forgive having been surprised in a compromising situation. Instead of denouncing her, she sent eunuchs daily to ask after the malingerer's health and to urge her to return to the discharge of her duties.

'Now, it so happened that at this time a memorial had come in from one of the provinces, recounting the heroic chastity of a certain young widow, who, though starving, had died rather than accept the advances of a wealthy neighbour. The Governor memorialised the Empresses, asking for the honour of a memorial arch to be conferred as an encouragement to "faithful women who would die rather than lose their virtue." Tzŭ An came across to show this document to Tzŭ Hsi, and to ask her decision. Possibly she may have thought to avert suspicion from her colleague's mind by talking frankly about the woman's virtue, which would lead Tzŭ Hsi to think that her colleague knew nothing of her recent intrigue. But Tzŭ Hsi's suspicions were not to be thus lulled. She answered Tzŭ An perfunctorily, her own mind working rapidly all the time. She came to the conclusion that this was a subtle way of informing her that her own lack of feminine virtue had been discovered, so she determined to delay no longer. Tzŭ An said: "This memorial will show you how you are needed at Court; pray come back at once." Tzŭ Hsi answered:

THE COURT OF PEKING

"The woman acted well; let her have her arch, as an example to the women of the day." No more was said, but on the following day Tzŭ Hsi sent her favourite waiting-maid to Tzŭ An with a present of honey cakes and her reverent greeting. Tzŭ An ate of them and died of poison within a few hours. When Tso Tsung-t'ang (who had only lately arrived to take up his duties on the Grand Council) came to Court next day, he was met by the announcement that Tzŭ An was dead. He stamped angrily up and down the Palace courtyard, exclaiming: "Why was no announcement made of her illness, and why was no doctor called in from the Imperial Court of Physicians? It seems very strange also that no decree was issued immediately after her decease occurred, as custom requires; its belated issue is highly suspicious."

'Tzŭ Hsi, who was in the main hall of audience, was speedily informed by her eunuchs of what Tso had said. She took an early opportunity of relieving him of his duties on the Grand Council by sending him to Nanking as Viceroy. She realised that he suspected her, and his death soon afterwards came as an immense relief. He was too powerful, with his army behind him, for her to adopt her usual drastic methods in his case. I was lucky myself in not incurring Tzŭ Hsi's suspicions; indeed, she has always treated me with much liberality. I am still in her service, although my present duties keep me in the Forbidden City.'

"Thus ended the eunuch's statement; a few moons later Tzŭ Hsi herself 'mounted the chariot drawn by fairies and went forth on her distant journey.' Doubtless she still has her imperious way in the Halls of the Lower World, and compels her colleague to yield precedence to her august shade!"

Finally, we reproduce an extract from the artlessly biassed writings of the Chinese essayist who signs himself

"Born out of Time." The monotonous regularity with which these pamphleteers credit the Old Buddha with selecting her lovers from the lowest classes, suggests a conspiracy of defamation, very characteristic of Oriental methods.

This writer observes: "During the lifetime of the Old Buddha, the following story was only whispered with bated breath in the precincts of the Palace, but its truth is universally acknowledged. It accounts for Her Majesty's illegal nomination of Kuang Hsü to the Throne, far better than the commonly accepted official version of the matter, whereby it is explained that Tzŭ Hsi appointed him because of his physical disabilities, so that she might look forward to a prolonged Regency.

"The Old Buddha was very fond of poached eggs cooked in chicken gravy, a popular dish in Peking restaurants, where it is commonly called 'tangwo kuo' (literally, 'fruits lying in gravy'). During her first Regency she insisted on having this delicacy brought to her every morning by the eunuch, An Te-hai, and after his death by Li Lien-ying. They bought it at the Chinhua (Gold Blossom) restaurant, which stands outside the West gate of the Imperial city, a house famous for this dish. [*En passant*, I may mention that the Old Buddha was charged twenty-four taels for four eggs served in this way, the usual price being about twenty cents, so An and Li must have made handsome profits.] After An's unlucky decease, Li made friends with one of the waiters at the restaurant, a handsome youth of twenty, named Shih, who had a remarkably white complexion. Li allowed this youth to accompany him within the forbidden precincts, and even into Tzŭ Hsi's Palace. One day the Empress observed him, was struck by his good looks, and asked Li who he was. On learning his name and origin, Tzŭ Hsi was pleased to say: 'He is the best-looking lad I've seen for many a long day. He shall have a post in the Palace, and he can wait upon me at table.' The result was that Shih was always at her side, and the intimacy, much to Li's disgust, resulted in Tzŭ Hsi becoming *enceinte*. She was then in her thirty-sixth year. When the child was born, it was obviously impossible to bring him up in the Palace, so Tzŭ Hsi appealed to her favourite sister, Prince Ch'un's wife, to help her. The infant was hurriedly removed to the West city, where Prince Ch'un lived. Doubtless the Prince was also in the secret, which would account for the Old Buddha's marked favour towards him. Tzŭ Hsi's next step was to put the unlucky Shih to death. This story serves also to explain Li Lien-ying's undisguised contempt for Kuang Hsü, for he could not forget his humble origin. When T'ung Chih died, Tzŭ Hsi defied ancestral tradition by placing this child, her second son, upon the Throne, as successor to his half-brother. One can realise what a bitter blow it must have been to her to find the boy growing up hostile and disobedient to his mother, to whom alone he owed the Throne. No doubt Wu Ko-tu [1] was in the secret of this matter, and if so, his historic protest requires to be read in a sense different from that which has hitherto been placed upon it. He would have wished to save the house of Gioro from being tainted by illegitimacy of this kind, and for this reason urged that the appointment of Kuang Hsü should be nullified at the first opportunity. On these grounds, also, the Old Buddha may have justified her design on the Emperor's life in 1900; she may have argued that she had a perfect right to dispose of her own son as she chose."

The frame of mind in which " Born out of Time " records these things is fittingly illustrated by his concluding observations : " If the purpose of the revolution

[1] The famous Censor who committed suicide at the grave of T'ung Chih to protest against the illegality of the succession of Kuang Hsü (vide *China under the Empress Dowager*, p. 132).

was to eradicate the Manchu dominion," he says, "it may appear to some to have been unnecessary, for that purpose had been to all intents effected by the Chinese paramours of the concubine of Yung Cheng, by Yehonala, and others."

It is interesting to compare the estimate of Tzŭ Hsi's character as presented by Young China, with that in which she was held by men like Tseng-Kuo-fan, Liu K'un-yi, and many other great officers of State, and to wonder which of these verdicts will be finally accepted in the histories written for the learning of the sons of Han in ages to come. It is certain that, making due allowance for bias of class, the opinion of the orthodox and sober-minded *literati* is the more sincere and nearer to the truth, and that it represents the instinctive judgment of the mass of Tzŭ Hsi's contemporaries. But the Republic's text-books for the use of schools are not likely to take their picture of the Old Buddha from the annals of the orthodox. History, as Froude has said, presents no subject matter for science: had he examined some of the material from which Chinese history is usually compiled, he might have expressed the same idea in more forcible terms.

CHAPTER XXI

THE COURT UNDER THE LAST REGENCY

AFTER the death of the Emperor Kuang Hsü on the 14th November, 1908, followed next day by that of the Empress Dowager Tzǔ Hsi, the Throne passed once more to a child of tender years, the Emperor Hsüan T'ung. The objections to the succession were many and valid, and the risks of a Regency obvious, but Tzǔ Hsi, always a law unto herself, overrode all opposition. Her motives in selecting this infant son of Prince Ch'un (brother of the late Emperor) were mixed, and her dying words showed that she herself was by no means blind to the dangers to which her autocratic decision would expose the State. One of the factors which chiefly influenced her choice, was a desire to perpetuate the influence of the Yehonala Clan in the person of her niece (Kuang Hsü's widow), the Empress Lung Yü; another, as she herself declared, lay in the promise which she had made to Jung Lu, at the time when she betrothed his daughter to Prince Ch'un, that the eldest son of this marriage should become Heir to the Throne, in recognition of Jung Lu's lifelong service to the dynasty and to herself.

But whatever her motives, the immediate result of her action was to create a condition of affairs in the Palace similar to that which had served her so well during the minority of the Emperor T'ung Chih, and again during that of Kuang Hsü. It is to be remembered that when she issued her Decree of the 14th November, appointing Prince Ch'un Regent and his infant son Emperor, she had every intention of living; and had she not died, it is perfectly certain that the Regent would have enjoyed no greater authority than she had allowed to his unfortunate brother Kuang Hsü. It was only on the following day, and at the very point of death, that she issued a decree conferring upon him the whole government of the Empire; and it will be remembered that, even then, she took from him the substance of authority, leaving only the shadow, by the concluding sentence of that decree, which ordered that " in any question of vital importance, in regard to which an expression of the Empress Dowager's opinion is desirable, the Regent shall apply to her in person for instructions, and act accordingly." [1]

The ill-starred Regent found himself, from the outset, sore let and hindered in the administration of the Goodly Heritage. Tzŭ Hsi's last act, indeed, was fiendishly ingenious, if her object was to create divided counsels and to perpetuate the old Yehonala Clan feud in the Palace. The Regent's position was effectively undermined by that last clause of the decree, which placed at the disposal of the new Empress Dowager and the Yehonala Clan powers of supervision and interference sufficient to thwart him at every turn. The Regent and his party were checkmated from the first move: the real powers behind the Throne must always be his sister-in-law, the Empress Lung Yü, and his wife, the strong-minded daughter of Jung Lu. Tzŭ Hsi with her last breath advised her high officers of State " never again to allow any woman to hold the supreme power," but her valedictory orders made petticoat government a foregone conclusion, complicated by the further certainty of a struggle for power between these two masterful women.

Had the Regent been a man of strong purpose and resource, he might have won through to supreme authority

[1] Vide *China under the Empress Dowager*, p. 465.

by a skilful policy of *Divide et Impera*; but he showed neither initiative, courage nor intelligence, and frequently played into the hands of Lung Yü by the perpetration of blunders which, in the eyes of the Court, made her interference in State affairs wholly justifiable and inevitable. History seemed, indeed, to be in a fair way to repeat itself with extraordinary fidelity. Had it not been for the *débâcle* of the revolution, whereby the Regent, the Yehonala Clan, and all the loves and hates of the Manchus have been swept into the limbo of things outworn, it is safe to say that the position between the Empress Dowager, the young Emperor's mother and the Regent would have reproduced nearly all the essential features which existed during the joint Regency of Tzŭ Hsi and Tzŭ An, Empresses of the Eastern and Western Palaces, after the death of Hsien Feng, at the time when Prince Kung was " Adviser to the Government "; and it is equally safe to say that Lung Yü, faithfully following in the footsteps of Tzŭ Hsi, would before long have deprived Prince Ch'un of the Regency and relegated his wife, the Emperor's mother, to an innocuous background.

Lung Yü, whose death occurred " in the profound seclusion of the Summer Palace," on the 22nd of February, 1913, was openly estranged from her lord for many years before his death. When Tzŭ Hsi selected her for the position of Imperial Consort, in 1889, it was more with a view to strengthening the hands of the Yehonala Clan [1] through her influence, than to increase the felicity of His Majesty Kuang Hsü; and as both parties were aware of the fact, it would have been strange had their relations been cordial. Kuang Hsü's senior Consort certainly never pretended to love, honour and obey him; nevertheless, she resented his devotion to the " Pearl Concubine," and frequently quarrelled with her husband. In appearance Her Majesty was unattractive, and her

[1] She was the daughter of Kuei Hsiang, brother of Tzŭ Hsi.

disposition anything but genial; but she possessed the shrewd mother-wit and genius for intrigue which had distinguished her august aunt.

After Tzŭ Hsi's death, Lung Yü, now Empress Dowager, lost no time in asserting her authority, with the result that the inmates of the Palace and the officials of the metropolis speedily ranged themselves into opposing camps, the adherents of the Empress and her Clan against the Regent and his party. A further element of disruption arose in the strife which divided the eunuchs of the Palace into two fiercely hostile parties, the followers of Tzŭ Hsi's aged major domo, Li Lien-ying, fighting for perquisites and power against the partisans of Lung Yü's favourite, the arrogant young eunuch, Chang Yuan-fu. Here again history repeated itself with almost monotonous observance of dynastic tradition, and with the usual deplorable results.

Lung Yü made Tzŭ Hsi her model in all things. Those who had hoped that the new *régime* would set itself to abolish the crying evils of the eunuch system and, by cleansing the Augean stables of the Palace, give an earnest of its desire to effect reforms in other directions, were speedily disillusioned. The new Empress Dowager, like her august predecessor, was profuse with good intentions, but in practice she followed the example of the Old Buddha's extravagant and licentious youth, so that her Court rapidly became a hotbed of scandals and abuses. Upon the plea of reorganising the Imperial Household on a basis of careful economy and good order she did, indeed, reduce the eunuch staff and dismiss many of the Palace women, but the individuals dismissed were invariably supporters of the Regent's faction. She displayed a keen interest in the affairs of government, metropolitan and provincial, but her interest arose unmistakably from the connection of these affairs with the replenishing of her own Privy Purse.

THE COURT OF PEKING

One day, in the autumn of 1909, Lung Yü was taking the air with her favourite handmaidens and eunuchs on the Lake near the Winter Palace. The conversation turned on certain criticisms which had recently been directed against Her Majesty by some of the Censors and even in the Press. "I care nothing for such criticisms," said Lung Yü. "Her late sainted Majesty suffered greatly from the irresponsible wagging of evil tongues. I am firmly resolved to make her my guide and pattern in all things. She knew well how to blend severity with kindness, and she knew also that public opinion is like a stream which requires damming at its source."

Her attendants were delighted at this outburst, taking it to mean that Her Majesty looked forward to asserting herself after the manner of Tzŭ Hsi, when the time should be ripe. All the eunuchs kotowed, and "Little" Chang Yuan-fu expressed their sentiments, saying: "Your Majesty's resolve will bring happiness to the Empire and to your unworthy servants as well." Lung Yü beamed graciously, and the entertainment proceeded amidst general satisfaction.

Following the example of her illustrious model, Lung Yü took early steps to secure control of the education of the young Emperor, and was particularly careful to select, for attendance on the child, eunuchs who should alienate his affection from the Regent and train him to recognise her own paramount authority. At the same time she complied faithfully with the traditions of orthodoxy and Court etiquette in the following decree (10th July, 1911), which for platitudinous insincerity is on a level with Tzŭ Hsi's most classical effusions. It was issued, under her orders, by the Regent.

"The personal commands of Her Majesty the Empress Dowager, Lung Yü, to the Regent are as follows:

"His Majesty, the Emperor, succeeded in tender

infancy to the goodly heritage and glorious patrimony of the Throne. He has now reached an age when wise training becomes needful, and it behoves him to enter upon his education in due time, so that he shall accomplish notable results and build up a solid foundation for his rule.

"I command, therefore, that the Court of Astronomers shall select an auspicious day in the 7th Moon, for the Emperor to begin his studies in the Yü Ching Palace. I hereby appoint the Grand Secretary Lu Jun-tsiang, and the Vice-President Ch'en Pao-chen, as preceptors to His Majesty. They shall bestow instruction upon him early and late, and shall display their utmost diligence in sowing the fertile seed in his mind. It is incumbent upon them to impart in fullest detail the causes from which proceed good government or anarchy in ancient and modern times in every country of the world, since this is essential to a sovereign's training, and they are to point the moral as circumstances may require. At the present time, when intercourse between all parts of the world is widely developed, and civilisation is ever advancing, it behoves them, above all, to inculcate a clear impression of the progress of constitutional government during its first few decades, and of the development of sound learning, especial stress being laid on the needs of the day. The highest examples must be selected and scrupulous attention given to detail, it being understood that the cardinal principle of Confucius shall be faithfully instilled whereby the attainment of knowledge produces sincerity and righteousness, and the cultivation of the moral nature leads to a state of ideal government. Thus shall a daily increase of virtue be imparted to his mind, and thereby a good foundation be laid for perfect governance.

"The Regent is to exercise a general superintendence over the Emperor's curriculum and the procedure in the

THE COURT OF PEKING

Yü-ching Palace. The Manchu language, spoken and written, being inseparable from our Dynasty, I hereby appoint I-k'o-t'an, Deputy-Lieutenant-General-designate of a Banner, to bestow such instruction therein as may be requisite; of this also the Regent is to exercise a general control. The words of the Empress."

A few weeks later we find Her Majesty taking steps to prevent the "illicit diversion of funds" from her Privy Purse. Her decree on this subject, preaching the gospel of "circumspect parsimony," bears an unmistakable family likeness to those which Tzŭ Hsi was wont to issue in the heyday of her tumultuous and spendthrift youth. The reference to building operations is particularly barefaced, inasmuch as Her Majesty was at the moment conniving, as will be shown, at enormous peculations by her Chief eunuch under this very heading. It reads as follows:

"The Ministry of Finance has impeached the Comptroller and staff of the Imperial Household for recording false and excessive accounts of expenditure incurred, and for conniving at illicit diversion of funds in connection with the Imperial Silk Factory at Hang-chou. Such conduct is grossly improper, and I hereby command that the officials concerned be referred to the Cabinet for determination of a penalty proportionate to the respective offenders' rank and position.

"In addition, I hereby convey my severe rebuke to the Comptrollers of the Imperial Household for their gross lack of vigilance in the performance of their duties. Hereafter they are to examine all accounts of expenditure and of building operations with the most rigid and particular scrutiny, so as to conform with the earnest desire which animates me, in the profound seclusion of my Palace, to maintain in all things a circumspect parsimony. The words of the Empress."

This ingenuous declaration of high principle was made

in August 1911. Four months earlier, a certain Manchu Censor, named Ch'ing Fu, had expressed the sentiments of all who cared for the dignity of the Court, in an extremely outspoken memorial, which laid particular stress on the notorious malpractices of the eunuch Chang Yuan-fu in connection with the contracts for building works and repairs at the Palace. Abuses of this kind, exposing the incorrigible corruption of the Manchu *régime*, provided the revolutionary party in the South with arguments of a kind that appealed, far more than political ideals, to the man in the street.

In this memorial the Censor said : " Whenever money is needed in the Palace, this eunuch Chang Yuan-fu actually dares to make direct requisitions on the Board of Finance and the Imperial Treasury, out of which he helps himself freely. Quite recently he made an arrangement with three Manchus connected with the Works department of the Household for the rebuilding of the two Throne halls, the Hall of the Correct Mean and the Hall of the Empyrean, and another for the supply of musical instruments used in the Palace for sacrificial rites. The actual amount requisitioned was 490,000 taels in silver and 30,000 taels in gold (say, £180,000). For repairs of the main hall of audience at the Palace of Heavenly Purity, he has received 570,000 taels, while for re-painting some of the Forbidden City's inner enclosures, no less a sum than 260,000 taels has been charged in the account. For repairs to the Palace drains, the sum of 7,000 taels was actually expended, but this eunuch has drawn 80,000 taels from the Board of Finance on this account. For repairing the courts of the Palace, the Board of Revenue has paid over to him 1,200,000 taels. Not satisfied with these peculations, out of which he must have made at least 2,000,000 taels, he proceeded to rebuild the Palace of Perpetual Spring (which was in excellent repair). For this work the contract called for about 1,000,000 taels, but on the 26th of the 8th Moon of last year (September 1910), the Imperial Household memorialised the Throne that the Board of Finance should be ordered to pay over half as much again under this heading. To this memorial the Empress Dowager appended the rescript 'Noted.'

"Now the fact is, that on this contract no more than 300,000 taels were expended, so that the greater part of the balance of 1,200,000 taels has found its way into Chang's pocket.

"Worse than all this, Chang has purloined many valuable pearls and precious stones from the Palace, the value of which amounts to millions of taels. He and two tradesmen named Li Lo-t'ing and Liu Pu-ch'ing have also opened numerous pawnshops and building yards. At a crisis like the present, when funds are so urgently needed for Army reform, and when the provincial budgets all show huge deficits, it is passing strange that this all-powerful eunuch should be allowed to manipulate these large amounts at his own sweet will. I would humbly ask Your Majesty the Empress Dowager to issue a decree ordering the confiscation of all his ill-gotten gains, and the arrest and condign punishment of this baneful and iniquitous eunuch, in order that the National Treasury may receive an accession of much-needed funds."

This memorial was suppressed, and Her Majesty administered a severe rebuke to the Censor. The eunuch's power and insolence were greatly increased by the incident; he waxed fat and began to kick even the highest. Soon there were none at Court who dared oppose him, and even the Regent quailed before him. He became Lung Yü's inseparable and intimate companion, following her wherever she went. Shortly after his impeachment he made another large haul out of theatrical performances in the Palace. By his influence the compilation of the proposed Civil List was effectually blocked. Soon his fame spread, as that of Li Lien-ying had done before him, to every quarter of the city; his little finger became thicker than the loins of his predecessor, so that in two years all men spoke of him with hatred and fear. In that time he amassed a fortune of about £1,000,000 out of Palace squeezes alone, and this is without reckoning bribes and " grants-in-aid " from officials.

Li Lien-ying weakened visibly after the death of his mistress and protector; his proud spirit was broken and his stomach for fighting permanently deranged. He died on the 4th of March, 1911, at the age of sixty-nine, after two years of chronic dysentery. On the day of his death some of his most valuable pearls were stolen from his apartments by eunuchs of the Chang faction: they were subsequently claimed by a eunuch named Li Yi-ch'un on the plea that he was Li Lien-ying's foster son. Chang subsequently intrigued against him and secured his banishment for life, and the pearls are now in Chang's safe keeping, or were until the abdication of the dynasty.

The extraordinary influence which this man rapidly established over the Empress Lung Yü, his unbounded presumption and haughty bearing, naturally led in his case to rumours similar to those which were widely circulated about the favourite companion of Tzǔ Hsi's halcyon days, the " false eunuch " An Te-hai. His antecedents were peculiar, for it was not till his eighteenth year that he " left the family " (to use the Chinese euphemism) and became a eunuch. Previous to that he had been married, and was the father of two children. When he came from Ho Chien-fu to Peking, in 1899, seeking employment in the Palace, he was quite without influence or friends, but was able to persuade one of his fellow-townsmen, a head eunuch, to employ him in a menial capacity. Being of extremely handsome appearance, a good musician and a first-class actor, he soon made his way to the front, and was eventually employed to wait at table upon Lung Yü, whom he accompanied to Hsi-an in 1900.

His way of living lent colour to the rumours which reflected on the virtue of his Imperial mistress, for in 1911 he kept up the establishment of a family man. Three of his chief clients in the building contract and stolen-jewellery businesses (of whom one was the shopkeeper Li Lo-t'ing, mentioned in the Censor's memorial above quoted) presented him during that year with three maidens of respectable parentage, whom they purchased in Tientsin for the purpose. No great importance need be attached to these facts, however, nor to the rumours thereby created, for such domestic arrangements are by no means unusual with the wealthier eunuchs at Peking, and may be regarded as " face-making " expedients.

Of the enormous power and wealth which this individual gathered into his supple hands during the brief course of the Regency, there is no doubt. Towards the end he was, in fact, the Government of China. The semi-regal dignities which he assumed, his insolent attitude towards the highest Manchu and Chinese officials, had become a public scandal greater than anything Peking had known since the days of Ho Shen. As his career fittingly adorns the tale and points the moral of the Manchus' decline and fall, we make no apology for describing the most notorious of his achievements and habits.

Before the Court mourning was over, with Lung Yü's knowledge and consent, he organised sumptuous theatrical entertainments at the Palace, a gross breach of piety and decorum. In the course of these entertainments an incident occurred which showed that the new Empress Dowager had studied her illustrious prototype to good effect, in that she regarded herself and her affairs as above the law. At this time the leaders of the Opium Abolition movement were displaying great activity in Peking and

Tientsin, and the Government was affording them moral, if not material, support in the form of decrees, regulations and Bureaus. In theory there were no opium smokers left, either in the Palace or in any public office. Now, the most famous actor and singer of North China was a man named T'an, nicknamed " The Heaven-compelling Singer "; he was then sixty years of age, but still in full vigour and a confirmed opium smoker. Lung Yü had sent for him to give a command performance, but the summons, though thrice repeated, was ignored. The Ministers of the Household sent for him, intending to punish him for his contumacy, but T'an said to them : " I need an ounce of opium every day, as the craving is very strong, and without it I cannot sing a note. Now that officials have been forbidden to touch opium, how should an actor dare to break the law and smoke in the Palace ? " The Ministers proceeded to consult Lung Yü, who said : " Let him have his opium in peace." She even signed a special decree, saying : " The actor T'an is permitted to enter the Palace and to smoke opium during the intervals between the acts."

Lung Yü also imitated the Old Buddha in displaying the keenest interest in everything connected with her theatrical entertainments, and in her criticism of the performers. This criticism sometimes expressed itself in a manner which Europe has outgrown. On one occasion, for instance, the well-known actor Yang Hsiao-lou was performing an emotional piece, " The Long Mountain Slope," before Lung Yü and the Court. Her Majesty took umbrage at his lack of expression in delivering his lines and " at his failure to exert his best energies in her presence." She commanded the Chief eunuch (Chang) to have the actor chastised with forty strokes of the whip, after which he was to be expelled from the Palace precincts and permanently struck off the list of Palace actors. It is true that there were many at Court who declared that his disgrace had nothing to do with his acting, but was due to his having failed to placate Chang with the usual " squeezes," in addition to which, he was a *protégé* of the late Li Lien-ying.

By dynastic houselaw, all building operations in the Forbidden City are supposed to be suspended during the period of mourning; yet Chang persuaded the Empress to sanction the expenditure of vast sums upon a large building in foreign style—the Yen Hsi Kung, or Palace of Continual Prosperity. For the construction of this inappropriate edifice, no official supervisors were appointed, as precedent required. The estimates were all drawn up by Chang and carried out under his own supervision by the Yung Te ("Everlasting Virtue") firm of contractors. The same firm was simultaneously engaged in the complete reconstruction of Chang's private residence, in the lane of the Temple of Supreme Felicity. The result was a Palace, fitted with camphor wood furniture and lacquer screens. The style of architecture (except that the roofs are not yellow) is identical with that used in the Ning Shou-kung, which in itself constitutes an act of *lèse majesté*.[1] His mansion was equipped throughout with electric light fittings taken from the Palace of Ceremonial Phœnixes, where Her Majesty Tzŭ Hsi died. Many curios were also taken from the same place, including the golden image of the Goddess of Mercy, four feet high, which was presented to the Old Buddha at Hsi-an. His garden also contained a famous jade fish-bowl, taken from the private Imperial garden in the North of the Forbidden City. The rockery was made as an exact replica of the one in the Palace, and six ornamental kiosques, of the Imperial design, were erected in the grounds.

His residence was connected by a private telephone with Lung Yü's apartments in the Palace of Perpetual

---

[1] *Vide*, the impeachment of Ho Shen, *supra*, p.

Spring, which also constitutes *lèse majesté*. His tables were covered with bronzes and sacrificial vessels removed from the Palace; many of them, no doubt, presents from the Empress to her favourite.

He gave orders for the demolition of the Imperial studio, known as the "Studio of Long-Lived Uprightness," and directed that all its fittings of camphor and black wood were to be deposited with the Yung Te contractors, to be used in decorating a new wing of his own residence.

As his hold over Lun Yü increased, so did he wax in insolence towards the Regent, who, towards the end of 1911, was obviously afraid of him. On one occasion, when the Regent had ventured to remonstrate with him for removing Palace valuables, the eunuch produced Lung Yü's golden tablet and said: "Here is my authority." The Regent glared angrily and began to fume, whereupon Chang haughtily remarked: "Palace matters are not your business. When the Empress and I require your advice we will ask for it. Meanwhile, your apartments and your duties lie at the San So" (the Three Departments set aside for the Regent to the East of the Palace): "what business brings you here?"

In like manner, when Li Chia-chu was appointed Vice-Chancellor of the Senate, he put in a memorial denouncing the entire eunuch system as unworthy of a State with any pretentions to civilisation. Li had only recently returned from investigating the constitutional system of Japan. He himself felt no divine despair in this matter, but since he was obliged to put in a report of some sort, and to discuss changes desirable in the interests of the State, it would have been absurd not to attack the eunuch system, as to the evils of which all Chinese rulers, statesmen and moralists, have agreed for centuries. But Chang Yuan-fu was, none the less, exceeding wrath, and made no secret of his anger. One day, in April 1911,

THE COURT OF PEKING

Li, having been summoned to audience, was sitting in the ante-chamber, awaiting his turn to be called to the Presence. Suddenly the Chief eunuch, resplendent in sumptuous apparel, came in, and seating himself, without preliminary ceremonies, in the place of honour, addressed Li, *de haut en bas*:

"We read your memorial advocating our dismissal," he said, "at which both Her Majesty and I are much displeased. What is it fills your head with these ideas, utterly opposed to all dynastic tradition?" Li, much embarrassed, replied: "Not at all: you misunderstand my meaning. I would not have any of you gentlemen lose your posts. All I have ventured to advise is that henceforward no more eunuchs should be engaged, so that the system might gradually die a natural death. You see, no other civilised State employs eunuchs, and China must come into line with the rest of the world in this matter. I hope that you may be pleased to cooperate with me in my humble efforts, and explain my views to Her Majesty, that she take not umbrage. If you oppose us, we shall never succeed." Chang replied: "The Empress is very wrath with you, and declares that you are interfering with Palace matters, which concern you not. Beware of meddling." With that Chang rudely shook his sleeve, and left the room.

An incident occurred two months later which opened the eyes of the citizens of Peking, and forcibly brought home to them the fact that a new power had arisen in the Palace. Li Lien-ying, after many years, had chastised the mandarin world with whips of craftiness, but here was one who, almost at his first coming, chastised them with the scorpions of his contemptuous wrath.

Every year, for fifteen days in the moon of June, a sort of horse show, with racing, is held just outside the Southern gate of the "Chinese" city of Peking. It is, or was, a fashionable resort at which most of the young bloods and sprigs of the Manchu aristocracy were wont to display themselves, either riding their pacers or watching the sport. On these occasions brawls constantly occurred between the henchmen and followers of high officials, especially if local etiquette and the rules of the game were infringed. The sport was not exactly racing as the term is understood elsewhere : the track is narrow, lined by the spectators, and on it the riders display the paces of their fast trotters and amblers, amidst the plaudits of the crowd. It is more a parade than a contest of speed, and it is improper for one horse to pass another, except when the owners are on intimate terms.

The Palace eunuchs always looked forward to this festival, which gave them an opportunity to show off their horses and mules in public. The crowd often included the most fashionable Manchu women and the *élite* of the gay world, so that to " lose face " at the " Nan Ting " (as the fair is called) meant a discomfiture from which a ruffling blade might never recover.

In June 1911 the eunuch Chang Yüan-fu attended at this festival, accompanied by a faithful myrmidon named Shen (also a favourite with Lung Yü). He brought with him a large retinue of servants and four beautiful black mules, one of which was ridden by Shen. Chang himself looked on. Suddenly, as Shen was pacing down the track, a certain Tientsin man, named Wang, deliberately raced past him. Shen, furious at this loss of face, ordered his servants to pull Wang off his horse. Nothing loth, they did so and belaboured him soundly, Chang all the while reviling him from the stand. In the midst of the disturbance Duke P'u Shan,[1] who was sitting close to Chang, interposed. " We all know your power," said he, " but you will probably admit that a member of the Imperial family is not to be insulted.

[1] A great grandson of Chia-ch'ing and second cousin to the young Emperor.

This man Wang is my friend. If you do not obtain an immediate apology from eunuch Shen, I shall complain to Prince Su" (Minister of the Interior). At this Chang laughed scornfully: "You had better complain to the Empress Dowager while you are about it," said he, "and I will give you something to complain for." Whereupon he called his satellites, who pulled Duke P'u Shan from off the stand and flogged him soundly with a horse-whip. The police, who up to this time had been standing by, deep in thought, with their hands in their sleeves (anxious to avoid getting into trouble with either party), now came up and besought the eunuch to spare the Duke, if only for their sakes—in a broil of this kind the police are always severely punished. Their officer, Yüan Te-liang, tried to patch up a peace; as the hour was late and the city gates would soon be closing, the eunuchs allowed the Duke to rise and depart, while they returned to the Palace, vowing further vengeance.

On the following day they turned up at the races in force, supported moreover by about a hundred sturdy contractors' men from the firm of "Everlasting Virtue," all of whom were armed with carpenters' tools; the eunuchs carried staves. There was also an extra large muster of police on the scene, while Duke P'u Shan, burning to avenge the insult of the previous day, had brought a goodly number of Manchu retainers. There was, therefore, every prospect of an interesting meeting; but (as usual, when serious personal injury is likely to ensue) it first took the form of a fierce bandying of abuse between the parties, during which another Imperial duke came up and offered to mediate. He said he would apologise, in Duke P'u's name, for the latter's infringement of etiquette, and he begged the three eunuchs to meet him and Duke P'u at dinner in a fashionable restaurant on the following evening, when the *amende honorable* would be formally concluded. To this the

Chief Eunuch felt that he could agree without loss of dignity. P'u Shan then uttered a few words of grudging apology, in the presence of a huge crowd of spectators. Naturally the sole topic of conversation at Peking, for several days following this incident, was the power of the eunuch, against whom even a scion of the Imperial house was helpless.

Duke P'u reported the matter in due course to Prince Su, who condoled with him on his loss of face, but frankly said he could do nothing. "Do you expect me to ask the Empress Dowager to dismiss Chang? She would be much more likely to dismiss you. Better stomach the affront, and avoid offending him for the future."

But to return to the Regent. His troubles and difficulties were not all made for him in the Palace of Lung Yü. His own wife, the daughter of Jung Lu, gave him furiously to think. A woman of remarkable intelligence and independence of character, she has always inspired the Regent in his own home with a dull, steady kind of fear, harder to bear and more nerve-stretching than the swift slings and arrows of the late Empress Dowager. The Regent's wife is, indeed, one of the most remarkable results of the impact of the West in China—a woman who only awaits the coming of the illustrated halfpenny paper to fill the eye and cheer the heart of the Chinese public, and in other ways to emulate her vivacious and emancipated sisters, and the suffragettes of the Western world. Until the abdication of the Regent, she was everywhere and anywhere in Peking; business, politics, society, the play—all felt her restless hand and knew her shrill voice. To the man in the street, who regarded her with open awe, as a strange manifestation of the latest ways of Providence, she was known as the "Eighth Married Sister," she being the eighth of Jung Lu's daughters.

The Regent, as a prudent politician, was greatly

troubled by many of his wife's doings, by her extravagance, her lack of modest decorum, and her revolutionary ideas on the subject of the emancipation of women. These she emphasised, *inter alia*, by going to the theatre escorted only by her adopted brother, Liang K'uei, a notorious spendthrift and ruffling blade. She was always to be found at the Temple fairs, at the bazaars outside the city, at race meetings and fashionable restaurants, and, being known to the populace, was generally followed about by an admiring crowd. She was for ever frequenting the shops which sell European articles, and would run up reckless bills, leaving her husband or her brother to pay them. On one occasion, when the Regent had screwed his courage to the sticking point and rebuked her for frequenting the Chinese city without an escort, she replied: " European Empresses and Queens go about incognito wherever they choose, and I shall do the same. I do not ask you to accompany me." At the time the revolution broke out she was planning a trip to Shanghai—having heard much praise of the shops and theatres of the " Model Settlement "—and treated with the contempt they deserved her husband's suggestions of revolutionary attempts on her life. She is quite fearless, with the courage of a woman who has no time to think of danger. In her independence she resembles the proud, uncurbed spirit of the American woman. It is recorded of her, that even in her youth she was one of the few people who dared to answer the Old Buddha, and that, on one occasion, Tzŭ Hsi said to Jung Lu: " Your daughter is incorrigible; she defies every one, she defies even Us!" Nevertheless, Tzŭ Hsi liked her, and arranged for her marriage with Prince Ch'un. The only person who could control and guide her actions during the Regency was her near relative, Kuei Chün.

Clearly the Regent's lot was not a happy one, and in judging the failure which he made of his little day of brief authority, allowance must surely be made for a man confronted on the one hand by Lung Yü, a woman of boundless ambition and power of intrigue, and, on the other, by the " mean one of his inner chamber," the excesses of whose frivolity he could neither anticipate nor check.

CONCLUSION

THOSE who have followed the course of events in the Far East during the past two years, that is to say, since the ignominious collapse of the Manchu power and Young China's little hour of brief authority, must have been struck by the general, almost unanimous concurrence of opinion, expressed in Europe and America alike, that, with the establishment of a Republican form of government, China had undergone a sudden and radical transformation; that the essential qualities of the people had been completely changed, and all its social and political institutions regenerated. Students of history and sociological science are familiar with this persistent and imperishable delusion. It arises, as Herbert Spencer has said, from " the difficulty of understanding that human nature, though indefinitely modifiable, can be modified but slowly; and that all laws and institutions and appliances which count on getting from it, within a short time, results much better than present ones, will inevitably fail." It may fairly be said that missionaries in China and philanthropists generally are subject to this delusion as a matter of vocational necessity; that special correspondents cherish it, because a belief in new eras and dramatic transformation-scenes appeals naturally to the journalist, whose business it is " to see history in the making;" and that many politicians encourage it for purposes which have nothing to do with philanthropy. Every new political scheme that has ever been commended to a hopeful world, counts on the imperishable vitality of this Utopian fallacy, and on the fact that it flourishes with particular vigour amongst those civilised nations whose habit it is to cloak the brutal realities of life with a tissue of more or less conventional ideals.

The idea of changing the social structure of a race, not to say human nature, by virtue of the Republican form of government, is one of the commonest manifestations of this perennial delusion. As applied to China, in her recent dynastic convulsion, it has been warmly welcomed by public opinion in Europe, and with even greater fervour in America, as heralding the dawn of a new and happy day in farthest Asia; and this, in spite of the startling demonstration concurrently afforded by Mexico, of the instability of the structure upon which all such hopes are founded. The "unexampled felicity," which the Monroe doctrine declares to be the inheritance and reward of a Republican form of government, takes the form, in Mexico, as in China, of prolonged and aggravated misery for the masses, proving once more that despotic authority remains necessary for the maintenance of law and order amongst peoples incapacitated by their character and circumstances from acquiring representative institutions. Remove that authority, for any reasons which are not slowly determined by the natural evolution of the race, and the result, as Mill says, must be another form of despotism—" a despotism, not even legal, but of illegal violence, which would be alternatively exercised by a succession of political adventurers and under which the names and forms of representation would have no effect but to prevent despotism from attaining the stability and security by which alone its evils can be mitigated and its few advantages realised." There is much food for thought in the difference between the American Government's attitude of to-day towards the Republic of China and that which it feels constrained to adopt towards the Republic of Mexico; nevertheless, and in spite of this remarkable illustration of the delusiveness of hopes based on the regenerative power of political formulae, we look in vain for signs, either at Washington or elsewhere, of recognition of the truth that " so long as the characteristics of citizens remain substantially unchanged, there can be no change in the political organisation which has slowly been evolved by them," [1] which is merely another way of saying that every people get the government it deserves, and that the sins of the fathers are visited on the children.

These conclusions, which most students of sociology will draw from the present condition of affairs in China, and from the restoration of despotic authority in the hands of Yuan Shih-k'ai, follow naturally from the history of the country, not only during the period covered by the present work, but for many centuries before the overthrow of the Mongol dynasty. Yuan Shih-k'ai, if he lives, must govern China by methods very similar to those by which Porfirio Diaz gave stability and security to the government of Mexico. In other words, what was true of China when the Manchus first established their dynasty at Peking, remains true to-day. As General Shih K'o-fa said in 1644, " a supreme ruler is needed to inspire the nation with courage and patriotism; without one, no national spirit can exist. History has approved of this principle, and has recognised that in no other way can the fortunes of the State be preserved." [2]

The daily life of the average educated European is so deeply affected by the political institutions which have been gradually evolved throughout the Western world; his material progress, which he has been taught to regard as a blessing, is so closely identified with political ideas and the laws which express them, that he is naturally disposed to be impressed by the surface phenomena of Young China's political activities and to attribute to them

[1] Spencer, *Study of Sociology*, Chap. VI.
[2] *Vide supra*, p. 181.

an importance far beyond anything that they inherently possess. It is true of China, as of India, Persia, and Turkey (and, for that matter, of Japan) that, on the surface of the deep sea of national life, rapid phenomena of disintegration are perceptible, and new structures are forming; but the social conditions of the masses and their incapacity for self-government remain at a stage generally similar to that which existed in Southern Europe before the Christian era. The average observer notes this fact, but he often fails to apply to sociological problems the laws of evolution.

As to the question of the moral preferability of one or the other type of civilisation, the active European or the passive Oriental, there can be no doubt that the main concurrence of opinion (even amongst moralists) in European countries is all against the passive ideal inculcated by the founder of the Christian religion. With this aspect of the question we are not here concerned, further than to observe, that if the test of a civilisation be sought in the average individual's opportunities of happiness, the East may well dispute the moral superiority claimed by the West, and resent our satisfaction at the prospect of a Europeanised China.

The principal conclusion which appears to be justified by these annals and memoirs, gathered from three centuries of Chinese history, is that it were folly to expect stability and efficiency from any political institutions in China which do not conform to the deep-rooted sentiments and traditions of the masses. The most cursory study of the country's history should prevent us from mistaking superficial for fundamental phenomena. It may be, as a distinguished American professor has lately written after a tour of China, that " in forty years there will be telephones and moving picture shows and appendicitis and sanitation and baseball nines and bachelor maids in every one of the one thousand three hundred districts of the Empire."[1] Remem-

[1] Prof. E. A. Ross, in *The Changing Chinese*, 1911.

bering the similar prophecies of Mr. Anson Burlinghame (similarly inspired), forty years ago, we are content to wait and see, only hoping that China, protected by her poverty, may escape these undeserved calamities. But even if they must fall upon her, neither these, nor any other results of our triumphant materialism are likely to disturb, for many generations to come, the Oriental's attitude toward the things that matter; his conception of the purposes and relative values of existence; his views on birth, marriage, and death; all the fundamental truths and beliefs which constitute the inner life, the very soul of a people. It may gratify the Wisconsin Professor's benevolent instincts to believe that " the renaissance of a quarter of the human family is occurring before our eyes, and we have only to sit in the parquet and watch the stage," because " nowadays world processes are telescoped and history is made at aviation speed," but all human experience and biological science proclaim, nevertheless, with one voice, that the racial instincts which find their expression in China's social and political systems can only be modified by a very slow process of evolution. If by "renaissance" we mean a complete change of the ethical ideals and traditional culture of a race, with whom reverence for the past has attained the force of instinct, if we look for a swift shedding of the accumulated experience of centuries, history (as contained in these Annals) forbids us to cherish any such comfortable fantasies.

The history of China shows clearly that the greatest danger which can threaten the nation during its inevitably recurring crises of economic and political unrest, lies not in foreign invasions, nor even in alien rule, but in a weakening of those ethical restraints, of that ancient moral discipline, upon which has rested the world's oldest civilisation; of those qualities from which the race draws its unconquerable strength. The history of Japan and the wisdom of her Elder Statesmen proclaim the same truth; if Dai Nippon has come safely thus far through her great perils of change, if she has been able to assimilate the material arts and crafts of the West and adapt them to her own needs, it is, as Lafcadio Hearn justly said, "because under new forms of rule and new conditions of social activity, she could still maintain a great deal of the ancient discipline." It was imperative for Japan, as it is imperative for China, that great changes should be made, but it is equally imperative that they should be of a character which shall not endanger the foundations.

Those who supported the inauguration of a Republican form of government in China, and believed in its practical utility, advocated something which seriously endangers the foundations, because it undermines the ethical basis of China's whole social system. The government which Yuan Shih-k'ai is administering at this moment is no more Republican than was that of Kublai Khan. He recognised instinctively, at the outset, as did Prince Ito in Japan, how vitally necessary is the preservation of the unbroken continuity of ancient traditions. He knows that all the instincts and experience of the race will accept his exercise of despotic authority, so long as his rule follows established precedent and conforms to popular sentiments and traditions. The annals upon which we have drawn reveal on every page the truth, that this people understands and accepts the government of a despot, whether his methods be benevolent or brutal, provided that he rule according to the patriarchal precedents of the Canons of the Sages. Let him, if he will, deck the surface of Chinese life with strange inventions from the West, but let him not disturb those silent depths wherein lie all the moral and social experience of the race.

Of the *zeitgeist* in Japan, where the outward and visible manifestations of materialism and commercialism have become so conspicuous, Hearn observed ten years ago:

" It were a grave mistake to suppose that the ancestor-cult has yet been appreciably affected by exterior influences of any kind, or to imagine that it continues to exist merely by force of hallowed custom. No religion—and least of all the religion of the dead—could thus suddenly lose its hold upon the affections of the race that evolved it. Even in other directions, the new scepticism is superficial; it has not spread downwards into the core of things."

If this be true of Japan, the observation applies with far greater force to China. For, because of their religious and social training, the Japanese brought into the crisis of their contact with the West, virtues of patriotism, courage and loyalty, which the Chinese lack. To China remain those passive virtues which spring from the religion of ancestor worship, chief of which and most powerful as a factor of cohesion, is the sentiment of duty to the dead. It is this sentiment which invests the world's oldest civilisation with a philosophic dignity and elements of happiness that the West instinctively respects and envies; with virtues which survive even when bereft of this world's goods. For the preservation of this sentiment, the unbroken continuity of ancient traditions, including the monarchical-patriarchal system of government, is evidently essential. Throughout the brief period of Chinese history with which we have dealt in this volume, the darkest hours of national humiliation and disaster have ever been lightened by the example of a minority, splendidly faithful to the Canons of the Sages, and to their stoics' tradition of courage and unselfish loyalty. Young China, or at least that section of it which has acquired its learning and its inspiration from abroad, mocks at the Sages. The student class, full of the wind of new doctrines from Tokyo, Harvard and Edinburgh, would destroy in a day the splendid edifice of Confucian philosophy and replace it by jerry-built structures of its own vain imaginings, tenements all uninhabitable by the sons of Han. These, more than invading hosts, the soul of the people fears and distrusts, not only because they would desert the old ways, but because their new ways have been weighed in the balance of morality and found wanting. Already, even at Canton, there are signs of the inevitable reaction, and portents of an orthodox revival.

The Throne and the Court remain, therefore, necessary integral parts of China's social system and cult of ancestors. To these, sooner or later, the instinct of the race must insistently return. It was perception of this truth, that caused Li Hung-chang to support the Manchus in 1901, not because they were good, but because they were *there*, and because, in his opinion, no individual or family in China, without fighting a successful civil war, could command the respect of the people in measure sufficient to found a new dynasty. Whether Yuan Shih-k'ai will be able to command it remains to be seen, but every day increases his chances of success. In biding his time, he is conforming strictly to precedent, as established by the soldier-priest founder of the Ming dynasty. He has made no secret of his contempt for the Republican mirage, which for him means " the instability of a rampant democracy, of dissension and partition." In these sentiments, he has not only the support of the *literati*, but the inarticulate approval of the masses. He realises that China's best hope lies, not in a sudden revolutionary distruction of the old order, but in slow steady growth, by educative processes, which shall enable the nation to adapt itself gradually to its changed environment. He knows that, whether as a sovereign State, or under foreign dominion, the unconquerable vitality of China, long tested in the crucible of time, lies in the moral qualities of her common people, in the unconscious heroism of a race of cheerful toilers, in the enduring qualities of body and mind which have preserved the soul of this nation steadfast and undismayed through countless generations. It is a people which, as Sir Robert Hart once said, " believes in right so firmly that they

scorn to think it requires to be enforced by might ";
a people which has often led captivity captive and will do
so again, because it has retained that elemental Christian
virtue which refuses to regard material advantage as the
be-all and end-all of existence. " The thoughts of the
heart, these are the wealth of a man," says the Sage.

The rough outline, contained in these annals, of that
period of China's history which leads up to her first
relations with the Western world, should enable the reader
to form a general idea of the economic and political
problems created by her ancient social system, of the
forces which have rough-hewed the character of the
people. In order to understand the problems which
perplex the nation to-day, it is necessary that we should
approach them with sympathetic knowledge of its religious
and sociological evolution. To this end, the voice of
Young China helps us but little, for Young China is
morally an alien in its own land; some hundreds or thousands
of foreign degrees taken by its students cannot
alter the fact that the Chinese people remains in the patriarchal
stage of development. It is unfortunate that Young
China (like Young India), being highly vocal, should have
commanded so wide an audience, and inspired so many
illusions, abroad, that superficial disintegration should
have been so widely interpreted to imply a vast upheaval
of the depths; because Young China, imbued with an
exaggerated sense of its own importance, becomes a danger
to itself and to the nation. Those who have followed the
history of the Ming and Manchu dynasties in their decline
and fall, must realise that this is true; and that
socially, morally and economically, the Chinese race, so
long a law unto itself, remains much the same to-day as
it was a thousand years ago. Even Young China, as
represented by its fiercest iconoclasts, unconsciously fulfils
the laws which ages of moral experience have written deep
in the heart of the race. Bravely it parades its foreign

clothes and foreign ideas from platform and press, but in the privacy of its home, in the market place and even in its foreign-built government offices, it yields atavistic allegiance to those laws of its inheritance which it can never evade, to authority of traditions from which it can never escape. *As has been finely said, in China " law is not a rule imposed from above, it is the formula of the national life and its embodiment in practice precedes its inscription on a code. Hence it is that in China, government is neither arbitrary nor indispensable. Destroy our authorities, central and provincial, and our life will proceed very much as before. Come what may, the family remains, with all that it involves, the attitude of mind remains, the spirit of order, industry and thrift. These it is that make up China."*

INDEX

ABBÉ HUC, *Travels in Tibet*, cited, n. 333, n. 399
Abbot of T'ien Tai temple, 237; also *vide* Shun Chih
Abtai, Prince, 155, 242–45
Alexander I of Russia, 236
Alexander VII, Pope, 223
A-Lu-te, Empress, 420–22, 468, 469, 477, 478
Amin, Prince, 144
Amherst Mission, 381 *et seq.*
"Anhui Official, An," Chinese annalist, 474
An Tê-hai, Chief Eunuch, 420, 477, 490, 502
Aomen, foreign traders' base near Canton, 327 *et seq.*
Ao Pai, Regent, 219, 242, 243, 257
Aristotle's sacrifice to Hermias cited, 18
Astrologers and soothsayers, 40, 226
Astronomers, Court of, 44, 106, n. 244, 498

BANNERS, Manchu, institution of, 139, 150, 359
Benedict XIII, Pope, 307, 308
Board of Ceremonies, 279
Board of Punishments, 76
Board of Regents, 242
Board of Rites, 273
Bocca Tigris, bombarded, 400
Book of Rites, quoted, 178
Borjikin, Empress, 242, n. 256
Borjikitu, Lady, 162, 231, 242, n. 475
"Born out of Time," Chinese Annalist, quoted, 230–32, n. 297, 490 *et seq.*
Bouvet, Joachim, 240, 243
Boxer indemnity, n. 367
Boxer leaders, 443, 448, 449, 459, 463
British at Canton, 391
British embassies to China, 311, 320 *et seq.* 381 *et seq.*
British trade in China, 311, 322, 326, 327, 381
 duties on British merchandise, 329

Brothers of Yung Cheng, 269 *et seq.*
 titles restored by Ch'ien Lung, 301
Buddhist All Souls' Day, 424
Buddhist arts of incantation, 346
Building operations in Palace, 500 *seq.*, 505
Burmese King, 218

CANON OF HISTORY, quoted, 39, 390
Canons of the Sages, 184, 185, 214
Canton, blockaded, 399
Canton, European trade at, 311, 325
Censorate, the, 57, 65, 351, 391
Censorate, suicide of President, 109
Chahal Mongols, 145
Chang Ch'ai, 448 *et seq.*
Chang Chih-tung, n. 303, 438
Chang Chin, 30 *et seq.*
Chang Fu, 463, 464
Chang Hsien-chung, 94
Chang Kuo-chi, 60, 63, 67
Ch'ang Lo, Prince, 47 *et seq.*, also *vide* Emperor Kuang Tsung
Chang Ming-ti, 262, 265 *et seq.*
Chang Tê, Emperor, 24 *et seq.*
Chang Yin-huan, 430
Chang Yüan-fu, Chief Eunuch, 496, 497, 500 *et seq.*
 and horse-show brawl, 508, 509
 and Regent, 501
 insolence of, 503 *et seq.*,
 quarrel with Li Chia-chu, 506, 507
 residence of, 505
Cheng, Concubine, 47–52, 55
Cheng Kuo-tai, brother of Concubine Cheng, 48
Cheng, Prince, co-Regent with Dorgun, 158
Ch'eng, Prince, elder brother of Chia Ch'ing, 349, 365, 368, 376, 412, 413, 418
Ch'eng Tê, 373, 374
Ch'en, Lady, the "Round-faced Beauty," 120–22
Chen Hsin-chia, 148, 149, 154

523

INDEX

Ch'en Liang-mi, 111
Ch'en Yen, 107
Chia Ch'ing, Emperor, 311, 322
  and Ho Shen, 345, 346, 349 *et seq.*
  and Amherst Mission, 381 *et seq.*
  character of, 336, 361, 373
  conspiracies against, 373 *et seq.*, 478
  death of, n. 350, 390
  decrees, 347, 350, 359 *et seq.*, 360, 361, 370, 375, 377, 379, 382, 385
Chia Ch'ing's sister, 359
Chiang Hsiang, 96, 97
Chiang Te-ying, 97
Ch'ien Lung, Emperor, 18, 59, 138, 234
  abdication of, 310, 345
  and Ho Shen, 344 *et seq.*
  and Macartney Mission, 321 *et seq.*
  and Stranger Concubine, 341
  campaigns, 310
  character of, 310, 334 *et seq.*
  death of, 347
  devotion to the chase, 334
  domestic affairs, 334
  escapades, 338
  his heir, 311 *et seq.*
  letter to George III, 331 *et seq.*
  restores title to sons of K'ang Hsi, 301
Chien Men quarter, 420
Chihli, Manchu raid into, 144
Chi Lu, 441
China Under the Empress Dowager, referred to, 9, 409, 417, 419, 423, 437, 442, 466
Ch'ing, adopted grandson of Ho Shen, n. 365
Ching Fu's memorial, 500
Ch'ing, Prince, brother of Chi'a Cheng, 365
Ch'ing, Prince, 446, 447, 450, 456
Ching Shan, 466
Ching Tai, Emperor, 438
Chinese poetry, 316
Chinese social system, 14
Chinese women debarred from entering Forbidden City, 475
Ch'i Hsiu, 412, 447
Chin Tartars, 150, 181
Ch'i Shan, 399 *et seq.*
Chi T'an-jan, 218
Chou Yü-chi, 95, 96
Christianity in China, 330
  conversion of Princes, 247, 273
  Jesuits at Court of K'ang Hsi, 241
  Palace missionaries forbidden to hold intercourse with Chinese, 330
  practised by Imperial clanswomen, 221
Chu Chih-feng, 98, 99

Chu Kuei, 331
Ch'ung Chen, Emperor, 82, 85, 92 *et seq.*, 187
  death of, 103
  burial of, 104, 105, 154
Chung Ch'i, 420, 422
Chung Hou-so, taken by assault, 158
Chung Li, 458
Ch'un, Prince, Regent, n. 302, n. 303, n. 433, 493, 494, 497, 501, 510
  and Chang Yüan-fu, 501, 506
  his wife, 510, 511
Ch'un, Princess, 473, 491
Chusan, British request for island near, 328
Ch'u Tsung, 278
Chü Yen-kuan, 99
Chu Yüan-chang, 23, n. 135, 220, 224
Civil service, 18, 390
Civil service examinations, 410 *et seq.*, 427
Coal Hill, 101, 276, 300, 301
Confucian philosophy, 14, 109, 167, 498
  tradition, 15
Confucius quoted, 181, 345, 350
  grave of, 82
Constitutional government, 498
Coup d'état of 1898, 430, 436, 437
Court, profligacy of, 187
Court of Astronomers, 44, 100, 498
Court of Imperial Clan, 275, 418

DALAI LAMA, 320, 321, 352
Decapitation, etiquette of, 418
Degenerate Manchus, 372, 444 *et seq.*
Department for Tributory States, 323
De Toqueville, quoted, 14
Diary describing sack of Yang Chou fu, 188 *et seq.*
Diary of Ching Shan, 466
Diary of Manchu official, 443, *et seq.*
Dice-throwing, 243, 244
"Discerning Concubine," 421, 477
Dominicans and Jesuits, 240
Dominic, Father, 222
Dorgun, Prince Jui, Manchu Regent, 85, 104, 132, 147, 157, 159, 168, 213
  appoints himself Generalissimo, 158
  becomes Regent, 157, 158
  correspondence with Wu San-kuei, 128-31
  death of, 233
  defeats Li Tzŭ-cheng, 131
  enters Peking, 127
  his march from Shan Hai-kuan to Chin Chou, 127
  posthumous degradation, 233, 242
  receives Ming officials, 127

INDEX

Dorgun, restitution of honours by Ch'ien Lung, 234
Dutch in China, 86
Duties on merchandise, 329
Dynastic ordinances, 334

EASTERN COURT, 68
East India Company, 381, 385
Eclipses as omens, 318
Edict of Toleration, 240
Eleuths subjugation of, 253, 281
Elliott, British Commissioner, 400
Ellis's Journal, quoted, 382, n. 383, n. 386
Empress Consort of Ch'ung Chen, 102
Empress Helen, 222
Eunuchs, Palace,
 and Government appointments, 430
 Christians, 222
 conspire against Chia Ch'ing, 378 *et seq.*
 factions of, 496, 508
 in command of military forces, 100
 power at Court, 17, 24, 46, 56, 100, 141, 268, 406
 power reduced by Shun Chih, 232
 system denounced by Li Chia-chu, 506
 tortured and beheaded by Li Tzŭ-cheng, 116
 under Yung Cheng, 306
European civilisation compared with Oriental, 14
European guns, 145, 158, 173
 merchants not allowed to enter city of Canton, 329
European missionaries compelled to adopt Chinese dress, 323
 forbidden to leave China, 323
Europeans classed with actors and soothsayers, 294
Examinations, civil service, reorganised by Chu Yüan-chang, 23
 classical, revised by Shun Chih, 229
 for public service, 410 *et seq.* 427

FALL OF PEKING, 166
Fang Tsung-che, 50 *et seq.*
Fan Wen-ch'eng, 127, 159
Fei, handmaiden at Palace, 103
Fontaney, Jean de, 240
Fortune-tellers and astrologers, 44, 135, 262
Fu Ch'ang-an, 349, 357 *et seq.*
Fu K'ang-an, n. 332
Fu Lin, Prince, son of Emperor T'ai Tsung, became Emperor Shun Chih, 231
Fu, Prince, son of Lady Cheng, 48, 55, 60

GENEALOGY OF HOUSE OF GIORO, 161
Gerbillon, Jean François, 239, n. 244
Ghoorkas of Nepal, 320, 332, 333
 ask aid of Great Britain, n. 333
Gioro, Genealogy of House of, 161
 alleged illegitimate descent of, 230, 232
"Goddess Chang," 79, 83
Gordon and the "ever-victorious army," 422, 423
Grand Council, 101
Grave of Confucius, 82
Great Wall, 113, 143
"Green Monkey" singing girl, 458
Grimaldi, Philippe, 240

HALL OF IMPERIAL LONGEVITY, 237, 291
Hanlin Academy, 25, 45, 258
Hara-kiri, Chinese influence in origin of, n. 109
"Harrier Prince," nickname of Li Tzŭ-cheng, 166, 175, 183
Heavenly Principles Society, 378
Heavenly Reason Society, 373
Heng Yi's reminiscences of Boxer Year, 453
Hermias, eunuch Governor of Atarnea, 18
Histoire Génerale de la Chine, Père Mailla's, n. 239, n. 305
Ho Lin, 320, 321
Honan-fu, siege of, 88
Hongkong, ceded to Britain, 395
Hongs, foreign, at Canton, 326 *et seq.*
Ho Shen, Grand Secretary, 18, 311, 319, 321, 373, 503
 career of, 345 *et seq.*
 collection of curios, 366
 death of, 368, 369
 disgraced, 349
 his pearls, n. 353
 indictment of, 350 *et seq.*
 investments of, 366
 origin of, 344
 power and wealth, 344, 364 *et seq.*
Ho Shen's adopted grandson, n. 365
Ho Shen's faction and anti-dynastic societies, 394
Ho Shih-t'ai, 387, 389
House laws of Manchus, 41, 230, 232, 248, 312, 349, 435, 475, 476, 505
House laws of Mings, 52, 56, 65
Hsiang, Prince, 89
Hsieh Fu-chen, Dr., 481, 483
Hsien Feng, Emperor, 403, 470 *et seq.*
 accession of, 405
 character of, 405, 409
 death of, 418, 422, 473

INDEX

Hsin, Prince, brother of Emperor Hsi Tsung, who succeeded him as Emperor Ch'ung Chen, 79, 80
Hsining, Yün Tang's mission to, 275, 278, 279
Hsi Tsung, Emperor, 55 et seq.
Hsing Ching, Nurhachi's capital, 140
Hsiung, Ming general, 141, 142
Hsüan-hua, 37, 94, 98
Hsüan Tsung, Emperor, 24
Hsüan T'ung, Emperor, 225, n 353
   education of, 497 et seq.
   parentage of, 493
Hsü Ching-ch'eng, 455
Hsü Ch'ing-yü, 449, 450
Hsü T'ung, 443, 447, 449, 450, 459
Hsü Yung-yi, 455, 459
Huai River, 187
Huang Hsing, 225, 226
Huang Taiki, fourth son of Nurhachi, 143
Huang Te-hung, Marquis, 189
Huang Tsun-su, 73
Hung Ch'eng-chou, 173
Hung Fu-lien, 425
Hung Kuang, Emperor, 184, 215
Hung, "the Heavenly King," 424

I-CHIANG-A, 354 et seq.
I-k'o-t'an, 499
Imperial cedar-wood, used in Palace, 352, 362
Imperial Clan, 236, 311, 443
Imperial Clan Court, 289
"Imperial Clansman, An," Annalist, 462
Imperial mandates to King of England, 322, 325, 382
Imperial mausoleum, 104
Imperial pearl, 242, n. 353
Italy, mission to Chinese Court, 324

JADE SCEPTRES, 381
Japanese samurai tradition, 109
Jehol, Court at, 311
   reception of British Embassy at, 321
Jen, Concubine, 67, 84, 85
Jesuit priests, 221
   and Manchu Princes, 273
   dissensions between Jesuits and Dominicans, 240
   Edict of toleration, 240
   expulsion of, 273, 307
   introduce European guns, 95, 141, 145, 173
   introduce quinine at Court, 240
   their zeal leads to persecution, 241
   under K'ang Hsi, 239–41
   under Yung Cheng, 307
Job, quoted, 12
"Journey Eastward, A," play cited, 137
Jui Ch'eng, n. 399
Jui, Prince, vide Dorgun.
Jui sceptres, 356
Jung Lu, 420, 448, 450, 459 et seq., 467, 471, 481, 493

K'AI FENG-FU, siege of, 90
   recovered for Mings, 170
K'ang Hsi, Emperor, 132, 133, 234
   abolishes semi-independent vassaldoms, 134, 158
   addicted to drinking bouts, n. 292
   and Jesuit Fathers, 237, 247
   death of, 269, 270
   deposition of Heir Apparent, 249–62
   dismisses Regents, 242
   his wars, 241
   homily to Ministers, 252–55
   obsequies of, 277, 280
   persecutes Christians, 241
   reign of, 238, 239
   rumoured conversion to Christianity, 241
   sons of, 245–68
   succeeds Shun Chih, 235
Kang Yi, Boxer politician, 443, 447 et seq., 451, 452, 459, 462
K'ang Yu-wei, 230, 436
Kao, Empress, 114
Kao Ti, General, 143
Keyte, J. C., work cited, 209
Khorchin Mongols, 146, 158, n. 256, 276
Kiakhta, Russian trade at, 328
Kings of Korea, become vassals of Manchu Emperor, 147
Kitchen God, 335
Koffler, Andrew Xavier, Jesuit, attached to Ming Court, 222
K'o, Madame, 56 et seq.
K'o, Prince, 446
Korea, Prince Amin's expedition to, 144
   invasion of, 146
   refuses to recognise T'ai Tsung, 146
   subjugated, 147
   T'ai Tsung's campaign against, 143
Kowtow, ceremony of, 321, 331, 382, 383, 386
Kuai Tzu, philosopher, 113
Kuang Hsü, Emperor, alleged origin of, 491
   character of, 429
   confined to Ocean Terrace, 440
   death of, 439, 469
   defies Tzŭ Hsi, 432
   his mean apartment, 439

INDEX

Kuang Hsü, last request to Old Buddha, 439
Kuang Hui, 386–89
Kuang Tsung, Emperor, 52–4
Kublai Khan, 23
Kuei Chün, 511
Kuei Wang, last of the Mings, 167, 213; (Reign title Yung Li).
  death of, 220, 221, 223
  flight into Burma, 213, 214
  letter to Wu San-kuei, 215–19
Kung, Prince, 419, 434, 435, 472
Kung Yi, 220, 221
Kung Yung-ku, 100

Le Comte, Louis, 240
Lhasa, 320, 321
Liang Kuei, 511
Liao Shou-keng, 459, 460
Liao Yang, fall of, 142
Li Chang-shu, 452
Li Chia-chu, 506
Li Chien-t'ai, Grand Secretary, 92, 93, 97
Lien Shan, 455
Lien Yüan, 458, 462, 463
Li Hsiü-ch'eng, Taiping leader, 423 et seq.
  his letter to Hung, 424
  his record of Taiping rebellion, 424
  his son, n. 424
Li Hung-chang, 450, 452, 453
Li Hung-tsao, 434, 435, 476, 478 et seq.
Li K'o-shao, 54
Li Kuo-chen, 116
Li Kuo-pu, Grand Secretary, 78
Li, Lady, 52 et seq., 68
Li Lien-ying, Chief Eunuch, 429, 433, 437, 439, 463, 473, 483, 490, 496, 507
  and Government appointments, 430
  death of, 502
  his pearls stolen by Chang Yüan-fu, 502
Lin Ch'ing's conspiracy, 378
Lin Chi-shih, 25 et seq.
Ling Yi-ch'ün, suicide of, 110
Lin Hsü, reformer, 436, 437
Lin Tse-hsü, Viceroy of Canton, 395, 397
  his despatch to Queen Victoria, 396
Li, Prince, 462
Li Shan, 455, 457, 458
Li Tai-po, poems of, 16
Literary examinations, 40 et seq.
Literary tradition, 15
Literati, 236, 301
Li Ting-kuo, freebooter, 214
Li Tzŭ-cheng,
  alliance with Wu San-kuei, 114, 123
  ascends Imperial Throne, 107
  assumes Imperial title, 114

Li Tzŭ-cheng (*continued*)
  defeated by Dorgun, 131, 132
  defeated by Wu San-kuei, 119, 123
  ends days as Buddhist priest, 116, 117
  enters the city, 104, 106
  flight to Hunan, 116
  his political genius, 107
  his tomb, 117
  punishes Palace eunuchs, 115
  rebellion of, 24, 82 et seq., 86 et seq., 104 et seq., 148
  takes Peking, 99
Liu Cheng, eunuch, 28, 49
Liu K'un-yi, Nanking Viceroy, 433, 492
"Liu, Mysterious," eunuch, 484
Liu Tsung-min, 121
Liu Wen-pin, 486 et seq.
Liu Wen-ping, Marquis, death of, 111
Liu Yi-ching, Grand Secretary, 54
Li Yen, rebel chief, 83, 84
Lou Te-na, 258
Lung K'o-to, 269, 271, 282, 285, 291, 292, 305
Lung Yü, Empress, 225, 242, 353, n. 421, 493 et seq., 497 et seq.
  and Eunuch Chang Yüan-fu, 496, 501 et seq.
  death of, 495
  "squeezes" in building operations, 499
  theatrical entertainments, 504
Lu Pin, Prince, 290
Lu Po-yang, 430, 431, 433

Macao, banquet at, in honour of Ming Envoys, 222
Macao, Portuguese at, 221
Macartney Mission, 311, 320 et seq., 344, 382
Ma Chang-hsi, 478
Magic and spells, 451
Mahomedan mosque, 340
Mailla, Père, author of *Histoire Génerale de la Chine*, n. 239, n. 305
Manchu invasion, 84
  capture of Wuchang, 116
  dynasty's Eastern tombs, 156
  etiquette, 355
  expedition to Korea, 144
  house laws, 41, 230, 232, 248, 312, 349, 435, 475, 476, 505
  march on Peking, 113
  Prefect at Tamsui, 378
  Princes, 335, 443; degeneration of, 444 et seq.
  Princes and Wu San-kuei, 132
  raid in Chihli, 144
  rulers and eunuchs, 17

INDEX

Manchus massacred by Chinese, 209
Market days in Forbidden City, 50
Market fair, 335
Ma Shih-ying, 168, 170, 172
Massacre of Chinese by Manchus, 195
  of Manchus by Chinese, 209
Mencius quoted, 302, 319
Metropolitan Museum, New York, n. 367
Mien Ning, Prince, son of Chia Ch'ing, became Emperor Tao Kuang, 375
Military organisation, 18, 390
Ming Heir Apparent, 97, 100, 101, 107, 121, 122, 124, 166
Ming mission to Vatican, 222
Ming nobles squeezed, 116
Mings at Nanking, 84, 167, 168
Mings, last of the, 104, 106, 137, 235
Missions to Chinese Court from Portugal and Italy, 324
"Model Beauty, The," 341 *et seq.*
Mongol Empire, finally shattered, 23
Mongol Princes' tribute, 250
  and smallpox, 352
Mongol Tushetu Khan, 157
Mongolian Superintendency, 277
Mongolia subjugated by T'ai Tsung, 143
Moukden, 142
Mu Ch'ang-a, Grand Secretary, 391, 395 *et seq.*, 401
Mu Ching-yuan, European, at Court of Yung Cheng, 299
Mu Yung-a, 242

Nanking, sack of (1913), 12
  fall of, 406, 425, 428
Napier, Lord, 385
Nepal campaign, 320, 321, 332, 333
Ning, Prince, 32, 33
Ning Yüan, last of the Ming strongholds, 112.
  defence of, by Wu San-kuei, 118, 143, 148, 154
Nurhachi, 217, 225
  appointed Warden of the Marches, 138
  assumes dynastic name of Manchus, 140
  declares war on China, 140
  his army, 139, 143
  his capital at Hsing Ching, 140
  his capital at Moukden, 142
  organises tribes under four banners, 139
  rise of, 86, 138
  ruler of five Manchu tribes, 139

"Ocean Terrace," 437, 440
Odes, Book of, quoted, 474, 477
Omens and portents, 43, 87, 88, 224, 243, 244, 318, 400

Opium abolition, 395, 503
Orientals, jealousy of, 242

Pa Chung, General, n. 333
Palace actors, 487, 502, 504
Palace Amazons, 475
Palace concubines, 60, 406
Palace pearls, 501
Palace of Prince Hsiao, n. 365
Palace of Tranquil Longevity, 362
P'an Achilles, Chief Eunuch of Empress Helen, 222
  in command of land and sea forces of Mings, 223
Pang Pao, eunuch, 48, 49
Panshen Lama, n. 233
P'an Tsu-yin, 469
Pao Tai, Resident at Lhasa, n. 333
Parker, E. H., work cited, 223
Peace Protocol (1901), 449
Pearl Concubine, 440, 468, 495
Pearl necklaces, 353, 363, 369, 370
Peking Court Gazette, 293
Peking *Gendarmerie*, 338, 509
Peking horse show, 507
Péreira, Anthoine, 239
Pescadores, seizure of, by Dutch, 86
Ping Ling, 411 *et seq.*
Pi Ting-ho, 444
Pi Yün-ssü, 75
Poison, use of, 81, 134, 166, 246, 464, 483, 484, 487, 489
Polygamy, 13 *et seq.*, 245, 270
Portuguese in China,
  aid Mings, 141
  at Macao, 221
  language used by Princes, 307
  Mission to Chinese Court, 324
  supply Mings with cannon, 145
Po Sui, Grand Secretary, 409 *et seq.*
  execution of, 414–17
Pottinger, Sir H., 395
Precious Pearl, Empress, 59 *et seq.*
  death of, 82–5
President Yuan Shih-k'ai's Palace, n. 341
Price of eggs, 337, 490
Priesthood, Shun Shih's regulations for entering, 229
  not reverenced by *literati*, 236
Princedom of Jui re-established, 234
Prophecies, 224, 225
P'u Shan, Duke, 508 *et seq.*
Pu Ying-ch'i, 427, 428

Random Notes from the Chamber of the Cloudy Sea, 469
Ransom for Proscribed Mings, 109

INDEX

Rebellions against Manchus, 347, 373
Reformers, 436
Regents, Board of, 242
    harsh treatment of Jesuits, 242
Regents, Prince Abtai, 242–45
    Ao Pai, 219, 242, 24? 257
    Prince Ch'un, n. 202, n. 303, n. 433, 493 et seq.
Regents, usurping, 418, 470
    dismissed by K'ang Hsi, 242
Regency, Joint, of Prince Cheng and Dorgun, 158
    of Tzŭ Hsi and Tzŭ An, 419, 4C5
Republic, the, 442
"Restore the Mings," battle cry of Taipings, 221
Ricci, 221
Ritual of mourning, 271
Roman Catholic religion, 221, 272 et seq.
"Round-faced Beauty," 120, 122, 125; also vide Lady Ch'en.
Russian merchants at Peking, 327, 328
Russian trade at Kiakhta, 328

SAGES, teachings of the, 141
San Ku-niang, literary courtesan, 338, 339
Schall, Adam von, 242
Secret Societies, 373, 378
Shanghai Taotaiship, 430
Shan Hai-kuan, 95
    siege of, 113
Shen, Eunuch, 508
Shih, alleged paramour of Tzŭ Hsi, 490, 491
Shih K'o-fa, General, 168, 188, 189, 207,
    his memorial, 169, 170
    correspondence with Manchu Regent, 174–84
    death of, 174
Shou Fu, 464 et seq.
Shun Chih, Emperor, 138, 157, 158, 160, 229
    alleged to have joined priesthood, 236, 237
    birth, 231
    character of, 229, 232
    curtails power of eunuchs, 232
    death of, 235
    marriage, 234
    reputed illegitimacy, 230
Shun (Obedient), title of Li Tzŭ-ch'eng's rebel dynasty, 121
Sianfu, sack of Tartar city, 209
"Signs of a Decaying Dynasty," 443 et seq.
Singing-girl and Wu San-kuei, 119; also vide "Round-faced Beauty."

Sister Phœnix, 37 et seq.
Smith, Dr. Arthur, work quoted, 225
Song of the Cakes, quoted, 224, 226
Soochow, fall of, 424
Soothsayers and fortune-tellers, 40, 226
Spirits and omens, 43, 44
Spring and Autumn Annals, quoted, 174, 178, 265
State seal of Mongol dynasty, 146
Staunton, Sir George, cited, 311, 319, n. 320, 321, n. 386
"Stranger Concubine," 341 et seq.
Su, Prince, Minister of the Interior, 509, 510
Su, Prince, son of Emperor T'ai Tsung, 145, 157
Suicide of two hundred women of the Palace, 103
Sungaria, campaign in, 340
Sung Ch'i-chiao, 108
Sung Fan, Viceroy of Kansuh, 450, 451
Sung, Prince, 218
Sung Yün, Resident at Lhasa, 321
Superstitions, characteristic, 243
Sun Yat-sen, 221, 225
Su Shun, Imperial clansman, 406 et seq.
    death of, 417, 418, 470 et seq.
Symptoms of demoralisation, 372

T'AI HU, Magistracy, 36
Taiping Court at Nanking, 406, 410, 423
Taiping rebellion, 391, 405 et seq., 422 et seq., 475
    genesis of, 423
T'ai Tsu, 217
T'ai Tsung, Emperor, 143
    ambitions of, 143, 144
    correspondence with Ming Emperor, 148, 149, 151, 153
    death of, 157
    invades Korea, 146
    raids China, 147
    receives State seal of Mongol dynasty, 146
    subjugates Charhar Mongols, 145
    takes Port Arthur, 145
T'ai Yüan-fu, siege of, 93
T'an, "Heaven-compelling" singer, 504
Tantla Pass, n. 333
Tao Kuang, Emperor, 375, 390 et seq.
    and Tseng Kuo-fan, 400 et seq.
    character of, 391, 394
    signs Nanking Treaty, 399
Taranatha Lama, 280
Tashilhunpo, sack of, n. 333
Temple of Ancestors, 57, 93, 359
Temple of Heaven, 93, 115, 342

INDEX

Teng, " the large-thighed," 231
Tê, Prince, cousin of Ming Emperor, 147
Theatricals, palace, 136, 172, 335, 501, 503
Tibet, 320
    British mission to, 332
    China's suzerainty over, 320
    war with Nepal, 321, n. 333
T'ien Ch'i, Emperor Hsi Tsung, 55 et seq.
T'ien, Concubine, 104 et seq., 122
T'ien Ming, reign title of Nurhachi
T'ien Tsung, reign title of Huang Taiki, 143
T'ien Wen-ching, 305, 306
Ting, Prince, 122
Ting, Prince, grandson of Ch'ien Lung, 364, 369, 370
Trading centre at Peking, 322
Treaty of alliance between Li Tzu-ch'eng and Wu San-kuei, 114, 119, 122
Treaty of Nanking, 395, 399
Tsai Chen, son of Prince Ch'ing, 446
Tsai Ch'u, 479
Tsai Lan, Duke, 458 et seq.
Tsai Lien, Beileh, 446, 447
Tsai Yüan, n. 271, 481
Ts'ao Chen-yung, Grand Secretary, 393, 403, 404
Tseng Kuo-fan, 400 et seq., 419, 422, 426, 492
Tsin, eunuch, 440
Tso Kuang-tou, Censor, 51, 52, 56, 76
Tso Tsung-t'ang, 419, 422, 477, 484, 489
Tsui Wen-hsia, eunuch, 52, 53
Tuan, Prince (Boxer), 455
Tu Hsün, eunuch, Commander-in-Chief, 94, 96, 98, 99, 115
Tu Shou-t'ien, Imperial tutor, 391, 392
Tung Chia, Empress of Shun Chih, 234
T'ung Chih, Emperor, 419, 469, 477
    character of, 419
    death of, 478–80
    escapades of, 420, 478
    marriage, 420
Tung, Lady, Concubine, 234, 235
Tzŭ An, Empress, 469, 473, 476 et seq., 481 et seq.
    death of, 483–84, 486 et seq.
Tzŭ Hsi, Empress Dowager, 337, n. 367, 394, 400, 419, 422, 461, 466 et seq.
    and astrologers, 226
    and Censor Wang P'eng-yün, 436
    and Tzŭ An, 481 et seq.
    character of, 336, 466 et seq.
    coup d'état, 430, 364
    en retraite, 434
    executes Su Shun, 417; and usurping Regents, 418

Tzŭ Hsi, Empress Dowager, her pearl-embroidered jacket, 364
    her relations with Kuang Hsü, 429 et seq.
    homilies of, 272
    sympathy with Boxers, 455
    the verdict of history, 492
    usurps power, 433, 476

VERBIEST, 221, 239
Visdelon, Claude de, 240

WAN CHING, Board Secretary, 74
Wang An, eunuch, 56, 58, 70
Wang Ch'eng-en, eunuch, 98, 100, 103
Wang Ch'eng-yün, General, 98
Wang Kao, alleged father of Shun Chih, 230–32
Wang P'eng-yün, Censor, 434 et seq.
Wang Ting-lin, Grand Secretary, 397
Wang Wen-shao, 450, 457, 460
Wang Yung-chang, Diary of, 119, 122, 124
Wan Li, Ming Emperor, 47 et seq., 313
    Heir Apparent of, 47–52, 377
Wei Ching-yuan, Governor of Ta T'ung-fu, 96, 97
Wei Chung-hsien, the infamous eunuch, 47, 55 et seq., 142, 168, 232, 360
Wei Liang-ch'ing, 79
Wei Ta-ching, 74, 76
" Wen Ching," writings of, 230, 466
Wen Hsiang, 419, 480
Western Market, place of execution, 415
White Lily Conspiracy, 346, 347, 373
" Writer on Court Subjects, A," 486
Wu Ch'ang, captured by Manchus, 116
Wu Chao-ping, 324
Wu Hsiang, General, 113, 119
Wu Ko-tu, Censor, 491
Wu Len-cheng, suicide of, 110
Wu San-kuei, 98, 110, 118 et seq.
    allies himself with Manchus, 126 et seq.
    allies himself with Li Tzu-ch'eng, 119, 123, 125
    and last of the Mings, 124, 214
    and the " Round-faced Beauty," 113, 119 et seq.
    character of, 134 et seq.
    death of, 132
    defeats Li Tzu-ch'eng, 123
    defence of Ning Yuan, 112, 118
    his career, 119 et seq., 132
    his father, 125
    his rebellion in 1674, 128, 133–35
Wu Su, 111, 112
Wu Tai Mountains, 85

INDEX

Yang, Chou-fu, sack of, 168, 172, 185, 188 et seq.
Yang, Colonel, 188
Yang Hsiao-lou, 504
Yang Hsin-ch'eng, rebel Prince, 427
Yang Jui, reformer, 467
Yang Lien, Censor, 51, 52, 55, 56, 68 et seq., 75
Yang Ssu-ch'ang, Ming Commander-in-Chief in Hupei, n. 89
Yang Yueh-lou, actor, 487
Yao, Emperor, 312
Yeho tribe, 139, 474
Yehonala clan, n. 139, 493 et seq.
Yen Ching-ming, Grand Secretary, 483
"Yellow Lotus Holy Mother," 452, 453
Yi, General, 170
  murdered, 172
Yi Hsing, reign title of Ming Heir Apparent (1644), 122, 124
Yi, Prince, brother of Chia Ch'ing, 396, 413, 418
Yi, Princedom created, n. 271
Yi Yuan-lu, Board President, 109
Young China, historical writings of, 230, 492
Yü, Prince, brother of Dorgun, 170, 172, 205
Yüan Ch'ang, 455, 457
Yüan, General, 142
Yuan Shih-k'ai, 225, 340, 450
  his dismissal by Empress Lung Yü, 242, n. 479
  his respect for Confucian tradition, 15
Yü Hsien, 450, 451
Yü Lu, 452

Yü Ming, 431–33
Yün Ch'ih, eldest son of K'ang Hsi, 245, 255, 262, 263
Yün Chih, son of K'ang Hsi, 246, 301
Yung Ch'ang, Imperial title of Li Tzu-ch'eng, 91, 123
Yung Cheng, Emperor, 246, 269–309
  alleged illegitimacy of, 290, n. 297
  alleged murder of, 309
  and disloyal brothers, 289–301
  character of, 270, 284, 297, 304
  end of reign, disturbed, 301
  executes Yün T'ang and Yün Ssu, 298–300
  his literary style, 303
  letter to Pope, 307
  limits authority of eunuchs, 306
  persecutes Christians, 304
  relations with Jesuits, 307
  reported drunkenness of, 291, n. 292
  rescripts, 303
Yung Li, reign title of Kuei Wang (last of the Mings), 213, 219
Yung Lo, Emperor, 23, 217
Yün Jeng, Heir Apparent of K'ang Hsi, 246 et seq.
  death of, 276
  deposition of, 249–62
  imprisonment of, 257
Yün O, son of K'ang Hsi, 246, 273, 275, 280, 300, 301
Yün Ssü, son of K'ang Hsi, 246, 262, 264–67, 269, 271, 273–301
Yün T'ang, son of K'ang Hsi, 246, 278, 289, 290, 298, 299
Yün Ti, son of K'ang Hsi, 247, 280, 289–91, 297, 300

PUBLISHED BY

CH'ENG WEN PUBLISHED CO.,

P.O. Box 22605

Taipei, Taiwan

The Rep. of China

發行人：黃　成　助

發行所：成文出版社有限公司

地　址：台北市羅斯福路三段279號之2

印刷所：正　大　印　製　廠

地　址．台北縣三重市長生街2號之1